A Conservation
Ethic for
Architecture,
Urbanism, and
Historic
Preservation

THE
FUTURE
OF THE
PAST

C.1. New entrance pavilion, Cour Napoléon, the Louvre, Paris, by I. M. Pei & Partners, 1981–89.

The stark juxtaposition of an abstract image realized in industrial materials—like Pei's pyramid and its entourage—with an articulate classicism rendered in carved stone—like the surrounding wings of the Louvre—is currently a conventional approach to relating new and old in historic settings. A provocative gesture, but at what cost to the protected landmark?

C.2. Corcoran Gallery of Art, Washington, D.C., by Ernest Flagg, 1897, and Charles Platt, 1928, with proposed addition by Gehry Partnership, 1999–2005.

C.3. Corcoran Gallery of Art, Washington, D.C., with proposed addition by Elizabeth Frick LaDuke, fifth-year thesis project, School of Architecture, University of Notre Dame, 2003.

Juxtaposing classical landmarks with contrasting modernist additions often diminishes the setting while detaching the institution from its historic identity. Gehry's proposed addition erupts in violent opposition to Flagg's building, while Frick LaDuke's counterproposal opts for continuity with the original language. The Gehry project was dropped in 2007 after a disappointing fundraising campaign, and the museum building is now being restored without an addition.

C.4. Hearst Building, New York, by Joseph Urban, 1929, with Hearst Tower by Foster & Partners, completed 2005.

Foster's glass tower and internal gutting of the landmark building were approved by the Landmarks Preservation Commission in 2001 without opposition. Despite the project's similarity to Marcel Breuer's 1968 proposal for Grand Central Terminal (see Figure 1.4), the commission found Foster's tower not an "aesthetic joke" but a "completion." Three decades of preservation successes were thus overturned. (See Chapter 1.)

C.5. Paul Cushman III International Financial Center, Dupont Circle, Washington, D.C., by John Blatteau Associates, 1989–97.

Not all contemporary architecture takes an oppositional stance toward historic contexts: The work of Blatteau and other contemporary classicists illustrates the recovery of the traditional formal languages as well as the competence to execute new works that equal or exceed the quality of traditional designs of the 1920s and 1930s. (See Chapter 1.)

C.6. An analytique of Carolands, San Mateo, California, by Sheldon R. Kostelecky, a graduate student of the School of Architecture at the University of Notre Dame, 2007.

The compositional premises of traditional architecture are fundamentally different from those of modernist design. A characteristic drawing type, the analytique, illustrates an architectural subject in several views at different scales, arranged so that the drawing itself reveals the compositional logic of the whole work. This example depicts an early twentieth-century house near San Francisco designed by Achille Duchene and Willis Polk. (See Chapter 2.)

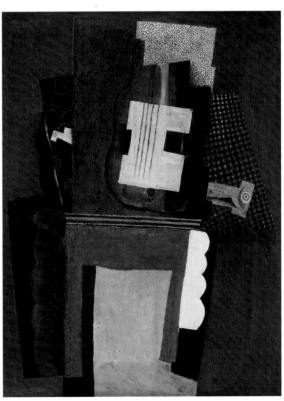

C.7. Guitar and Clarinet on a Mantelpiece, oil on canvas, by Pablo Picasso, 1915.

Cubism, a formative influence on the Modern Movement in architecture, presented the viewer with a collage-like juxtaposition of indivisible but fragmentary shapes offering different views of an object simultaneously. The differences between the analytique and the cubist collage continue to distinguish traditional and modernist approaches to composition. (See Chapter 4.)

C.8. Monument and fabric: Jerusalem Church and surroundings, Bruges, Belgium.

Traditional urbanism enacts the compositional premises of classical architecture at the scale of the city. The fabric of private dwellings and interspersed public monuments reflects a parallel rapport between vernacular and monumental character. Both are products of a common building culture sharing the principles of traditional design. (See Chapter 3.)

C.9. Katrina Cottages, Cottage Square, Ocean Springs, Mississippi, Tolar LeBatard Denmark Architects, based on a design by Marianne Cusato, 2005.

Intended as a substitute for the infamous FEMA trailer, the Katrina Cottage has redefined industrialized housing. Unlike modernist competitors, these models have entered production in large numbers, are in demand outside the intended market, and can be grouped to form urban neighborhoods. (See Chapter 1.)

C.10. Infill housing and urban conservation, San Leonardo district, Bologna, by Pier Luigi Cervellati and Commune di Bologna, 1972.

Departing from the typical approach of its time, this infill housing employed local building typologies and materials palettes to replace deteriorated buildings without displacing residents or diminishing the historic character of the neighborhood. Note the continuous street arcade characteristic of historic Bologna. (See Chapter 3.)

C.11. French Ministry of Culture, Paris, former office building by Georges Vaudoyer, 1919, as remodeled by Francis Soler and Frédéric Druot, 1999, detail.

Continuity must be sought on terms favorable to the landmark buildings we wish to preserve. In this case, the metal screens with which the architects wrapped the 1919 classical building and its 1960s glass box neighbor, intending to unify them, effectively obscure the traditional building, which appears to have been vandalized by a three-dimensional form of graffiti. (See Chapter 4.)

C.12. The Grand' Place, Brussels.

Continuity of character is not dependent on style or age. The character of the Grand' Place is clear and memorable despite varied building types, uses, styles, and construction dates because these differences are harmonized by the congruence of the formal principles shared by all the buildings. (See Chapter 3.)

C.13. Arch of Titus, Rome, first century, restored by Raffaele Stern and Giuseppe Valadier, 1817–23.

At its best, modern preservation practice seeks a balance between authenticity and permanence. Using surviving Roman marble supplemented by additions in travertine to replace missing parts, the restorers of the ancient Roman arch subtly differentiated historic from new material while rendering whole the original design of the monument. (See Chapter 5.)

C.14. Allen Memorial Art Museum, Oberlin College, Oberlin, Ohio, by Cass Gilbert, 1917, with addition by Venturi & Rauch, 1976.

Modernist and postmodernist architects have tended to emphasize "difference" rather than continuity between new and old buildings. Despite the ornamental pattern intended to link the addition (right) to the older building (left), the addition to the museum boldly asserts its difference. (See Chapter 4.)

C.15. Trinity Church, Boston, by Henry Hobson Richardson, 1872–77, with John Hancock Building by Cram and Ferguson, 1948, and John Hancock Tower by I. M. Pei & Partners, 1976.

Throughout the postwar decades, architects tried to relate new and old buildings without abandoning the element of contrast. When first built, the Hancock Tower (right) was praised as "contextual" because its glass skin "reflected" (literally) Richardson's church (left). As glass buildings increasingly reflected only one another, the older Hancock building (rear) appeared as a more appropriate model. (See Chapter 5.)

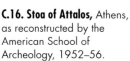

C.16. Stoa of Attalos, Athens, as reconstructed by the American School of Archeology, 1952–56.

A concern for authenticity need not preclude didactic reconstruction. Several bays of the rebuilt Stoa incorporate fragments from the original building (see lower cornice and frieze, right), subtly differentiated by the evident difference in the age of the material. Although banned by the Venice Charter as a "falsification," such reconstruction is of inestimable value for scholarship and interpretation. (See Chapters 5 and 7.)

C.17. Lever House, New York, by Gordon Bunshaft of Skidmore, Owings & Merrill, 1951–52, restored 1998–2003.

Authenticity is harder to define when industrial systems and materials are involved. Less than fifty years after its completion, the curtain wall of Lever House had to be completely replaced. The new exterior is not seen as "false" because industrial materials, unlike handicraft products, are seen as replaceable—an illogical distinction. (See Chapter 7.)

C.18. Ponte Santa Trinità, Florence, by Bartolomeo Ammanati, 1567–69, reconstructed 1957.

After its demolition by the Nazis, Ammanati's bridge of elliptical arches was rebuilt, using salvaged original materials. While such reconstructions have often been condemned as "false," in what way is the new bridge less "true" than a conspicuously different modernist design would be? (See Chapters 5 and 6.)

C.19. Baker Street buildings, London, by Quinlan & Francis Terry Architects, 2001–2, detail.

An exemplary study in continuity: Gracefully joining their Georgian neighbors, the new structures demonstrate the architects' deep identification with the architectural culture of the place as well as a commitment to superb craftsmanship. (See Chapter 7.)

C.20. New townhouse, 829 Greenwich Street, New York, Matthew Baird, 2007.

Modernist designers often struggle with contradictory impulses toward compatibility and contrast, and baffled authorities often take refuge in glib rationalizations. Here a new façade (center), featuring a slab of rusting steel, was judged compatible because it suggested the "gritty" character of the nearby former meat-packing district—in disregard of its historic immediate neighbors. (See Chapter 7.)

C.21. Grand Central Terminal, New York, by Warren & Wetmore and Reed & Stem, 1910–13, restored 1994–98. General view of Main Concourse.

One of America's greatest public interiors, the Main Concourse was saved from destruction by the U.S. Supreme Court in 1978. Departing from preservation orthodoxy, the room was restored not to its original appearance but according to the architect's intentions, including addition of the unbuilt east staircase.

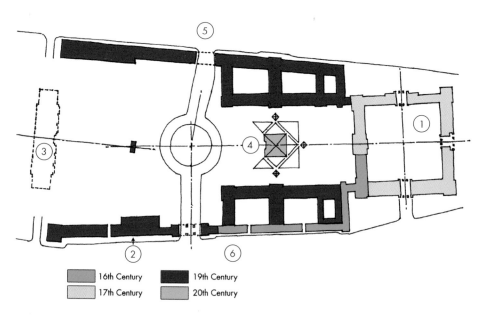

	16th Century		19th Century
	17th Century		20th Century

1. Cour Carré
2. Napoléon III wings flanking the Cour Napoléon
3. Site of Tuilleries palace, destroyed in 1871
4. Pyramid entrance pavilion of I. M. Pei
5. Rue de Rivoli
6. Quai du Louvre overlooking the Seine. (See Chapters 8 and 9.)

C.22. West façade on the Cour Carré, the Louvre, Paris, by Pierre Lescot, 1546–59, extended by Jacques Lemercier, 1624–43.

Literal Replication is a legitimate strategy for harmonizing new and old construction. Lescot's façade (the bays left of the center pavilion) was the first important realized design of the French Renaissance. A century later, Lemercier replicated it to the right of his new center pavilion to create a harmonious, symmetrical façade. (See Chapter 8.)

C.23. Plan of the Louvre, Paris, 1546–1989.

C.24. Duomo (Cathedral of Santa Maria del Fiore), Florence, entry façade designed by Emilio de Fabris, 1867–87.

Invention within a style allows the completion of an older building consistent with its historic character or the original architect's unrealized intentions. The nineteenth-century façade of the Duomo successfully complements the preexisting medieval and Renaissance elements, rendering the setting whole. (See Chapter 9.)

C.25. Saint Bartholomew's Church, New York, by Bertram Grosvenor Goodhue, 1918.

Styles may be combined as long as their underlying principles are sympathetic. Goodhue's design preserves Stanford White's entrance, relocated from the congregation's previous building and set off as a separate volume, but joins it to the new church by interweaving its limestone with the new structure's warm brick. (See Chapter 9.)

C 26. Scholastic Building, New York, by Aldo Rossi with Gensler & Associates, completed 1997.

Rossi's designs often suggested nostalgia for the traditional city, but his building is assembled from abstract shapes acting as mere signs for the traditional elements in the neighboring buildings. The new façade is, at best, an inoffensive placeholder. (See Chapter 10.)

C.27. Carhart Mansion, 3 East 95th Street, New York, by Horace Trumbauer, 1913–16, with addition by Zivkovic Connolly Associates with John Simpson & Partners, 2002–5.

An addition in a closely related style readily supports both subtle differentiation and unambiguous compatibility. The recent addition (right) is a respectful neighbor to Trumbauer's earlier façade—by virtue of similar massing, materials, and formal language—although in a recognizably different style and with a different compositional sensibility. (See Chapter 9.)

C.28 and C.29. Jorge M. Perez Architecture Center, University of Miami, Coral Gables, Florida, by Léon Krier, with Merril Pastor & Colgan and Ferguson Glasgow Shuster & Soto, 2005.

The strategy of relating old and new by abstracting from composite form to simplified shapes can also operate in reverse. Krier cleverly applies this strategy to an intervention in a modernist setting, but standing the usual relation between new and old on its head. Here, the new building adds visual interest rather than deriving value parasitically from its preexisting neighbors. (See Chapter 10.)

C.30. The Harvard Club, New York, by McKim, Mead & White, 1892, with addition by Davis Brody Bond Architects, 2004.

Formal and material contrast remains the most common strategy for additions to historic settings today. Typically, the modernist addition responds to the massing of the older building and registers its major horizontal lines; but in this case the strong material and character contrast violates an otherwise harmonious streetscape. (See Chapter 11.)

C.31. The Harvard Club, New York, with rendering of counterproposal by Cameron Cameron & Taylor, 2004.

A Georgian-style alternative to the addition as built would have extended the original structure's composition, material palette, style, and character, maintaining continuity with the predominantly masonry and classical context of West 44th Street.

C.32. A historic façade in the Piazza del Duomo, Arezzo, Italy, as restored.

Historic structures may be seen by many as "documents of their time," but that does not mean each building must register in its physical appearance "the way it has come down to us in history." Uncritically revealing layers of historical development typically leads to confusion, not to mention visual dissonance. (See Chapter 12.)

C.33. Gorham Building, New York, by McKim, Mead & White, 1906, detail of ground-floor existing conditions.

The future of the past depends on our judgments among mutually exclusive aspects of that past. One of Stanford White's finest buildings remains trapped in an unsightly "mid-century modern" alteration. Will the original design be restored, or will the alteration be preserved as a "document of its time"? What distinguishes mere "history" from the "historic"? (See Chapter 12.)

A Conservation Ethic for

Architecture, Urbanism, and

Historic Preservation

THE FUTURE
OF THE PAST

STEVEN W. SEMES

in association with

THE INSTITUTE OF CLASSICAL ARCHITECTURE
AND CLASSICAL AMERICA

W. W. NORTON & COMPANY
NEW YORK • LONDON

The art of progress is to preserve order amid
change, and change amid order.

—ALFRED NORTH WHITEHEAD (1929)

page 23: Hearst Building with Norman Foster addition (see page 27).

Copyright © 2009 by Steven W. Semes

For information about permission to reproduce selections from this book, write to
Permissions, W. W. Norton & Company, Inc., 500 Fifth Avenue, New York, NY 10110

For information about special discounts for bulk purchases, please contact
W. W. Norton Special Sales at specialsales@wwnorton.com or 800-233-4830

Manufacturing by Edwards Brothers
Book design by Abigail Sturges
Production manager: Leeann Graham

Library of Congress Cataloging-in-Publication Data

Semes, Steven W.
  The future of the past : a conservation ethic for architecture,
urbanism, and historic preservation / Steven W. Semes. — 1st ed.
    p. cm.
  Includes bibliographical references and index.
  ISBN 978-0-393-73244-3 (hardcover)
  1. Architecture and history. 2. Architecture—Psychological aspects.
3. Historic preservation. I. Title. II. Title: Conservation ethic for
architecture, urbanism, and historic preservation.
  NA2543.H55S43 2009
  720.1'03—dc22
                                    2009017360

ISBN: 978-0-393-73244-3

W. W. Norton & Company, Inc.
500 Fifth Avenue
New York, N.Y. 10110

www.wwnorton.com

W. W. Norton & Company Ltd.
Castle House
75/76 Wells Street
London W1T 3QT

0 9 8 7 6 5 4 3 2 1

Contents

The Classical America Series in Art and Architecture

The Golden City by Henry Hope Reed

The American Vignola by William R. Ware

The Architecture of Humanism by Geoffrey Scott

The Decoration of Houses by Edith Wharton and Ogden Codman, Jr.

Italian Villas and Their Gardens by Edith Wharton

The Classic Point of View by Kenyon Cox

What is Painting? by Kenyon Cox

Man as Hero: The Human Figure in Western Art by Pierce Rice

Greek and Roman Architecture in Classic Drawings by Hector d'Espouy

Monumental Classic Architecture in Great Britain and Ireland by Albert E. Richardson

Monograph of the Work of McKim, Mead & White, 1879–1915, Student Edition

The Library of Congress: Its Architecture and Decoration by Herbert Small

Letarouilly on Renaissance Rome by John Barrington Bayley

The New York Public Library: Its Architecture and Decoration by Henry Hope Reed

The Elements of Classical Architecture by Georges Gromort

Palaces of the Sun King: Versailles, Trianon, Marly, the Chateaux of Louis XIV
by Berndt Dams and Andrew Zega

Bricks and Brownstone: The New York Row House 1783–1929 by Charles Lockwood

The Architecture of the Classical Interior by Steven W. Semes

Classical Architecture for the Twenty-First Century: An Introduction to Design
by J. François Gabriel

The United States Capitol: Its Architecture and Decoration by Henry Hope Reed

Arthur Brown Jr.: Progressive Classicist by Jeffrey T. Tillman

Classical Swedish Architecture and Interiors 1650–1840 by Johan Cederlund

Carolands: Ernest Sanson, Achille Duchene, Willis Polk by Michael Middleton Dwyer

The Theory of Mouldings by C. Howard Walker, Introduction by Richard Sammons

Building Details by Frank M. Snyder, Introduction by Peter Pennoyer and Anne Walker

Antiquities of Athens by James Stuart and Nicholas Revett, Introduction by Frank Salmon

Get Your House Right, Architectural Elements to Use & Avoid
by Marianne Cusato and Ben Pentreath with Richard Sammons and Leon Krier

The Study of Architectural Design
by John F. Harbeson, Introduction by John Blatteau, and Sandra L. Tatman

The Institute of Classical Architecture & Classical America (ICA&CA)
is dedicated to the classical tradition in architecture and the allied arts in the United States.
Inquiries about the ICA&CA mission and programs are welcome and should be addressed to:

The Institute of Classical Architecture & Classical America
www.classicist.org

Acknowledgments

The phrase "The Future of the Past" was coined in 1953 by Sir Osbert Lancaster for an essay in the *Journal* of the Royal Institute of British Architects. This was followed by a lecture given by Jane Fawcett in 1970 at the Smithsonian Institution in Washington, D.C. An exhibition with the same title, sponsored by the Victorian Society at the London Central School of Art and Design in 1971, was curated by Fawcett and Nikolaus Pevsner and is now in the collection of the Victoria and Albert Museum. Sir Osbert's phrase also provided the title for the book of essays edited by Fawcett and published in 1976 as *The Future of the Past: Attitudes to Conservation, 1174–1974*. It has subsequently appeared in the titles of several other books on subjects far removed from historic preservation and urban conservation. Developments in the theory and practice of architecture, urbanism, and historic preservation in the decades since Fawcett's book appeared suggest that a reconsideration of the sentiment implied in the first half of her title might be timely now. Those same developments form the bulk of the story that I hope to tell in these pages. I have appropriated the phrase once again, with all due respect to its originators, because it so succinctly captures the spirit that I wish to promote.

The second part of my title refers to a "conservation ethic," a phrase I must credit to Anthony Tung in his *Preserving the World's Great Cities*, a book whose in-depth analysis of permanence and change in a dozen cities around the globe is a model of patient scholarship, astute judgment, and passionate advocacy.

The point of view presented here is the fruit of my lifelong involvement with preservation projects and the relationship between modernist and historic buildings, interests that extend back to childhood and that were encouraged by my parents. My first thanks, accordingly, are offered to them. Among the mentors whose teaching, work, and writings have been crucial for the development of the arguments in this book are Henry Hope Reed, Alvin Holm, Léon Krier, Jaquelin T. Robertson, and Robert A. M. Stern. Among my colleagues at the Institute of Classical Architecture & Classical America, I wish to thank in particular Anne Fairfax, Richard Sammons, Seth Weine, Francis Morrone, John Massengale, and Brian Connolly. I gratefully acknowledge the generous grant support of the ICA&CA, and extend my thanks to its board of directors; its president, Paul Gunther; and its managing director, Henrika Taylor.

Since joining the faculty of the School of

Architecture at the University of Notre Dame in 2005, my colleagues and students have greatly enriched my perspectives on architecture and urbanism. For their advice and encouragement I wish to thank in particular Dean Michael Lykoudis and Professors Thomas Gordon Smith, Richard Economakis, Philip Bess, John Stamper, Carroll William Westfall, David Mayernik, Ingrid Rowland, Steven Peterson, Barbara Littenberg, and Ettore Mazzola. My thanks to Kara Kelly of the School of Architecture staff and Marsha Stevenson of the Architecture Library for their assistance during my research. I must also express my gratitude to my students, whose enthusiasm for architectural ideas provided an invaluable stimulus. In particular, thanks to Sheldon Kostelecky and Aaron Helfand for their contributions of drawings and photographs. I cannot avoid mentioning the unparalleled experience of teaching at the School's Rome Studies Program, where immersion in the "palimpsest" of Rome and other cities in Italy has been an essential factor in the evolution of the views presented here.

Other friends, colleagues, and correspondents whose assistance and encouragement have earned my special gratitude include Professor Elizabeth Meredith Dowling at Georgia Tech, Professor Emeritus Jean-François Gabriel of Syracuse University, architectural critic Catesby Leigh, architectural historians Calder Loth and Mark Alan Hewitt, and architect Milton Grenfell.

Despite our different views on matters of architectural style, I wish to pay my respects to the late Paul Spencer Byard, whose commitment to the cause of historic preservation was the centerline of his distinguished career as architect, author, advocate, and teacher. Our public presentations and published exchanges of views in 2005 and 2006 provided opportunities to bring issues we both thought important to a broad audience within the architectural and preservation field.

The practical genesis of this book was an invitation from Clem Labine in 1997 to address the Restoration and Renovation Conference in Boston. My comments there appeared in the form of an article, "Paradigm Shift: The New Classicism and Historic Preservation," published in his Traditional Building magazine in 1999. Since then, Clem and his successors as editor-in-chief, Michael Carey and Martha McDonald, have provided numerous opportunities for the public presentation and publication of the ideas developed more fully in this book.

I want to thank the National Trust for Historic Preservation, and in particular Royce Yeater of the Midwest Office, for offering their platform for the presentation of my views and publishing a related article in the Summer 2007 issue of the National Trust's Forum Journal. Other material in this book appeared previously in the American Arts Quarterly, whose editor, James F. Cooper, deserves my thanks, together with Sandra Sanderson and the members of the Advisory Board of the Newington-Cropsey Cultural Studies Center, sponsor of the publication and related cultural events. Additional material related to this book was presented to the International Network for Traditional Building, Architecture, and Urbanism (INTBAU), whose 2006 conference, "The Venice Charter Revisited: Conservation and Modernity 1964–2006," aired emerging perspectives on international conservation standards and policies. Thanks especially to its director and the conference organizer, Dr. Matthew Hardy.

I acknowledge also the many practitioners and activists in the locations I visited in the course of my research who courageously work to change attitudes toward our architectural heritage, often in the face of fierce resistance. In particular, I salute the National Civic Art Society of Washington, D.C., Peg and Truman Moore and the Committee to Save the City in Charleston, the Nantucket Preservation Trust, the Alexandria Association, the Historic Districts Council of New York, the Greenwich Village Society for Historic Preservation, the Preservation Foundation of Palm Beach, and the Preservation Foundation for Greater Philadelphia. Many thanks to all the architects and project sponsors who contributed their points of view and essential documentation regarding the various case studies included in this book.

Production of the book was greatly aided by the capable assistance of Ruth Mandel of Images Sought & Found. Philip Langdon, Royce Yeater, Ashley Robbins, and Andrew Berman read an early draft proposal and I thank them for their support of the project. My gratitude, finally, to copyeditor Fred Wiemer, and to Nancy Green, Vani Kannan, and Nancy Palmquist at W. W. Norton & Company, whose professional guidance brought this project to realization on the printed page.

THE
FUTURE
OF THE
PAST

1.1. The Acropolis with the Parthenon, Athens, fifth century B.C.

Even the Parthenon replaces an earlier building—a Doric temple destroyed decades earlier in the Persian wars. In a constantly changing built envirnoment, a new structure is not always to be resisted, nor an older one always to be preferred.

CHAPTER 1

New and Old Architecture Together

[S]tructures with special historic, cultural, or architectural significance enhance the quality of life for all. Not only do these buildings and their workmanship represent the lessons of the past and embody precious features of our heritage, they serve as examples of quality for today. Historic conservation is but one aspect of a much larger problem, basically an environmental one, of enhancing—or perhaps developing for the first time—the quality of life for people.

—The United States Supreme Court, June 26, 1978, in *New York Central and New Haven Railroad v. The City of New York*, majority opinion by Justice Brennan

Every building that is now considered a historical monument was once new and encountered a preexisting context that it gracefully joined, disregarded, or sought to transform. Many buildings have replaced earlier structures, demolished to make way for the new one or destroyed by fire, war, or natural disaster. Whatever context it enters and whatever conditions accompany its birth, no new building rises bereft of relationships, whether intended or inadvertent, with other buildings or landscapes around it.

Especially when designing and building in cities long inhabited, the architect cannot avoid taking an attitude toward the city in its historical and morphological development. Every new building enters a conversation already in progress, but whether the colloquy is joined with tact and grace or with rudeness and disrespect depends on the intentions of the newcomer's designers, patrons, and builders. An issue as old as the second building ever constructed by human beings, the problem of how to add new architecture to old takes on added urgency when we survey a built heritage of unprecedented diversity and seek to enter and add to it from within a contemporary architecture that is similarly diverse, if not also increasingly polarized by conflicting attitudes

toward the past and objectives for the future. The modern condition, more than in the past, confronts us with the issue of the "difference" between contemporary and historic buildings and townscapes, and this has led to a rising debate about how this difference should be expressed in architectural terms.

The intensity of the disparity between the aesthetic intentions of a new building and its historic setting depends on the degree to which the architectural culture represented by the new structure is distinct from that of the older ones. New buildings in a setting where the new and old represent similar or closely related building cultures are unlikely to arouse significant controversy, at least with respect to the outward form of the new construction. For example, the Parthenon on the Acropolis in Athens, completed in 438 B.C., was a replacement for an earlier temple on the site destroyed while still under construction during the Persian invasion a half-century earlier. The new temple, though larger and perhaps more refined, did not depart radically from the design of its predecessor. Both temples were peripteral types—with Doric colonnades on all four sides—both represented similar aesthetic and architectonic ideas, and both would have been embellished with significant

1.2. Loggias of the Palazzo della Ragione (the "Basilica"), Vicenza, by Andrea Palladio, 1546, completed 1597.

Palladio's arcades wrap the medieval town hall with a classical rigor that conceals the irregularities of the earlier building. The white stone and classical orders presented a marked contrast to the existing context but became a model for imitation by others.

sculptural decoration. (Rhodes, 1998, pp. 28–34, 40–41, 86–87.) (Fig. 1.1)

Similarly, the buildings that have been proposed to date on the site of the World Trade Center in New York, destroyed on September 11, 2001, while departing from the specific form of the Twin Towers, nonetheless display the same conception of the tall office building as a figural object set in an extensive spatial field. Despite the changes in architecture and building technology in the four decades since the original World Trade Center was built, the style of mainstream contemporary architecture is still essentially continuous with that of the fallen towers. While considerable controversy has accompanied the planning for rebuilding the site, the question of what style of architecture should be adopted was not foremost among the contested issues. (Stephens, Luna, and Broadhurst, 2004, and Goldberger, 2004.)

On the other hand, there are cases where an alteration or addition to a historic setting presents a striking departure in terms of style, scale,

materials, or composition, representing a significant difference between the aesthetic intentions of the new and old construction. When in 1545 Andrea Palladio proposed wrapping the medieval town hall of Vicenza with white marble arcades embodying the principles of classical architecture, his intention was to repudiate the Gothic style—which he saw as a barbarian innovation—and return to the style of the ancient Romans, thereby reestablishing a connection with an older and, in his view, far superior civilization. There was little controversy at the time about Palladio's makeover of the older building because his views were widely shared by the learned culture of his day, and resistance to the artistic and urbanistic programs of the Renaissance—if any—has not survived in the historical record. It is nonetheless essential to remember that Palladio's opposition to medieval architecture was not motivated by his commitment to something new but, rather, by his ardent struggle to recover something old. (Fig. 1.2)

The issue is more complicated today. Richard Meier's new museum to house the ancient Ara Pacis in Rome is located in the midst of a historic setting that has been built up over the last two millennia. It is adjacent to the ancient Mausoleum of Augustus and houses a masterwork of early Imperial Roman sculpture. Adjacent to the new building are an eighteenth-century neoclassical church and a series of "stripped classical" buildings from the Fascist era on one side, and the heavy traffic of the Lungotevere on the other. Celebrated by architects and academics but largely detested by ordinary Romans, the new museum is the first unambiguously modernist structure to rise in the historic center of Rome since the Second World War, and its vivid contrast with its historic neighbors has been a source of heated debate and even proposals for its demolition. (Fig. 1.3)

Many other cities in Europe and the United States have faced similar instances of new structures in historic settings that seem to celebrate their differences from their surround-ings in ways that many observers find erodes the historic character of the place. Even in an archetypal modern city like New York, the contrast of a modernist high-rise office building on top of a low-rise classical masonry landmark building can galvanize vigorous protest. Such was the case with the 1968 Marcel Breuer project for Grand Central Terminal that resulted in the 1978 Supreme Court decision upholding the right of the City of New York to regulate new construction affecting designated landmark sites. In the decades since that case, other proposed towers have been rejected in similar circumstances, although the 2001 approval by the city's Landmarks Preservation Commission of the new tower by Norman Foster above Josef Urban's 1929 Hearst Building reversed this long-standing policy. (Fig. 1.4) (See fig. C.4 and page 23.)

The question of how to evaluate the appropriateness of new construction adjacent to or on top of historic buildings or joining an ensemble

1.3. Museum of the Ara Pacis, Rome, by Richard Meier & Partners, completed 2005.

The new structure's formal language and palette of white stucco and plate glass present a striking contrast to the classical composition and warm brick and travertine around it. The new building cannot be a model, since imitation would only undermine the impact of the "difference."

1.4. Grand Central Terminal, New York, by Warren & Wetmore and Reed & Stem, 1910–13, with proposed office tower by Marcel Breuer Associates, 1968.

The Supreme Court's 1978 decision upholding the city's rejection of the proposed office tower put preservation on a sound legal footing. Preservation of the exterior shell despite the destruction of the interior and the building's relationship to its context was recognized as an "aesthetic joke."

Because our attitudes toward the architecture of the present are shaped largely by our attitudes toward the architecture of the past, and vice versa, the dialogue of new and old architecture becomes an intersection of memory and invention often more revealing about our cultural assumptions than the production of new designs for contexts relatively untouched by reference to the past. This explains why proposals for new buildings that visibly depart from the character of their historic surroundings often arouse intense feelings: such departures challenge our sense of collective and personal identity, revealing conflicting ideas and values that extend well beyond questions of architectural form. Defenders of the existing condition fear that change will result in loss of cultural value; defenders of the new condition see preservationists as obstructing progress, of being "afraid of the future." (Maltese, 2007.) But preservation cannot be thought of as only a negative force; indeed, it is no less creative than new construction. The very act of preserving something changes it, and every conserved monument becomes "a testament not only to its initiators but to its inheritors, not only to the spirit of the past but to the perspectives of the present." (Lowenthal, 1981, p. 412.) On the other hand, the belief that a historic site can reveal unambiguously what the past was "really like" is mistaken; it rests on a fundamental philosophical misunderstanding that has distorted and exaggerated our perception of the differences between the past and the present, leading to a misguided and ultimately disappointing search for material authenticity and verisimilitude while overlooking the important lessons and artistic enrichment that the vestiges of the past still available to us legitimately offer.

One of the difficulties we face in our discussions about how to build new structures in historic settings is that most of us—members of preservation commissions, citizen activists, academics, and architects—do not properly understand the differences between "traditional" and "modernist" architecture. We tend to see them in terms of the rather unsophisticated ideas of style taught in standard architectural history courses. We assume that historical styles are the unique expressions of precise time periods and that what determines the way buildings look is the time and not the place of their construction. We believe that to define architectural style in any other way leads to

or streetscape in a historic district—especially when significantly different in scale, style, and materials—has become a matter of increasing public debate. The matter can be framed as a search for an appropriate response to the conflicting claims of continuity and change applied to a built environment displaying a range of conditions from noisome wastelands to cherished heritage sites. Any architectural response to these claims and this range of conditions is also analyzable according to a spectrum of alternatives between differentiation from, and compatibility with, the preexisting context. The current public debate will be greatly advanced if we can think and speak clearly about our attitudes toward this range of questions and options.

kitsch and the historic-district-as-museum. We maintain a strong sentimental attachment to historic places while remaining intellectually committed to what we believe are the contrary imperatives of the modern world. Because the differences between periods are exaggerated by simplistic theories of stylistic succession, we see the difference between "traditional" and "modernist" styles in contemporary architecture as one between familiar but "phony" historical imitation and dissonant but "authentic" modernist departures from historical models. We seem to be faced with a stark choice between "copies" and "experiments."

Historic places from Santiago de Compostela to St. Petersburg, from Nantucket to Santa Barbara, have been caught in the dilemma posed by this conflict between historic character and contemporary innovation. At the heart of the debate we can identify two conflicting views of how buildings relate to history: On one hand, there is the view that historic buildings are primarily to be seen as documents of their time, deserving of preservation because of their historical significance but having little relevance to how we design buildings and cities today. This view is the source of the seemingly unbridgeable gulf separating historic and contemporary art and architecture as viewed by the professional and academic mainstream. On the other hand, there is the belief that historic places are or ought to be living entities that not only can grow and accommodate change without losing the character that qualified them for preservation in the first place, but can also provide models for new work in other places and times. In this view the criterion that matters most is the appropriateness to its setting of a proposed intervention rather than conformance with currently fashionable ideas. While this is not the mainstream view today, it is growing in acceptance. It is the view that I advocate in this book.

While the debate between traditionalist and modernist positions often seems to be about architectural style, it is more accurately understood as an argument about the nature of time, history, and progress, and the ways our conceptions of these influence the kinds of interventions we find appropriate in any given setting. My objective is to persuade the reader that the architecture of the past and that of the present need not be antagonists, at least not in those places where preservation regulation aims at safeguarding our cultural heritage. In such settings we can choose continuity instead of contrast—without copying historic buildings and without introducing alien forms and materials that erode the historic character of the places we love. It is not our time that demands contrast between the new and the old but an aesthetic theory and a philosophy of history that have long since proved inadequate.

To prompt thinking about this debate in new ways, I propose the adoption of a *conservation ethic* that can be shared by architects, urban designers, and preservationists based on the assumption that the century-old gulf between the architecture of the past and that of the present is not permanent and need not exclusively determine our approach to historic places. (Tung, 2001, pp. 9–10.) As a starting point, I examine values that transcend style and necessarily draw together the now disparate fields of architecture, urbanism, and historic preservation. I propose a common ethic for all three of these specializations that is based on an attitude of respect toward, and understanding of, valued elements of the past. If we believe that safeguarding historic structures, districts, and landscapes is legitimate and noble, then we may reasonably prioritize those approaches most likely to further this intention and deemphasize those likely to inhibit it. While there ought always to be room in our cities for architectural innovation and experimentation, there must also be places dedicated to the continuity of valued architectural character. Keeping these two desiderata in balance is the challenge now faced by architects and preservationists alike. Though the delicacy of this balance should not be underestimated, I believe there is ample room for common ground among diverse viewpoints.

In order to limit an already expansive subject, I confine my inquiry to the specific case of new additions to historic buildings in urban settings or new buildings in urban historic districts. It is in these instances that the dilemmas raised by the relationship of new and old architecture are most intensely presented and where the opportunities for the development of a new conservation ethic are most abundant. While this discussion inevitably touches on restoration practice, the primary focus is less on the technical treatment of designated sites and structures than on the new features, additions, or infill buildings that we choose to introduce into a historic setting, whether that is an individual building, an ensemble of structures, an urban neighborhood, or a historic landscape.

1.5. Façade of 1001 Fifth Avenue, New York, by Johnson/Burgee Architects, 1980.

Philip Johnson attempted to render the new façade (left) "compatible" with its historic neighbor (right) by mechanically continuing the older building's horizontal lines across the new façade, but genuine dialogue requires coherent language on both sides.

As readers will have already surmised, this book is written from a particular point of view with respect to the larger debate it describes. For this reason it aims at fairness rather than objectivity. One cannot state the terms of a debate with utter neutrality while also taking a position within it. I acknowledge this difficulty and try to state the arguments of different positions as fairly as I can; however, I also disclose at the outset that I draw conclusions and make judgments that I hope will be accepted as not unreasonable, even when the reader disagrees with them. Debate on the subject explored by this book has not been conducted publicly at a high level until very recently, and the criteria for evaluating different arguments are still emerging. The comments and judgments I make are offered in a spirit of dialogue and will, I hope, contribute to the emergence of a new consensus on the conservation of cultural resources in our built environment. Further, I hope that this book will empower professionals, academics, students, and informed citizens to question fashionable but uncritically assumed views about architecture and the city that currently obstruct the instinctive drive to make places, monumental or modest as the case may be, that aspire to beauty, sustainability, and justice.

Changing Ideals in Architecture, Urbanism, and Preservation

In the four decades since the passage of the National Historic Preservation Act of 1966, the historic preservation movement has grown from a small grass-roots campaign protesting against ill-advised utopian urban renewal schemes and short-sighted commercial development to a multi-billion-dollar industry and social reform movement with broad support in both the public and the private sectors. Elaborate mechanisms for financing, extensive public review processes, corporate and government project sponsorship, and university-trained professionals have institutionalized the movement. But it could be argued that, in becoming mainstream and professionalized, preservation has lost its original idealism and dissident character, especially its opposition to utopian visions of architecture and the city. Today the products of modernist design are themselves increasingly the subjects of preservation efforts. As the purview of the preservation movement advances into the era of the buildings it once sought to prevent being constructed, it must face anew the question "What should we preserve and why?"

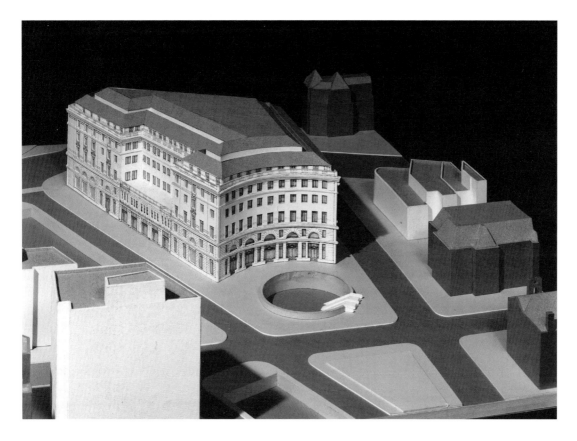

1.6. Paul Cushman III International Financial Center, Dupont Circle, Washington, D.C., by John Blatteau Associates, 1989–97, model.

The Cushman Center (see fig. C.5) is the only constructed part of a proposal to rebuild the entire site, incorporating new and historic structures at a scale appropriate to the monumental setting. The project was blocked by preservationists committed to the defense of an inferior status quo.

Many preservationists are reluctant to be seen as obstructing the progress of contemporary architecture, but "contemporary" design today is not what it was when the preservation movement came of age in the 1970s. By the end of that decade, the once-impregnable dominance of orthodox modernism, as represented by firms like Skidmore, Owings & Merrill and the architecture and design department of the Museum of Modern Art, faced growing challenges from postmodernist critiques. By the 1980s a new pluralism allowed even frankly classical designs (which began to appear in the professional press in the mid–1970s) to garner awards from leading publications like *Progressive Architecture*, and debates about the value and appropriateness of "historical allusion" were the mainstay of the academies. Self-conscious quotation of motifs derived from historical architecture or literal replication of features drawn from the immediate context were used to adorn otherwise modernist buildings and make visual connections between new construction and preexisting conditions. (Fig. 1.5) This was the intent of the "contextualism" that the *New York Times* saw as the "watchword" of the New York Landmarks Preservation Commission's deliberations prior to the

Hearst Tower decision. (Dunlap, 2001.) In the late 1980s and through the 1990s, however, a more aggressive strain of modernism emerged that was less accommodating toward traditional architecture. An uncompromising new attitude—typified by the designs of Frank Gehry, Rem Koolhaas, Zaha Hadid, and Peter Eisenman—seemed to render the "sympathetic addition" untenable, and a sound basis for compromise between historic and contemporary design seemed to disappear. (See figs. C.2 and C.4.)

While the modernists reconnected with the heroic phase of Modern Movement abstraction and expressionism, the more traditional-minded postmodernists gradually dropped their "allusive" and "ironic" pose and explored a more learned application of traditional formal idioms, pursuing what their modernist colleagues referred to as "literal" or "historicist" designs. Gradually, the new traditional work moved beyond "paper architecture" as interest in the recuperation of traditional construction also increased. Thanks to the success of historic preservation programs, many traditional building crafts and materials became feasible for new construction, and new technologies and materials made the execution of traditional details

1.7. Church of Our Lady of the Rosary (Shrine of St. Elizabeth Ann Seton), New York, by Shanley & Sturges, Architects, 1965.

Stylistically harmonious additions found favor in the early years of the preservation movement in New York. The Georgian-style chapel (left) adjoins the 1794 James Watson House (remodeled and enlarged by John MacComb in 1806), both now besieged by enormous office towers.

OPPOSITE

1.8. Master Plan, Battery Park City, New York, by Cooper Eckstut Architects & Planners, 1978–83.

Battery Park City's plan continued Lower Manhattan's historic street grid into the site along the Hudson River, allowing the street-and-block pattern to "make more of itself" while establishing a superb new public resource, the riverfront Esplanade. (See figs. 12.3A and B.)

more economical. New traditional architects began to produce contemporary buildings comparable to those produced by the last generation of traditional designers and builders a half-century earlier. (Fig. 1.6 and see fig. C.5.)

To their surprise, the traditionalist architects often encountered resistance from preservation authorities when proposing stylistically sympathetic interventions in historic settings. Initially—in the 1970s and 1980s—bodies like the New York City Landmarks Preservation Commission looked favorably upon extensions of landmark buildings in the same style as the original building (or in a closely related style) and typically denied approval to projects that, however allusive to the historic setting in abstract terms, presented significant departures in formal language and character. (Fig. 1.7) By the late 1990s, in parallel with the new assertiveness of the modernist designers, the commission's "contextual" criteria shifted in favor of a more strongly contrasting character, and traditionalist proposals were subject to greater scrutiny and occasional rejection. A similar shift occurred nationally, including in programs of new construction for federal government facilities. (Dunlap, 2000, 2001, and 2007, and Alderson, 2006, p. 9.)

Far from seeing new traditional design as a natural ally of preservation, many professionals and policy-makers in the field disapproved of attempts at stylistic continuity on the grounds that additions or infill structures should be clearly distinguishable from landmarks and give evidence of the "architecture of our time," which was typically identified with an exclusively modernist aesthetic. This stance was often justified by reference to *The Secretary of the Interior's Standards for Rehabilitation*, which discouraged new construction that might blur the distinction between new and old, as new designs in traditional styles were believed to do as a matter of course. This document, which has for decades served as the de facto national preservation policy in the United States, was written in 1977 when new traditional architecture was not yet visible as a viable alternative to modernism. Subsequent revisions and interpretations have not reduced the confusion that has grown up around the interpretation of its principal terms. (See Chapter 7.)

New movements emerged in urban design during the same period. By the late 1970s, there were few advocates left for the large-scale urban redevelopment schemes of the previous decades, and many urbanists—inspired by the writings of Jane Jacobs and William H. Whyte—found a new appreciation for traditional city neighborhoods. Opposition to high-rise housing projects, freeways slicing through dense urban districts, and suburban sprawl became the focus not only of social reformers but of dissident architects and planners as well. By the 1980s, supporters of the movement called New Urbanism launched their remarkably successful campaign to change the paradigms of American city planning—away from monocultural zoning and automobile-centered design and toward higher-density, mixed-use, pedestrian-scaled communities. The pioneering master plan for Battery Park City in Manhattan and the new town of Seaside, Florida, were the first of hundreds of Traditional Neighborhood Developments (TNDs) intended to reconstitute traditional urbanism while accommodating contemporary life. New Urbanism also attracted support from a growing number of modernist architects and planners who recognized the disastrous effects of Modern Movement urban theories but who continued to support a modernist style for individual buildings. (Fig. 1.8)

Among critics of New Urbanism, a reaction against the emphasis on small-scale neighborhood development prompted new schemes for large-scale redevelopment reprising themes from the heroic phase of the Modern Movement, a revisionist reappraisal of the "visionary" projects of Robert Moses in New York, and a revival of what the *New York Times* called "Big Urbanism." (Haskell, 2006, and Jackson and Ballon, 2007.) Consequently, modernist designers have been left with the choice of embracing a New Urbanist critique that rejects modernist urbanism or embracing models of the city that have proved disastrous in the eyes of everyone but the current avant-garde.

While the connection between preservation and urbanism has still not received much theoretical attention, preservationists since the 1920s have increasingly focused on ensembles rather than isolated buildings. The very idea of a historic district implies a view of urbanism in which the fabric and character of the whole take precedence over individual structures. Today a vast number of protected buildings fall within designated historic districts and the management of these districts precludes a "one building at a time" approach. Moreover, one

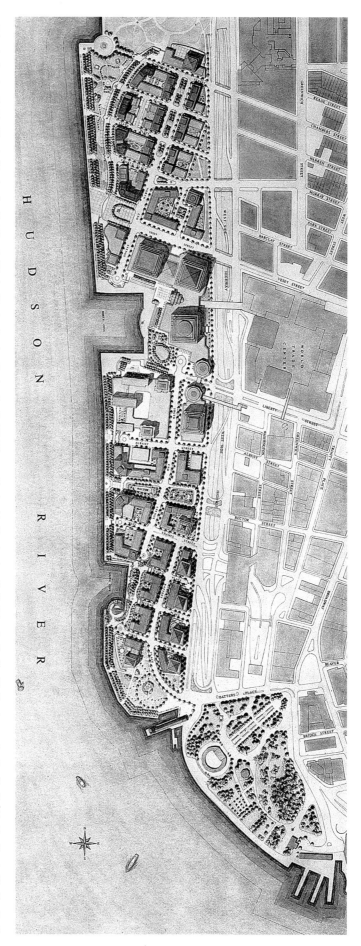

cannot imagine the success of New Urbanism today in the absence of intact historic neighborhoods like Williamsburg, Georgetown, Nantucket, New Castle, and Charleston, to name only a few American examples that have served as textbooks for a new generation of town planners. The use of pattern books and form-based codes in new TNDs is essentially an extrapolation from the physical survey techniques long used by preservationists to identify and evaluate areas under consideration for historic district designation. The pattern books employ these survey methods to define a local style of building that can then be extrapolated into new fabric that sustains the existing fabric or applies historic patterns to newly developing areas. Pattern books also envision the development of a community over time, despite the participation of many individual designers, in much the same way as unselfconscious design traditions and codes operated in the past. (UDA, 2005, and Mouzon, 2007.)

As a consequence of the developments in architecture and urbanism, which have split the design community between traditionalists and modernists, "contemporary design" can no longer be identified with a single style. The new condition challenges the belief, still held by many in the mainstream, that modernism uniquely and inevitably represents the "architecture of our time." Clearly the *Zeitgeist*—if there is one—is changing. As views of what constitutes contemporary architecture are debated, so, too, attitudes toward historical architecture and the obligations it places on preservationists and practicing architects and planners must be redefined. New construction in historic settings will inevitably have a "contemporary stamp," as the Venice Charter of 1964 called for, though the character of that stamp may no longer always be a modernist one. (ICOMOS, 1964.) A large and increasing segment of the architectural profession now seeks to fully recover the formal languages, bodies of knowledge, technical skills, and craftsmanship that produced the environments we now consider worthy of preservation, inevitably blurring the distinction between historical buildings and new ones. Indeed, the current separation between the fields of architectural history or preservation and the design of new environments is historically unprecedented and most likely culturally unsustainable. The criteria for evaluating new construction in historic settings must now be revised to account for the increasingly diverse stylistic conditions of contemporary architectural practice and the need for architects, urbanists, and preservationists to collaborate fruitfully in what James Marston Fitch called "the curatorial management of the built environment." (Fitch, 1982.)

A Conservation Ethic

In addressing the issue of the proper relation of new and old architecture in the traditional city, there must be agreement among architects, urban planners, and preservationists about their goals. The interests and expertise of these three classes of professionals overlap too much to permit them the luxury of autonomy; a common scale of values and a common ethic must unite them. My argument proposes that this common ethic be based on the concept of conservation, both in the narrower sense of preserving historic structures, neighborhoods, and landscapes, and in the broader sense of conserving values, meanings, skills, and building cultures. The new ethic will promote respect for the lessons we draw from the past while bringing civility and beauty to whatever conditions new ways of life and new technologies may create in the future. Taking natural resources conservation as its model, the new ethic will support and cultivate self-sustaining communities and the building traditions that enable their physical realization and maintenance, promoting an ecology of the built environment. Just as the environmental movement has brought into mainstream American culture new awareness of environmental conservation, so an emerging awareness of cultural resource conservation should be seen as a related and parallel aspect of our caring for the world—the world we make as well as the natural world we depend on.

Conservation, as I use the term, does not mean embalming something that is dead, like insects in amber; rather, it means managing and cultivating something that is alive, as one conserves an endangered species, a rain forest, or a garden. Natural resources are conserved by maintaining the ecosystems that sustain them; sometimes this involves clearing away invasive growth and taking remedial action to repair damage. In the same way, cultural resources remain alive when they continue to be used and assume new roles in the ongoing life of the man-made ecosystem of the city that surrounds them. Not everything is of equal value; conditions must be assessed and decisions made, including decisions to remove noxious or unsafe environments in order that better and safer ones may grow. The conservation ethic does not mean a ban on change; rather, it means the management of change to avoid unnecessary loss. Conservation is tied to the concept of culture, which, as Hannah Arendt reminded us, is of Roman origin, deriving from *colere*—"to cultivate, to dwell, to take care, to tend and preserve"—a term that ultimately "indicates an attitude of loving care." (Arendt, 1977, p. 211.) Extending that "attitude of loving care" to the built environment is the main purpose of the conservation ethic.

Historic buildings and districts are not stage sets or the setting for a theme park; nor are they museum artifacts to be protected under glass. They are our own homes, workplaces, gathering places, monuments, places of leisure, and the sources of several things necessary for human happiness, including the sense of pride, orientation, belonging, and participation in a community life longer and greater than one's own individual life span. A sense of place, recognized and supported over a long period of time by the community residing in that place, is a cultural achievement of a high order, whether in a New Mexico pueblo, a colonial town like New Castle, Delaware, or Rome's ancient Campo Marzio.

The desire to sustain and conserve the character and spirit of such a place—even when the community that formed it has disappeared or been transformed into something different—is an essential part of the ongoing development of any culture. In response to the furious pace of social and cultural change today, the counterbalancing drive to retain some things that either do not appear to change or change relatively slowly has only intensified. In the realm of architecture, this drive to sustain the old need not be associated with any particular political program or values drawn from other aspects of life. Indeed, the longevity of our historic built environments has repeatedly allowed them to survive the obsolescent social, economic, political, or religious ideas that may have become attached to them in the popular imagination. Hence, sophisticated urbanites enjoy living in loft spaces formerly devoted to manufacturing, and traditional housing stock comes to be occupied by successive waves of residents representing different social and economic classes, ethnicities, and ways of life.

1.9. 500 Park Avenue, New York, by Gordon Bunshaft of Skidmore, Owings & Merrill, 1960, with office tower by James Stewart Polshek & Partners, 1991.

Employing the same style and material palette as the original building without imitating it, the new tower (right) demonstrates a continuity rarely evident in recent additions to traditional buildings, where current policies all but mandate a contrasting style.

Because the issues under consideration here are primarily (though not exclusively) urban issues, I take it as axiomatic that architects, urbanists, and preservationists must recognize the city as their primary concern: The city—meaning the historic centers of organized settlement, ranging from country hamlets to metropolitan capitals—is the stage on which the performance of civilization presents itself. If the best life for human beings is, as Aristotle believed, "the life of moral and intellectual excellence lived in communities," and if the city is the physical form taken by a community to represent itself, then the conservation of our cities is tantamount to the care and promotion of civilization itself. (Bess, 2006, pp. 11–15.) Architects, urbanists, and preservationists must, therefore, be advocates for and curators of the cities in which they work. Each decision they make should be "an act of urban craftsmanship." (Davis, 2006, pp. 235–36.) The principle proposed here is that neither preservation nor design can afford to look upon any given site as a blank canvas, but must always look to the larger whole of which any individual building site is a part. Moreover, they must not look upon that whole as raw material to be mined or transformed; nor should they see it as sacrosanct and unchanging, but as a setting deserving of respect and that with proper care and cultivation holds the long-term promise of beauty, sustainability, and justice.

The conservation ethic does not represent or dictate any style of architecture. This book is not an argument against modernism or in favor of classicism; rather, it is an argument for *continuity and wholeness*, regardless of style. A new modernist building in a modernist setting may be as welcome as a new traditional building in a traditional setting. Modernist architects have already adopted something like the conservation ethic when dealing with modernist landmarks; they proceed on the basis of understanding and respect toward a work from the tradition in which they themselves were trained. (Fig. 1.19) Indeed, the works of the leading modernist designers have become the objects of intense scrutiny when alterations or additions to their works are proposed. Controversies over proposed expansions of Frank Lloyd Wright's Guggenheim Museum and Marcel Breuer's Whitney Museum in New York, Louis Kahn's Kimbell Museum in Fort Worth, and Eero Saarinen's Dulles Airport Terminal near Washington, D.C., focused on the inviolability of the author's original conception. (See fig. 8.6.) In general, these landmarks have been treated with more delicacy than many traditional or classical landmarks. We cannot imagine, for example, the New York City Landmarks Preservation Commission approving a glass office tower on top of the Whitney. On the contrary, after several successive and increasingly deferential schemes by Michael Graves and then Renzo Piano were withdrawn in response to protests, no addition to this building is now planned. (Byard, 1998, pp. 151–52, and Vogel, 2006.)

While one cannot deny that differences exist between contemporary architecture (however it may be defined) and the architecture of the past, exaggeration and dramatization of that difference for its own sake reinforces the perception that disruption, distortion, and disorder uniquely characterize modern life, a view that denies the parallel and equally inescapable persistence of continuity and coherence—both as historical realities and as fundamental necessities for human flourishing. Promotion of or acquiescence in an avant-garde cult of rupture simply reinforces a self-fulfilling prophecy that threatens the destruction of our historical built environments. In truth, the view that new architecture should confront the old in a spirit of opposition is probably the easiest solution; it certainly makes the least intellectual or artistic demands on the architect or critic. One can hardly expect designers to treat with sympathy the products of architectural traditions that they do not understand or care to learn about. But it is also reasonable to ask that those who cannot accept and respect the architectural heritage that precedes them have the integrity to leave it alone, and those charged with defending heritage values ought to see that they do. Following the example of members of the medical profession, architects and planners working in historic settings should take a version of the Hippocratic Oath: "First, do no harm."

I do not probe deeply here into the question of what structures or neighborhoods should be designated as landmarks or how individual candidates for such protection should be evaluated. I conduct my argument on the assumption that most of the historically and architecturally significant sites constructed before the ascendancy of modernism have already been identified and protected. I realize this is not, in fact, the case, but to pursue further the criteria for designation would take us too far from our main subject—the way we treat and build alongside the landmarks we already have or are likely to have. I urge preservationists everywhere to continue to work for the safeguarding of our architectural heritage, especially the works of the modern traditional architects undervalued or overlooked by mainstream historians and critics.

The related issue of how to evaluate and treat modernist buildings that are increasingly receiving landmark protection is likewise beyond the scope of this book. The identification of cultural resources deserving of protection, no less than the study of how to integrate such designated sites into the larger context of the ever-changing city, will become increasingly urgent in the coming decades as more of the "recent past" becomes eligible for landmark protection. The possibility of designating as city landmarks Penn Plaza and Madison Square Garden, which rose on the site of the demolished Pennsylvania Station, was discussed in 2006 at a panel discussion on "Landmarks of the Future" sponsored by the Municipal Art Society in New York. The suggestion that we should extend protection to the buildings that rose on the rubble of the demolished landmark whose loss prompted the legislation that empowered preservation designation in the first place is a bitter pill for longtime preservationists to swallow. Without some publicly supported scale of values, without a high standard for what is considered "historic," the temptation to consider worthy of preservation everything that survives for the requisite fifty years will be increasingly hard to resist. (Leigh, 2001.)

The Role of Tradition in Architectural Practice

If some valued element of the past is to have a future, it must be transmitted across the existential gap of the present—by us. In the present moment we decide what aspects of the past shall have a future by choosing what to take with us and what to leave behind. That act of selection—whether conscious or unconscious—is tradition. The contemporary is whatever we remember at any given time; the act of remembering changes that which is remembered, making it new. "The backward glance transforms," as the classical architect John Barrington Bayley reminded us, and this is why the architecture of the Renaissance is not simply a revival of Roman architecture but a new creation inspired by the ancient models. (Bayley, 1984, pp. 2–3.) Tradition is not something we have—an unchanging set of "rules"—but, rather, something we do—an active cultivation of models, examples, and experiences to inform our work in the present. The more conscious, reflective, and inclusive our selection of models, the more rich and fertile the tradition will be. I explore further the workings of such traditional processes in Chapter 3.

As used in this book, the terms "traditional architecture," "traditional urbanism," or "the traditional city" indicate aspects of historic architecture and urbanism that have long been part of an ongoing balance between constancy and change in local building cultures. The practice of traditional architecture entails the gradual accrual of a body of knowledge that changes slowly, rather than a search for unprecedented solutions or unique gestures. Traditional urbanism is the art and science of building and caring for cities as places that persist in time for the benefit of their citizens rather than as a ratification of market forces or a realization of currently fashionable ideas about style. Similarly, historic preservation is a conservatorship of the best achievements in architecture and urbanism, not an embalming of individual fragments culled from a now vanished world or the uncritical immortalizing of the past.

Historic preservation is now in a position to broaden its view of its own subject, moving away from an exclusive concern with built artifacts toward a cultivation of the processes that build and sustain historic environments. The "loving care" implicit in the notion of conservation extends from individual built works to the skills, procedures, and technologies that made those valued works possible. Judgments of what is deserving of conservation must also be made publicly and transparently, taking into account the views of responsible stakeholders from the professions, the academy, the building trades, government, and—most important—the community most affected by such decisions. Neither new building nor preservation can afford to operate "one building at a time." Traditional architecture and urbanism offer us a viewpoint from which we may observe community-building as a social and cultural process—a *building culture*—rather than as an object fixation or a closed aesthetic accessible only to initiates. (Davis, 2006.)

While the term "language" applied to architecture should not be taken literally, it is a useful metaphor. It is natural to see classical architecture, for example, as a fluid system of conventions—a *grammar*—within which either conformance to or departure from those conventions can be meaningful. Without agreement as to the relationship between supposed meanings and the forms that supposedly embody them, there can be no real communication and no true innovation. Only within constraints can we freely invent. Other artistic disciplines have recently returned to their own respective traditional languages: Composers again write tonal music, poets again write verse in meter and rhyme, and painters again represent the known world in paint on canvas. Now architects and urban designers again propose buildings, districts, and landscapes that use the historic languages of their craft to negotiate and hold in balance the competing claims of memory and invention. Together, these movements constitute a true cultural paradigm shift—a revolution and a renaissance. They also reintroduce the idea that the arts are both a creative and a preservative force; innovation in one's medium and conservation of relevant models from the past are both essential functions of the artist's calling.

The Recovery of Building Cultures

Improving technical knowledge of the materials and methods of historic building construction has enabled us to make leaps in preservation technology, greatly facilitating diagnostics, stabilization, and—where necessary—replacement of historic materials. The current restoration efforts on the Acropolis in Athens, for example, would be unthinkable without the use of computerized databases, high-tech construction equipment, and contemporary materials such as titanium. (Fig. 1.10) But technical sophistication alone is not enough to preserve or restore cultural resources. Without understanding and respecting the artistic aims of those who placed a particular entablature on top of a particular column, we cannot hope to know how to replace a missing piece, remove a nonconforming alteration, or add a wing to accommodate the growth of the building's program without risking diminishment of the qualities that made the building eligible

for protection in the first place. Our growing knowledge about traditional architecture and urbanism, and our recovery of design skills that allow us to apply this knowledge in contemporary practice, are helping to bridge the gap between making new buildings and caring for old ones.

As an illustration of the preservation of building cultures, let me relate an experience I had as a young architect with the National Park Service in the mid–1970s. Traveling to New Mexico to inspect National Register sites applying for federal matching funds to undertake preservation projects, I visited one of the ancient Native American pueblos near Santa Fe. The residents of the pueblo—a massive but intimately scaled megastructure of adobe and timber dating back half a millennium—were seeking support for ongoing conservation of their historic home. New adobe bricks lay baking in the sun as they had for centuries, and workmen applied mud plaster to the walls just as their ancestors had done. (Fig. 1.11) The state had denied funding for the project because the community was making changes to the building, altering it from its appearance in photographs from a few years before: Here a door was changed to a window, there a window was added, elsewhere another opening was removed, etc. Each of these changes was being made in a way consistent with traditional practices. I argued that the grant should be approved because what needed to be preserved was not the specific appearance of the pueblo at any given moment, but the *living culture of building* that had continued unbroken for centuries, conserving the whole while allowing necessary and reasonable change in the parts. My superiors were convinced by this argument and the grant was approved.

I have since come to see that the same logic applies to other building traditions, such as the American Georgian and Colonial Revival styles in which my grandfather worked, building modest houses in Plainfield, New Jersey, in the 1920s, and which I have continued to explore in my own professional design work. In places like Nantucket, Massachusetts, contemporary designers and builders continue to erect houses following a design tradition based on eighteenth- and early nineteenth-century models, guided by codes designed to protect the area's unique character. (Fig. 1.12) (Lang, 1979.) These examples show us that what we ought to preserve is not only specific individual build-

1.10. The Parthenon, Athens, fifth century B.C., under restoration, 2007.

New stone elements carved in Pentelikon marble (from the same quarry used by the original builders) replace pieces damaged by atmospheric pollution and disastrous consolidations with reinforced concrete undertaken in the 1930s. Only ideological resistance prevents a more complete restoration of the temple.

TOP

1.11. Taos Pueblo, Taos, New Mexico.

Taos Pueblo developed over centuries as the community maintained and altered the structure using the materials and techniques of their ancestors. The survival of a building culture is more important than preserving the structure's appearance at a given moment.

BOTTOM

1.12. Aerial view of Nantucket, Massachusetts, from the tower of the North Meeting House.

Blessed by a wealth of early nineteenth-century buildings and streetscapes, Nantucket has managed growth and change by means of a strict urban code. Appropriate new buildings need not be feared and change need not necessarily bring loss of historic character.

ings or even large urban districts (as important as they undoubtedly are), but also the design and craft traditions that brought them about. Architect and author Howard Davis defines a *building culture* as "the coordinated system of knowledge, rules, and procedures that is shared by people who participate in the building activity and that determines the form buildings and cities take." (Davis, 2006, p. 3.) It was the building culture, not the state of the building at a particular time, that the National Park Service saw as the cultural resource to be preserved in the case of the New Mexico pueblo. Many such building cultures are still practiced or recoverable today, and in such traditions the loss of an individual building is not necessarily tragic if the building culture remains alive to maintain the character of the place despite losses and additions. At the very least, preservation authorities cannot logically discourage new work that seeks to continue the building culture that originally produced the landmarks entrusted to them.

The Architecture of Our Time Versus the Architecture of Our Place

Much damage to our historic environments has been done in recent years by misguided policies that defer to "the architecture of our time" when faced with proposed new architecture within historic settings. This theme has been a frequently heard leitmotif in recent public debates on the subject in New York, Charleston, the University of Virginia, and elsewhere. While it is true that our judgments about the art and architecture of the past are inevitably colored by our interests in the present, it does not necessarily follow that we are obligated to contrive our designs today so that they will appear "different" when juxtaposed with historic examples, as some preservationists have insisted. (Fitch, 1982, and Byard, 1998.) In truth, the architecture of our time is whatever we choose to make it as it emerges from the conditions of contemporary practice. There is no guarantee that architecture today will be uniquely identifiable as belonging to the present moment, and it may even closely resemble the architecture of some other time. We should design what seems most appropriate for the character of the historic settings in which we build, without slavish imitation of current fashion or a contrived evocation of "difference" simply so the work will be seen as ours.

If we observe the conservation ethic proposed here, the architecture of our place will flourish in beautiful disregard of chronology and the architecture of our time will naturally take care of itself—it will inevitably be our own but will only be recognizable as such in retrospect.

This viewpoint entails a different view of history—and specifically the history of architecture—than is generally assumed and taught in the professional and academic mainstream today. If we are concerned to show the uniqueness of each historical era, we will naturally concentrate on the ruptures and breakthroughs that have dominated the historiography of architecture since the waning of the Renaissance. If, on the contrary, we look at architecture from the point of view of continuity of languages and building cultures, we see a different picture. While both emphases reflect reality, the prevailing emphasis on discontinuity in contemporary culture prompts a closer examination of the continuities that have too often been overlooked. I address these historical questions more thoroughly in Chapter 6.

Nearly fifty years ago, Henry Hope Reed opened his book *The Golden City* with a chapter called "The City of Contrasts," showing on opposite pages photos of modernist and classical buildings representing the alternative visions of these two antagonistic building cultures. (Reed, 1971.) Despite occasional critical interest in revealing abstract analogies between some modernist works and some aspects of historical practice, modernism has largely embraced contrast as its default mode in relation to the preexisting environment. This stance has been the source of much of the power of modernist icons to engage the public imagination—from the Seagram Building to the latest tower by Jean Nouvel—but it has also sparked public opposition, fueled the historic preservation movement, and empowered the recovery of traditional architecture and urbanism in contemporary practice. Today we can place alongside views of the City of Contrasts alternative views depicting the City of Continuity, a fine-grained network of places whose character is the product of building traditions centuries old, seamlessly interwoven with new constructions that seek wholeness rather than rupture with their surroundings. The City of Continuity is the historical city no longer subject to a stylistic monopoly for new works and freed to assume the forms best suited to the context regardless of the date of construction. In the City of Continuity, the demands of place supersede those of time.

Beauty, Sustainability, and Justice

Vitruvius, author of the sole surviving architectural treatise from ancient Roman times, defined good building as satisfying the conditions of *firmitas*, *commoditas*, and *venustas* (or "firmness, commodity, and delight" in Sir Henry Wotton's seventeenth-century English translation), and this formulation has remained the centerline of Western architectural thought for two millennia. (Vitruvius, 1999, p. 26.) All architecture must deal with the realities of building construction, accommodation of human need, and the satisfaction of the aesthetic sense. In the modern world we may properly emphasize the need for environmentally sustainable construction and development; for just and equitable accommodation of the physical, social, and spiritual needs of the inhabitants of buildings and cities; and for the healing power of beauty. It is not enough to seek separate solutions to each of these demands; nor can we elevate one or two of the three above the others. Instead, we must seek the simultaneous and optimal resolution of all three in a single synoptic proposal. In my view, this ancient insight remains the foundation of any serious architectural discourse.

While the primary focus of this book will be on the physical appearance of buildings and cities, it is essential that this discussion be framed by equally important concerns about environmental sustainability and social justice. The conservation ethic's commitment to the beautiful city is more than a call for cosmetic prettiness; it envisions healthy, environmentally sustainable, pedestrian-centered, and economically viable places. Furthermore, as our society enters what may very well be an era of continuing environmental crisis, the longevity, material economy, and lifetime energy efficiency of buildings and cities places traditional building methods and urban settlement patterns in the forefront of an enlightened response. We now recognize that many traditional building materials and methods naturally tend to be long-lived, renewable, and energy-efficient. Traditional urbanism, having arisen in the eras prior to the availability of inexpensive fuels, is inherently conserving of energy and natu-

ral resources. The combination of these time-tested materials and methods of building with new technologies that allow us to maintain comfort while reducing depletion of nonrenewable resources promises to be the most effective strategy for realizing more ecologically sound built environments. (Kunstler, 2005, and Rypkema, 2007.) (Fig. 1.13)

The preservation of successful models of urban architecture, neighborhoods, housing stock, and communities is also a matter of social justice. While many of the pioneers of the Modern Movement proclaimed their commitment to improving conditions among industrial workers

1.13. Arcade on the north side of the Piazza Grande, Arezzo, Italy, by Giorgio Vasari, mid-sixteenth century.

Virtually all construction before the age of inexpensive petroleum was "green." Building in accordance with local conditions is the hallmark of traditional architecture, as in the familiar arcades that shade both people and buildings from solar gain in hot climates.

and the poor, the urban renewal experiments following World War II in the United States not only destroyed thousands of buildings, but brought dislocation and suffering to countless individuals, families, and communities. The realized projects often became places of crime and despair as the negative impacts of social-engineering failure fell disproportionately on poor and immigrant communities, often the people least able to opt out of unwanted changes to their environment. (Bluestone, 1994, and Charleston Charter, 2005.) Similarly, numerous researchers and observers have noted the social and cultural deficits associated with suburban sprawl, which is particularly harsh in its effects on children, low-wage workers, and the elderly. (Kunstler, 1994, and Hamilton, 1999.) Whatever moral advantage the modernist reformers may have held in the 1920s, it would be difficult to find anyone now who thinks that the housing types innovated by the European avant-garde nearly a century ago remain viable models for social housing today. Programs like the United States Department of Housing and Urban Development's HOPE VI have succeeded in replacing dysfunctional public housing projects with newly constructed mixed-income urban neighborhoods based on traditional models, and organizations like Habitat for Humanity are commissioning and building new prototypes for affordable housing from traditional architects. (Gartner, 2006.) Perhaps the most important and innovative recent entry into the arena of affordable housing has been the Katrina Cottage program, which promises to revolutionize the industrialized housing industry and deliver, for the first time, dignified and permanent housing to populations displaced by disasters or simply poorly housed for a host of other reasons. (See fig. C.9.) Today modernist housing schemes typically attract only the luxury residential market, where the allure of "retro-modern" remains strong.

It is also true that the traditional cities that we admire today have not always been salubrious or just places. Even the best-designed housing fails under conditions of overcrowding or deferred maintenance. Nor can architectural design compensate for social arrangements based on exploitation, discrimination, or slavery. We cannot be insensitive to painful memories of the past that may have become attached to certain styles of architecture; but neither should we disregard how styles have been appropriated by many different groups and causes throughout history. No style of architecture has a monopoly on either virtue or vice—all kinds of buildings have been used by political and social elites to project their power and values, for better or worse. While architectural monuments and styles are never entirely morally or politically neutral, we must exercise caution when judging the uses made of architecture by a wide variety of movements and regimes, including progressive and democratic ones. Accordingly, the conservation ethic seeks to promote a more just and equitable management of the urban environment, taking into account the viewpoints of a large and diverse group of stakeholders, many of whom lack the economic or political clout to make their voices and interests known in the normal course of urban development. The growing use of community-based planning processes—such as the public design charrette—has demonstrated that planning and development can be responsive to the interests of a broad spectrum of constituencies.

Because this book is primarily an investigation of architectural aesthetics in historic urban settings, I devote the bulk of my attention to how buildings look, how new buildings are designed, new cities planned, and historic built environments preserved. This is not to suggest that considerations of politics, economics, technology, or sociology are unimportant—on the contrary, they are very important—but simply to focus the present inquiry on those issues most directly affecting the physical appearance of harmonious and culturally rich urban environments. If the making of satisfactory and beautiful places is not determined by nonarchitectural matters alone, it is likewise not solely reliant on the vagaries of individual genius—though that is not unimportant, either. My inquiry investigates how architects and preservationists discern and realize the *appropriate*, which I define as the fitting and the exemplary, in the course of designing, restoring, altering, and adding to buildings and cities over time. In this way, the cultivation of beauty by means of the development of styles, building cultures, and communities of taste remains a proper subject for public discussion. It is neither objective nor subjective, but a matter of thoughtful judgment and, therefore, of moral and political significance in the broadest sense of these terms.

The history I draw upon in making my argument is limited to the cities and traditions I know best—that is, those of western Europe and North America—but I believe that other cities and other traditions will prove equally susceptible to parallel investigations and interpretations. Indeed, the imposition of inappropriate preservation standards on existing traditional communities in non-Western countries has prompted recent criticism of the outlook enshrined in the Venice Charter as it has been interpreted around the world. (Hardy, 2008.) It is my hope that this book will empower professional architects, urbanists, preservationists, citizen activists, and lovers of urban environments everywhere to resist the forces contributing to the continuing isolation and loss of our cultural resources and argue for the values that promote beautiful, sustainable, and just cities, wherever they may be.

A Note on Terminology

In this book my use of the term "modern" refers to the present time and the conditions of contemporary life, irrespective of style. "Modernism" refers to the current mainstream style of architecture descended from the Modern Movement of the 1920s, as exemplified by the work of Le Corbusier, Ludwig Mies van der Rohe, Walter Gropius, and their followers around the world. Current practice of modernism is extremely varied in appearance and intentions but, as I try to show in Chapter 4, remains definable in terms of certain constant principles that distinguish it from traditional architecture. The term is intended to be descriptive, not pejorative. "Historicism" denotes a philosophy of history arising in the nineteenth century in the writings of Hegel and Marx, which I examine critically in Chapter 6. "Traditional" architecture and urbanism are those practices of design and production rooted in local building cultures or inspired by Western classicism, in contrast to the universalizing and abstract ideals of the modernism that arose as a reaction against them. By "building culture" I mean the body of knowledge, technical skills, and craftsmanship that characterize the design and construction practices of a particular community, place, or period in history. The term is therefore independent of style and fashion, though possibly influenced by them, and they by it. (Davis, 2006.)

The terms "preservation" and "conservation" have different meanings in American and British usage. In this book "preservation" is any activity designed to sustain cultural resources, historic sites, or protected buildings and districts, employing a range of treatments from simple maintenance to rehabilitation for new uses, to restoration of missing or damaged fabric, to complete reconstruction of buildings or elements no longer extant. By "conservation" I refer to practices of a kind well established in the field of natural resources to maintain the life and health of living systems. The conservation of cultural heritage as proposed in this book is analogous to the care and cultivation that one directs toward ensuring the survival of any natural environment, hence my call for a "conservation ethic."

2.1. Piazza Navona, Rome.

The piazza is enclosed by a
mixture of ecclesiastical and
private buildings of diverse
ages, in a variety of styles,
and reflecting a range of
characters from monumental
to vernacular. This diversity
is harmonized by a set
of seven shared formal
principles.

CHAPTER 2

The Principles of Traditional Architecture

Attaining a greater degree of visual coherence in our architectural surroundings is one of the main tasks of architects, planners, and developers. I did not arrive at this conviction by theorizing about the meaning
of Architecture, or by considering the architect's rather vague political
or philosophical responsibilities, but by looking around and realizing
that visual continuity was a major component of those places which
I found beautiful. It should be clear from the historical examples that
these felicitous relationships do not depend on copying. But to achieve
such visually coherent surroundings once again does require a change
in the way we have been taught to see these relationships and a delicate redefinition of architectural creativity.

—Brent Brolin, "Architecture in Context:
Fitting New Buildings with Old" (1981)

Observers of historic European cities are often impressed by the way buildings, districts, and landscapes sustain a remarkable continuity of scale and character
despite having been built over long periods of time. Many familiar architectural works, like
a number of Gothic cathedrals or the massive complex of the Louvre in Paris, were completed by a succession of architects many years after construction began but yet retain a sense
of wholeness that is not diminished by subtle variation. Not just buildings but entire urban
ensembles reflect the same consistency. While a number of familiar European urban squares—
the Place Vendôme in Paris or the Piazza del Campidoglio in Rome, for example—were
built to a unified design with uniform wall treatments around the outdoor rooms they
enclose, many others form lively but coher-
ent ensembles representing a variety of different styles and periods. The Piazza Navona in
Rome, the Piazza San Marco in Venice, and
the Grand' Place in Brussels are harmonious
spaces enclosed by buildings in a variety of
styles and from different eras, each of which
was once new and took its place as an intervention within a preexisting setting. American
buildings such as the United States Capitol and

urban ensembles like Jackson Square in New
Orleans provide similar examples of growth
with continuity. While it is clear how buildings
or urban spaces designed as wholes to begin
with can display consistency and integrity,
what accounts for the coherence we see in the
buildings and places built up over the course
of centuries? Do buildings of different styles
share common principles that allow them to
form ensembles despite their differences? Why
do we often feel that modernist buildings introduced into such settings sound a discordant
note? Is the difference between modernist and
traditional architecture simply a matter of style
and subjective preference or indicative of more
fundamental disparities? (Fig. 2.1)

Consider two architectural icons of traditional and modernist sensibility, respectively:
Charles Garnier's Paris Opéra of 1861–74 and
Ludwig Mies van der Rohe and Philip Johnson's Seagram Building in New York, completed in 1959. The Opéra looks like a complex
and articulate body: it is a whole revealing its
parts, and its parts compose other wholes, all
of them exhibiting pattern similarities at different scales. Portions of the building—particularly the pavilions on the sides of the main
block—seem to be budding buildings in them-

45

2.2. Opéra (Palais Garnier), Paris, by Charles Garnier, 1861–74.

Four views of the Paris Opéra show how a classical building reveals different information at different scale levels and depending on the distance from which it is viewed. This "fractal" quality extends beyond the building to engage the city around it.

selves, as if the Opéra were growing additions from its own genetic material. The structure reveals different aspects as we observe it from varying distances: From down the Avenue de l'Opéra, we see the building as a whole, extending its influence beyond its own footprint as it engages the surrounding buildings and streets, themselves designed to provide a

consistent setting for the climactic monument in their midst. As we approach, new information appears as worlds of detail gradually come into focus. (Fig. 2.2)

The Seagram Building, with its appearance of technical virtuosity and calm restraint, is based on the repetition of a single module, in this case a window unit in a bronze-mullioned curtain-

2.3. Seagram Building, New York, by Ludwig Mies van der Rohe and Philip Johnson, 1957–59.

Organized on a regular grid, the building displays few distinct scale levels and does not reveal different information as one approaches. A freestanding object in a neutral spatial field, the building inverts the traditional relationship between private buildings and public space.

wall system. The building is not so much a whole composed of hierarchically subdivided parts as a meticulously detailed assembly of machined components. From a distance the building appears as a handsome object subtly articulated into ground-floor lobby, office floors, and a crowning band concealing the mechanical floors. The arrangement of the whole recalls the base-shaft-capital tripartition of a classical order, although without the sequences of smaller parts and molding profiles: there is only the scale of the whole and the scale of the detail. Unlike the Opéra, the building does not yield significant new information as we approach, but, rather, the individual components that make up the pattern of its elegant bronze curtain-wall system come more into focus. Because of the strong object quality of the building, it is difficult to imagine how an addition might be designed that would not ruin it. When originally built, it stood as an isolated object behind its austere plaza, related axially to its classical neighbor across Park Avenue (the New York Racquet Club of McKim, Mead & White, 1916–19) but otherwise in sharp contrast to the traditional

masonry buildings that surrounded it. Today it fades into a background of similar metal-and-glass curtain-wall buildings of considerably less interest. (Fig. 2.3)

In the Garnier building and the Mies van der Rohe work, we see not only differences of style and period, or of material and technology, but fundamentally different conceptions of formal order and of the relation between the individual building and the city in which it stands. My purpose in juxtaposing these two structures is not to make an invidious comparison—I personally admire both of these works—but to suggest that traditional architecture, like Garnier's Opéra, may be understood as a reflection of the ways nature organizes and orders itself, generating stupendous variety by the application of a handful of relatively simple principles operative at a variety of scales. The Seagram Building, on the other hand, represents a different view of nature and science—one based on linear and repetitive systems of the sort introduced by industrial production. If the first example reveals patterns of emergent complex order, the second defines a system of fixed ele-

ments and relations that are then iterated independently at different scales. (Glieck, 1987, pp. 116–17.)

This distinction, admittedly based on broad and arguable generalization, is nonetheless useful for taking account of the continuity we see in traditional urban environments and the contrast between them and the modernist interventions in their midst. If we take the comparison further to include many more examples representing different periods, styles, building types, and scales, we can identify and compare the principles we observe operating in traditional and modernist architecture, respectively, based on their conceptions and use of the common attributes of *space*, *structure*, *elements*, *composition*, *proportion*, *ornament*, and *character*. At the risk of further excessive generalization, I undertake such a review of the formal principles underlying traditional architecture with respect to these seven attributes and illustrate how their operations singly and all together inform the architectural richness we commonly observe in valued historic places. Limitations of space do not permit more than an outline

of such an analysis here, but even this brief review may yet reveal useful perspectives on the sources of the continuity or contrast characterizing relations between new and old architecture in historic settings.

Space

In traditional architecture, space is typically conceived of as if it were a solid body. Space takes the form of a recognizable figure, which is to say a traditional architectural space may always be seen as a room, whether interior or exterior. A street is simply a long and narrow exterior room, a city square is a more regularly proportioned room, and any room—however grand or modest, whether interior or exterior—is potentially describable as a discrete figural volume or collection of volumes in terms of solid geometry. Traditional space has a distinct shape, scale, proportion, and size, as if the volume were a molten substance that had taken the shape of its mold. Traditional space is always bounded, and the nature and quality of

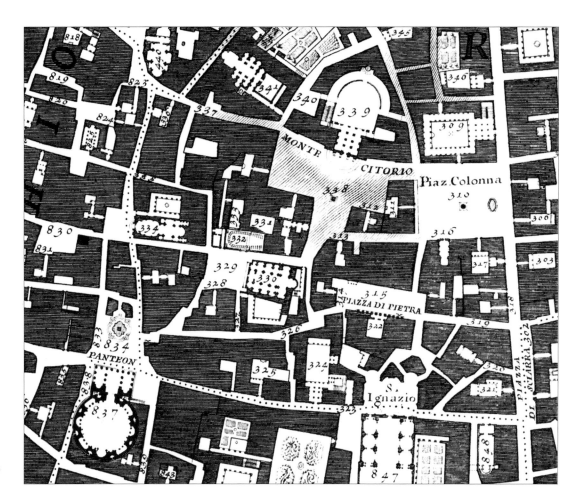

2.4. Plan of Rome (detail) by Giambattista Nolli, 1748. © 2006; reprinted by permission of the University of Oregon Nolli Map Project.

Nolli's map illustrates the traditional city as a network of public rooms—both exterior and interior. The solid masses of the buildings form the ground against which the public spaces stand out as figures. The space is keyed to the pedestrian observer, not an abstract system.

the bounding surfaces and the linkages between one space and another are essential aspects of the built environment. An archetypal example of traditional space is the interior of the Pantheon, although the same principle applies in outdoor urban spaces as well. (See Fig. 2.1)

This concept of space has profound implications for the design of the city, as illustrated by the eighteenth-century plan of Rome by Giambattista Nolli. In this remarkable document the public spaces of the city—both interior and exterior—are shown as a series of linked rooms. Space is the figure and buildings are the ground; the fabric as a whole predominates over the individual building. Even when buildings are freestanding, they are not isolated objects, but always participate in the definition of some larger figural space. (Fig. 2.4) (Norberg-Schulz, 1980, pp. 160–64.)

The geometrical construction of traditional space is governed by axes that provide a sense of orientation and movement. The axis is not only an instrument of bilateral symmetry, but also directs where we look—it is a line of vista. Where the eye goes, the body wants to fol-

low, and a space in a recognizable shape with a discernible axis (or series of axes of graduated importance) invites us to move, making the traversal of the space into a journey with a beginning, middle, and end. This is the source of much of the animation we find in great spaces, even when they are occupied by only a few people. A longitudinal space like the Piazza Navona may be contrasted with a centralized space in which the most important axis is the vertical one at the center, as in the Place Vendôme in Paris. However it may be organized, a traditional space is always a form of embodied geometry. This is the case whether the space is an irregular shape—like the Piazza del Campo in Siena—or a regular one—like the Place Stanislas in Nancy. While the first instance is less geometrically formalized than the second, they have in common a strong figural character defined by enclosure, center, and vista—which implies movement. (Fig. 2.5)

This traditional understanding of space is reflected in the Renaissance conventions of perspective, which sustained an analytical coherence between space and form. In perspective, space becomes visible, not only as a quantity or implied ground, but, crucially, as a figure. Perspective locates and organizes both space and objects in ways that reveal hierarchy, scale, and orientation. Sharing the traditional conception of space allows buildings, streets, and squares built up over long periods to sustain a sense of place, whatever other aspects of the environment may change. Additions or alterations that conform to the preexisting space conception are likely to reinforce or clarify the implied embodied geometry and movement; conversely, introducing a different spatial conception threatens to destabilize or destroy the character of the place by confusing its sense of enclosure and implied movement. (Peterson, 1980, pp. 88–113.)

The geometrical construction of traditional space need not be restricted to the Euclidean solids. In projects like the churches of Sant'Ivo alla Sapienza or San Carlo alle Quattro Fontane, both in Rome, Borromini introduced geometries that seem to defy closure and promote uncertainty. The Baroque vistas created by Vanvitelli at Caserta, Neumann at Würzburg, or Guarini in Turin all suggest extension into indefinite spatial realms reflecting the contemporary discovery of infinity. These are not, however, undifferentiated neutral fields—they suggest indefinitely large but still enclosed and geometrically ordered spaces whose centers and circumferences might be beyond our powers of

perception at the moment but which nonetheless are potentially discoverable and knowable. Similarly, the grand vistas and complex, scenographic spaces of the Baroque city reveal a sense of extension that seems nearly infinite, but is nonetheless terminated and contained. Traditional space is never simply defined by an abstract system, but always presents us with a model of the cosmos—a cosmos in which humankind has a rightful, if modest place.

Structure

By "structure" I mean the rational and visually convincing representation in the building's design of the tectonic and material forces acting upon and within it. Because all earthbound structures are subject to gravity and because our sense of well-being demands that we feel secure inside and outside of buildings, not only must a structure succeed in resisting gravitational forces to remain standing, it must be seen to be doing so. Apparent loads superimposed on building elements must be visibly and convincingly brought down through the structure to the ground. Buildings that are top-heavy or that feature elements with no visible means of support produce anxiety, whether or not they are, in fact, engineered sufficiently to resist collapse. The proportion of a building's height to its width, the apparent robustness of its visible

2.5. Three models of urban space.

Squares typically display embodied geometry and an implied directionality, as in the longitudinal Piazza Navona, Rome (A), the centralized Place Vendôme, Paris (B), and the non-orthogonal Piazza del Campo, Siena (C).

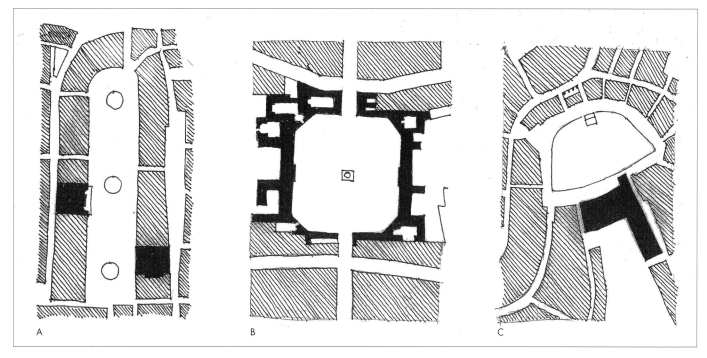

A   B   C

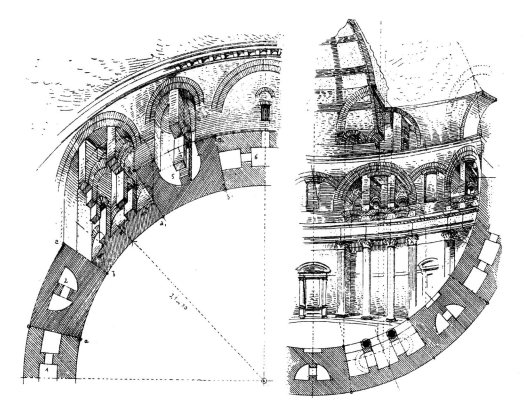

2.6. The Pantheon, Rome, second century, from G. B. Milani, *L'Ossatura Murale,* 1920.

This Roman masterwork illustrates "fictive structure" inside and out: The visible articulation is largely a cosmetic cladding concealing the actual structure, designed on an altogether different system. But even the fictive elements appear to be load-bearing.

structural support system, the proportions of its openings and their relation to solid wall, the thickness of walls or other supports, and the grace with which implied loads are carried down through the structure to the ground—all are indicators of conformance to or departure from tectonic logic. (Fig. 2.6)

Structural systems may be either skeletal or massive; hence, traditional construction falls into two broad types: trabeated systems based on a timber framework of posts and beams and arcuated systems based on masonry arches and vaults. Usually, these systems are given distinct expression in buildings, but they may also be combined, as they were artfully in ancient Roman construction. The varied uses and expressions of these systems, singly or in combination, are an essential matrix out of which all traditional construction grows. One may, for example, understand classical architecture in terms of the relations between columns and walls, illustrating the architects' fascination with structural systems that can be perceived as simultaneously rational and expressive.

The necessities of statics and stability require that buildings constructed of load-bearing masonry adhere to tectonic logic, which is why almost all such buildings appear regular and well-proportioned. But the apparent tectonic structure need not be the actual means of supporting the building; traditional architecture often includes elements that are more decorative than strictly tectonic. Such decorative structure may be either consistent with the actual load-bearing structure of the building or in opposition to it. What is essential is that whatever looks like structure be designed as if it were load-bearing. For example, a building elevation articulated into horizontal layers recognizes the reality of gravity by making the lowest level appear relatively massive and the uppermost relatively lighter in weight. Similarly, vertical divisions across a façade suggesting a series of columnar supports are typically rendered in a way that represents a logical arcuated or trabeated system, whether or not these vertical elements actually provide structural support. Window openings are supported on string courses or pedestal-like panels rather than "floating" on the wall surface. This principle, which I have called "fictive structure," is followed by virtually all buildings of any pretension to distinction throughout the history of Western architecture prior to the ascendancy of modernism. (Norberg-Schulz, 1965, p. 163, and Semes, 2004, pp. 22–31.)

Materiality is another aspect of structure. Naturally, the materials used contribute to the total impression of a building and may influence its form, though they can rarely be said to determine it. A clear, rational, and expressive presentation of structure, whether actual or fictive, cannot be conceived apart from the materials constituting it, and much of the richness of traditional architecture comes from the satisfaction we derive from observing well-crafted materials at work. The introduction of iron, steel, glass, and reinforced or precast concrete, while to an extent liberating the designer from the limitations of older materials and methods, does not change our expectation of tectonic logic, which includes recognition of the capacities of different materials to perform according to their natures. While the familiar systems of load-bearing masonry and timber construction have been proven by long experience, alternative materials and methods have also been used as instruments of traditional architectural expression, enriching and refreshing the building culture. In truth, advanced structural systems and materials have yet to be exploited by contemporary traditional architects in ways that fully reveal their expressive potential while remaining faithful to the traditional principles of design.

Elements

One way of identifying traditional architecture is to try to describe a building or an urban ensemble in words. Traditional buildings and neighborhoods are made of smaller bits of architecture, each of which has a name, a history, and a characteristic role to play in the larger composition in which it occurs. An example of such an element is the *aedicule*: a miniature "building" consisting of a pair of columns rising above a pedestal and supporting an entablature and pediment, which in Roman times formed a shrine for the statue of a divinity. Aedicules continue to be used as framing devices, often for painted or sculpted human figures, or as surrounds for door and window openings. Such a composite element may also be a link in a chain of related elements making up a larger composition: A series of aedicules might compose a *façade*; a series of façades define a *street*, several of which make up a *district* centered on a small public *square*. We recognize such elements as potentially beautiful and useful constituents of our built environment, but they are also subdivisions of larger architectural compositions that also have names, histories, and roles to play. Different building traditions or styles may have different elements or call them by different names, but all our traditions create new architecture out of bits of other, older architecture. (Fig. 2.7)

Each individual element in a composition is a transformation of an ideal type, and so appears both familiar and new at the same time. For example, a new entrance door might be so designed that it reminds us of all other important doors we have seen, and yet reproduces none of them. The same could be said of other elements of buildings—windows, stairs, ramps, pediments, domes, balustrades, courtyards, etc.—as well as various elements of the city—fountains, benches, flagpoles, kiosks, waterways, bridges, statues on pedestals, rows of trees, even a common letter box. These elements of a building, district, or city make the

2.7. The aedicule as an architectural element: Church of Orsanmichele, Florence, fifteenth century, with sculpture of "Doubting Thomas" by Verrocchio.

Traditional architecture is typically composed of recognizable elements like the aedicule—a temple-like shrine for a sculptural figure later widely adapted for window or door surrounds and other uses at a variety of scales.

A

B

2.8. Variations on the aedicule in urban architecture.

Variations on the aedicule include a door surround at the 1830s Merchant's House Museum, New York (A), the fifteenth-century wellhead in the piazza at Pienza, Italy (B), a twentieth-century subway kiosk on Michigan Avenue in Chicago (C), and a standard letterbox in Bruges, Belgium (D).

built environment readable and facilitate orientation; at the same time, they allow for invention, as the designer finds new meaning in the adaptation of familiar forms. At a larger urban scale, spatial types like streets, boulevards, piazzas, squares, and districts give order and coherence to the city, acting as individual elements in the fabric that they collectively compose. It is primarily these architectural and urbanistic elements that we mean when we speak of the "character-defining elements" of a historic site or district. (Fig. 2.8)

The elements that most strongly demonstrate adaptability and inventiveness are the ancient orders (also referred to as *genera* or "types") of classical architecture—the Doric, Ionic, and Corinthian types, plus the derivative Tuscan and Composite—a "cast of characters" that governs the proportions and ornament of wall surfaces, articulates structure and rhythm, and carries iconographical meaning. Like many other aspects of traditional architecture, the orders are at once universal and particular, pragmatic

C

D

and poetic, timeless and invented anew with each use. It is appropriate to think of the orders not as something applied—a kind of extraneous decoration—but as something latent in the architectural composition, a veritable "genetic code" governing the proportions and ornament of walls and spaces. (See Wilson Jones, 2000, p. 109, and Semes, 2004, pp. 32–41.) (Fig. 2.9)

While buildings prominently displaying complete orders on their elevations are familiar from many classical monuments, it is not the presence of columns that makes a building classical. A building with no visible columns or pilasters—called "astylar," from the Greek meaning "without columns"—may nonetheless be designed with an *implied order*. By this means, buildings of different type and character can be composed into coherent ensembles by what the contemporary architect Robert Adam calls "progressive omission," meaning that the orders appear on their façades with varying degrees of explicitness. (Adam, 1990, pp. 138–39.) (Fig. 2.10) These variations allow

buildings to respond to the suitability-to-purpose that Vitruvius called "decorum"—while the implied order sustains continuity among different buildings despite their superficial differences. (Vitruvius, 1999, p. 25.) The streets and squares of Paris offer numerous illustrations of such "progressive omission," from the full columnar orders on buildings associated with the monarchy to the astylar façades of ordinary apartment houses.

The classical orders embody the compositional, proportional, and ornamental possibilities of the classical tradition. Other traditions have elements that fulfill analogous roles. For example, Gothic architecture may be analyzed in terms of such elements as the aedicule, rib vault, bundled column, lancet window, flying buttress, and center-occupied opening. Entire cathedrals may be understood as elaborate sets of nested aedicules. (Summerson, 1949.) Such elements—however selected or defined—are the building blocks from which traditional buildings and urban settings are made, regardless of style.

DORIC ORDER

A Sima
B Corona
C Bed Mold
D Triglyph
E Metope
F Taenia
G Regula
H Guttae
I Abacus
J Echinus
K Necking
L Cincture
M Flute

IONIC ORDER

A Sima
B Corona
C Modillion band
D Bed mould
E Frieze
F Cymatium
G Architrave
H Abacus
I Volute
J Eye
K Echinus
L Flute

2.9. The classical orders as elements of architecture.
Drawn by Sheldon R. Kostelecky, graduate student, School of Architecture, University of Notre Dame, 2006.

The classical orders are a family of "types" governing the proportions and ornament of a wall composition. The three principal orders in antiquity were the Doric, the Ionic, and the Corinthian, later codified in the Renaissance with the addition of the Tuscan and the Composite.

CORINTHIAN ORDER

A Sima
B Corona
C Modillion
D Bed mould
E Dentil band
F Frieze
G Cymatium
H Abacus
I Fleuron
J Lip
K Calathos
L Helices
M Volute

N Cauliculo
O Cincture
P Flute

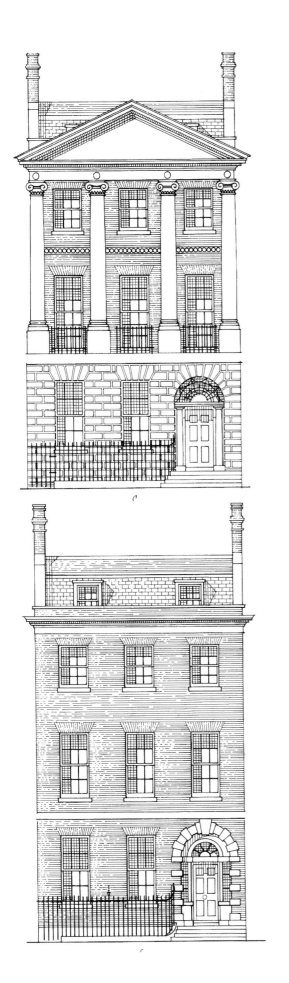

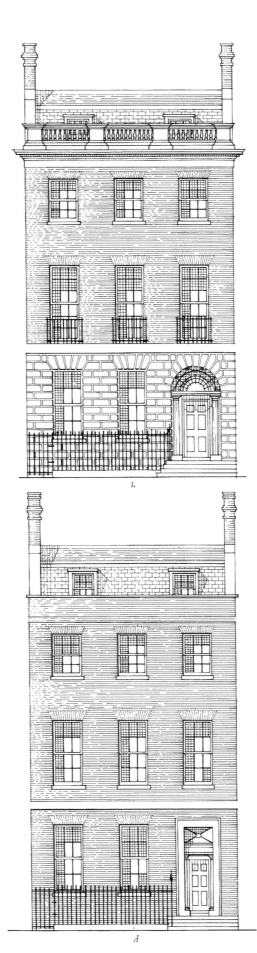

2.10. Progressive omission in the use of architectural orders, from *Classical Architecture,* by Robert Adam, 1990.

Many traditional buildings display classical proportions and ornament without visible columns or pilasters. A composition governed by one or more classical orders can be edited or enriched depending on the demands of decorum.

Composition

Composition is the principle that distinguished the Paris Opéra from the Seagram Building in the comparison made earlier: these two buildings are put together in fundamentally different ways. Composition, meaning literally "putting it together," defines the elements and relations of an architectural work, embracing the concepts of *arrangement* and *scale*. Traditional buildings are *arrangements of nested composite forms*; that is to say, they are so arranged that the parts assume precise and mutually defining relationships with one another and with the whole. Every form is a whole composed of parts, and each of these parts is also a whole composed of still smaller parts. For example, a classical column appears whole in itself but is also composed of a capital, shaft, and base, each of which is a whole composed of molding profiles or other smaller components. The column is also a part of a larger order including, potentially, a pedestal and entablature which, in turn, might compose a larger building façade that is part of an urban ensemble of buildings on a street or square. This ensemble, finally, is part of a city.

In virtually all traditional styles, composition moves from the whole to the detail and back again by means of a process of hierarchical subdivision in which every whole is a part and every part is a whole, depending on the scale level at which it is viewed. This compositional process may be extended indefinitely at larger or smaller scales, limited only by the practical limits of our perception, our production methods, or our interest. This idea of composition has been fundamental throughout the classical tradition, from Vitruvius (who described it as the basis for beauty, or *venustas*) to Alberti (in his theory of *concinnitas*) and into the modern era. (Tzonis and Lefaivre, 1986, p. 98, and Semes, 2004, pp. 47–52.)

Traditional composition is reflected not only in finished buildings but also in the ways they are conceived and represented graphically, and there is no better demonstration of this than the classical type of drawing known as the *analytique*. This drawing convention, a staple of the educational program of the École des Beaux-Arts, involves the depiction of a building or element in multiple views and at various scales within a single drawing. All the parts of the drawing are so arranged and sized on the sheet that they appear to represent a composed tableau of actual fragments—a depiction of real objects in real space—as if the elevation of a building in the background were viewed through a frame of architectural elements, drawings on scrolled parchment, or other similar features in the foreground. The drawing itself, as well as the object depicted, is an example of the classical composition of parts and wholes. (See fig. C.6.)

As the views of the Paris Opéra from varying distances reveal, different scale levels within a composition allow us to direct our attention to different parts of a composition without losing a sense of the whole, and vice versa. The whole and the smaller parts work in parallel, tied together by recurring self-similar patterns across scales but still allowing each part to reveal its own new information. For example, the parts of a classical entablature are composed in a way that mirrors the compositional strategy of the entire order and, in turn, the building façade in which the order occurs. In the most beautiful buildings the details and the whole explain one another; the details present themselves with maximum vividness without diminishing the vitality of the whole. In the same way, the buildings of a well-designed city may recall and reflect the compositional patterns operative in the city as a whole.

A well-composed building or architectural element follows three simple canons of arrangement: those of *number*, *punctuation*, and *inflection*. (Edwards, 1926 and 1944, p. 2.) (Fig. 2.11) The most important goal of any composition is to create a strong center or focus (even if not the geometrical center of the composition). The canon of number expresses a preference for an odd number of elements or bays, since this allows for an open center, as in the space between the center pair of columns in a temple front. An even number of bays or spaces sets up a duality, which may have its uses in composition but is not typically resolvable into a strong center. (Gothic architecture developed ways of resolving such dualities by its use of a different proportional system, discussed below.) The canon of number embraces the classical concept of *tripartition*, in which elements tend to occur in groups of threes: left, center, right; bottom, middle, top; base, shaft, capital; architrave, frieze, cornice; etc. The canon of number does not require symmetry, but it does promote balance and the avoidance of dualities.

The canon of punctuation allows parts to

OPPOSITE

2.11. Three canons of composition.

Trystan Edwards defined three canons of architectural composition: the canon of number (A) seeks to avoid duality and create a strong center; the canon of punctuation (B) links and separates elements by introducing frames, borders, and transitions; and the canon of inflection (C) promotes vitality through rhythm and hierarchy.

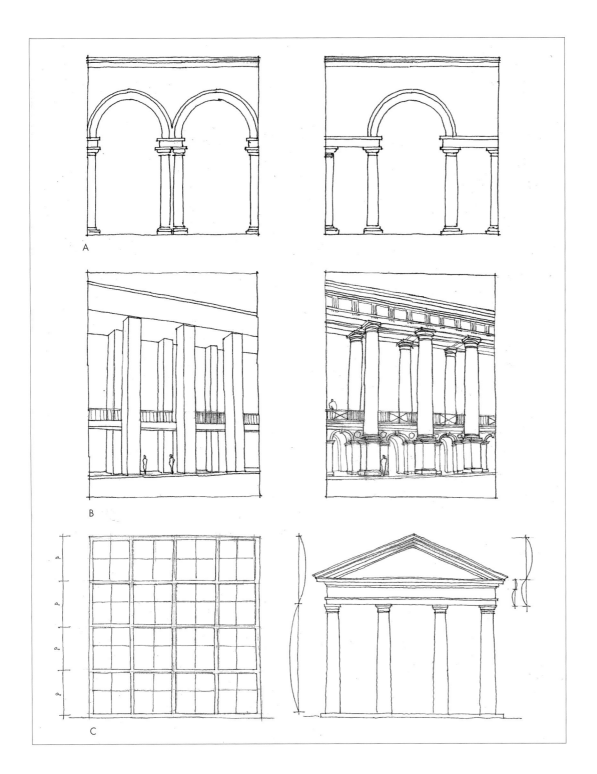

A

B

C

be joined gracefully by means of a transition, border, or frame that both separates and links adjacent parts. Punctuation in formal design is analogous to the commas, semicolons, and colons of written language. Architectural elements are not merely juxtaposed or collided, they are brought into an articulate and unified arrangement by transitions and nested frames. Punctuation prompts us to give special treatment to important moments of transition, such as the point where a beam rests on the top of a column (yielding the punctuating capital), or where a wall meets the ground (a water table), or a building turns a corner (quoining). At an urban scale, we might say that a city composed of traditional streets and squares uses punctuation to establish the relationship between continuous fabric and intermittent monuments and open spaces.

Finally, the canon of inflection introduces hierarchy, so that the parts are not monotonously repeated, but form dynamic composi-

A

B

C

D

2.12. Four compositional models.

Four compositional options are bilateral symmetry, as in Palladio's Villa Barbaro (A); asymmetry, as in the lagoon façade of the Doge's Palace in Venice (B); local symmetries composing a global asymmetry, as at the Erectheum in Athens (C); and asymmetries composing a global symmetry, as at the Villa Aldobrandini at Frascati (D).

OPPOSITE

2.13. Comparison of scale and scale levels.

A. Arc de Triomphe, Place de l'Étoile, Paris, by J. F. T. Chalgrin, 1806–36.

B. Arc du Carrousel, the Louvre, Paris, by Percier & Fontaine, 1807–9.

The eye expects the number of scale levels to match the size of an object: the bigger the structure the more subdivisions one expects to see. A very large structure with few scale levels (A) will seem to loom even larger, while a smaller structure with more scale levels will seem intimate by comparison (B).

tions on the analogy of the human body and other natural systems. In any composition some one element must be dominant and the others must inflect toward it, although such domination and submission need not be blatant or conspicuous. Subtle inflection is often the secret of vitality in compositions which, appearing regular, prove upon closer scrutiny to be carefully nuanced. Such is the secret of the ancient Greek temples, which achieve a perfect harmony of line by being, in fact, compositions of very attenuated curves. Inflection is the compositional defense against monotony, which is why the orthogonal grid—with its mechanical repetition of a single unit—is usually avoided in traditional architecture.

Perhaps the simplest model of arrangement is that of bilateral symmetry, in which the two halves of a composition are mirrored about an axis. While this arrangement is undoubtedly the easiest to see and understand—and most clearly answers the desirability of a strong center—symmetrical arrangements produce a predictable, static quality that ultimately fatigues the eye. Symmetry can often be relieved by inflection, removing the duality about a centerline and producing an asymmetrical but balanced arrangement. Asymmetry can animate a composition but is limited by the sense of unpredictability it can introduce if repeated excessively. A combination of the two devices, which might be called pseudo-symmetry, is often capable of sustaining interest by using symmetry at one scale and asymmetry at another, as when local asymmetries enliven an arrangement governed by an overall symmetry at a larger scale. The façade of the Villa Aldobrandini at Frascati is a classic example. None of these devices can be declared normative or canonical—we find them all throughout traditional architecture and urbanism—but their use requires judgment. Neither an arbitrary symmetry nor an arbitrary asymmetry will hold our attention in architectural design, but only a judicious mixture that seems to grow naturally out of the contingencies of the site and program. (Fig. 2.12)

Finally, traditional composition is governed by scale, which reveals the perceived "grain" of the compositional subdivisions, allowing us to estimate the size of a building or element in comparison to our own bodies. The "scaling factor" is the number of distinct scale levels (subdivisions) a composition has in comparison to its size. (Salingaros, 2006, pp. 45–55.) We naturally tend to assume that the larger the composition, the more subdivisions there will be; departures from this expectation have psychological effects. The Paris Opéra, being a very large building, predictably reveals a full spectrum of regularly graduated scale levels, from the whole building down through several intermediate levels to the smallest, which can be measured in fractions of inches. By my count there are at least seven distinct scale levels visible in the exterior of this building. Our visual interest is maintained at each level, which underscores the vitality of the whole composition. (See fig. 2.2)

Departures from our expectations of scale can be used for expressive effect. A large but coarse-grained composition (i.e., one with fewer distinct scales than we expect) can surprise us when we grasp its actual size, and a small but fine-grained one may delight us by its intricacy. For example, the Arc de Triomphe at the Place de l'Étoile in Paris (Jacques-François-Thérèse Chalgrin, 1806–36) has but three or four scale levels, lending the 150-foot-tall arch an undeniable grandeur, while the more intricately detailed 63-foot-tall Arc de Triomphe du Carrousel at the Louvre (Charles Percier and Pierre-François-Léonard Fontaine, 1809), with its five or six scale levels, appears much more intimate by comparison. (Fig. 2.13)

A

B

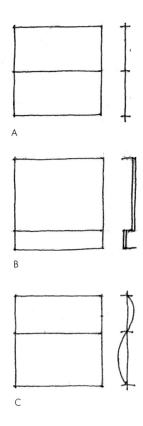

2.14. Three proportional relationships.

Three possible proportional relationships are identity or equality (A); punctuation, in which a subordinate part is reduced to a border or frame (B); and differentiation, in which the second part is neither the mean nor the extreme (C).

Calculated adjustments of scale allow buildings in entirely different styles to be visually related to one another within larger compositional ensembles; conversely, the absence of clearly defined and related scales and subdivisions increases the apparent isolation of buildings from one another. Indeed, traditional architecture consistently seeks "scaling coherence," or the resolution of multiple scale levels in building designs, in recognition that our psychological well-being depends on our perceptions of such coherence. However it may be explained scientifically, there is no denying that the close coordination of arrangement and scale is an essential contributing factor to the deeply satisfying compositions we commonly find among historic buildings and urban ensembles, even among buildings built in widely varying styles and over long periods of time. (See fig. 2.1) (Alexander, 2002, and Salingaros, 2006.)

Proportion

The qualitative, nonmetrical relationships established among parts by composition are given a more precise set of quantitative relations by means of proportion. The essence of proportion in architecture is a pattern of similar relationships between analogous parts at different scales. In other words, proportion is a means of unifying into a larger order the differences between similar things. The relationships among the shapes in a composition are calculated to give vitality to the individual parts in relation to one another and to the whole. Proportion can be most simply understood as an ordered set of ratios governing the shapes and sizes of parts, such that these parts are regulated by a common measure or module, and are also visibly identifiable as subdivisions of the whole. "The secret of proportion seems to lie, not in the shapes themselves, but in the relationships between them." (Scholfield, 1958, p. 5.)

Three proportional relationships reflect the three possibilities for parts to be related to one another: Two elements can be equal; one can be so much larger than the other that the smaller is reduced to the status of a border or frame; or the two can be in a balanced hierarchical relation, with neither being the extreme nor the mean. These relations are called *equality, punctuation,* and *differentiation,* respectively. (Fig. 2.14) Historically, punctuations have tended to range

from a part-to-whole ratio of 1:5 to 1:9, while differentiations have tended to approximate 5:8 or, more precisely, 1:1.618, commonly known as the Golden Section. Ideally, all the punctuations within a composition employ the same ratio and, similarly, all the differentiations are defined by a second repeated ratio. Consistency in the ratios yields that sense of "sympathy and consonance of the parts within a body" which both Vitruvius and Alberti thought an essential aspect of beauty. Such proportional self-similarity across scales exudes unmistakable liveliness and unity-with-variety; the absence of this kind of proportional refinement is equally noticeable. (Sammons, 2006.)

Numerous methods have been proposed historically to facilitate proportional refinement, mostly employing the arithmetical regulation of linear dimensions (referred to as "analytical" methods) or the geometrical ordering of shapes and areas (called "geometrical" methods), or a combination of the two. While it is apparent that the ancient Greeks and Romans and medieval builders employed sophisticated proportional systems, the absence of literary or documentary evidence severely limits our understanding of how they were conceptualized and employed. Analysis of buildings to determine how their designers might have determined their proportions has proved inconclusive. Documented proportional theory first appears in the Renaissance treatises and became a matter of intense critical interest only in the nineteenth century. What all the proposed systems have in common is that all are attempts to derive patterns that can be applied throughout a composition with greater or lesser facility, depending on the skills and temperament of the designer. None of them is definitive or guarantees successful design.

While proportional relationships governing the plans of buildings and urban ensembles are important, the proportions of elements in section and elevation are more evident to the eye. The fundamental principle to be observed is that building façades are composed as series of vertically oriented rectangles, like the ranks of figures in a sculptural frieze. While many buildings may at first appear to be horizontally layered—especially if they are multistory buildings whose floors are expressed on the elevation—traditional architecture nearly always seeks a balance of the horizontal and vertical line in building elevations and then tips the balance slightly in favor of the vertical. Windows, doors, and other similar elements are typically proportioned such that the width is to the height in a ratio of approximately 1:2 or 2:3. This preference for verticality reflects the principle of fictive structure, with its evocation of load and support, but also responds to the paradigm of the standing human figure: Architecture is always, at the most basic level, a frame for the human person—like the classical aedicule housing the statue of a divinity. (See fig. 2.7.) The taller a classical building, the

more it takes on the proportions of an order, so that the base, middle, and top of the building reflect the pedestal, column, and entablature of the order itself. (Fig. 2.15)

Different proportional systems can lead to very different results. For example, Gothic architecture is based on a system that typically yields a center-occupied composition (a column or solid element on the centerline), whereas the proportions of the classical styles typically result in compositions with an open center.

2.15. The Municipal Building, New York, by McKim, Mead & White, 1908–13, proportional analysis after Richard Sammons.

The elevation of this classical skyscraper can be analyzed for proportional similarities at different scales. Recurring relations of punctuation and differentiation give unity and vitality to the whole.

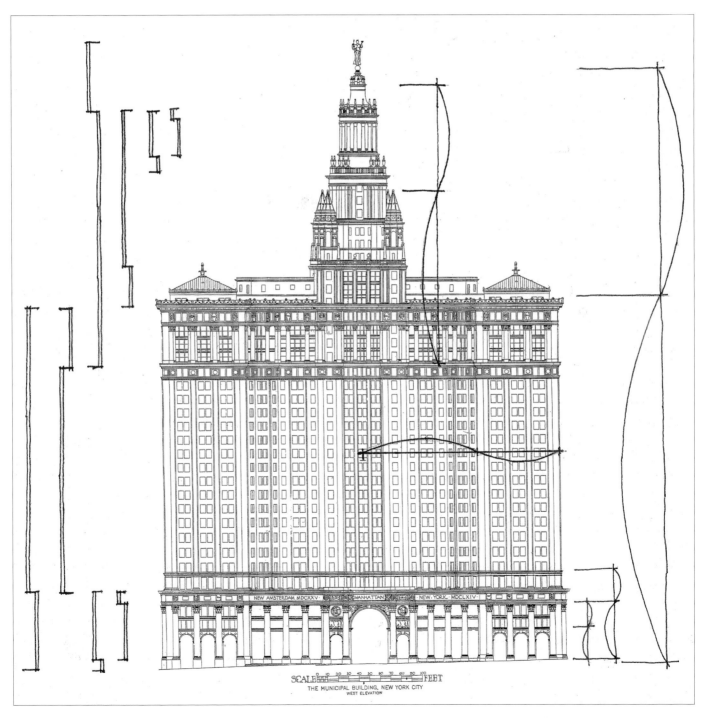

SCALE [FEET]
THE MUNICIPAL BUILDING, NEW YORK CITY
WEST ELEVATION

A

B

ABOVE AND OPPOSITE

2.16. Ornamental motifs.

Traditional ornament draws motifs from the human figure, as at the Palazzo Spada, Rome (A); animal forms, as at the Basilica of Neptune, Rome (B); botanical motifs, as at the entrance to the church of San Zanipolo in Venice (C); and geometrical patterns, as on the façade of San Miniato al Monte in Florence (D).

While in practice the consistency of ratios is more important than the ratios themselves, the selection of ratios is an important indicator of style. For example, adjusting the ratio of punctuation from 1:5 to 1:7 underlies the increasing attenuation of form visible in the transition from the Georgian to the Federal styles, or from Louis XV to Louis XVI. Edith Wharton and Ogden Codman, Jr., point out that proportion, not ornament (as often thought), is the key to understanding any style, and the ornament of any composition must conform to the

style indicated by its proportions. (Wharton and Codman, 1897, p. 14.)

While proportion has historically been viewed as the key to an objective standard of beauty, it is not an end in itself: It is an instrument of composition and governs the precise relationships among parts and between parts and the whole. It is also an essential means by which buildings may be allowed to grow and accept additions without losing their original identity and visual character. An addition that is not only in proportion to the original building but also maintains internally the same proportions as the building to which it is added will more likely form a coherent whole.

Ornament and Decoration

Virtually all premodernist architecture of any consequence includes ornament and decoration. Although the two terms are often used interchangeably, it is useful to distinguish between embellishment in the form of repeating pattern (ornament) and in the form of pictorial imagery (decoration). In the first category we might find a row of acanthus leaves on a molding and in the second a sculpted relief or a painted mural. Ornament must be understood not as something added to a form, but as something a form does to complete itself in its subdivision into parts. The smallest parts at the smallest scale within any composition can be considered ornament—the articulation of an underlying form, rather than something added to the form to make it "pretty." Ornament on buildings directs the eye to the parts of the design that are about the same size or smaller than we ourselves are; when this small-scale articulation is missing, the building seems unfinished, as if intended to be seen only from a distance. Properly understood and designed, ornament is no more superficial or dispensable to a building than leaves are to a tree; we might even describe ornament as the foliage on the trunk and branches of composition. (Semes, 2004, pp. 65–74.)

Classical ornament is typically derived from five categories of motifs: human, animal, botanical, geometric, and man-made artifacts. (Bayley, 1984, pp. 102–3.) The human figure appears in the form of herms, caryatids, masks, and figures in varied poses. Animals depicted in ornament include both naturalistic and mythological creatures and animal derivatives like the eggs in an egg-and-dart molding. Botanical motifs are perhaps the richest source of ornament, from the ubiquitous acanthus leaf to spiraling rinceaux to bundled wreaths and swags of leaves and flowers. Geometrical figures abound, from the repeated shapes of squares, circles, and diamonds to elaborate Greek frets and the radiating elliptical paving pattern of Michelangelo's Piazza del Campidoglio. (See fig. 11.3.) Forms of man-made artifacts include weapons, artists' or craftsmen's tools, or musical instruments. These and other motifs formed the cumulative visual culture of twenty-five centuries—what Brent Brolin quite aptly called "the borrowing tradition." (Brolin, 2000.) Throughout the tradition, designers borrowed motifs but felt free to adapt them to their expressive purposes or recast them as necessary to keep them fresh and relevant. (Fig. 2.16)

If ornament entails rhythmically repeated elements, decoration presents us with pictorial imagery. The decorative enrichment of buildings includes murals in paint or mosaic, sculpted reliefs and panels, as well as statuary placed on the building or freestanding. The sculptural figures filling the pediments of classical temples, the carved metopes of the Doric frieze, or the saints lining the portals and animating the skyline of a cathedral are familiar examples of classical and Gothic decoration. The scale of ornament is relative: What is principal form at one scale may be considered ornament at another. At an urban scale a civic building may well be considered an ornament to the city. Such elements as statuary, murals, fountains, landscape treatments, and paving patterns provide embellishment to the streetscape analogous to the ornamental carving on a molding or the wreaths and swags adorning a piece of furniture.

Ornament and decoration also introduce specific narrative and symbolic content that underscores and amplifies the generalized meanings that the nonrepresentational forms of architecture typically evoke. For example, the acanthus-clad Corinthian capital represents life and rebirth, and the statue of a historical figure at the center of an urban square may remind us of civic virtue. This narrative or symbolic content of ornament is regulated by the concept of *decor*, or decorum, as developed by both Vitruvius and Alberti. (See Vitruvius, 1999, pp. 24–25 and 150–51, and Alberti, 1988, pp. 311–14.) Decorum calls for

C

D

ornament to be commensurate with the purpose and status of the building or ensemble in terms of its quantity and placement as well as its content; a church is therefore ornamented or decorated differently than a parking garage. But the absence of embellishment altogether is typically felt as a deficiency, except in buildings of the most modest character or utilitarian function. Some observers have even argued for the mathematical and neurological "necessity" of ornament, and there is now evidence that the urge to make ornament and decoration is indeed a cultural universal. (Salingaros, 2006, pp. 77–78, 84–92.) However they may be explained and wherever they are found, ornament and decoration represent a spirit of generosity and abundance—a kind of offering that goes above and beyond necessity or, as Alberti expressed it, an additional splendor that gives more particular expression to the general and abstract beauty already inherent in an underlying form. (Alberti, 1988, p. 156.)

Character

The summation of the principles enumerated so far is *character*, which may be considered the phenomenological aspect of architecture as it is actually experienced. The Romans understood character as *genius loci*—the spirit of a place—which they took literally as a god dwelling in that place. We can speak of the spirit of place as analogous to the character of a human person; it is that which is defining and memorable about a room, a building, a street, a square, a neighborhood, a landscape, or a city. It is the culmination of the other principles, because it coordinates them all to arrive at a specific concrete combination that distinguishes this building or place from all others. In Aristotelian terms, character is what makes similar things different; it allows us to recognize and discuss the accidents that articulate and embody an essence.

While character includes the modern idea of function, it transcends pragmatic considerations of use and includes the concepts of economy, decorum, and appropriateness. For eighteenth-century French theorists, character was the expressive dimension of architecture that allowed it to evoke ideals and aspirations—personal, typological, or communal. (Egbert, 1980, pp. 121–35.) On a deeper level character is the ineffable, poetic quality of a place not describable in words. Character is what most attracts people to historic architecture and urbanism and why we go to considerable trouble to see it and, if we are fortunate, to live and work within it. Buildings and cities with strong character attract us and can stimulate strong feelings of attachment and a sense of belonging. (Davis, 2006, p. 154, and Norberg-Schulz, 1980.)

We can further understand architectural character as a specific combination of *scenography*—the visual order and expressiveness of form and material that allows buildings to appear as individual entities while simultaneously composing larger urban settings—and *parti*—the rigorous three-dimensional composition of space, structure, and elements in response to a particular site and program. The close coordination of scenography and parti is essential to the evocation of distinct character and the creation of built ensembles that satisfy our need for both visual and intellectual order. For example, in evocative works of the Italian Renaissance—such as Michelangelo's Piazza del Campidoglio in Rome—we may say that the character of the place results in large part from the architect's mastery of both of these desiderata. (See fig. 11.3.) What makes the place memorable is not only the compositional rigor of the design or the strongly dramatized rhetorical gestures, controlled vistas, and warm materiality that dominate our perceptions of the place, but also the synthesis of these features in ways that are mutually reinforcing and mutually illuminating.

While character is the culmination of an observer's perception of a place, it becomes the starting point for the designer, for whom it is an answer to the question "What would it be like to be in this place?" Character is the evocation of purpose. Form does not, as Louis Sullivan suggested, "follow function"; rather, form *embodies character*. Traditional architecture avoids a narrow functionalism by producing rooms and spaces that are somewhat generic: they are good for certain kinds of activities but are not necessarily tailored too literally to any one, allowing for multiple uses or different uses over time. When the architect grasps the character of a contemplated room or building before beginning to design, decisions about space, structure, elements, composition, proportion, and ornament flow logically and authentically from that initial conception.

Character leads to considerations of meaning and significance but is distinct from these to the extent that it is inferable from the formal and tactile properties of the work itself rather than from thoughts about it derived from nonarchitectural content. Character is not limited by the abstract ideas buildings and places are thought to express. Character is not the concept or idea itself, but the manner in which it is materially embodied, the totality of its realization in physical terms. Indeed, character often persists long after the original purposes of a building or the original inhabitants of a place have disappeared. Furthermore, when works of diverse styles and periods form an ensemble characterized by a strongly unified sense of place, as in the examples noted at the start of this chapter, we can say that the buildings jointly define a collective character greater than that contributed by any one of them. Character is, therefore, the principal way in which diverse buildings relate to one another to form strongly identifiable and memorable places. "Historic character," the value we strive to safeguard in preservation efforts, is simply this sense of identity in a place sustained by the decisions of multiple authors over an extended period of time. It is therefore vulnerable to erosion or loss due to the removal of features that define it or the introduction of new features that might alter or diminish it. The objective of any preservation program should therefore be to identify the "character-defining elements" of a historic place and take measures to sustain them by managing change to prevent unnecessary loss. (Alderson, 2006, pp. 3–4.) (Fig. 2.17)

Application of the Principles

The seven principles just enumerated are descriptive of characteristics found in traditional architecture and urbanism irrespective of style; they are not prescriptive for design or a set of rules that will guarantee a good result. They help us to evaluate those parts of the built environment we value most highly and to grasp the continuity and variety found in the historic cities we most admire. The principles help us to understand how buildings as diverse as those enclosing many historic streets and squares, with their variety of styles, ages, materials, and uses, can nevertheless form an ensemble marked by congruity and what we might call *neighborliness*. Harmonious ensembles of buildings *get along* with one another. Like good human neighbors, they observe unspoken rules of civility and mutual deference. (Edwards, 1924.) They achieve this degree of civility *because they want to*: traditional buildings are designed with this kind of harmony in view as a design objective from the beginning. The simultaneous and mutually supportive operation of the seven principles is the instrument that allows ensembles of buildings to achieve this aim.

The buildings enclosing the Grand' Place in Brussels, for example, date from the four-

teenth century to the end of the seventeenth, with considerable alteration and restoration in the nineteenth. (Choay, 2001, pp. 129–30, and Zucker, 1970, p. 129.) Styles represented include Gothic, Renaissance, Baroque, Neoclassical, and Gothic Revival. The buildings vary in width and height, their average heights punctuated by the bell tower on the medieval town hall. Many of the individual houses were originally built for the "corporations," or trading companies, that were the backbone of the medieval mercantile economy, but they have subsequently been occupied by quite different uses. In keeping with regional tradition in this part of northern Europe, the individual houses have steeply pitched roofs set perpendicular to the façades, their gable ends and silhouettes animated by ornamental figures in carved stone and gilded metal. (Fig. 2.17)

2.17. The Grand' Place, Brussels.

Architectural character, the nonabstract experience of buildings and places as physical entities, is the summation of the six other principles reviewed in this chapter. Despite considerable diversity of style and period, the character of the Grand' Place is unified by the features and principles that the varied buildings share.

Despite the differences among these buildings, they compose a strong ensemble because they share similar adaptations of the seven principles. They acknowledge a common conception of urban space in the way they maintain aggregate façades forming the walls of a large outdoor figural room. They employ a small set of structural techniques and a limited material palette but also consistently observe tectonic logic. The elevations are composed of identifiable elements, including large windows, stepped gables, implied and explicit orders, aedicules, and balustrades. Every façade is a composite form of nested parts and wholes arranged in tripartite divisions vertically and—in most cases—horizontally. Three-part arrangements predominate, but two- or four-bay units are interspersed for a varied rhythm. Punctuation and inflection are observed in the joining of parts and the way the buildings defer to one another and meet the sky. The façades maintain a generous range of scale levels. The coordinated proportions of the classical façades are governed by explicit or implied orders and revealed also in the consistency of window openings and punctuating ornament. The Gothic buildings use a different proportioning system but likewise maintain consistent self-similar relationships between scale levels.

The abundant ornament in the Place includes all five categories of motifs and, despite its occasional extravagance, remains subordinate to the compositions and proportions of the underlying forms. The overall character of the square is one of private ostentation in harmonious balance with civic pride: it exudes an atmosphere at once exuberant and decorous. The complicated histories of Brussels and Belgium preclude a narrowly political or nationalistic reading of the Place; instead, it is an expression of a building culture and an economic community articulating its aspirations in a remarkable ensemble that has taken on very different programs, uses, and meanings over the course of the centuries. Finally, it is an entirely satisfying exercise in what the poet Gerard Manley Hopkins called "likeness tempered with difference," as in a piece of complex but beautiful music in which all dissonances are resolved and there are no wrong notes. (Hopkins, quoted in Smith, 1987, p. 65.)

While I have reviewed the seven principles of traditional architecture singly, examination of places like the Grand' Place prove that in practice they act simultaneously as a common matrix whereby architectural form leaves the realm of abstraction to take on concreteness and specificity. The concept of space, for example, collaborates with that of composition; ornament cannot be considered apart from proportion. All seven of the principles are simultaneously operative and generative at every scale. Though different values and emphases may be given to each of the principles, they must be able to work together as a network or a fabric that gives life to architectural wholes. It is the capacity of these principles to engender both similarity and difference that allows buildings of different sizes, ages, styles, and characters to compose a larger ensemble whose character is stronger than that of any of its constituent parts without diminishing the individuality of those parts.

All the historic styles of European architecture before modernism can be combined because they present a series of variations on the seven principles, even though the variations remain within a narrow range of deviation. Small changes might yield disproportionately significant differences in the built results: For example, relatively minor variations in tectonic system, proportioning, and ornamental motifs define the essential differences between Gothic and classical architecture. One tectonic system might succeed another, or one architectural style with its distinctive proportions and ornament might supersede another, but all of the styles addressed the issues of spatial, structural, and formal composition, proportion, ornament, and character in fundamentally consonant ways. In general, the affinities of different styles of traditional architecture are sustained by a common conception of the first four principles—space, structure, elements, and composition—while the differences between them are due largely to subtle variations in applying the last three principles—proportion, ornament, and character. This explains the unity-with-difference that so strongly impresses us in many traditional urban settings, but it also cautions us to respect the boundaries beyond which the affinities among styles can no longer be sustained.

While this kind of analysis of traditional buildings and urban space may be helpful, ultimately the secrets of aesthetic and stylistic harmony in our most beautiful built environments elude our attempts to rationalize them or reduce them to formulas. Harmony can be neither described nor prescribed by any series of merely verbal desiderata, which is why written design guidelines cannot produce beauty, although they may prevent the most egregious ugliness. The most that a theoretical exercise like the present inquiry can do is to suggest a framework within which the architect might search for harmony. There is no guarantee that the architect will succeed, but what is certain is that the opposite aim—a deliberate desire to create disharmony by subverting the prevailing formal order in a place—cannot lead to beauty and continuity in built environments where these attributes are already established. This is why styles are so important: they increase the chances of success by defining a framework within which harmony can be pursued. "Style reduces uncertainty." (Smith, 1987, p. 102.) (I consider style in more detail in Chapter 3.)

All architecture must be judged by the same standards; there can be no special rules or exemptions for particular periods or styles.

Buildings either conform to the principles of traditional architecture or they do not. That conformance does not determine their aesthetic quality but it does give us a common set of premises upon which to base our judgments. What sounds so simple when stated this way, in fact, runs counter to the way we habitually make judgments today. But as an examination of our valued historical places demonstrates (and as many of the examples illustrated in this book prove), the styles that have defined Western architecture prior to modernism are inherently consonant with one another because they share such a set of common premises. In our living building traditions, cities have been designed, altered, expanded, and transformed according to these same principles for millennia, and their endlessly reiterated application has yielded the nearly inconceivable richness and particularity of the places we admire today.

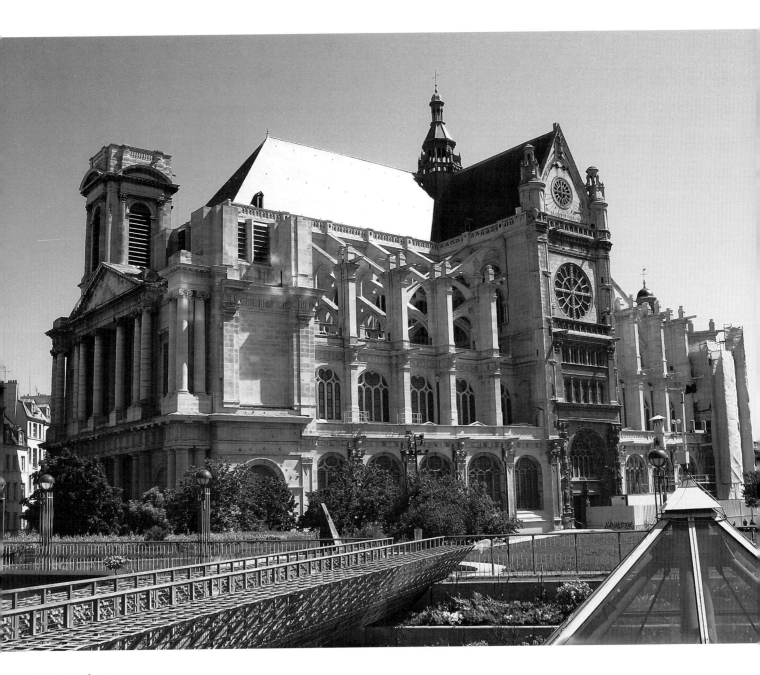

3.1. St.-Eustache, Paris,
sixteenth century.

Sixteenth-century
French builders applied
Renaissance ornament
and decoration to what
remained essentially Gothic
buildings, like the unfinished
St.-Eustache. Such hybrids
are often devalued or
overlooked in favor of
"pure" examples of the
styles.

CHAPTER 3

How Traditional Architecture Works

> Contrary to what is called the architecture of accompaniment, which seeks to stay unpretentious, and contrary to the architecture of rupture, which seeks to stand out at all costs, my architecture simply seeks to be loved and admired. . . . Originality, for me, comes not from submission to techniques or the systematic recourse to a form never seen before but, rather, from new combinations of eternal elements perfectly adapted by their form to human nature.
>
> —CHRISTIAN LANGLOIS (ca. 1980)

The principles reviewed in the previous chapter establish the underlying formal agreements that unite traditional buildings into harmonious ensembles. What, then, accounts for the multiplicity of styles that we can see represented in historic urban ensembles? Style is related to character, although I reserve the latter term to denote the specific qualities of individual places, while the former points to recognizable and repeatable manipulations of architectural language by which different characters may be evoked. Our modern concept of architectural styles as discrete manners of building associated with specific historical periods was unknown before the mid-nineteenth century. Instead, styles were fluid, vaguely defined, and certainly not limited to specific time frames. The two largest families of styles, the classical and the Gothic, were different ways of making buildings that long coexisted, sometimes used by the same architect and sometimes appearing simultaneously in the design for a single building, as at the fascinating Gothic-Renaissance church of St.-Eustache in Paris. (Fig. 3.1)

Language and Style

A style gives varied but coherent expression to certain perennial concerns under particular circumstances. For example, we can identify in different times and places a sensibility that loves complexity, ambiguity, elaboration, ornament, symbolism, and theatricality. We can see this sensibility in Hadrian's Villa at Tivoli, in the late Gothic churches of northern Europe, and in the fantastical works of seventeenth- and early-eighteenth-century Italy and Austria. We might call this the "Baroque" spirit. In contrast, we can also see a love of simplicity, clarity, austerity, regularity, and restraint, such as we might find in the temples of Republican Rome, Cistercian abbeys, Brunelleschi's church interiors, and eighteenth-century New England houses and churches. These we might label as sharing a "rationalist" sensibility. We can see both of these attitudes repeatedly played out in history, one following the other in reaction to the perceived "excesses" of the other, and occasionally coexisting within the same group or even in the works of a single artist.

We may then understand a style as a recognizable and repeatable way of evoking such perennial motives within a craft or building culture in response to the exigencies of a given place and time. A style establishes the likelihood that a certain form will be used to communicate certain content: a style is a "statistical ensemble," a characteristic arrangement of elements based on the notion of "repeatable form." (Norberg-Schulz, 1965, p. 156, and

A

B

3.2. Two houses in the Georgian style.

A. The George Read II House, New Castle, Delaware, 1801.
B. The Richardson Dilworth House, Philadelphia, 1957.

Two houses built a century and a half apart in the Georgian style: The Read House is a treasured house museum; the Dilworth House was nearly demolished because it was not viewed as consistent with the official narrative of Philadelphia's architectural history.

Scruton, 1979, p. 11.) We may add a communitarian dimension to this concept by saying that a style is the conscious and public cultivation of the appropriate—that is, the fitting and exemplary—in architectural form as discerned by a community of builders and designers. To the extent that it addresses perennial themes by means of broadly accessible concepts and skills, a style may continue to develop and remain in active use well beyond the time and place of its first appearance. For example, the style now commonly described as "Georgian"

is a complex and highly nuanced tradition now over two centuries old and continuing to find new expression. (Wilson, 2004.) A later example of the style cannot be simply dismissed as a "copy" of earlier models, but must be recognized as a contemporary manipulation of the formal ideas, materials, proportions, ornament, and character associated with the stylistic tradition in which it participates. Within the framework of a traditional architecture, style is utterly independent of "period" or any overriding conception of history or progress. The construction date of a traditional building may be of interest to the historian, but it has nothing whatever to do with judgments of aesthetic quality. (Fig. 3.2)

Because styles and their uses reflect changing interests and changing attitudes toward the perennial themes mentioned above, we should understand the intermittent appearance and reappearance of styles genealogically rather than chronologically. Adaptability and applicability, rather than temporal sequence or some criterion of progress, are the key to judging the value of a particular style. Like a literary genre, style imposes limits and boundaries so that some particular aspects of the fitting and exemplary may disclose themselves while others are foreclosed. Styles live on so long as they prove meaningful and useful, and so long as they retain the capacity to take on new content and reveal new formal possibilities.

The terms "language" and "style" are closely related and are frequently used interchangeably by architectural writers, but the distinction between them is worth observing. A number of styles may have a single language in common; for example, the styles of the Italian Renaissance, French Classicism, and Edwardian Baroque have in common the classical language of architecture, but they make use of it in distinctive ways in response to the exigencies of the times and places they are employed. Language is the more fundamental reality of the two: it is the grammar of forms independent of rhetorical or narrative content. (Tzonis and LeFaivre, 1986.) So while the three styles just mentioned have different rhetorical or expressive contents, they all make use of the classical language, and their varying uses of this common language define them as distinct styles.

A healthy architectural culture understands style as a positive inducement to cultivation and refinement rather than a limiting or divisive ideology. When Demetri Porphyrios writes

3.3. Façade of the Duomo, Milan, thirteenth to nineteenth centuries.

The front of the Milan cathedral remained raw masonry until the seventeenth century, when Baroque door and window surrounds were added. In the late eighteenth century, construction began on an elevation conforming to the original Gothic, interweaving the two styles.

that "classicism is not a style," he intends to isolate the classical language from the art-historical understanding of style and from accusations that classicism is "only" style—a kind of obsession with empty appearances. (Porphyrios, 1982.) A Renaissance architect like Alberti saw style as the application of a formal language in the service of a noble rhetoric that articulates the highest ideals. Style becomes, in fact, "the architectural equivalent of Cicero's art of 'the good man (or woman) speaking well.'" (David Mayernik, quoted in Carey, 2004, p. 13.) We

cannot understand the practice of traditional architecture, either historically or in contemporary work, without understanding this rhetorical and aspirational aspect of style.

As I argued in the previous chapter, the styles that have defined Western architecture prior to modernism are inherently consonant with one another because they share common premises. These common premises also allow different styles to be combined, as they were in St.-Eustache. In many cases, it is not the "pure" expressions of any style but precisely

3.4. Piazza S. Pietro, the Vatican, by Gian Lorenzo Bernini, 1656–57.

This view of the elliptical colonnades illustrates Geoffrey Scott's idea that architecture is a translation into built form of our bodily states: the piazza is a metaphorical embrace. Beyond, the Via della Conciliazione plows through a former historic, intimately scaled neighborhood.

those buildings and places representing stylistic hybrids that are of the greatest interest. The Gothic and Baroque styles, once seen as adversarial, today appear to us as sharing deep affinities, as demonstrated by hundreds of buildings built or altered between the thirteenth and the eighteenth centuries and revealing superimposed layers of successive styles. It is not their superficial appearance but their underlying formal principles that allow buildings or elements drawn from different styles not only to coexist but to collaborate in architectural works of great complexity and beauty. (Fig. 3.3)

Architecture and Meaning

Meaning is the aim the seven principles of traditional architecture serve and the ultimate goal of the expression of character in buildings and places. Character serves and in part defines meaning but is both more concrete and more elusive. Meaning is the product of our reflec-

tion on character, supplemented by our awareness of content that may derive from sources outside the field of architecture. Because it is the product of reflection rather than a property of the visible forms themselves, meaning is also ephemeral and changes along with our changing ideas and perceptions.

It is essential to remember that the necessarily nonrepresentational nature of architectural form limits the kinds of meaning that buildings can evoke and the manner in which that meaning can be conveyed. In representational arts like literature, drama, painting, or sculpture, recognizable events, states, ideas, persons, places, or objects are readily depicted and this content could, theoretically at least, be described in words. In the nonrepresentational arts of architecture and music, no precise objects are depicted or described and their meaning or content is not usually expressible in words. Who can describe the meaning of Beethoven's Seventh Symphony? Or of the Pantheon? The meaning of a nonrepresentational work, especially to the degree that it is recognized as profound, cannot readily be translated into verbal formulas. In the same way, a building's meaning cannot communicate explicit points of view about social conditions or a particular political program without assistance from representational media. Just as composers set words to music when literary content is required, architects call upon painting, sculpture, and textual inscriptions to reinforce specific contents in buildings. (See Scott, 1914, pp. 61–62, and Scruton, 1983, pp. 77–100.)

So what do we mean when we speak of buildings as having something to "say"? We may classify architectural meaning as either direct or indirect, having to do with meaning inferable from the forms themselves and with meaning projected onto the forms by our associations, respectively. (Scott, 1914, p. 59.) Direct meaning may be divided into three types. The first involves the capacity of architectural forms to be expressive of emotional states or mental attitudes by virtue of *empathy*: We are able to discern the character of a building in the same way we judge the character of a person, by scrutiny of "posture" or "bearing." For example, the colonnades of the Piazza S. Pietro at the Vatican are usually seen as "embracing"

the space of the square in a gesture that is usually interpreted as welcoming, and implying the universality of the Catholic Church. (Fig. 3.4) Such interpretations are based on the empathic translation of our bodily states into physical form and the perception in the forms of recalled physical movements and states. These empathic meanings tend to be imprecise with respect to content, evoking general character rather than denoting specific thoughts expressible in words. (Scott, 1914, pp. 157–77.)

Another kind of direct meaning is *symbolic*. Few architectural elements are recognizable purely as symbols, but there are numerous elements that nonetheless carry a symbolic charge. The modification of the rectangular Roman basilica into the Latin-cross early Christian church plan is a rare direct use of symbolism. In classical architecture the Corinthian capital, with its acanthus leaves entwined around a woven basket, is traditionally seen as a symbol of life and rebirth. When the symbol is understood, the capital takes on an added resonance, reinforcing the inherent beauty of the form and endowing buildings articulated in the Corinthian order with a lofty, honorific, and ultimately life-affirming character. (Fig. 3.5)

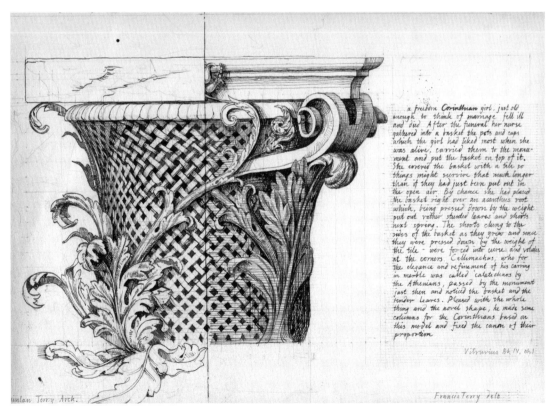

3.5. The Corinthian order, from designs for Corinthian House, Hyde Park, London, by Quinlan & Francis Terry Architects, 2000–2002.

The Corinthian order is a symbol of life and rebirth: A basket containing personal effects and covered by a roof tile was placed on the grave of a maiden. An acanthus plant sprang up around it, conventionalized in the capital's canonic design. Francis Terry's drawing illustrates both the origin (left) and its development (right).

Third, buildings may imply meaning on the basis of conventions that arise within a style as it pairs specific repeatable forms with particular recognizable contents. For example, in classical architecture we see a pediment supported on a row of columns as representing a temple front and understand this as an honorific device—perhaps indicating a sacred place or simply an entrance—whose significance is understood by anyone familiar with the convention. (Fig. 3.6)

The three direct sources of meaning in architecture are mutually reinforcing, so that symbol and convention work to underscore the more generalized character evoked by empathetic reading. We infer direct meaning from the visible and tactile form of the architectural work itself, deriving content from the specific operation and interaction of the seven principles. The Parthenon or the Pantheon, the Gothic cathedrals, and the great urban ensembles of the Renaissance and Baroque "speak" to us by means of direct meaning, but we can only understand what they have to "say" by learning the formal languages, styles, symbols, and conventions through which they convey their meaning. Failing this, we will have an impoverished sense of what historic buildings and sites can offer us, and we may also misjudge their importance as objects worthy of preservation.

Finally, there is indirect meaning, not inferable from the forms themselves, but projected onto them by the observer based on what nineteenth-century commentators called the "association of ideas." Such ideas tend to be nonarchitectural, perhaps drawn from literature, politics, religion, or other artistic disciplines, or they may simply reflect the memories of people whose experiences are bound up with certain buildings. There is no question that nonarchitectural content is an essential component in the evocation and recognition of character in the built environment, and indirect meanings are often important considerations in evaluating the historical significance of buildings and sites for preservation. Indirect meaning allows us to discuss architecture in terms of our historical experience, yielding such associations as the popular nineteenth-century equation of Greek temple architecture with democracy and the consequent adaptation of the Greek temple to a wide variety of public and private buildings. (Greenberg, 2006.)

As central as indirect meaning can be to our understanding of architecture, it can also be exaggerated. Our feelings about the ideas believed to be represented in particular forms can distort our perception of the forms themselves. Associational meanings are as unreliable as they are unavoidable, revealing an instinc-

3.6. Main Building, Girard College, Philadelphia, by Thomas U. Walter, 1833–48.

The appropriation of the Greek temple for a variety of uses often reflected nonarchitectural values (the temple as an emblem of democracy) rather than the form's suitability to the program or site, inhibiting the development of an urban vernacular.

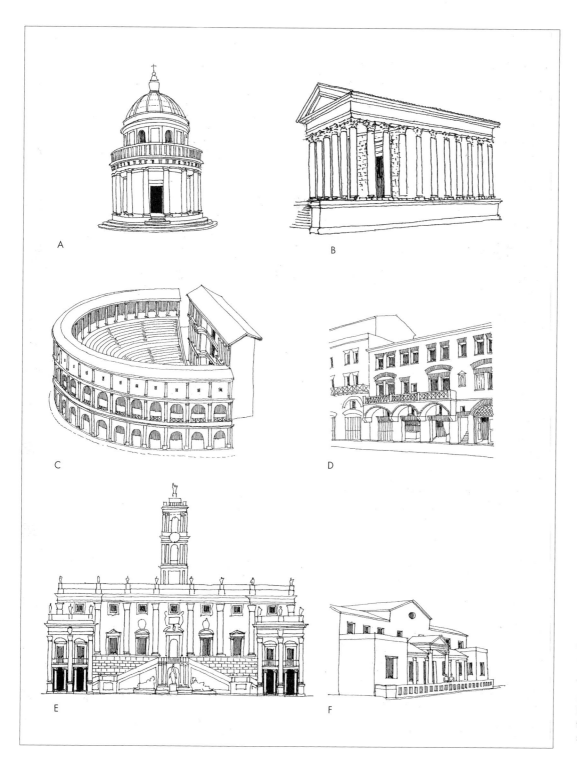

3.7. Six building types, after Carroll William Westfall.

At least six primary typologies may be identified, based on compositional and iconographical morphologies: the Tholos (A); the Templum (B); the Theatrum (C); the Bottega (D); the Regia (E); and the Domus (F). More than one type may appear in the same building.

tive tendency of human beings to personalize objects and places. We have no choice but to seek to understand and respect associational meanings when we become aware of them, but we must also critically evaluate them in relation to the direct meanings inferable from the forms themselves, guarding against the substitution of ideological prejudice for architectural understanding.

Typologies of Traditional Building

The study of traditional buildings of all styles reveals recognizable patterns of organization repeated in a variety of settings and for varied purposes. Certain forms or ways of organizing buildings recur regularly and can be named. Carroll William Westfall has identified six building types based on recurrent patterns first developed in Roman antiquity: the commemorative form of the *tholos*, the ecclesiastical form of the *templum*, the political-performance space of the *theatrum*, the institutional seat of the *regia*, the commercial space of the *bottega*, and the residential unit of the *domus*. (Fig. 3.7) Four of these six types are visible, for example, in the United States Capitol building in Washington, D.C.: the *tholos* in the central commemorative Rotunda, the *templum* in the entrance portico of the East Front, the theatrum in the House and Senate chambers, and the *regia* in the overall palace-like form of Thornton's original design. (See fig. 9.8.) The growth of the building during the century and a half or more after its inception maintained this formal, visual, and typological linkage between ancient and modern sources. (Westfall and Van Pelt, 1991, pp. 155–60.) Virtually any traditional building can be understood in terms of similar types (there may be more than six) that govern the distribution of mass, surface, and space in plan, elevation, and section. These architectural typologies should not be confused with the "building types" defined by specific functions. On the contrary, the traditional typologies have proven fruitful for organizing very different uses, as when the Roman basilica became the model of the Christian church or the palace that of the modern museum. The architectural type under consideration here is independent of particular functions or historical periods: it is a kind of "form" or "genre" like the sonnet in poetry or the sonata in music—a clear and distinct organizing idea that is independent of its content.

In contrast to later theories of functionalism, traditional designs aim for a certain "generic" quality (which is another way of saying they remain true to type) in the sense that the expected longevity of the building suggests the advisability of what we might call a "loose fit" between form and function. Buildings need rooms that are good for different kinds of activities, although what specific activities occur in them may change from time to time. The same is true of urban spaces: those who have lived in European towns with traditional squares know that a good *piazza*, *place*, or *platz* is one that graciously hosts a wide variety of activities, often simultaneously. In summary, traditional architecture and urbanism are essentially typological rather than functionalist in their intentions and methods. The study of traditional design draws on a broad selection of models to allow the student to find the most appropriate type (or combination of types) for a given program and site. (Curtis, 1935, and Collins and Collins, 1986.)

Typology gives us a frame of reference that allows us to judge whether we have been successful in fulfilling our intentions for a certain kind of building or urban environment: The type provides the "universal" of which the "particular" we have designed is an instance. Understanding the type gives us the criteria by which reference to a universal can be made; understanding the particular needs and contingencies of a site in its physical and historical context gives us the materials with which to design what is programmatically fitting. The greatest success occurs when a particular character embodies a universal typology in a way that simultaneously fulfills the promise of the type and vividly evokes the unique concreteness of the individual building program and site.

Architectural Traditions at Work

The embodiment of a universal in a particular case is an aesthetic achievement but also a social and cultural one. Architectural traditions, with their languages, styles, and accumulated experience, establish the mechanisms by which individual buildings fulfill the promise of their typological universality by taking on the particular materials, methods, styles, and meanings appropriate to their place. Tradition is a way of making successful outcomes more likely by establishing a common frame of reference and a common set of tools that are then used by individual designers to propose specific projects exhibiting a broad variety of different characters. The main components of any architectural tradition are a collection of models representing the best examples of the accumulated experience of the tradition and a set of methods of analysis and systems of composition that allow those models to be adapted and readapted to make new works.

A tradition is essentially a body of knowledge or a collection of practices that is inheritable. From the Latin *tradere*, *traditio*—to "hand on" or "what is handed on"—the tradition subsists in the commitment of its adherents to sustain it rather than in any fixed content. A tradition is not a set of rules, but an extended conversation about a canon of models, which are the examples that participants in the tradition recognize collectively as defining the boundaries of what falls within the tradition. Each model represents a particular species of excellence—a "classic" that is considered "timeless," not because it is considered eternal or incapable of change, but because we recognize it as having reached a degree of fulfillment of its potential that cannot be substantially improved upon and which also in some way transcends the limitations of its moment. The Parthenon in Athens and the Pantheon in Rome are classic models in this sense. (Eliot, 1975, pp. 37–44, and Settis, 2004.)

We may think of the collection of models as constituting a kind of genealogy or "family tree": They are positioned along imagined branches at varying distances from a metaphorical trunk, which is the presumed core or "centerline" of the tradition and in relation to which all the models may be evaluated. The centerline is knowable only by the models that appear along it in relation to those more distant from it. The selection and placement of models is decided thematically without regard to temporal sequence. Some models wind up on the edges of the collection, testing the boundaries of what is "in" and what is "out." Groups of models comprising various styles assemble themselves or are dispersed. New models are occasionally added and old ones retired.

The selection of models and their distribution and placement within the family tree are the subject of active discussion and debate among the participants in the tradition, who may have different views of the relative merits and genealogy of the models. In truth, the tradition is defined as much by the ongoing conversation about the models as by the models themselves: The tradition is not established by fixed consensus but by ongoing discussion about which models to include, how they should be valued and placed within the whole scheme, and how they should be used as precedents to inform new work. For example, the tradition of French classicism was enlivened by the debates between the "ancients" and the "moderns"—those who based their theory and practice on antiquity versus those who looked to the Renaissance—that animated the otherwise systematizing tendencies of the Royal Academy in the seventeenth century. (Egbert, 1980, pp. 99–108.) What is essential is that this process of discussion be conscious and public. Each new work places itself in relationship to those that have come before and contains the unspoken wish that it, too, might become a model, offering itself as a general pattern or rule. The tradition is not passive, but active; one doesn't *have* a tradition, one *performs* it. (MacIntyre, 1984, p. 222.)

Two essentials of any artistic tradition are, first, that the conversation that defines and sustains it be conducted in a common formal language and, second, that it consciously cultivate the fitting and exemplary, potentially yielding new models. We know from modern linguistics that there can be no such thing as a private language; all language is shared and public or it is of no consequence. (Pinker, 2002.) The common language in an architectural tradition allows works from different authors, places, and times to constitute a collection of exemplars rather than merely a random sampling of preferences. The language of classical design, for example, is the central thread that weaves together the models composing the main tradition of Western architecture. This language is durable and it is public, in the sense that it is not the property of any one artist, location, or period.

Secondly, the point of assembling the models in the first place is not simply antiquarian interest, but emulation. To work in a tradition entails not merely the reproduction of accepted models, but their thoughtful adaptation and transformation in response to present needs and circumstances, and that is the source of the invention and creativity that allows the canon, and the tradition it defines, to expand and replenish itself over time. Emulation is not copying. The models identified as exemplary by a tradition inform new work by means of characteristic methods of analysis and systems of composition. These are employed in the transformation of precedent in response to new problems, programs, and sites. To cite but one example, the tradition associated with the École des Beaux-Arts in the second half of the nineteenth century devised elaborate and highly sophisticated methods of analysis and compositional systems that had—and continue to have—a widespread influence beyond France, especially for the design of large, monumental buildings and ensembles. (Curtis, 1935; Harbeson, 2008; Gabriel, 2004.) These methods and systems are rational and can be learned; they define operations that may logically be performed on a series of recognizable models and building typologies, mostly derived from Roman antiquity and the great age of French

3.8: Musée d'Orsay, formerly the Gare d'Orsay, Paris, by Victor Laloux, 1900.

Laloux's station skillfully both accommodates a modern program and construction technology and provides an appropriately monumental urban amenity. The station's 1986 conversion into an art museum demonstrates its adaptability to changing uses and meanings.

classicism of the seventeenth century. While often criticized as rigid and antiprogressive, the truth is that this tradition has never been surpassed for the flexibility with which entirely unprecedented programs—such as the large urban train station, the public museum, or the department store—and new construction technologies—such as iron-and-glass structures—could be given convincing form in a familiar and coherent formal language. (Fig. 3.8)

A tradition survives as long as the conversation about the models continues. Once that conversation stops and the participants retreat to the comfort of simple rules, or break out on their own in search of unique and inimitable gestures, the tradition stiffens into a kind of habit, lapses into dormancy, or ends. Finally, the value of a tradition depends on the breadth and depth of its selection of models—a tradition that embraces models drawn from a wide range of different building tasks is likely to last longer than one with a more limited range. The tradition of classical architecture in the West is

perhaps the broadest, most versatile, and longest-lasting tradition of all, due to its nearly infinite adaptability.

Similarly, the methods of analysis and systems of composition identified with a tradition must be adequate to allow the range of models to be adapted and transformed in response to new ideas and new requirements. The greater the universality, abstraction, and flexibility of these operations, the greater the arena within which the tradition can promote innovation and development. This is how a tradition continues to develop and grow, sometimes slowly and incrementally, and at times dramatically, as when a master accomplishes a work that is accepted as a new model, realigning the entire collection. (See fig. 11.3.) While a tradition allows the practitioner of modest ability to achieve a high average level of achievement, the master is the one who "knows how to go farther," knowing the tradition well enough to push it forward into the future without breaking its ties to the past. (MacIntyre, 1990, pp. 64–66.)

At the same time, every tradition is vulnerable. It takes but a generation or two of disregard to wipe away what a tradition spanning centuries has slowly built up. Hence, the education of new practitioners is essential to the mission of the tradition itself rather than a task to be left to independent experts. To learn traditional architecture is, in this sense, to submit to a discipline or apprenticeship: One must somehow learn the models and the operations that may be performed on them. But the discipline itself must sustain a just balance between permanence and change, between inheritance and innovation, avoiding the opposite risks of ossification and disintegration.

The notion of tradition described here is based on a genealogical rather than a chronological organization of precedent and method. The models are considered relevant or irrelevant on the basis of their fruitfulness for inspiring new work, not on the basis of their position on a time line or their conformance to some overriding idea of progress. In a sense, all the models known to us at any given moment are "contemporary" because we remember them and consider them normative in the present. In jurisprudence, a legal precedent is either valid or superseded irrespective of the time in which its validity was first affirmed. In the same way, "Whether the precedent was decided two days ago, two decades ago, or two centuries ago, it is still a precedent; indeed it is this majestic indifference to mere historical chronology which makes the legal concept of precedent so much more relevant to the theory of architecture than the art-historical concept of 'style.'" (Collins, 1971, p. 101.)

The divergent views of the historian or scientific restorer and the traditional practitioner—seeing a work of historic architecture as primarily a document of its time or a potential model or precedent to move the tradition forward, respectively—create a tension that has come to dominate contemporary preservation philosophy, with its competing claims for historical objectivity (differentiation) and visual continuity (compatibility). The architect's respect for the tradition as a whole and for its concrete embodiment in the historical site during its life until now allows for modifications and additions consistent with the preestablished pattern. Outside the tradition, boundaries must be consciously defined within which a designer from a different tradition (or from no tradition) can enter into a relationship with the historic setting without diminishing or destroying it. (I return to this theme in Chapter 7.)

Today traditional architecture is not solely a historical phenomenon; new traditional architecture and new urban environments are being designed and constructed in Europe and North America following models and principles similar to those that produced valued historic places, and the relationship between these two kinds of traditional work—historical and contemporary—is one of the major concerns of this book. Since our views about historical architecture are inevitably colored by our views of contemporary practice, it follows that an interest in contemporary traditional design raises both opportunities and challenges for preservation. These will be the subject of a more detailed examination in the following chapters.

Decorum and Appropriateness

I have suggested that a style is a public search for appropriate form within a community or building culture; I further suggested that the appropriate is the fitting and exemplary. In this way, style is more than a concern with superficial appearances but is grounded in the search for appropriate expression of the perennial concerns of the architect and the community in which one builds. Looking more closely, the fitting is that which conforms to our sense of what is consistent with a preexisting pattern or level of expectation. The appropriate entails the embrace of things belonging together and the avoidance of the incongruous; indeed, the apprehension of consistency or inconsistency is the logical basis of all aesthetics. (Whitehead, 1968, p. 52.) This concept is developed by Vitruvius in his idea of *decor*—translatable as "correctness" or "decorum"—which he relates to function, tradition, and nature: In the first case, a building should conform to cultural rules, as when a temple design is consistent with the character of the divinity to whom it is dedicated. In the second case, a design should be formally consistent in all its parts, so that elements from different orders (or types) of columns and entablatures should not be mixed together. In the third case, designs should be in conformance with the health-giving properties of nature, including considerations of siting and orientation for warmth, ventilation, and light. In sum, *decor* is "the refined appearance of a project that has been composed of proven elements and with authority." (Vitruvius, 1999, pp. 24–25, and 150–51.) For example, decorum decrees that a church should be distinguishable from a private house because the status and cultural meaning of these two types of building are different, requiring distinctive expressions. In this way, the building's architectural significance is a function of the social and cultural content of the form as defined by decorum, represented by specific typologies, and articulated in a particular style. Style, therefore, is a key to judging the appropriateness of a proposed intervention, because only within a style (or within a small number of related styles) can such judgments have a rational basis.

The exemplary is the projection of this fittingness into the future by means of the potential imitability of a new work. In an analogy with Immanuel Kant's "categorical imperative"—according to which every act should lend itself to becoming a maxim to be followed by others without contradiction—new works are considered valuable insofar as they may serve as precedents to be imitated by others, enriching rather than diminishing the city. (Kant, 1929, p. 302.) Imitation is fundamental to the operation of a traditional architecture and, likewise, to the formation and maintenance of any particular style. We should not be concerned when our designs are imitated, as they almost certainly will be if they are deemed successful or interesting by others. Architects should always design in a way that "sets a good example"; good buildings are those that, even if imitated by lesser talents, nonetheless inspire more good buildings. The conscious and public cultivation of the appropriate then becomes the driving force behind the development of a style; a breakdown in this process causes the style to lapse into uncritical repetition or desuetude. The development of a style (or a set of closely related styles) then promotes the creation of the city as a coherent work, even when its individual buildings are the products of architects and builders of varying talent, knowledge, or ability.

The Construction of an Urban Vernacular

The pursuit of the appropriate extends beyond the design of individual buildings; indeed, the design of cities rests on appropriateness as a means of sustaining civility, establishing a kind of "building ethic" in which liberty and community are in balance. This is not always or only the product of conscious design. Our cities are filled with buildings that were designed by amateur architects or anonymous builders and craftsmen working within an unselfconscious building culture. For every "high-style" monument or building complex, we can find tracts of simple houses and commercial structures nearby that participate in the same building culture as their more refined neighbors but direct the materials and forms of that building culture to more modest purposes. John Ruskin first pointed to the artistic importance of the modest and often undervalued structures and streets surrounding celebrated monuments—what we now call "urban fabric." (Ruskin, 1971, p. 172.) This insight has profoundly affected preservation practice during the last century, leading it from a preoccupation with single monuments to recognition of the importance of conserving entire urban neighborhoods, cities, and landscapes.

If we think of the city as composed of a *res publica* of monuments and a *res privata* or *res economica* of fabric, the first is typically the realm of high-style design and the second the territory of the vernacular. (Krier, 1998, pp. 30–31.) (Fig. 3.9) The monuments may represent aspirations that transcend the local time and place while the fabric may faithfully embody local building traditions. But this distinction does not mean that we have two different architectures. On the contrary, the close, reflexive relationship of the high-style and the vernacular means that urban building forms a continuous spectrum from the civic monument to the "classicism of everyday life" that gives character to a private house or a newspaper kiosk. (Semes, 1998, and Davis, 2006, pp. 10–11.) The interplay of the principles of traditional architecture, as adumbrated by a particular building culture, becomes the matrix within which an identifiable vernacular can develop.

If high-style design is a "top-down" process in which individual architects pursue the public cultivation of the fitting and exemplary through the conscious imitation and transformation of historical precedent, vernacular design is a "bottom-up" process of building according to custom, unselfconsciously, although often referring to models gleaned from high-style precedents or disseminated by published sources. Vernacular and high-style architectures ideally engage in a creative dialogue in

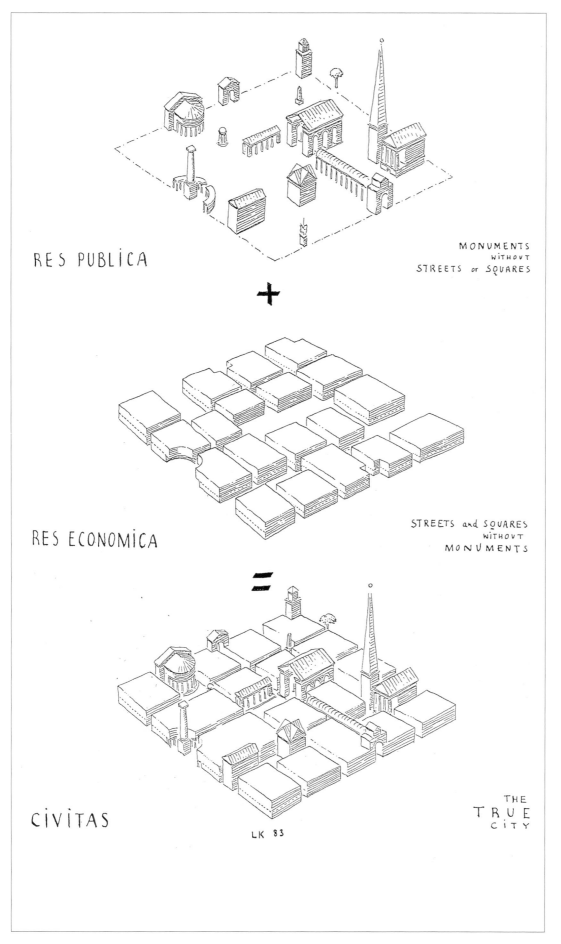

RES PUBLICA

MONUMENTS
WITHOUT
STREETS or SQUARES

+

RES ECONOMICA

STREETS and SQUARES
WITHOUT
MONUMENTS

=

CIVITAS

LK 83

THE
TRUE
CITY

3.9. The elements of the traditional city, drawing by Léon Krier.

Krier's diagram applies the concept of decorum at the urban scale, distilling the essence of the traditional city as a largely vernacular fabric of private buildings into which singular civic monuments and their associated public spaces are woven.

which each draws lessons from the other. A close relation between high-style and vernacular building is often the key to the continuity of character we find in traditional urban settings, where the most conspicuous monuments and the most modest dwellings participate in a common language. (For more on vernacular architecture, see Scruton, 1995; Brand, 1994; and Davis, 2006.) (See fig. C.8.)

For a vernacular building culture to make use of them, the high-style models must be imitable and their imitation must support the generation of more modest versions of themselves. Style is then the sine qua non of a vernacular because there can be no stable vernacular without a style that predictably unites repeatable forms with recognizable contents, as did the designs of Robert Adam, Sir William Chambers, and James Gibbs that supplied the models for the anonymous buildings of Georgian London. These, in turn, were translated into the townhouses, churches, civic and commercial buildings of New York, Boston, and other American cities during the Colonial era. A century later these American models were adapted in the Colonial Revival, which became a truly national vernacular style and which is still alive today. (Wilson, 2004.) (See fig. 3.2.)

Vernaculars can be powerful generators of a sense of urban continuity difficult to achieve through conscious design of individual buildings. The style acts as a kind of genetic code for the city, allowing large numbers of buildings to be produced consistently and inventively. Individually, the buildings may not be in any way exceptional or distinguished; collectively, they form ensembles and districts of harmonized urban fabric within which monuments and public spaces stand out as exceptional moments. The manner in which these elements of the city are formed and composed—no less than the elements of the individual buildings—lends the resulting environment a strong sense of character, a "spirit of the place" that has little to do with any purported "spirit of the time." In vernacular traditions the craftsman-builder is informed by a sense of "how we build here" rather than by a set of fixed rules, a desire for individual self-expression, or a concern with differentiating the new work on the basis of its place in a temporal sequence. (Mouzon, 2007.)

In most traditional settings, "how we build here" is a complex constellation of practices and bodies of knowledge, partly formulated in urban codes, building regulations, master plans, and design guidelines, and partly the product of a multitude of individual decisions, some carefully studied and others unselfconsciously following a preordained, if probably unwritten, law or pattern. To what extent the seemingly serendipitous framed views and picturesque conjunctions of streetscape and building articulation that we find everywhere in the historic center of Rome, for example, are designed and to what extent fortuitous is difficult to say. There is no question that in Rome the key element in the development of the historic center that we enjoy today was an architectural culture within which both architects and their patrons placed a higher value on visual consonance than on efficiency of movement or economy of construction. (Fig. 3.10)

In seventeenth-century Paris, explicit urban design regulation produced an urban fabric utterly unlike that of Rome. As a consequence, the character of Paris is more generalized and abstract—the patterns larger in scale, the vistas longer—in contrast with the more scenographic and composed vistas of Rome. In American cities of the nineteenth and early twentieth centuries, vernacular building cultures produced a large part of the housing stock we now consider historic, much of it controlled by specific building regulations but much of it also the product of a building culture that prioritized the single-family house and the orthogonal grid that organized most of the streets and spaces of the cities. In some such way, the vernacular building culture of a city or region collaborates with the monumental, high-style architectural culture to produce the distinctive character that identifies the historic cities we admire.

It is also worth noting that not all styles have historically given rise to rich urban vernaculars. The nineteenth-century Greek Revival style, for example, was characterized by a very limited range of building types and characters as architects tended to emphasize what they took to be the ancient Greek paradigm of the freestanding object-building heroically dominating its hilltop site. Strangely ignoring models of ancient Greek urbanism that used quite different typologies for a variety of buildings, Greek Revival architects designed all kinds of structures in the form of freestanding peripteral temples. The style was more an emblematic homage to the ideals of democracy than an architectural pattern lending itself to the dense and versatile cities built by the ancient Greeks. Works like

Robert Smirke's British Museum (from 1823 onward) or Thomas U. Walter's Girard College in Philadelphia (1833–47) reveal the difficulties posed by appropriating the Greek temple model for more complex programs on urban sites. Despite distinction in individual monuments, the Greek Revival was never successful at assembling diverse functions into a varied but coherent fabric. (See fig. 3.6.)

In contrast, we can look to the Georgian styles, the Victorian Gothic Revival of James Renwick and Calvert Vaux, the Romanesque Revival of H. H. Richardson, and the Renaissance Revival of McKim, Mead & White for examples of versatile and adaptable styles that were readily applicable to a variety of building tasks in varied physical and cultural contexts. Each of them presented a sufficient number of different models and spatial types to allow these styles to accommodate nearly every conceivable use and scale of building, monumental and vernacular alike. It is no accident that those styles represent the vast majority of American buildings under preservation regulation today.

Understanding an urban vernacular is not only a matter of antiquarian interest: Adding to a historic environment requires knowledge of and respect for the vernacular architecture characteristic of the place, if one can be identified. To the extent that the evidence of the vernacular is a reason for the setting to have been deemed worthy of preservation in the first place, either we must allow it to grow according to its own tradition or we must intervene with extreme caution and tact to avoid destroying the values that preservation seeks to safeguard. (See fig. C.10.)

Architecture and Urbanism

The character of an urban district, like that of the individual buildings within it, is the product of consistent application at all relevant scales of the seven principles enumerated in the previous chapter. This insight underlies the important continuity linking architecture and urbanism, which, after all, are disciplines distinguished by the scales at which they are typically enacted—and the different types of expertise required by each—rather than by any essential difference in fundamental objectives. The main difference in practice is that urban design specifies a general pattern of building massing and public spaces independent of the architectural resolution of the individual buildings. A good urban design plan does not overspecify the building designs, but establishes conditions of enclosure and linkage between public spaces that should be further developed by the individual designs of architects working within the urban designer's master plan.

At the urban scale we can identify at least four models for the traditional city in Europe and North America: the geometrical grid of regular streets and blocks, the medieval pattern of winding streets and piazzas carved out of a solid building fabric, the radioconcentric Baroque plan defined by extended vistas and ritual movement, and the English pattern of residential squares. (Choay, 1968, p. 11.) (Fig. 3.11) Each of these types has its own characteristic elements and relations, its own opportunities and limitations, and its own criteria for success. For example, the grid type (dating back at least to the fifth century B.C.) defines a hierarchy of streets and public spaces within an overall abstract geometrical pattern. Open spaces are typically defined by leaving one or more adjacent blocks unbuilt upon. The medieval plan is governed by visual cues relating one public space or monumental building to another in a series of linked piazzas best appreciated from a pedestrian's viewpoint. The long vistas of the Baroque plan—in which the points of origin and destination are more important than what one passes on the way—are intended to impress not the pedestrian but the occupant of a moving conveyance, whether a horse-drawn carriage or an automobile. The squares of the West End in London or the New Town in Edinburgh serve as the centerpieces of separate interventions related to one another by contiguity rather than by a larger-scale circulation pattern.

Within these four models of the city we may identify urban spatial types consistent with some but not all of them: streets, boulevards, piazzas, squares, parks, etc. (Bess, 2006, pp.

116–22.) We must be clear about which model or spatial type is operating in any given case: A square (usually a landscaped area surrounded by streets) cannot be judged by the standards of a piazza (usually a paved open space defined by buildings), but is a different kind of space altogether. The relation between buildings and open space also varies among the models. For example, the medieval plan carves public space out of a continuous and solid built fabric in order to provide settings for the monuments embedded in that fabric, while the grid plan subordinates all buildings to the abstract pattern of streets, and the radioconcentric plan typically uses vistas to connect freestanding monumental buildings or objects. We need not judge among these models but may simply recognize that there are different ways to plan cities and many reasons for finding any particular solution appropriate or inappropriate within the tradition in which one is operating.

It is essential for the architect and preservationist evaluating new construction in a historic setting to understand the urbanistic dimension of historic monuments—the way they are embedded in and generate urban fabric according to one or more of the models of the traditional city and making use of a selection of urban spatial types. No building, whether historic or new, can be evaluated simply as an isolated artifact but must always be viewed in the context of its physical as well as its historical milieu. Preserving the historic character of an urban district requires that we understand and respect the specific qualities and intentions of the local building culture operating at all scales, from the individual buildings to the urban spatial types to the models defining the city as a whole. Only in this way will we avoid the error of introducing new construction that imposes alien models or typologies, potentially violating or diminishing the very character the preservation effort is supposed to sustain.

The imposition of interventions drawn from a different model need not be destructive to the city, however: The transformation of Rome by the straight streets and axial vistas planned and realized by the Renaissance popes introduced a new model of the city without invalidating the earlier one. (See fig. 3.10.) Indeed, in Rome one may find examples of all four models of the traditional city juxtaposed and superimposed. Similarly, Pierre-Charles L'Enfant's plan for Washington, D.C., is a fascinating, if somewhat problematic, layering of the radiocon-

3.11. Four models of the traditional city.

Exemplifying four models of the traditional city are the gridiron of Manhattan (A); the "organic" plan of the medieval Campo Marzio quarter of Rome (B); the Baroque pattern of radiating avenues at the Place de l'Etoile, Paris (C); and the English residential squares of the Bloomsbury district in London.

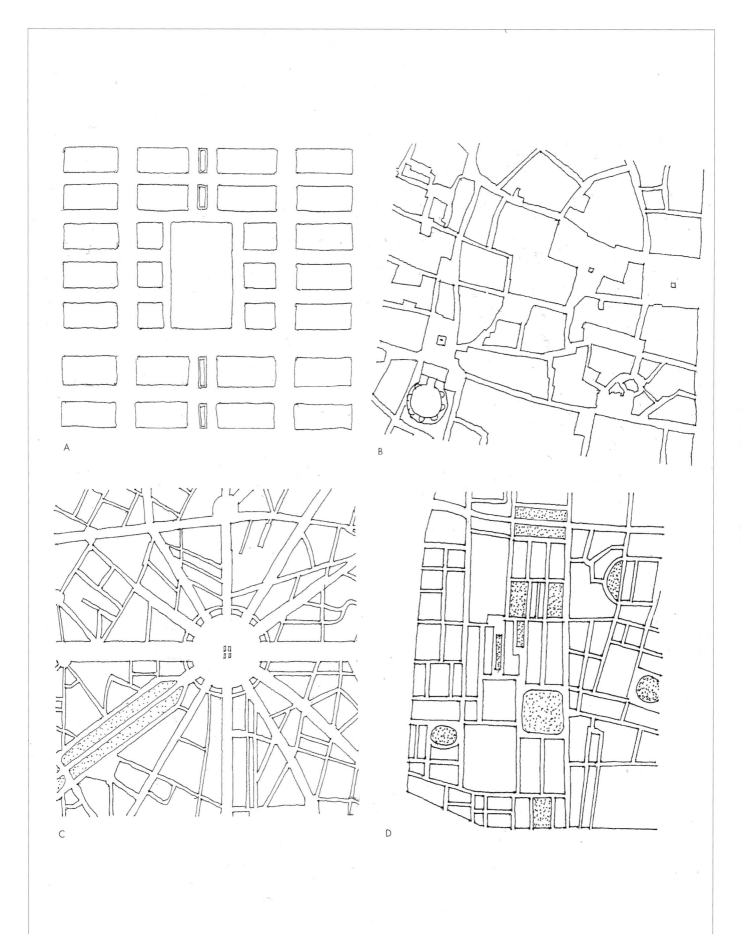

A

B

C

D

centric Baroque plan on top of an underlying grid or plaid. The complexities arising from such multiple layers of models in a single city are a source of much of the visual richness of our historic urban environments, but they also challenge us to analyze carefully the models and spatial types implicit in any site where we propose to introduce new construction.

Beauty in Traditional Architecture

The beauty of architecture, like that of music and dance, is a nonrepresentational beauty; which is to say that it does not depend on its resemblance to some other thing thought to be beautiful, in the way a painting might be thought beautiful because it depicts a beautiful subject. After decades in which the attribution of beauty to specific objects or places was thought to be an entirely subjective matter, developments in contemporary science are revealing underlying universals that form the basis for many of our judgments, rooted perhaps in the workings of our brains. (Pinker, 2002, pp. 400–420.) As part of nature, our gravitation toward such patterns as the logarithmic spiral or the Golden Section is simply a consequence of our minds being embedded in, rather than standing in opposition to, the natural world. Our arts are not unrelated to our evolutionary development, but a fulfillment of it:

> Thus the traditional disciplines of the arts— drawing, harmony and counterpoint, rhyme and meter, dramatic mimesis, proportion in architectural design, storytelling and so on—are not a bunch of dead rules but a live evolutionary process. And that process is not merely a technique for making beauty but the continuation of the creative unfolding of the world whose experience defines what we call beauty itself. (Turner, 2006, p. 13.)

Beauty is "the sign of the fruitfulness and inventiveness of the universe." (Turner, 2006, p. 11.) Since we ourselves are part of that "fruitfulness," our recognition of beauty is a form of remembrance and a sense that we can indeed be at home in the world. Amid the change that inevitably characterizes all life and time, something endures; we can "elicit the permanent from the transient." (Gadamer, 1977, p. 47.) Our recognition of beauty reveals the persistence of pattern, relationship, and consonance within the transient. This same insight

is the foundation of the theories of Vitruvius and Alberti, each of whom defined architectural beauty in terms of the relations of parts and wholes, of good proportions, and fitness of appearance to purpose in imitation of nature. (Vitruvius, 1999, pp. 25, 47, 188–89, and Alberti, 1988, pp. 302–3.)

We can now understand art as something more than the indulgent expression of the individual ego. "Art," George Santayana wrote, *"is skill in the service of beauty."* (Santayana, 1955, p. 140, emphasis added.) The combination of skill—ranging from technical mastery to artistic imaginativeness—and beauty—in the not entirely subjective way described here— allows us to understand art as a participation in the creativity of life itself. Architecture and urbanism, as hybrids of art and science, are uniquely situated to bring our skills into the service of beauty in the environment that is our common home. The beauty of the built environment may now be understood not as a fixed ideal or a subjective preference, but as an idealization and revelation of what Christopher Alexander calls "forms of order" or, more simply still, "life." (Alexander, 2002.)

Traditional environments, as instances of organized complexity, operate within a range between monotony and confusion. Regularity, but not too much, is enlivened by incidents, but not too many. A balance among binaries such as unity and variety, novelty and familiarity, explosive energy and formal limits, is a powerful source of much of the beauty we find in traditional architecture and urbanism. "Aesthetic success is conditional upon the victory of order, but there has to be sufficient complexity to make the victory worthwhile." (Smith, P., 1987, p. 14.) A Baroque church appears as a kind of controlled explosion held in check by the ordering frame of the classical orders. A city derives visual interest from the play of a uniform grid plan against dramatic topography, as in San Francisco. A classical cityscape modulates between uniformity and surprise, generating a hierarchy ranging from unique monuments like the Paris Opéra to the more regular façades of the buildings surrounding it and the typical *architecture Hausmannienne* of a modest Paris street, producing beauty at every stage. (See fig. 2.2.)

Each of the principles of traditional architecture outlined in Chapter 2 contributes to our perception of beauty in architecture, from the ordered geometry of figural space, to the articulation of distinct elements, to their compositional arrangement and refinements of scale and proportion, to the embellishment of ornament and the culminating character that is the product of all of the principles working in harmony. This more "rational" view of beauty does not, however, exclude an equally decisive subjective component: Beautiful architectural works impress us with an ineffable and inexpressible quality in much the same way as natural beauties do, and we are ultimately unable to account for these qualities in exclusively rational terms. Beautiful works of architecture, being the products of human invention, reflect the full range of human faculties from the rational to the spiritual in ways that reinforce the unity rather than the separateness of these faculties. The greatest beauty will be found in those works that, along with all the other things they need to do in order to be successful as architecture or urbanism, also present us with the maximum degree of complexity and the maximum degree of unity at the same time. Beauty points beyond the occasion on which we recognize it to a reality of harmonized dualities, to a peace that lies beyond the joys and sorrows of life.

Beauty is not limited by scale: The beauty of a city is analogous to the beauty of the individual buildings in it but, arguably, is more important. While, of course, the cumulative effect of its beautiful buildings supports and reveals the beauty of the city, it is equally true to say that a beautiful city inspires the design of beautiful buildings. Beautiful buildings are to the city what beautiful ornament is to the building—an example of the fitting articulation of a whole into its parts. While not all traditional architecture is beautiful—or at least not to the same extent—traditions increase the odds that even a modest beauty will be the result of the architect's work, without limiting the freedom of the unique talent to reveal beauties previously unknown and redefine the tradition itself in the process. Any preservation philosophy that does not take seriously the obligation to beauty, especially in settings valued specifically for being beautiful, risks ruining the very qualities that preservation is charged with defending. We must recognize beauty as the ultimately decisive factor—not as an excuse for subjective preferences or formal self-indulgence, but as a value often present in historic settings that requires the utmost respect and nuance when new elements are added. What is more compatible with a beautiful historic building than an equally beautiful new building next to it? In this sense, conservation can never be solely a technical enterprise; it is always and everywhere also a creative act, but one that acknowledges the primacy of the beauty of the historic setting. The difference between a creative act and a destructive one lies in the degree to which the intervention adds new beauties that reinforce rather than diminish the beauty preexisting or latent in the historic setting.

4.1. Maison Carré, first century B.C., and Carré d'Art, Nimes, by Foster Associates, Nimes, 1991.

Despite abstract formal analogies that purportedly relate the new building (rear) to its ancient neighbor, the preponderant visual effect of the new building is to isolate the Roman temple from its otherwise consistent setting.

CHAPTER 4

The Modernist Paradigm

> Painters, poets, musicians, and architects felt themselves being suf-
> focated by the sheer massive presence of the past everywhere—in the
> landscape around them and in the attitudes of institutions and indi-
> viduals who peopled it. That generation demanded that the way be
> cleared for wholly new artistic idioms that would be congruent with
> the new potentials which seemed to be promised by science, industry,
> political democracy. . . . But from the Chicago of Louis Sullivan right
> on down to the Weimar Republic of Walter Gropius, the battle was on
> to liberate building and landscape alike from aesthetic thralldom to
> what seemed to them a corrupt and ineffectual past.
>
> —James Marston Fitch, *Historic
> Preservation* (1982)

The previous chapter's introduction to traditional architecture and urbanism naturally leads to an examination of whether modernist work follows analogous principles. If it often appears that traditional buildings of different styles and eras compose ensembles that are both varied and unified, it is also the case that many observers find that the introduction of modernist structures into a pre-existing traditional setting alters or erodes the historic character of the place. While it is too easy to say that there should be no modernist interventions in historic settings, it is also glib to say that resistance to modernist design— either as interventions in historic places or as a style now being recognized as eligible for preservation protection—would be overcome if the public were sufficiently "educated" about the language and intentions of modernism in order to appreciate its role in the contemporary built environment. (Lyon, 2003, pp. 13–14, 51.) The visual dissonance between the ancient Roman temple of the Maison Carré in Nimes and the adjacent Carré d'Art designed by Norman Foster, for example, is a fact that no amount of further education will change. (Fig. 4.1) But what is the source of this contrast between new and old, and how should we evaluate its impact on historic environments? Can an architecture that

is fundamentally motivated by a determination to "liberate [us] from aesthetic thralldom" to "a corrupt and ineffectual past" fit gracefully among traditional buildings and districts that are the product of that past? (Fitch, 2006, pp. 22–23.)

About a century has now passed since the first pioneers of the Modern Movement— Frank Lloyd Wright, Tony Garnier, Adolf Loos, Antonio Sant'Elia, and others—declared their independence from the prevailing traditions of Western architecture. The early modernist architects sought a radical break with the past, but, as in many such revolutionary movements, the break was not a clean one. Some aspects of traditional form and practice were consciously rejected while others were, perhaps uncon-sciously, retained. Our evaluation of modernist architecture and urbanism today must there-fore recognize a complex layering of intentions that prevents us from accepting uncritically either assertions of wholesale rejection of the past or claims for continuity with it—whether from critics or defenders of modernist design.

To understand both the continuities and the discontinuities, we can analyze modern-ist architecture under the same seven head-ings used in Chapter 2. Modernist designers address the same concerns as their traditional colleagues, but for each of the principles of traditional architecture, the modernist architect typically takes the opposite position. This reversal of values explains why the juxtaposition of modernist and traditional architecture is often perceived as confrontational, not only by critics of modernist design but also by the architects themselves. That such contrast was intentional can be adduced from the vast literature dating from the 1910s to the present in which a cultivation of "difference" with respect to the tradition has been a predominant theme. While not all modernist designers or built works present an adversarial stance toward traditional environments (and some have consciously sought to establish new forms of relationship between new and old works), the claim for a fundamental historical rupture between modernist and traditional aesthetics in architectural theory, criticism, and education establishes the framework within which all modernist responses to the preexisting built world must be understood. (For a fuller discussion of the theoretical positions of the leading modernist designers since 1910, see Banham, 1960, and Frampton, 2007.)

The Search for a New Architecture

Architects' attitudes toward buildings of the past are informed by their attitudes toward the buildings they wish to make in the present, and vice versa. In the genesis of what would become modernism in architecture, the predominant attitude toward the past was that it was finished and that built work of the present day should be recognizable as "different." Most of the leading late-nineteenth-century and early-twentieth-century architectural thinkers assumed a chronological and evolutionary view of history and its correlative—the idea of progress. But what was the end toward which architecture was supposed to be progressing? After the middle of the nineteenth century, positivism, industrialization, revolutionary social theories, nationalism, and Marxist dialectics seemed to be driving society toward new forms of economic and political organization. Since architecture was supposed to express ideas of social and cultural importance, why should it not also evolve a new style expressive of these new realities? In an architectural culture defined by traditions and models, the "difference" between the present and the past

could be expressed most clearly by rejecting the historical styles and the academic apparatus that supported them in favor of something entirely new. Influential architectural historians, theorists, and critics demanded that architects evolve a new style that, when unearthed by future archeologists, would be datable to their own age with the same certainty that fragments from the Renaissance, the Middle Ages, or classical antiquity seemed to be datable to their respective times. (Collins, 1967, pp. 131–32.)

This aesthetic objective was combined with a utopian social and political program inherited from the critiques of nineteenth-century reformers but given a more radical focus by the nascent Modern Movement. Between 1900 and 1935 the pronouncements of Frank Lloyd Wright ("The Art and Craft of the Machine," 1901), Adolf Loos ("Ornament and Crime," 1908), Le Corbusier (*Vers une Architecture*, 1923), Mies van der Rohe ("Architecture and the Times," 1924), and Walter Gropius (*The New Architecture and the Bauhaus*, 1935) set out a program drawing on the historicism of Hegel and Marx, the moralistic exhortations of Ruskin, the rationalism of Viollet-le-Duc, and a secularized version of the religious fervor of Pugin, but emptied of their original stylistic contents. All the leading ideas of nineteenth-century architecture—what Geoffrey Scott catalogued as the Romantic, Ethical, Mechanical, and Biological Fallacies—were brought together in the service of the new architectural movement, but now directed at justifying a radical new aesthetic language that claimed fidelity exclusively to function and reason. (Scott, 1924.)

At least in its public declarations, the Modern Movement claimed to reject virtually the entire inheritance of Western architecture. As Le Corbusier wrote in *Towards a New Architecture*, "If we set ourselves against the past, we are forced to the conclusion that the old architectural code, with its mass of rules and regulations evolved during 4,000 years, is no longer of any interest; it no longer concerns us: all the values have been revised; there has been a revolution in the conception of what Architecture is." (Le Corbusier, 1986, pp. 266–68.) This "revolution in the conception of what Architecture is" is the heart of the matter. Modernism did not present itself as simply a new style among other styles: All of the styles, together with the very concept of style

4.2. Villa Savoye, Poissy, France, by Le Corbusier, 1929–31.

Serving as a virtual emblem of the Modern Movement, Le Corbusier's iconic object-building standing in an open field represents a conscious rejection of history and a reversal of nearly every principle of traditional architecture.

itself, were repudiated. Architecture was to be conceived according to a new pattern based on the imperatives of the modern world. Consequently, traditional architecture and the historical city were viewed with skepticism, if not antagonism, since they represented the inheritance that needed to be cleared away in order for the new modernist vision to be realized. (Fig. 4.2)

Only around the turn of the twentieth century did technologies capable of fulfilling this desire for an entirely new architecture emerge with such innovations as the steel frame, reinforced concrete, the high-speed elevator, and curtain-wall systems for building envelopes. Gradually, the building industry caught up with—or was pressed into the service of—the aesthetic visions and social objectives of the Modern Movement, allowing it to present its ideas in an architectonic language apparently independent of traditional construction techniques and historical styles. The founding of the Congrès Internationaux d'Architecture Moderne (CIAM) in 1928 institutionalized and internationalized the modernist positions. As new iconic buildings were designed and constructed, schools were established—or redirected—to teach the new architecture and the theories of urbanism that were its logical extension at the scale of the city and region. Governments and corporations alike were convinced that modernism represented the future

in contrast to the familiar attitudes and habits of the past. A couple of generations later, modernist architecture itself began to look like a tradition—the Tradition of No Tradition.

A comprehensive history of the ascent to power of the Modern Movement in Europe and the United States has yet to be written, but even now we can only marvel at the breathtaking speed and thoroughness with which the new paradigm of modernism took command of the design professions, academia, and the construction industry. (For part of the story, see Alofsin, 2002.) And yet the victory was not complete: The design of private houses and the field of restoration remained open to those drawn to traditional design—thereby ensuring its survival, albeit in weakened form. A few practitioners of traditional architecture continued to work and build admirable buildings, but these were ignored by the mainstream of the profession, the academics, and the media. Where the new design ideas were introduced into historic settings, the opposition between the modernist and traditional sensibilities produced, on one hand, startling contrasts in form, materials, and scale and, on the other hand, the rapid expansion of the historic preservation movement in reaction to the replacement of traditional buildings and districts by modernist projects.

My aim in this book is neither to demonize modernist design nor to argue that traditional architecture is right and modernist architecture wrong. Rather, I want to set out as clearly as possible the differences between them and why I believe the two traditions are antithetical. They cannot easily be combined or hybridized in the way that the Gothic and the classical were from the fifteenth to the eighteenth centuries, for example. In that case, the Gothic and Renaissance or Baroque styles were different in their respective formal languages but their underlying principles were fundamentally reconcilable. (See fig. 3.3.) On the contrary, when traditional and modernist architecture come together, we find an opposition of aims as well as procedures, of fundamental premises as well as forms. This opposition has complicated all attempts to synthesize or harmonize new and old architecture in historic settings. The pages that follow do not attempt to offer a comprehensive description of modernism, nor a thorough critique, but only to begin an inquiry into the ways its divergent principles tend to subvert the kinds of relationships between new and old construction that we typically see in the encounters of other, premodern architectural styles. To begin with, we will examine the

seven principles of formal design in modernist architecture, paralleling those of traditional architecture but positing a reversal of values.

Space

If traditional space is a metaphorical solid body bounded and governed by Euclidean geometry and a hierarchy of axes, modernist space is the opposite—a fluid, moving force, creating the seductive illusion of boundlessness, freedom, and speed. Modernist space is not a body; it is a void typically conceived as extending infinitely in all directions, and its essential characteristics are neutrality and endlessness. (Norberg-Schulz, 1969, p. 215.) Modernist space is not itself a form, but "the form of the in-between"—that which exists between solid objects. (Peterson, 1980, pp. 91, 98.) Contrary to the traditional concept, in modernist architecture objects are the figures and space is the ground. With rare exceptions, the plans of early modernist buildings—those of Frank Lloyd Wright, Le Corbusier, and Mies van der Rohe in the 1920s, for example—accommodate space as if it were

4.3. Farnsworth House, Plano, Illinois, by Ludwig Mies van der Rohe, 1946–50.

A flowing space is channeled by abstract planes floating in a neutral spatial field and ordered by an implied three-dimensional Cartesian grid. In more recent modernist work, designers have abandoned the grid and, in many cases, Euclidean geometry altogether.

a kind of flow that may be deflected and cor-ralled, but not enclosed, by walls, ceilings, and floors that are rendered as abstract floating planes. This powerful spatial idea is a common thread linking virtually all modernist design, from Mies van der Rohe's Farnsworth House to the streamlined swooshes of Zaha Hadid. It has become a convention in the representation of contemporary buildings and interiors to ren-der architectural elements as weightless screens suspended in a limitless spatial field, with the powerful suggestion of instantaneity, mobility, and ephemerality. (Fig. 4.3)

This conception of space has profound consequences for the city: If the traditional city was envisioned as a series of discrete, figural spaces defined by continuous solid buildings, the modernist city is seen as a kind of "anti-space," a collection of freestanding

objects arrayed in an extensive spatial field. (Peterson, 1980.) The imposition of modernist space on an existing traditional environment inverts the former relation between space and building. Streets and squares are no longer enclosed outdoor rooms but areas left over between buildings; individual historic struc-tures become stranded as freestanding objects isolated from the continuous fabric that for-merly formed their context. "Differentiation" between new and old is prioritized over the composition of a unified space embracing diverse times and typologies, resulting in a decontextualized historical setting. While it is true that some traditional buildings were con-ceived and built as freestanding object-build-ings without direct connection to a specific context, in modernist design this exceptional case has become the paradigm. It is this diver-

4.4. Master plan for the Illinois Institute of Technology campus, Chicago, by Ludwig Mies van der Rohe, 1939–41.

The traditional fabric of buildings and streets is exploded and replaced by a limitless spatial field in which object-buildings are placed according to an abstract system. The destructive imposition of the modernist model on the traditional city gave impetus to the preservation movement.

A

4.5. Two views of modernist structure and systems.

A. Drawing from *La Nuova Città*, by Antonio Sant'Elia, 1914.

B. Centre Pompidou, Paris, by Piano & Rogers, 1977.

For Sant'Elia and his successors, the structural and service systems of buildings—representing the process of production itself—assumed the role of primary expressive elements, even if often exaggerated or dramatized to appear more "interesting."

B

gence in the conception of space, more than any other single factor, that separates the traditional and modernist attitudes toward the individual building and its relationship to landscape, to urban fabric, and to nearby historic structures and sites. The city of continuity has been replaced by the city of contrasts. (Fig. 4.4)

Structure

Modernism as a style properly emerged only after the advent of new steel and concrete technologies introduced alternatives to load-bearing masonry systems, metal-and-glass assemblies allowed the development of lightweight curtain-wall systems for building envelopes, and the invention of the elevator facilitated rapid vertical circulation. With these new resources, modernist designers sought to dramatize structure by exhibiting longer spans, more daring cantilevers, thinner slabs, taller towers, and audacious forms that seemed to defy gravity. These moves were justified as the "honest expression of structure," even when the drama and complexity of the configuration exceeded what pragmatic and economical engineering would have required. Instead of being readable as a visual expression of stability and repose, structure became a means of declaring independence from the supposed imperatives of gravity.

In truth, structural technologies themselves rarely drove the appearance of buildings; rather, the architects' formal intentions drove the development of the technologies. It was not pure efficiency or engineering elegance but aesthetic audacity that motivated the futuristic drawings of Antonio Sant'Elia, with their celebration of exposed structure, elevators, high-flying bridges, and other technical feats. Renzo Piano and Richard Rogers's Centre Pompidou of 1977 in Paris, perhaps more than any other building, realized Sant'Elia's vision and stands as an icon of a dramatic, if exaggerated, exhibition of structure and mechanical systems, representing pure instrumentality and technical prowess as the basis for architectural form. The exposed structural framework becomes the primary visual and spatial ordering system of the building, a formal as well as physical armature upon which, or within which, the separate space-defining and compositional elements are constructed. (Fig. 4.5)

To the extent that traditional building often emphasized obtaining the maximum amount of internal space consistent with the minimum amount of solid structure (walls, columns, etc.) plus whatever additional structure might be required to convey an effect of permanence, modernist designs tend to seek the maximum amount of internal space that can be enclosed by the minimum amount of solid structure, and the visible portion of that structure tends to be articulated in such a way as to appear even slenderer and more evanescent than one expects. While not all modernist architects have practiced structural minimalism, most of the major figures have advocated it at one time or another. (Ford, 1997.) If traditional architecture presents us with displays of fictive structure, modernist design often offers a fictive dematerialization and weightlessness. (See, for example, figs. 4.1 and 4.3.)

Among the early leaders of the Modern Movement, the rationalization of the materials and methods of construction was seen as a primary determinant of architectural form. Today construction technology has advanced to the point that almost anything we can imagine can be built. Technology can no longer be said to determine form; if anything, it is the other way around. Computers have vastly increased our power to envision shapes and spaces that would have been nearly impossible to imagine only a couple of decades ago, and construction technologies have developed to realize them. Buildings now celebrate their freedom to assume the shapes they do because they can. On the other hand, the structure that makes the new shapes possible is no longer expected to be "rational." In a conspicuous display of "irrational" structure, the billowing titanium draperies of Frank Gehry's Pritzker Pavilion at Millennium Park in Chicago are supported by an ad hoc configuration of struts, braces, and catwalks that would have dumbfounded Le Corbusier or Mies. It is difficult to imagine how such a display of seemingly random shapes and elements could create a relationship with traditional buildings on any other basis than conspicuous opposition. (Fig. 4.6)

There is no reason why the juxtaposition of modern construction systems and traditional materials and methods must necessarily be dissonant. Lightness of structure was, after all, pursued as an aesthetic aim even by Roman mural painters (possibly representing

A

B

4.6. Pritzker Pavilion, Millennium Park, Chicago, by Gehry Partners, 1999–2004.

A. Front view.

B. Rear view.

If "rational abstraction" was essential to early modernism, contemporary practice has emphasized what can only be called "irrational abstraction." The arbitrary shapes of the pavilion are supported by equally arbitrary structural elements.

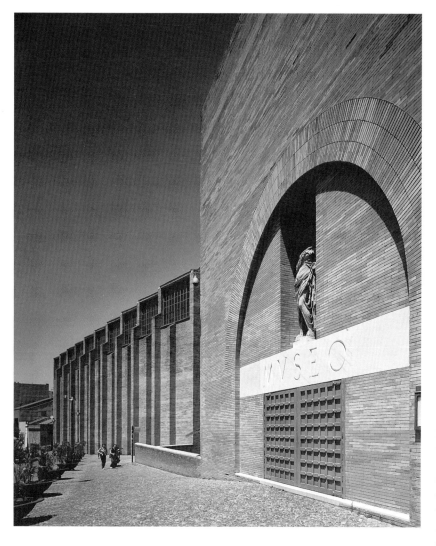

the ancient ruins excavated below. (Fig. 4.7) In most cases, it is not the structural design itself, but the exploitation of structure by the other six principles that lends many modernist buildings their oppositional character in relation to historic neighbors.

Elements

Modernist architecture often presents us with configurations of form and space that we recognize with difficulty, and sometimes not at all, as architectural elements. The realism of traditional elements with their familiar names, typologies, and meanings is replaced by what appear to be abstract sculptures offering few clues to their meaning or use, like the multicolored shapes hanging off the side of Jean Nouvel's Musée du Quai Branly or the graffitilike metal grilles masking the exterior elevations of Francis Soler and Frederic Druot's offices for the French Ministry of Culture, both in Paris. (Fig. 4.8 and fig. C.11)

Not all modernist design avoids the use of recognizable elements. Le Corbusier's "Five Points of the New Architecture" proposed *pilotis*, ribbon windows, free plans, free façades, and roof gardens as repeatable elements rendered in what he called the "engineer's aesthetic." He was fascinated by the products of industrialized manufacturing, which he celebrated as *objets-type*s. (Le Corbusier, 1986.) (See fig. 4.2.) Mies van der Rohe, too, devised a systematic set of elements and details which, like Le Corbusier's, embraced mass-production techniques and could be learned and imitated by his followers. (See fig. 4.3.) But the search for typological consistency in conventional architectural objects must compete with the allure of the unprecedented object in a global consumer marketplace that rewards novelty and originality. Critics often praise a new work by saying, "And here the architect *calls into question* what a door can be"—or a window, a bathroom fixture, or a building. This calling into question of what might otherwise have been taken for granted exerts a strong fascination for many followers of contemporary culture, but it precludes the formation of a stable visual language or set of models, without which there can be no consistent criteria for judging the merits of new designs or sustaining a formal tradition, to say nothing of maintaining dialogue between old and new in historic settings.

4.7. National Museum of Roman Antiquities, Mérida, Spain, by Rafael Moneo, 1980–84.

A legible structural rationalism organizes this museum constructed over excavated Roman ruins. Using load-bearing masonry as a bridge between modernity and antiquity, Moneo achieves a visual rapport with barely a trace of the rhetoric of "difference."

actual slender structures in wood or bronze) and the Gothic cathedral builders. Many of the innovative structural systems developed in contemporary projects by Ove Arup or Santiago Calatrava likewise suggest an analogous pursuit of expressive lightness. Alternatively, several modernist architects—including Le Corbusier and Louis Kahn—have explored massive masonry and concrete systems that are anything but minimal, and the use of these massive systems links these examples, however tenuously, to the tradition. And yet, when intervening in traditional settings, modernist designers often use lightweight or advanced modern structures and materials to project the maximum contrast with load-bearing masonry or heavy timber construction. An exception to this pattern is Rafael Moneo's use of massive brick walls and arches in his museum of Roman antiquities in Mérida, Spain, a building that visually connects the visitor with the world and architectural values represented by

Composition

If traditional composition is concerned with composite form, modernist design is concerned with *assembled shapes*—objects juxtaposed rather than composed. In contrast to the classical analytique, the paradigmatic modernist formal device is the *collage*, invented by Picasso and Braque around 1910 as a way to break out of what they saw as the oppressive conventions of classical pictorial composition and perspective. The components of the collage are not composite forms, but indivisible and irregular shapes subject to aggregation, superimposition, rupture, collision, or interpenetration. (See fig. C.7.)

Buildings designed on the collage model are likewise assemblages of indivisible parts, arranged in additive sequences, subtractive erosions of larger shapes, collisions of components, or some combination of these. The avoidance of hierarchically organized traditional composition—with its canons of number, punctuation, and inflection—in favor of the unresolved juxtaposition of figures against a neutral ground make the collage the ideal visual device to project an architecture of difference.

Prominent among the compositional patterns characteristic of modernist architecture and urbanism are two paradigmatic devices: the orthogonal grid and the "blob" or "organic" shape resulting from a topological, non-Euclidean geometry. The first has often been associated with rationality per se and the second with irrational or "subjective" motives. Exemplifying the first category, Giuseppe Terragni's Casa del Fascio in Como (1932) and Gunnar Asplund's addition to the Law Courts at Göteborg (1937) display similar large-scale grids as the chief organizing device of their elevations, employed in both cases as a symbol of rationality despite the antithetical political programs of their respective patrons. Terragni's building is freestanding, although adjacent to the historic center of Como, whereas Asplund's is an

4.8. French Ministry of Culture, Paris, former office building by Georges Vaudoyer, 1919, with 1960s addition, joined and remodeling by Francis Soler and Frédéric Druot, 1999, detail.

Modernist buildings often display invented elements whose intended meaning and use are puzzling. Here the architects wrapped a scrim of camouflage-like metal screens around a traditional building and its modernist neighbor. While adding visual interest to the banal curtain wall of the newer building they obscure the classical detail of the older one. Their purpose is clearly not functional, but "transgressive." (See also fig. C.11.)

4.9. Modernist abstraction: the grid.

A. Casa del Fascio, Como, Italy, by Giuseppe Terragni, 1932–36.

B. Addition to Law Courts at Göteborg, Sweden, by Erik Gunnar Asplund, 1937.

The orthogonal grid became a symbol of "rationality" transcending other content. Asplund and Terragni, despite the divergent values implicit in their respective building programs, use the grid to express radical opposition to their contexts.

addition to a classical building of the late seventeenth century by the Swedish master Nicodemus Tessin. In both cases the grid distances the new structure from its traditional neighbors. The immediate juxtaposition of Asplund's grid and Tessin's classical composition illustrates the distance between the modernist and traditional conceptions of compositional arrangement: Asplund's grid is weighted toward the horizontal and the windows are set asymmetrically within the grid frame; Tessin's façade, alternatively, is vertically inflected and classically punctuated, its proportions and ornament governed by the Doric order. The alignment of

key horizontal features on the two buildings is insufficient to establish a harmonious relationship between them in the face of their visual dissonance. (Fig. 4.9)

In contrast, a so-called "irrationalist" strain in modernist design has yielded the amorphous or nongeometrical shapes identified with German Expressionism and its successors, as exemplified in the work of Erich Mendelssohn, Hans Scharoun, and Frederick Kiesler. Appearing as an atavistic return to a kind of primitive topology in Le Corbusier's pilgrimage chapel at Ronchamp, amoebic or "organic" shapes have more recently come to be associated with freedom—in the billowing curves of Frank Gehry—or daring and speed—in the hyperenergetic designs of Zaha Hadid. These freely developed shapes may be collaged together or played against gridded surfaces and spaces, or both. Le Corbusier often synthesized the "rational" grid and "irrational" curves in the same building, as in his collage of a geometrical *brise-soleil* and protruding kidney-shaped volumes at the Carpenter Center for the Visual Arts at Harvard University (1963). In recent work of Frank Gehry, Rem Koolhaas, and Steven Holl, the use of computer modeling and computer-directed production techniques has permitted the deformation of gridded surfaces into shapes of unprecedented complexity. (Fig. 4.10)

In the absence of subdivided and articulated composite form, modernist buildings develop

A

B

A

B

4.10. Modernist abstraction: the "organic" shape.

A. Einstein Tower, Potsdam, by Erich Mendelsohn, 1917–21.

B. IAC Building, New York, Gehry Partnership, completed 2007.

C. Simmons Hall, Massachusetts Institute of Technology, Cambridge, by Steven Holl, Architects, completed 2002.

If the grid represents the "rationalist" side of modernism, the "organic" shape represents the "irrational" or subjective side, suggesting freedom, uncertainty, or semantic emptiness. The grid and the organic shape can also be combined, as in the Holl building.

C

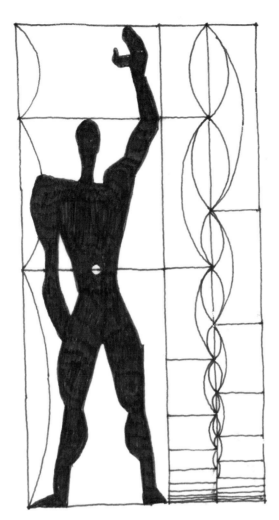

4.11. Le Corbusier's Modulor, 1948 and 1954. Drawing, after Le Corbusier, *Oeuvre Complete 1938–1946.*

The Modulor is a dimensional, rather than a proportional system, intended to standardize industrial production on an anthropometric basis. Two scales defined by the Fibonacci series are separated by a ratio of 1:2 and calibrated to the figure of a six-foot-tall man. Le Corbusier replaces the classical idealized human figure with a misshapen one.

shape or volume added horizontally or vertically to the historic structure, it can burrow into or penetrate the older building, or it can appear to be breaking out of the older building in an act of violence. What it can rarely do is engage a traditional historic building as a partner in respectful dialogue or as anything other than an objet trouvé. The compositional means to unite a new and an old building on equal terms despite differences in typology, materials, size, and style—as premodern buildings were typically able to do—are largely unavailable to the modernist designer who intervenes in a traditional historic setting. (See figs. C.2 and C.4.)

Proportion

Some modernist designers have employed what appear to be proportional systems analogous to those found in traditional work, the best-known being Le Corbusier's "Modulor," a double scale of standard linear dimensions purportedly based on the standing human figure and regulated by the Fibonacci series. Applied to a set of plan and façade elements, the Modulor system produces consistent differentiations throughout the composition, but it can only be carried so far. In order for relations between parts and wholes to be regulated, there must be parts and wholes to regulate. Le Corbusier employs his dimensions at the middle and large scales, but the building as a whole is not "in the system" and the Modulor does not extend to ornamental detail because there is none. (Le Corbusier, 1980, and Scholfield, 1958, p. 124.) (Fig. 4.11)

The same difficulty is illustrated by published sketches purporting to demonstrate "proportional kinship" between Norman Foster's Carré d'Art and the adjacent Roman temple, the Maison Carré, in Nimes. (See Byard, 1998, pp. 57–60.) (See fig. 4.1.) The "regulating lines" derived from a set of three rectangles related to major façade subdivisions suggest a proportional affinity between the two structures that is not borne out by close inpection of the figures. The rectangles and their diagonals are not, in fact, congruent between the two buildings. Indeed, they cannot be so because the modernist building, with its predominating orthogonal grid, is clearly based on an arithmetical system of repeated units, while the ancient temple is baesd solely on geometrical proportions, which necessarily involve quantities that are incommensurable. But the prob-

a different sense of scale from that typically seen in traditional models. Iconic modernist buildings—from Le Corbusier's ideal villas to the crystalline office towers of Norman Foster—appear as unitary shapes, without hierarchically organized parts and revealing few distinct scale levels, typically only the scale of the whole and the scale of a typical component of the building envelope system. (See figs. 4.2 and C.17.) This is what critics mean when they claim that modernist buildings lack "human scale," and it is undoubtedly a primary cause for the popular sentiment that finds modernist interventions out of scale with historic settings. (Salingaros, 2006, pp. 71–74.)

Their differences in fundamental compositional strategies pose difficulties for the encounter between modernist and traditional architecture. The devices of collage enable the designer to confront, but not to weave together, disparate kinds of architecture. A modernist structure can engage an older traditional building compositionally by appearing as a discrete

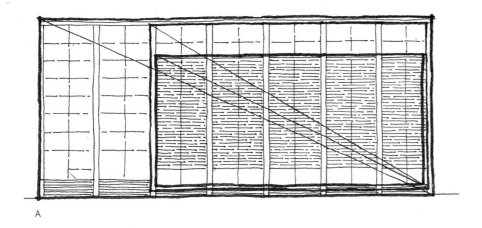

A

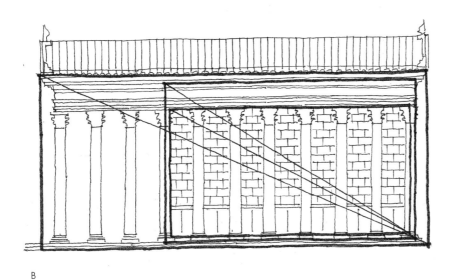

B

4.12. Proportional affinities between new and old buildings.

A. Carré d'Art, Nimes, Foster Associates, 1991.

B. Maison Carré, Nimes, first century B.C. Drawing, after Paul Spencer Byard, *The Architecture of Additions*, 1998.

Claims that these two buildings share proportional affinities are spurious. The overlaid rectangles are not congruent because Foster's modular building uses an arithmetic system, while the ancient temple uses geometrical proportions. Even if correct, the similarities would apply to only the largest scale levels in the two compositions. (See also fig. 4.1.)

lem lies deeper: the crude proportional device of the diagram, even if correct, would regulate only subdivisions at the largest scale of the two elevations. The absence of a more diffused proportional conformance among the parts of the modernist building or between the two structures contributes to the sense of opposition with which the new building meets its ancient neighbor. (Fig. 4.12)

These examples are symptomatic of a general modernist indifference to traditional theories and practices of proportion, which were roundly attacked by most of the polemicists of the Modern Movement. The subjectivist, intuitive approach of modernist design, rooted in the values of originality and individual genius, would seem to be unsympathetic to a practice that implies an objective standard of beauty. Curiously, the disinclination toward proportional systems is not primarily a technical issue—one can imagine a thoroughly modern building (in terms of its materials and construction methods) employing a rigorous clas-

sical or even Gothic proportioning system fully functioning at all scales. The design of such a building, theoretically possible, has yet to be accomplished, yet it presents a challenge that contemporary designers of all stylistic persuasions should take seriously.

Ornament

One of the ironies of twentieth-century architectural history is that the early modern "pioneers" wanted to *reform* ornament, not eliminate it; its elimination came, nevertheless, as a consequence of their work. Figures like Morris, Loos, Wagner, Sullivan, and Wright all integrated ornament into their designs, but sought to reestablish its relationship to underlying form and to impose a more limited and idealized selection of motifs—whether naturalistic or geometric—in the interest of expressing what they saw as the nature of machine production. The more radical figures of the Modern Movement saw *all* ornament, especially anything resembling handicraft, as impermissible within the "engineer's aesthetic" they championed. (Brolin, 2000, pp. 106–66.) We now understand that ornament is a perennial human interest that, if prohibited, finds surreptitious ways of expressing itself. (Salingaros, 2006, pp. 77–78, 84–92.) If the embellishment of surfaces and forms by ornamental patterns was not allowed by modernist theory, then the designer's ornamental impulses would come out in other ways. Mies van der Rohe and Carlo Scarpa, for example, made ornament out of the luxurious surfaces of their interiors and out of the meticulously detailed reveals and joints between the materials and components from which their buildings were made. (See fig. 2.3.)

Alternatively, the entire building could be designed as if it were a gigantic piece of ornament. Frank Lloyd Wright's National Life Insurance Company Building proposal for Chicago (1924) features a row of high-rise office blocks in the form of the "hollyhock" motif the architect used at the Barnsdall House in Los Angeles, but here colossally magnified. While more recent designs by the current avant-garde do not resemble any recognizable species of ornament, their powerfully gestural shapes likewise give them the appearance of objects intended to be only inches high that have been preposterously enlarged. In such cases one cannot say that modernist architecture has no ornament; rather, the entire building became a colossal ornament without an underlying form to reveal and articulate. (Collins, 1967, p. 127; Brolin, 2000; and Beeby, 1977.) (Figs. 4.13, 4.6, and 4.10)

Robert Venturi and his colleagues reintroduced ornament as the superficial application of pattern to a pragmatically arranged structure (the "decorated shed") in contradistinction to the building as a sculptural and ornamental object (the "duck"). (Venturi, Izenour, and Scott Brown, 1977.) While the firm's own work in historic settings mostly followed the "decorated shed" model and introduced polychrome ornamental surface patterns intended to harmonize the addition with its older host—as in the Allen Memorial Art Museum at Oberlin, Ohio, or the recent addition at Dumbarton Oaks in Washington, D.C.—the application of a strictly two-dimensional pattern, with its Pop Art graphic qualities, does not remove but rather underscores the conspicuous contrast between the new and old buildings. The new ornament lacks a compositional or scaling relationship to either the building it embellishes or the one to which it makes allusion. As a result, the architect misses the opportunity to draw the new and old buildings together into what Venturi elsewhere called "the difficult whole." (Venturi, 1965, p. 89.) (See fig. C.14.)

What modernism abandoned definitively was ornament as an instrument of composition—punctuating and articulating frames, borders, and thresholds between parts and weaving them into wholes. Without ornament of this kind, modernist buildings have difficulty establishing complementarity with adjacent traditional buildings. An entire scale level—that of the small part rewarding the near view—is missing. But in the eyes of an increasing number of professionals and virtually the entire lay public, it is the absence of conventional ornament that most sets modernist buildings apart from the historic structures around them, making them appear blank in comparison to their more embellished neighbors.

Character

In modernist design as in traditional work, attitudes toward space, structure, elements, composition, proportion, and ornament evoke an overall "spirit of place" that is critical for our understanding of the work as architecture. And yet, despite its obviousness to even the most casual observer, architectural character has rarely been discussed in modernist theory, nor is it a term often used by contemporary practitioners. Christian Norberg-Schulz's analysis of architecture as "the concretization of existential space" perhaps comes closest to a modernist theory of architectural character, although this promising line of inquiry seems to have had little influence on contemporary thought or practice. (Norbert-Schulz, 1980.)

The absence of character from discussions of modernist architecture is both a cause and a symptom of the architects' displacement of significance from form to technique and from what buildings look like to the "ideas" they are believed to express. Character does not present itself as an issue for theoretical exploration if the phenomenological dimension of architecture—the experience of its material reality, its light, its tactile concreteness—is considered subordinate to the "concept," which might be one or more abstract formal ideas, a

4.13. National Life Insurance Building (project), Chicago, by Frank Lloyd Wright, 1924.

Wright never rejected ornament but often manipulated its scale, and in some cases the whole building appears to be a kind of ornament. Here the shape of the office slabs recalls the "hollyhock" motif from the Barnsdall House in Los Angeles of 1921.

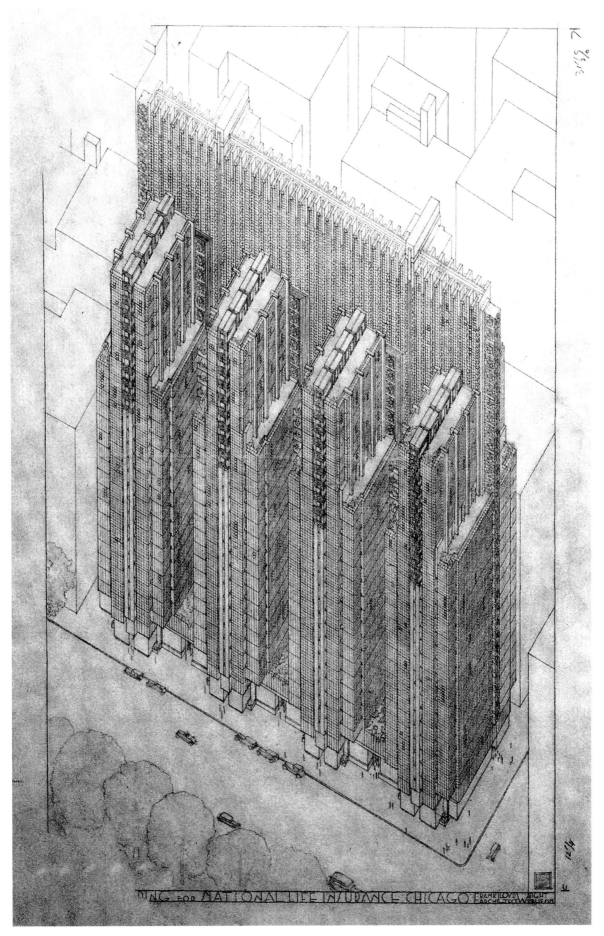

...NG FOR NATIONAL LIFE INSURANCE CHICAGO FRANK LLOYD WRIGHT ARCHITECT TALIESIN

protest against social or cultural conditions, or an innovative technical design or production method. This conceptual bias is not found in all modernist work, but it does characterize an important—and apparently growing—segment of modernist practice.

On the other hand, one may cite works by Louis Kahn, Alvar Aalto, and Carlo Scarpa in which the architect seems intent on exploring not only a "concept" but a definite physical means of embodying it that lingers in the memory as a distilled sense of identity and "spirit of place." We cannot understand Kahn's Kimbell Art Museum in Fort Worth, for example, without grasping both the universality of its formal and structural order and the particularity of the material substance, light, and texture of the realized building. Such qualities have prompted critics to remark on the "tragic," "humanistic," or "ineffable" qualities of the work, citing these same qualities as evidence of a vestigial relationship to tradition. But it is precisely their memorable evocation of character—rather than simply a schematic representation of abstract ideas or technical processes—that separates these works from many of their contemporaries and tenuously links them to traditional architecture.

Among the current generation of designers, we are more likely to find forms, configurations, and materials palettes calculated to underscore the difference between modernist and traditional buildings. The character of much modernist architecture is, accordingly, derived from its assertion of a self-referential formal autonomy in disregard of, or in opposition to, traditional sensibilities. While the production of the "heroic" phase of the Modern Movement often evoked a confidence in the promise of new technologies and new forms of social order, the character of much mainstream architecture today provokes a sense of instability, anxiety, and doubt. Going a step further, a number of current avant-garde designers have pursued an architecture that seems to escape the semantic dimension altogether. A vision of what might be called the "nihilistic sublime"— a breathtaking emptiness of content expressed at the largest possible scale—pervades such monumentally scaled but semantically empty works as Peter Eisenman's Memorial to the Murdered Jews of Europe in Berlin, Steven Holl's Simmons Hall at MIT, or Rem Koolhaas's Chinese Television Center in Beijing. (See fig. 4.10C.) Proposals for the rebuilding

of the World Trade Center in New York were, with the exception of the historically informed scheme by Peterson/Littenberg, uniformly in this same category. (Stephens, Luna, and Braodhurst, 2004.) From the New Brutalism of the 1970s to the "monsters" of more recent production, the character evoked by modernist buildings, whether intentional or inadvertent, is often perceived by the public as intimidating or disturbing and, in any case, rarely conducive to partnerships between new and old structures within larger urban ensembles.

The seven principles described in this chapter certainly do not exhaust the possibilities for modernist design, and counter-examples for any of the categories can be found. Even so, and keeping in mind the inevitable risks of such broad generalization, they do assist us in evaluating the very different premises on which modernist and traditional buildings operate. As with the traditional versions of the same principles, they must be understood not as separate precepts but as a field of mutually defining and mutually modifying values acting simultaneously. The principle of illimitable space goes hand in hand with collagist composition and minimalist ideas of scale, proportion, and ornament. The summation of the first six principles yields a character that is conspicuously distinguishable from that projected by most traditional buildings. It is the coordinated action of the principles together that defines the quality of conceptual abstraction popularly identified with modernist design, and vice versa.

And this is the heart of the matter: *Traditional and modernist architecture in their "pure" states are fundamentally irreconcilable, not because they are different styles representing different tastes, ideologies, or historical periods, but because the formal premises on which they operate are antithetical.* The introduction of new modernist buildings into a preexisting traditional setting results in a jarring contrast precisely in proportion to the conviction and rigor with which the modernist building and surrounding traditional ones embody their respective principles. Only with significant compromise on either or both sides can the two architectural conceptions collaborate on the production of places characterized by continuity and wholeness. In my view, this does not invalidate modernist architecture but, rather, suggests that the proper place for new modernist buildings is *with other modernist buildings,* not as interventions within historic districts whose character and significance are threatened by the imposition of new work embodying contrary principles.

Modernist Urbanism

More problematic than modernist prescriptions for individual buildings are the effects of modernist urbanism. The greatest threat to the preservation of historic settings arose from the sweeping reconceptualization of the city that followed logically from the application of the principles of modernist space and composition at the scale of the city: Le Corbusier's Plan Voisin of 1925 proposed the wholesale demolition of the monumental center of Paris, to be replaced by an array of high-rise office and apartment towers widely spaced in a landscaped park crisscrossed by highways. (Fig. 4.14) Frank Lloyd Wright's Broadacre City plan from

the middle of the following decade proposed the transformation of American cities and countryside into a low-density sprawl of isolated "Usonian" houses punctuated by intermittent office and apartment towers served by both automobiles and curious flying machines, all organized on a grid pattern of roads and highways stretching indefinitely across the land. (Fig. 4.15)

These schemes, bereft of the signature architectural styles that provided much of their initial appeal, defined the patterns of urban development that have been adopted throughout the developed world up to the present: Le Corbusier's vision became the model for the "urban renewal" schemes of the 1960s, exemplified in the redevelopment plans of Robert Moses and the 1961 Zoning Law that nearly destroyed the historic urban texture of Manhattan in favor of object-buildings set in plazas. This pattern would be imitated uncritically in cities across the United States. Wright is the unacknowl-

4.14: Plan Voisin, Paris, by Le Corbusier, 1925.

There is no clearer statement of the modernist attitude to the historical city than this proposal to replace central Paris with widely spaced high-rise towers separated by broad highways and open landscape. A handful of monuments (note the Louvre in the foreground) were to be retained as isolated artifacts.

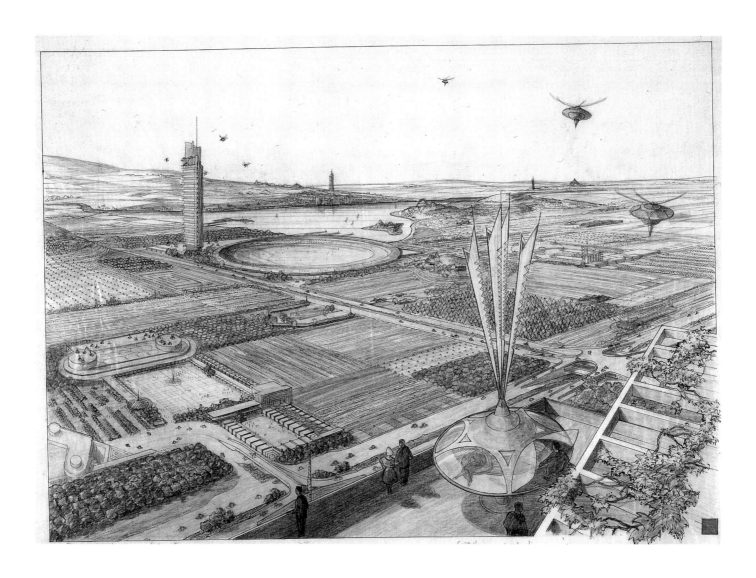

edged progenitor of postwar suburban sprawl, the indefinite "geography of nowhere" that has dispersed the activities of social and family life into separate zones accessible only by private automobile. (Kunstler, 1994.) While one may safely speculate that both architects would be horrified to see the ways in which their ideas have been implemented, and while neither of them arrived at those ideas without historical precedents stretching back a century or more, we cannot absolve them from introducing virulent "viruses" into the codes of modern city planning, transportation, real estate development, economics, and politics. As a result, traditional patterns of city-making were abandoned in favor of a new code of monocultural, single-use zones connected by highways. Worse, the traditional patterns were actually prohibited by postwar zoning laws so that, however much Americans might appreciate New England townscapes, tree-lined residential streets, or early twentieth-century town

centers, these became for the most part illegal wherever conventional zoning was implemented. Even though the consequences of the modernist urban vision have long been plainly evident to everyone without a vested interest in their continuation, the underlying "viral" concepts are nonetheless proving difficult to dislodge.

Most relevant to our present inquiry is the way the modernist conception of space, with its fixation on the freestanding object-building, impacted preexisting historic fabric. Le Corbusier's Plan Voisin preserved a handful of monuments—such as the Cathedral of Notre-Dame and the Louvre—within his radically altered cityscape of towers, parks, and freeways, but these survivors from the past were presented as decontextualized artifacts extracted from the dense urban fabric that had formerly surrounded them. The same motive drove the "liberation" of ancient monuments in Rome during the Fascist era, and after the

Second World War, American cities were similarly "cleared" for freeways and large-scale redevelopment proposals, except that in the American case few monuments were spared. (See figs. 4.4 and 5.6.) The successful resistance to large-scale redevelopment projects by citizen activists like Jane Jacobs has become legend, but many committed modernists were also among the protesters, including James Marston Fitch and Lewis Mumford, who believed that the destructive consequences of modernist urbanism could be avoided without abandoning the modernist aesthetic for individual buildings. (Fitch, 2006, p. 183.)

This same belief has been expressed more recently by several leading figures in the Congress for the New Urbanism who embrace traditional town-planning principles but reject the practice of new traditional architecture. For these critics and practitioners, the mistakes of modernist urbanism do not invalidate the modernist program as a whole, which many of them still regard as progressive. In my view, the attempt to decouple the urban theories of modernism from the formal language used for the design of individual buildings, ensembles, or landscapes founders on the reality that the modernist urban vision is the logical extension of its formal language and conception of space at the scale of the city. Can one design a coherent urban environment with one conception of architecture at the scale of the building and a completely different, even contradictory one at the scale of the city as a whole? More simply, can the urban code and the architectural code inhabit two different conceptual worlds? Perhaps so, but does the adoption by some modernist architects of New Urbanist notions of mixed-use, high-density, pedestrian scale, and "walkability" not represent an enormous concession by them of virtually the entire field of urbanism in the face of the failure of the modernist urban vision?

On the other hand, a new generation of academics and professionals has reacted to this bifurcation of modernist design and New Urbanism by unapologetically embracing the Modern Movement vision of the city. In such developments as the new commercial center of Lille in France, schemes for the rebuilding of New York's World Trade Center site, and a new quarter of skyscrapers proposed for Milan, we see defiant new editions of the Plan Voisin at even greater scale and featuring updated technology and imagery. (Stephens, Luna, and Broadhurst, 2004.) The *New York*

Times noted a growing reaction by ambitious developers, architects, and planners against what they see as obstruction by Jane Jacobs–inspired neighborhood activists and design review processes. Instead, these groups promote the return of "Big Urbanism" to maintain the city's competitive edge. Cities, noted the *Times*, "are once again planning with grandiosity," as evidenced by the enormous Atlantic Yards project in downtown Brooklyn, designed by Frank Gehry and demonstrating a disregard of nearby historic neighborhoods that recalls the "grandiosity" of the 1960s—or, more ominously, of the 1930s. (Haskell, 2006.) Recent publications and exhibitions have called for the reappraisal of Robert Moses and the impact of his freeway, bridge, and superblock redevelopment and housing projects in the New York metropolitan area. In commentaries on Moses's legacy, praise of this complex figure's positive achievements was accompanied by an unconcealed envy of the power that allowed him to achieve astonishing, mammoth projects in a short time, for the most part unaccountable to governmental checks and balances, undeterred by public opposition, and heedless of the human cost. (Ballon and Jackson, 2007, and Goldberger, 2007, p. 85.)

Resolution of this larger debate over the merits of "Big Urbanism" is crucial for defending historic settings in the modern city because it was the rise of modernist urbanism that fueled the exponential growth of the historic preservation movement in the first place. The legislation and infrastructure put into place over the last four decades to safeguard historic environments against "Big Urbanism" are now coming under threat, and this must prompt dismay not only among those who value historical architecture but also among modernists who see the heritage of the "recent past" as likewise threatened. (Lambin, 2003.) The combination of a resurgent totalizing urbanism and an endemic culture of "star" architects devoted to novelty, if not contained and counterbalanced by opposing tendencies, portends a grim outlook for the preservation of historic resources in cities.

Modernism and Historic Settings

An architect who believes that the models of the past are a hindrance to progress in the discipline might logically propose new build-

4.16. Skyscraper for Friedrichstrasse (project), by Mies van der Rohe, Berlin, 1921.

Mies van der Rohe's prismatic glass tower rising in striking contrast to surrounding buildings— rendered as mute, dark masses—is the paradigm for generations of modernist object-buildings whose visual interest similarly depends on contrast with older neighbors.

ings intended as alternative models. Less consistent have been architects' attitudes toward the continued presence of the old models and the survival of traditional buildings and urban districts adjacent to proposed new construction. In many cases it was simply assumed that the existing built environment would be demolished to make way for the new; hence, little concern was given to accommodating or harmonizing with it. When it was not in the architect's power to determine the future status of the existing context, the architect might view the preexisting context as an unmovable fact to be grudgingly accommodated or as a "foil" against which the new building appears to good advantage by virtue of contrast. Such an approach is visible in the early projects of the Modern Movement, such as Mies van der Rohe's 1921 scheme for a glass skyscraper in Berlin. In the architect's rendering, preexisting historic buildings appear as shadowy presences lurking in the background, their primary significance apparently to provide the contrast that gives interest to the prismatic, minimalist object rising in their midst. (Fig. 4.16)

In cases where the designer wishes to evoke an intentional connection between new and old buildings, the modernist architect might adopt an approach in which aspects of the traditional design are abstracted and incorporated into the modernist composition, an approach illustrated by the diverse works of Philip Johnson and the postmodernist architects who followed his example. In his addition to the Boston Public Library (1965), a series of formal analogies yields a building that is neither entirely modernist (because of the seemingly arbitrary and nonfunctional arrangement of shapes and volumes) nor convincingly traditional (for the same reason). The addition is differentiated from its original "host" by its reduction of the older building's formal language to two or (at most) three scale levels, the absence of articulation or ornament, and the generally opaque character of the addition. Compatibility with the older building is suggested by means of archlike shapes and horizontal alignments within an overall mass similar in height and bulk to the McKim building. In the absence of a common language, however, these formal analogies are incapable of drawing the new and old buildings into a larger whole. (Fig. 4.17)

The allusions to traditional forms of postmodernist architects such as Robert Venturi, Charles Moore, Michael Graves, Robert A. M. Stern, and Aldo Rossi may have been more obvious but they were similarly abstracted and—departing from modernist orthodoxy—were consciously framed within an enveloping irony. (Jencks, 1981.) As the allusions of postmodernism became more and more "literal"—meaning identifiable as direct references to specific historical forms—it appeared that a means of bridging the gap between modernist and traditional design might yet be found, although this experiment collapsed when the postmodern school of architects polarized into neomodernist and nonironic traditionalist camps in the mid–1980s. Only with the recovery of traditional formal languages were some of the protagonists of postmodernism— particularly Robert A. M. Stern and his colleagues—able to move from abstract allusion to a more historically informed and materially convincing character.

Typically, the modernist architect attempts an expression of "unity by contrast," but this oxymoronic approach often results in a new building that, if it were not juxtaposed with adjacent historic structures, would be of little visual interest, while the preexisting traditional buildings are seriously compromised by the intrusion of a discordant neighbor. Andrés Duany noted that "Modernist buildings to be successful must be located within traditional urban fabric. They are *parasitic*." (Duany,

4.17. Boston Public Library, Boston, by McKim, Mead & White, 1898, with addition by Philip Johnson, 1967.

The addition (right) seeks compatibility through abstract massing rather than formal language or specific character. McKim's building is an articulate body, while Johnson's is a mute object whose exterior reveals little about its structure or interior arrangement.

2005, emphasis added.) A building that cannot form relationships with its immediate context except on a crudely opportunistic or parasitic basis cannot be expected to compose coherent urban ensembles or maintain a sense of continuity with older neighbors. This incapacity to form continuous urban fabric produces instead a strong sense of decontextualization, both for the modernist work and for any traditional building that may come within its sphere of influence. (Fig. 4.18) What is rare in modernist projects designed for historic settings is a new structure that engages its historic neighbors as equal partners in the composition of a larger ensemble intended to sustain a sense of continuity in space and time. To do so, a modernist project would have to recognize the continuing validity of the preexisting buildings and the city in which they stand, as well as to find alternatives to the collage as a compositional model. (I examine strategies for relating new and old architecture in historic settings in more detail in Chapters 8 through 11.)

The Future of Modernism

After nearly a century of modernist ascendancy, we must ask: What is the prognosis for the continued survival of historical sites in the midst of an environment shaped by very different premises? And what is the likelihood that contemporary architecture might evolve in ways more conducive to the design of neighborhoods and cities characterized by continuity rather than contrast? Are there strains of modernism more likely to maintain sympathetic relations with traditional contexts, or does the fundamental divergence of languages and aims render any such compromise out of the question?

Modernist architecture has been no more monolithic in its development than traditional architecture. Numerous dissenters within the modernist community have addressed particular deficiencies or gaps they saw in the overall architectural and urbanistic program. These have included the Scandinavian modernism of Alvar Aalto, the formal analyses of Colin Rowe and his followers, the study of symbolism and allusion by Robert Venturi and Denise Scott Brown, the New Rationalism of Aldo Rossi, and the "critical regionalism" promoted by Kenneth Frampton. A detailed discussion of any of these strains within modernism is

beyond our present scope, except to point out that some of these critiques and alternatives may offer possibilities for the growth of more nuanced and inclusive strains of modernist thought and practice in the future. Indeed, certain of them have been incorporated or adapted by new traditional architects and New Urbanists, for whom the more nonideological and less abstract aspects of modernism still offer important lessons, particularly in the areas of programmatic and technological innovation. On the other hand, in my view none of these dissents adequately addresses the fundamental problem of architectural language and its relation to the building of successful ensembles and cities.

Another alternative might be found by rediscovering what has been called the "Other Modern," the modernity that did not reject history or tradition entirely, but sought instead to weave new insights and new experiences into the fabric of the world we have inherited. (Tagliaventi, 2000.) The ascendancy of the Modern Movement largely erased the works and reputations of architects such as Sigurd Lewerentz, Jože Plecnik, and Bernard Maybeck, but their persistent attachment to a critical transformation of traditional models and languages now appears prescient and valuable. A new generation might yet follow the examples of these artists, redefining modernism as a richly allusive, reflective, syncretistic medium which, like the turn-of-the-twentieth-century eclectics of Henry-Russell Hitchcock's "New Tradition," draws on whatever is relevant and appropriate, integrating the past and present and handing the inheritance on, transformed, to the future. (Hitchcock, 1970, p. 44.)

The neat symmetry that binds the diametrically opposed traditional and modernist outlooks together suggests possibilities for dialogue. It is possible to envision architectural positions that draw from both traditional and modernist versions of the seven propositions explored in Chapter 2 and above, defining architectures on some other basis than a pure traditionalism or a rigorous modernism. For example, one could design buildings that maintained traditional concepts of space, elements, and composition, while exploring modernist concepts of structure, proportion, and ornament. The Jorge M. Perez Architecture Center at the University of Miami by Léon Krier suggests the kind of building that might result

WHAT IF Nº 10 DOWNING STREET HAD NOT BEEN REBUILT BY RAYMOND ERITH ?   LK 85

4.18. "What If Number 10 Downing Street Had Not Been Rebuilt by Raymond Erith?", Drawing by Léon Krier, 1985.

Krier's satirical cartoon perfectly captures the consequences of a policy of introducing "the architecture of our time" into historic settings—a streetscape of architectural clichés in opposition to, rather than in harmony with, the preexisting context.

from such an eclectic selection of principles. (See figs. C.28, C.29, and 10.9.) It is in this borderland between the traditional and modernist sensibilities that perhaps the most interesting work is yet to be done. One cannot say with certainty that a rapprochement between traditional and modernist architecture is possible on any grounds that would not entail unacceptable levels of compromise on either side. I simply wish to suggest here that the possibilities have not been exhausted and perhaps merit further investigation, especially in modernist settings (like the University of Miami) that are increasingly subject to preservation regulation.

The development of an appropriate architectural language remains the fundamental challenge of modernist architecture, but it is difficult now to conceive how a repeatable formal language might emerge from the practices of the most well-known contemporary designers. While some of the first generation of modernist architects sought to develop new formal languages as an alternative to classical and vernacular usages—foremost among them Le Corbusier, Mies van der Rohe, Alvar Aalto, and Louis Kahn—the recent designers who have inspired the most widespread imitation are paradoxically those—like Frank Gehry, Rem Koolhaas, and Zaha Hadid—who reject repeatable language altogether in favor of grandiose, if semantically empty, projections of the "nihilist sublime." But ultimately buildings have meaning only in relation to other buildings across space and time. The disinclination of modernist architects to establish a stable formal language that can sustain long-term relationships with a world of other buildings on a basis other than contrast and oppositional self-assertion makes the prospects for a mutually respecting rapprochement between modernist design and traditional architecture dim. Consequently, preservation policies or urban design practices that induce reliance on some such creative encounter or synthesis between historical and modernist architecture raise challenges that no contemporary architect may be able to meet.

5.1. Round Temple by the Tiber, Rome, first century B.C.

Like most visible Roman remains, this round temple has been altered and restored numerous times. Several columns were replaced in antiquity, two centuries after the temple's construction, and one Corinthian capital was re-carved in the twentieth century.

CHAPTER 5

A Brief History of Preservation Philosophy

Architecture may be frozen music, but it melts.

—OSBERT LANCASTER, "What Should We
Preserve?" (1974)

Philosophies of preservation cannot be considered separately from philosophies of contemporary architecture: the relation between new and old architecture is always defined in terms of the perceptions, values, and interests operative in the architectural culture of the moment. It cannot be otherwise, since we can only look at the past through the eyes we have in the present and our eyes are inevitably trained to see both the new and the old in accustomed ways. In this sense, preservation and restoration, no matter how meticulously based on documentation or scientific analysis, is always also a creative act of imagination colored by the expectations we knowingly or unknowingly bring with us to the process. Philosophies of preservation have indeed changed over time, closely paralleling the interests and tastes of the architects and patrons. Even a cursory examination of the issues that have preoccupied our predecessors will help us arrive at a more conscious and critical view of the field. (For a detailed history of the theory and practice of architectural conservation, see Jokilehto, 1999.)

We know that preservation activity dates back to antiquity. The ancient Romans repeatedly restored important monuments, including the temples associated with their political and dynastic history. Bronze Age huts thought to be the original settlement of Romulus were preserved on the Palatine throughout the Republican and Imperial periods, and Roman restorers observed some of our modern preservation principles: At the Round Temple by the Tiber, familiarly known as the Temple of Vesta and dating from the late second or early first century B.C., ten of its twenty Corinthian columns were replaced a century and a half after its construction using a different white marble and capitals slightly varied in design. (Fig. 5.1) (Claridge, 1998, p. 255.) Medieval builders maintained a "crudely cannibalistic attitude toward the past," especially in Rome, where many new buildings were constructed and decorated almost entirely with spolia scavenged from antique buildings that were used as improvised stockpiles of construction materials. (Mayernik, 2003, p. 46.) Ancient and medieval exercises in preservation, however, lacked a sense of historical distance; only with the coming of the Renaissance, a thousand years after the fall of Rome, does a more "objective" view of the remains of antiquity and systematic attempts to identify and study them slowly emerge.

Close study of the ancient monuments was fundamental to the renewal of architecture that the architects of the fifteenth and sixteenth centuries sought to bring about, and yet the Renaissance and Baroque periods continued the systematic destruction of many ancient structures still standing at the time. The artists of the Renaissance "were excited more by the spirit of ancient times than by their remains. . . . [T]hey cared less to preserve the past than to have it inspire their own work." (Lowenthal, 1981, p. 406.) Their attitude toward the work of medieval builders was even less sympathetic; medieval architecture was rejected by Palladio, for instance, as a new "barbaric" style defacing the beauty of the antique style, whose superiority he assumed as beyond dispute. In opposition to this attitude, the Renaissance architect and theorist Leon Battista Alberti called upon architects to complete a work left unfinished by earlier builders in the style of the original rather than imposing new ideas and styles on what another architect had begun well. (Alberti, 1988, pp. 318–19.) This statement is a key document in the evolution of a self-conscious and historically informed philosophy that comprehends both preservation and the design of new architecture in harmony with the old.

In the eighteenth century, the discoveries of Pompeii and Herculaneum, the opening of Greece to European study, and the dawn of modern historiography brought a neoclassical viewpoint to bear on the preservation of ancient monuments. The *beau ideal* that Johann Joachim Winckelmann (1717–68) identified in Greek sculpture seemed a source of timeless and undisputed beauty. The birth of modern archeology and a more scientific classification of historical evidence lent a new sense of academic correctness to restoration work and new design alike. Only gradually, however, did appreciation for the Gothic and medieval heritage take shape, initially under the influence of Romanticism. Nineteenth-century architectural practice was dominated by stylistic revivals and a restless eclecticism that sought inspiration in a broad range of historical precedents. Architects who identified their own design work as continuous with traditions rooted in the past felt justified in retroactively altering historical monuments to conform more faithfully to what they saw as the purest expressions of the styles.

The ascendancy of the Modern Movement brought a forceful reaction against this commingling of restoration and traditional design.

The radical separation of modernist architecture from received design traditions was reflected in the theory of "difference" calculated to reinforce that separation. This view is now in turn being questioned in light of the reappearance of historically informed design in contemporary architectural practice. With architects once again seeking criteria for evaluation and models for emulation in historical precedent, the restoration of old buildings and urban neighborhoods and the addition of new construction in historical styles raises a new set of questions. Where, precisely, is the boundary between sympathetic preservation intended to sustain the integrity of the historic built environment and creative interventions that introduce new elements and character in response to the ongoing conditions of life? The debate that has prompted this book is only the latest skirmish in the long border dispute between contemporary architectural ideas and our obligations to the heritage—both cognitive and physical—of the discipline. The following discussion explores some of the leading themes in this debate as it has emerged from the nineteenth century until today.

Viollet-le-Duc and the French School

The beginnings of a systematic, "scientific" identification and cataloguing of historic monuments appear in early eighteenth-century France with compilations like Bernard de Montfaucon's inventory of antiquities, published as *L'Antiquité Expliquée et Représentée en Figures* between 1719 and 1724. During the Revolution, scores of churches, palaces, public buildings, and houses of the aristocracy were vandalized or destroyed, and it was only with difficulty that revolutionary leaders convinced their followers to protect the monuments as an inheritance rather than attack them as emblems of oppression. Systematic conservation of monuments directed by state authorities began only in 1833 when Ludovic Vitet was named inspector of historic monuments and charged with undertaking a national inventory of the artworks bequeathed to the French people by the Revolution. The work of identifying the national patrimony was followed by theoretical speculation concerning its meaning and proper handling.

With few extant remains of classical antiquity the French heritage was dominated by monuments of medieval civilization, and architects and critics became aware that the rigorous classical training of the École des Beaux-Arts and the French Academy in Rome did not necessarily prepare young architects for the care and restoration of Gothic monuments. The educational program of the École emphasized clarity of composition and consistency in language rather than attention to the informal or idiosyncratic character often encountered in Gothic design, whether in monumental or vernacular examples. As a result, numerous "restorations" further aggravated the losses suffered at the hands of revolutionary mobs. Often the architect sought to render a building's style more "pure" by removing nonconforming later additions regardless of their age or significance. Such work might strip the building of irregularities and asymmetries in the fabric that were historical facts full of interest in their own right rather than deficiencies in need of correction.

As the century progressed and stylistic revivals led to an increased appreciation for historic Romanesque and Gothic buildings as well as prompting the design of new works in these styles, the question of the proper relation of new construction to historic monuments and their surroundings assumed new urgency. How was a contemporary architect working in the Gothic Revival style to approach a historic Gothic building, whether for purposes of restoration or simply to expand it in response to current needs and reflecting current tastes? Where should the balance be struck between the interests of the "scientific" restorer and the "artist" architect?

The leading figure in this debate—indeed the dominant figure in the scholarly champion of medieval monuments architecture in nineteenth-century France—was the scholarly champion of medieval monuments Eugène-Emmanuel Viollet-le-Duc (1814–79), a tireless advocate for their proper care. He proposed a robust theory of "stylistic restoration," famously defined in the eighth volume of his *Dictionnaire Raisonné de l'Architecture Française du XIe au XVIe Siècle*: "To restore an edifice means neither to maintain it, nor to repair it, nor to rebuild it; it means to reestablish it in a finished state which may in fact never have existed at any given time." (Viollet-le-Duc, 1990, p. 195.) This statement, more than any of his actual works, has been the source of much misunderstanding and subsequent diminishment of his repu-

tation as a restorer, but his importance in the history of preservation is such that thoughtful reconsideration of his achievement is long overdue. A scholar and architect of rare knowledge and insight, Viollet-le-Duc brought to his restoration work an unrivaled technical mastery of medieval design and construction. Also an exceptional artist, he was motivated by an ideal of beauty which, while derived from the study of the most esteemed monuments, was rarely realized by any one of them. The material fabric of a monument was, therefore, valued as a documentation of the building's style, but also as an imperfect attempt to achieve the ideal image of the style, which the restorer sought to reveal through meticulous analysis and prudent treatment.

Viollet-le-Duc's methods were, relative to the knowledge and practices of his time, scrupulously scientific and based on what he termed "critical analysis." He understood that the techniques and styles of the medieval builders varied not only from time to time but also from place to place, so he insisted on thoroughly researching local schools and traditions. He dismissed a priori formulas or fixed ideas in favor of judgment, weighing in the balance diverse and potentially conflicting values, choosing a course of action appropriate to the particular circumstances. (Viollet-le-Duc, 1990, p. 210.) While he directed considerable scorn at the classical system of the École des Beaux-Arts (where he was engaged to teach courses on medieval architecture until student protests drove him from the school), his understanding of Gothic composition and proportion remains largely consistent with classical and rationalist theory. (Viollet-le-Duc, 1990, p. 214.) In the more practical realm, he excelled in the "detective work" necessary to understand in detail the complete history of a given monument—in physical, tectonic, programmatic, and aesthetic terms—and his published works amply attest to the breadth and depth of his knowledge. On the whole, his work of strict restoration is a model of scientific, rather than personally creative, work.

But Viollet-le-Duc was also an artist and a superb designer who saw the medieval monuments not only as documents of their times, but as works of art, most of which had been damaged, altered, or left incomplete. His conviction of their greatness impelled him to work toward their restoration or completion so that their aesthetic achievement would become once again—or, perhaps, for the first time—readily

5.2. Cathedral of Notre-Dame, Paris, twelfth to fourteenth centuries, with restorations and additions by Eugène-Emmanuel Viollet-le-Duc, 1845–64.

A. West front of Notre-Dame.

B. Rooftop view of Notre-Dame with spire by Viollet-le-Duc.

C. Detail of restored sculpture at main portal of west front.

Viollet-le-Duc's restoration of Notre-Dame remains controversial but renders whole a monument severely damaged by revolutionary violence. The added spire and re-carved statues on the west front are unarguably medieval in style, if not of the period, calling into question our unexamined notions of authenticity.

A

apparent. It was inconceivable to him that one would not replace parts of a building of which no traces or documentation remained in the same style as the building or element in question, and "in a manner suitable to its own integrity." (Viollet-le-Duc, 1990, p. 211.) In such cases new work was scrupulously based on similar elements in buildings of the same region, date, proportions, and type. (Reiff, 1971, pp. 27–28.) Where no suitable model existed, the architect was forced to invent, but only within the boundaries of the style in question. The architect would have so internalized the characteristics of the original building culture that new design would come about as an unforced act of empathy: "In such circumstances, the best thing to do is to try to put oneself in the place of the original architect and try to imagine what he would do if he returned

to earth and was handed the same kind of program as has been given to us." (Viollet-le-Duc, 1990, pp. 222–23.)

For Viollet-le-Duc this empathetic exercise was not a mysterious or mystical process because Gothic architecture, like the classical, is a language that, once learned, can be used to say new things. "It is the grammar of this architecture that one must come into possession of; therefore, it is imperative that this grammar be mastered." (Viollet-le-Duc, 1990, p. 223.) Documentation of a monument's history and knowledge of the formal language inform the empathy of the restoration architect, validating it as an essentially rational process. At the same time, it was also an artistic enterprise aimed at producing something more than historical verisimilitude. "The idea would be, in a word, to give [the restored building] back its form and color and, if I may dare to say it, its original *life*." (Quoting Ludovic Vitet, in Viollet-le-Duc, 1990, p. 204, emphasis added.) To do this requires the building to, as it were, *complete itself*, reassuming its "original unity." (Viollet-le-Duc, 1990, p. 211.)

Viollet-le-Duc's restoration projects provoked considerable controversy at the time and continue to do so today. Close examination of individual projects is beyond our present scope, but it is nonetheless impressive to note how widely his professional portfolio ranges in type and scale, from the walled town of Carcassonne to the château of Pierrefonds to the Cathedral of Notre-Dame in Paris. His oeuvre included all scales from urban fabric to individual buildings to furniture and decorative arts. A superb designer, he did not hesitate to add elements to a building he thought should be present even if they had never existed historically. While Viollet-le-Duc was not shy about removing or replacing original fabric when he deemed it "inferior" or an impediment to a fuller, clearer presentation of the style, his critics' characterization of him as a reckless auteur bent on back-dating monuments to conform to his own stylistic prejudices is unjust. It was precisely the tendency to do this by the amateurish restorers who preceded him that Viollet-le-Duc strenuously criticized. (Reiff, 1971, p. 26.)

The pinnacle—literally—of Viollet-le-Duc's scholarship and artistry was his design for the missing spire, or flèche, at Notre-Dame, so perfectly adapted to the monumental ensemble that one cannot now imagine it not being there, even if its design is probably more complicated that the one originally built. (Fig. 5.2) (Reiff, 1971, p. 30.) Statues that had formerly decorated the west front of the cathedral and been destroyed by the revolutionary mob were replaced under his supervision. New statues were carved, using as models those visible on less-damaged works of the period in Amiens, Rheims, and elsewhere. While some have criticized the resulting "falsification" that gives the impression that the figures we see there today are original works of Gothic sculpture, Viollet-le-Duc's intent was to recover the lost integrity of the architectural work as a whole, and that he certainly accomplished. Who would prefer to see the cathedral bereft of the sculptural decoration that is an essential part of its three-dimensional design, even if what we see today is from the nineteenth century? And how would our understanding of the cathedral as a

B

C

work of art be deepened by the appearance of new statues in a nonconforming or alien style? (Ceschi, 1970, pp. 68–71, and Reiff, 1971, pp. 17–26.) (Figs. 5.2A and C)

The decline in Viollet-le-Duc's reputation since his death reflects dissatisfaction with the way his theories were put into practice in specific projects. Numerous critics found that Viollet-le-Duc went too far in his stylistic inventions, especially at Carcassonne and Pierrefonds, where a significant amount of the work visible today is from his own hand. Above all, he saw his restorations as demonstrations of the aesthetic achievement of the Gothic styles, as proofs of the artistry and skill of the medieval builders, which he sought to continue in the present. We must remember that at the time, Gothic architecture was still little understood and typically judged inferior to products of the classical tradition. Perhaps Viollet-le-Duc got carried away by his own enthusiasm at times, but, in truth, both he and his critics viewed the architecture of the past through the lens of their intentions for the architecture of the present, and the way medieval builders viewed their own work at the time they were doing it was yet another thing entirely. Here we must recognize the limits of relying on the empathy of the restorer-designer: In our empathetic engagement with the work of the past, we often see what we want to see.

Viollet-le-Duc's work thus revealed the unavoidable conflict between the concerns of the restorer-as-archeologist and those of the architect-as-artist. In truth, the boundary between restoration and new architecture cannot be precisely drawn because it is often impossible to make a self-evident distinction between the life that a monument has lived in the past and the life that it may yet have in the future if it is to continue as a living resource rather than as a decontextualized artifact. In Viollet-le-Duc's work the continuity of the old and the new is taken to unparalleled lengths, passing beyond the restoration of individual monuments to inspire a revived building culture incorporating design, craftsmanship, and artistic embellishment. In judging the results we must guard against excessive generalization, because Viollet-le-Duc's interventions ranged from minimal repairs to scrupulous restoration to painstaking reconstruction to fantastical invention. It would be too simple to say that any one of these possible options is not permissible, just as it would be irresponsible to say

that any one of them is appropriate in every case. The best treatment of any given monument, as Viollet-le-Duc well understood, is naturally based on the unique circumstances of its history, its artistic significance, its physical condition, the state of our knowledge of it, and the values we see in it and wish to project into the future. No formula or standard can substitute for thoughtful judgment, remembering that the state of our knowledge at any given moment is inevitably provisional. For this reason we ask of the restorer, in addition to technical and artistic skill, modesty of aim, probity of documentation, and an unflagging respect for the monument as a historic and artistic resource that remains part of our world. Despite his written statements and the evident success of his work at Notre-Dame and elsewhere, Viollet-le-Duc's performance with respect to these criteria remains in dispute to this day.

It seems that some part of this dispute arises from a misunderstanding of that famous definition of restoration quoted earlier, when he wrote that to restore an edifice means "to reestablish it in a finished state which may in fact never have existed at any given time." He did not mean that the restorer invents for the fabric as a whole an appearance that never before existed. Rather, as a consequence of restoring individual elements of the work in accordance with their respective styles one may see elements juxtaposed that never coexisted in the past because they were built and altered at different times. The scholarly, patient approach of Viollet-le-Duc sought to reveal the complete historical development of the monument by presenting each of its significant elements in the clarity of its respective style, even though the cumulative result might present an appearance that the contributors to that history would not have seen at any point along the way. While subsequent research may demonstrate that Viollet-le-Duc was mistaken about some aspects of the history of medieval building, his intention to do justice to the morphological development of the monuments in his care was conscientious and sound. (Reiff, 1971, p. 27, and Jokilehto, 1999, pp. 140–49.)

Following the precepts of its leading thinker and advocate, the French preservation tradition has more or less consistently taken a holistic view of the monument, tending to value the persistent form rather than focusing narrowly on preserving the aged material alone. New or replacement elements were often added, each employing the style and materials of the original. Indeed, after a century and a half of continuous conservation, much of the fabric of French churches and châteaux visible today is replacement material. It was in reaction against this alleged "falsification" that the generation after World War II definitively rejected Viollet-le-Duc's approach, and it is in response to their overreaction that a reappraisal of his thought and work is now required. Furthermore, however critics and theorists may view his writings and completed projects today, there is no denying that it is thanks to Viollet-le-Duc and his influence that we can now see and admire the principal monuments of France as largely intact and whole works of art instead of ruined fragments or isolated artifacts.

Ruskin and the English School

In contrast to the state-sponsored programs in France, English preservation has largely been led by private nongovernmental organizations, many established locally to protect towns, villages, country estates, and rural landscapes from the depredations of industrialization. A more national—but still privately sponsored—program emerged in reaction to the alterations of Gothic buildings, particularly the major cathedrals, which became the subject of a program of updating and remodeling starting in the late eighteenth century and continuing through the nineteenth. James Wyatt's demolition of late Gothic chapels at Salisbury around 1788 was particularly lamented, but such losses continued despite protests.

In the first half of the nineteenth century, both restorations of historic church buildings and the designs of new churches were influenced by the liturgical ideals of the Ecclesiologist Movement. As the Gothic Revival initiated by Augustus Welby Northmore Pugin (1812–52) generally promoted ideas associated with the Anglo-Catholic Oxford Movement, church officials saw the restoration of historic cathedrals—many of which were in dire need of remedial work—as opportunities to give clearer expression to the goals of ecclesiological and liturgical renewal, the physical refurbishing mirroring the cultural and spiritual renovations directed by the clergy and committed laypeople. (Lowenthal, 1985, p. 278.) A debate quickly emerged between those who sought to safeguard the documentary significance of the historic monuments and those who saw the churches as living structures susceptible to continuing adaptation to meet the changing needs of the religious communities for which they were originally built. Entering this debate, Sir George Gilbert Scott published his "Plea for the Faithful Restoration of Our Ancient Churches" in 1850, setting out a program that was seen as similar in spirit to that of Viollet-le-Duc. Scott distinguished between monuments that should be conserved as "testimonies of a past civilization" and those that remained in continuous use—Anglican churches in England being in the second category. In such cases a more liberal approach to restoration was justifiable, although each monument must be considered on a case-by-case basis. (Jokilehto, 1999, pp. 159–63.)

Scott was an intrepid "building detective" capable of sympathetic and sensitive restoration work: His remodeling of the central octagon and nave ceiling at Ely, the reconstructed interior of the chapter house at Westminster Abbey, and restoration of the façade at Salisbury are models of sensitive restoration work. On the other hand, despite the cautious and conservative tone of his writings, Scott's restorations were at times as invasive as the destructive remodelings he criticized. His handling of the exteriors of the cathedrals at Lichfield and Worcester has been severely criticized, while at Chester and Oxford cathedrals he destroyed the east-end Perpendicular-style windows and substituted Early English lancets and a Norman wheel window, respectively. He rebuilt the north transept porch of Westminster Abbey, removing Christopher Wren's modest eighteenth-century work, but his own efforts were in turn removed in 1884 because much of his stonework had rapidly decayed. (Fawcett, 1976, pp. 87–91.) Choir screens, communion rails, and other elements considered liturgically redundant by the Ecclesiologists were removed and late Gothic windows and decoration were replaced by new evocations of the earlier and more favored Middle Pointed style of the thirteenth century. Scott himself later admitted that his conscious beliefs and unconscious practices had sometimes diverged to his shame. (Lowenthal, 1985, p. 326, and Jokilehto, 1999, p. 163.) (Fig. 5.3)

In fairness, some of Scott's revisions should be evaluated as important works in their own right rather than as misconceived restorations. Work that fails to uphold the high standards of

5.3. Salisbury Cathedral,
Salisbury, England, twelfth
through sixteenth centuries,
as restored by Sir Gilbert
Scott, 1860–78.

At Salisbury, Scott avoided
treatments intended to
render a monument of
mixed periods more uniform
in appearance and a purer
representation of its most
favored style. Such practices
aroused Ruskin's wrath and
inspired "noninterventionist"
preservation philosophy.

restoration should not necessarily be dismissed
if it is justified by the new artwork that it brings
into being. Is the new cathedral more beautiful
than the old? Is it a more complete expression
of the religious values and ritual practices of the
community it houses? Why should the artistic
and ecclesiological intentions of nineteenth-
century architects and churchmen be seen as
less legitimate than those of earlier eras? Should
spaces deemed historic but still in active use be
deprived of the right to change and grow in
response to present need? Whatever answers we
give to these questions, the historical and aesthetic value of the old work must be weighed in
the balance with the aesthetic value of the new,
remembering that in the treatment of valued
historical monuments the burden of proof rests
with the proposed change.

John Ruskin (1819–1900) saw the alterations made by Scott and others as nothing less
than the destruction of a beloved segment of
the human cultural patrimony, and his crusade
against them was as subtle and complex in
its underlying thought as it was strident in its
verbal expression. Of restoration, he declared:
"It means the most total destruction which a
building can suffer: a destruction out of which
no remnants can be gathered; a destruction
accompanied with false description of the thing
destroyed. Do not let us deceive ourselves in this
important matter; it is *impossible*, as impossible
as to raise the dead, to restore anything that has
ever been great or beautiful in architecture."
(Ruskin, 1971, p. 184, original emphasis.) Of
the works of the medieval craftsmen, Ruskin
declared, "We have no right whatever to touch

them. They are not ours." He declared resto-ration unnecessary: "Take proper care of your monuments and you will not need to restore them." (Ruskin, 1971, p. 186.) Ruskin, and his follower William Morris, thus defined the "non-interventionist" approach, denying the legitimacy of any change beyond the require-ments of maintenance, what William Lethaby would call "building dentistry." Morris, for his part, declared that it would be better to aban-don the old building and build a new one than to remodel or add to a treasured monument. (Lowenthal, 1985, p. 280.)

The "anti-scrape" movement Ruskin and Morris began was formalized in the Society for the Protection of Ancient Buildings, founded by Morris in 1877 in protest against Scott's restorations and similar alterations across En-gland. Ruskin and Morris also introduced the doctrine that any necessary new material added to the historic structure must be differ-entiated from the historic fabric of the build-ing. This insistence on making new material conspicuous in relation to historic fabric inaugurated a contradictory logic that still plagues preservation practice today: While conspicuous disparities between old and new alerted viewers to the fact of restoration, they detracted from the perception of wholeness. (Lowenthal, 1985, p. 280.)

Ruskin's "hands-off" approach would seem to limit the preservationist-restorer's role to a passive stewardship of the monument "as it has come down to us in history" (in the words of a recent National Park Service official, per-haps unwittingly echoing the Ruskinian view), declining to make any interventions that might complicate its status as a document of its pre-vious life story and maintaining it in "as-is" condition until the natural processes of mate-rial decay take their inevitable toll. While there are monuments of such significance and beauty that such a limited standard of care seems appropriate, applying this same standard indiscriminately to the entire historic inheri-tance would impose a death sentence on all but the most durable construction. But Ruskin also demands that the architecture of the pres-ent become "historical"—suggesting that the tragic fate of the individual monument is miti-gated by the ongoing activity of a building cul-ture descended from or in sympathy with that which produced the older monuments. Ruskin is therefore concerned with two distinct but inseparable objectives: the safeguarding of the

monuments that we have inherited from the past and the cultivation of that "competence to build" that would allow the production of new monuments whose beauty compensates to some degree for the loss of those falling vic-tim to time. (Choay, 2001, pp. 102–3.) What this amounts to is a kind of life cycle, a built ecology in which different generations and spe-cies follow one another in a naturally occur-ring succession. While subsequent generations of preservationists tended to emphasize the first of Ruskin's objectives, the second has been largely ignored—but his insight into the "organic" processes of a traditional building culture within which the monuments are inex-tricably embedded offers an essential founda-tion for the conservation ethic argued in this book.

In my view, Ruskin was wrong about the sacred inviolability of historic material and the impossibility in principle of restoration. His view of Gothic architecture was limited by his nearly exclusive attention to sculpture and dec-oration: It was the artistic contribution of the individual craftsman—in particular the decora-tive stone-carver—that he prized above all else. He had little interest in the structural or typo-logical features that were of most importance to Viollet-le-Duc. He was certainly correct, though, to condemn the arrogance of restorers who mishandled historic fabric or recklessly removed accretions to historic buildings that did not conform to their predetermined sty-listic interests. But, in cases where incomplete, stylistically mixed, or unsalvageable material is encountered, the right treatment is more dif-ficult to judge and requires a degree of nuance quite out of Ruskin's reach. (I return to some of these questions in Chapter 7.)

While many of his views are now seen as extreme, Ruskin was prescient in his insistence that the buildings of the past are a common asset addressed to all of humankind and to all times, not simply documents of a particu-lar moment. Important monuments are there-fore by definition not "of their time." (Choay, 2000, p. 94.) Second, he steadfastly rejected the idea that changes in society require changes in art or in the configuration of urban space; or rather, loving as much as he did the older spatial configurations, he rejected the claims of social change to alter them. His criticism of the architecture of his day led him to criticize the society whose values seemed to be embodied in it. This "prophetic" role of the preservationist is rarely found among the professional class today but still motivates many in the "grass-roots" movement, who see preservation as an act of resistance against misguided progress. Third, Ruskin was the first to evaluate not just individual monuments but urban ensembles as worthy of preservation. For Ruskin, the houses of ordinary people—what we now call "urban fabric"—were as important as the cathedrals and other monuments in their midst. In fact, the monuments could not be understood without reference to the context of modest buildings that surrounded them and created their settings. He writes, "To this day, the interest of [France's and Italy's] fairest cities depends, not on the isolated richness of palaces, but on the cherished and exquisite decoration of even the smallest tenements of their proud periods." (Ruskin, 1971, p. 172.) We can credit Ruskin with the notion of the historic district as a segment of the built environment deserving protection as a whole rather than as a collection of disparate artifacts.

Giovannoni and the Italian Synthesis

It comes as no surprise that Italy, home to many of the oldest and most significant monuments in Western art, should have generated its own modern school of restoration philosophy and practice. Development of a specifically Italian theory begins with the rise of neoclassicism and the scholarly study of antiquities in the middle of the eighteenth century. A series of decrees issued by Pope Pius VII between 1802 and 1821 concerning the handling of historical monuments and works of art became models for legislation elsewhere in Europe. For the next century, Italian restorers explored a middle path between the positions that would be articulated by Viollet-le-Duc and Ruskin, seeking to render whole the historic form by restoring original fabric wherever possible and adding where necessary a modest and differentiated infill that kept the chronology of interventions clear while avoiding excessive contrast.

An excellent illustration of the new approach was the restoration of the Arch of Titus in the Roman Forum, carried out between 1817 and 1823. The architects—Raffaele Stern and Giuseppe Valadier—removed the medieval accretions (the structure had been incorporated into fortifications by the Frangipani family) and recomposed the arch from the remaining original fragments. Missing parts were reconstructed in travertine rather than the original marble, and the restorers reproduced only the architectonic elements, rendering these with simplified detail and omitting sculptural decoration. The visual distinction between the ancient weathered marble and the modern travertine is subtle, and the carving of the abstracted Composite capitals sensitively acknowledges the boundary between replicable architectural form and inimitable sculptural art. (They might have fluted the new column shafts to make the distinction even subtler still.) The added parts reveal the proportions and composition of the whole, enhancing our understanding and enjoyment of the surviving fabric while remaining identifiable as additions upon closer observation. The restoration of the Arch of Titus could well serve today as a model for restoration practice and the addition of new elements both subtly differentiated and unequivocally compatible. (Ceschi, 1970, pp. 39–42, and Jokilehto, 1999, pp. 83–85.) (See fig. C.13.)

This moderate approach received formalized expression at the end of the nineteenth century in the writings of Camillo Boito (1836–1914), who rejected what he saw as the arbitrary additions and falsification of the French school but also the fatalistic refusal to intervene of the English. Among his most valuable contributions was the demand that all parts of a building or site's fabric be evaluated for historical and artistic significance rather than assuming that only the "original" or oldest configuration is of value—sometimes beauty wins over age and later additions take on a value equal to or greater than the oldest fabric. Boito also distinguished appropriate treatments for different classes of monuments: Thus for antiquities he called for "archeological" restorations; for medieval, "picturesque" ones; and for modern (Renaissance and later), "architectonic" restorations, each of these having its own specific aims and criteria. The type, character, and history of the monument itself should determine the treatment, making a single set of guidelines or criteria impossible. (Del Bufalo, 1982, p. 119, and Jokilehto, 1999, pp. 200–203.) Boito, like Ruskin, insisted on differentiating new work from old—but without excessive contrast—as Stern and Valadier had done at the Arch of Titus; departing from Viollet-le-Duc, he sought to restrain the urge of the restorer to leave his mark, advising the architect instead

to "content yourself with the least possible" intervention. (Ceschi, 1970, p. 108.)

A distinctive aspect of the Italian School was its focus on the urbanistic context and significance of preservation efforts. Epitomizing the Italian approach was the reconstruction of the campanile of San Marco in Venice (under the direction of Luca Beltrami) after its sudden collapse into a pile of rubble on July 14, 1901. Public opinion demanded restitution *com'era, dov'era* (as it was, where it was) of a structure that had long been a principal symbol of the city, although the reconstruction proceeded only after considerable debate. The decision to rebuild the campanile, exactly as and where it was, acknowledged its irreplaceable role in the urbanistic ensemble, recognizing that this aspect of a monument may at times supersede its documentary, historical, or artistic value

considered only as an isolated artifact. In the case of the Venetian bell tower, the "monument" was not the tower but the piazza or, rather, the urbanistic ensemble of two piazzas, and the campanile was but one element in this larger monumental environment. A similar emphasis on the urbanistic dimensions of preservation efforts remained a feature of Italian theory and practice until the 1960s. (Ceschi, 1970, pp. 105–6, and Jokilehto, 1999, p. 206.) (Fig. 5.4)

Gustavo Giovannoni (1873–1947), the leading Italian figure of the following generation, linked the conservation theory of Boito with the historical analyses of the Viennese urbanist Camillo Sitte to become the heir of both. From Ruskin he derived his opposition to the demolition of the vernacular settings of important monuments in order to isolate them visually

5.4. Campanile, Piazza San Marco, Venice, sixteenth century, reconstructed after 1901.

The campanile was completely reconstructed following its collapse in 1901. Cesare Brandi denounced the new tower as a "falsification," but this reflects a misplaced focus on the material artifact rather than on its role in an urban ensemble or the cultural life of the city.

and temporally. Instead, great urban monuments were always to be seen as embedded in a fabric that he called "minor architecture" (*l'architettura minore*), constituting the ensemble of a street, a piazza, or a quarter. (Giovannoni, 1931, and Del Bufalo, 1982, p. 19.) Indeed, conditions surrounding the monument may have such importance in their own right that destroying them would be tantamount to destroying the monument itself. (Ceschi, 1970, p. 113.) He succeeded in including language defending urban fabric in the 1931 Athens Charter and the Italian Charter of Restoration of the same year. Despite his ardent efforts, Giovannoni's advocacy for maintaining historic monuments in their contexts was ignored and flagrantly violated in the heart of Rome itself by the building and clearance programs of the Fascist regime in the following years.

As a designer and restorer, Giovannoni showed remarkable knowledge and sensitivity in the handling of both classical and medieval monuments. His restoration and completion of the Church of Sant'Andrea in Orvieto (1928–30) began with a thorough physical analysis of the structure in all its historical phases. On that basis the architect proceeded to rebuild and complete the decayed and incomplete fabric—following the lead of Viollet-le-Duc—as if having empathetically entered into the spirit of the building culture that originally produced it. The upper part of the bell tower, the upper half of the main façade, and the entirety of the flanking loggia are new work. Some of the new elements and details are clearly of Giovannoni's invention in the absence of documentation, but they are all modest and consistent with the structure's overall character. Most important, the architect has recovered the monument as a vital protagonist in the ensemble of the piazza, with its multiplicity of periods and styles. (Fig. 5.5)

Giovannoni's intervention at Orvieto is not an archeological restoration but an architectonic one, in Boito's sense of the term: We are not seeing the building "as it was" at a definite time but as it has been imagined by an artist whose primary interest is the wholeness of the work, its architectural integrity, rather than the expression of his own personal preferences or the fashion of the time. This may not be the appropriate approach for monuments whose artistic or historical value places them in a category of inviolability, where the more demand-

5.5. Church of Sant'Andrea, Orvieto, Italy, restored by Gustavo Giovannoni, 1928–30.

Giovannoni's "philological" restoration completes the church using the historic style and matching materials. His respectful additions, such as the loggia at left or the upper portion of the tower, demonstrate his understanding of the original architecture and its urban context.

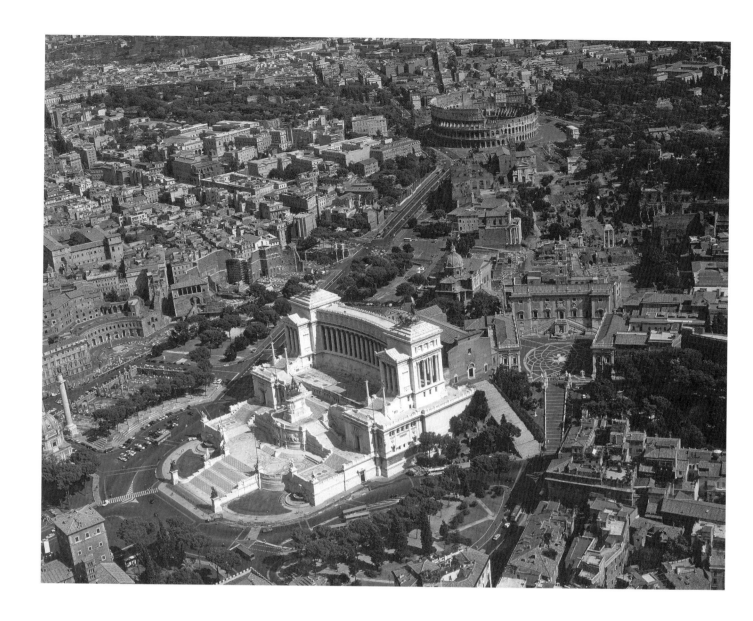

ing standards of archeology properly apply; but such monuments are the exception, especially compared to those that remain embedded in daily life and use, as well as in urban ensembles whose total character is of greater significance than any individual structure or element. The achievement of Giovannoni was to maintain such structures as living works of art, not hesitating to add modestly to their fabric but avoiding any change that would render them fragmentary or inconsistent with their own identities. It is a delicate balance resting on nuanced judgments with which we are free to disagree. Nevertheless, it is a fundamentally sound approach, as long as the knowledge and respect of the restorer outweighs the desire to put an individual or contemporary stamp on the work in question. (Del Bufalo, 1982, p. 197, and Jokilehto, 1999, pp. 219–22.)

The architectural and urbanistic programs of the Fascist dictatorship in Italy are conventionally associated with a resistance to modernism and the propagandistic exploitation of ancient Roman sites. A closer examination of the actual history of architecture and patronage in Italy in the prewar decades reveals a much more complicated, even paradoxical reality. (For a detailed history of architecture in the Fascist period, see Etlin, 1991.) In a 1925 speech, Mussolini himself declared his vision of *romanità*: "You shall create vast spaces around the Theater of Marcellus, the Capitoline Hill, and the Pantheon. All that has grown up around them in the centuries of decadence must disappear. *The millennial monuments of our history must loom gigantic in their necessary solitude.*" (Quoted in Fried, 1973, pp. 31–32, emphasis added.) This statement, the

5.6. Vittorio Emanuele II Monument, Rome, by Giuseppe Sacconi, 1885–1911, and the Via dei Fori Imperiali, Rome, 1925–36.

The monument represents a rejection of the form and materials of Baroque Rome and an appropriation of antiquity by the new nation. Clearance of medieval neighborhoods followed by excavation of the Imperial Forums and construction of the avenue traversing them (left rear) would be unthinkable today, but brought to light resources of incalculable value.

5.7. Basilica of San Lorenzo fuori le Mura, Rome, thirteenth century, reconstructed after 1945 by Alberto Terenzio.

The old basilica, originally constructed with antique spolia, was rebuilt after the Second World War, incorporating salvaged material. Such reconstructions violate the Venice Charter but are justified when used to ensure survival of the monument's historic form.

italicized portion of which might have been spoken by Le Corbusier in defense of his 1925 Plan Voisin for Paris, condemned the remains of the ancient city to the status of fragmented and freestanding artifacts summarily isolated from the intricate texture of the city that had grown up around them since antiquity. New highways and office buildings rose in newly created wide-open spaces, projecting a vision of military prowess, efficiency, and modernity, but at the cost of destroying layers of the city deposited over many centuries. The "liberation" of the Imperial Forums, the foot of the Capitoline Hill and Piazza Venezia, the Largo di Torre Argentina, and the temples in the Forum Holitorium involved the demolition of scores of buildings, blocks, and streets and the displacement of thousands of residents to permit the clearance and excavation of the antique sites. (Fig. 5.6)

To be sure, these urban interventions of the regime were not all cause for regret—the work of Corrado Ricci and Antonio Muñoz in the Imperial Forums and Alberto Calza-Bini at the Teatro Marcello brought to light ancient buildings that have immeasurably enriched our artistic and historical patrimony. Critics later charged that some of this work was motivated by political rather than archeological or architectural considerations, that the demolitions proceeded hastily without proper documentation or archeological analysis, and that a great deal of historical material was unnecessarily lost. These points remain in dispute. Undoubt-

edly, the archeological program was exploited for propaganda purposes, but there is also no denying the inestimable value of the expanded patrimony that the excavations and restorations of the 1920s and 1930s bequeathed to us. (Ceschi, 1970, pp. 117, 163.)

There were also dissenting voices against the clearance programs of the regime, preeminently that of Giovannoni, who argued in favor of *ambientismo*—the Ruskinian doctrine that urban fabric was worthy of preservation because the great monuments derived their authority and scale from coexistence with more modest construction. (Kostof, 1973, p. 15; Del Bufalo, 1982, p. 117; Etlin, 1991, pp. 101–28; and Giovannoni, 1931.) Like Sitte, Giovannoni saw the historic city as a place of ongoing significance which, with minor adjustments, could accommodate modern life. (For Sitte, see Collins and Collins, 1986.) Sympathetic new construction that continued the historic building culture could accommodate necessary changes without loss of character. The historical monuments would remain embedded in their historic, dense fabric rather than being isolated in an alien landscape. Where appropriate, Giovannoni's doctrine of *diridamento*—a judicious pruning and clearing—would enhance the legibility of the monument without removing it from its context.

Giovannoni's outspoken critique of the Fascist government's urban policies was doubly courageous: Not only did he openly criticize Mussolini's destructive clearance and road-building projects, but he did so at the same time that Le Corbusier's modernist urbanism and the pronouncements of CIAM dominated the architectural avant-garde, assuring that he would be denounced by both the left and the right. Unable to alter the course of the regime's plans, Giovannoni found his ideas rejected by the postwar modernists as well, and has only recently been the subject of renewed historical and critical interest. (Choay, 2001, pp. 131–37; Gurrieri, 2004; Torsello, 2005, pp. 87–90; and Mazzola, 2006.)

After the Second World War, architectural and conservation attention was focused on repairing the damage suffered by Italian cities and monuments during the years 1944–45. For the most part, bombed monuments were reconstructed along preexisting lines, often incorporating significant amounts of original material salvaged from the ruins. This was the case at the Basilica of San Lorenzo fuori le Mura in Rome, meticulously reconstructed under the direction of Alberto Terenzio. (Fig. 5.7) In some instances the war damage revealed earlier layers of construction, which were then restituted while destroyed later alterations were cleared away. At the Church of Santa Chiara in Naples, the destruction by fire of the Baroque decoration of the interior revealed the earlier intact medieval fabric, which was then restored. Full-scale reconstruction proceeded at such devastated sites as the Benedictine abbey of Montecassino, the bridges over the Arno in Florence, and entire urban districts in Naples, Palermo, and elsewhere in the south and Sicily, occupying Italian conservators and preservation architects in the decades following the war.

The remarkable quality of these projects is testimony to the skill and sensitivity of the Italian restorers, many of whom were trained by Giovannoni or practiced under his influence. Sadly, a younger generation of restorers reacted against this reasonable and judicious approach to historic monuments and formulated a rigidly oppositional attitude that was institutionalized in the Venice Charter of 1964. (I return to this development later in this chapter.)

The Preservation Movement in the United States

The American preservation movement, too, arose in the nineteenth century and, though starting modestly, soon took up all the issues raised by the European experience. As in England, the preservation cause was pressed by private individuals and organizations; government support, especially on the federal level, arrived only with the New Deal in the 1930s. Early efforts focused on sites connected with the Revolutionary and Civil War periods. Consistent with the nineteenth century's predisposition toward interpreting architecture in terms of the "association of ideas," the buildings in which important personages had lived or where historical events had occurred were valued as cultural shrines capable of arousing patriotism and civic virtue. Ann Pamela Cunningham, who can be credited with found-

5.8. Mount Vernon, Fairfax County, Virginia, eighteenth century.

The home of George Washington was the first successful preservation project in the United States. Such sites were presented as didactic historical shrines to inspire patriotism; their intrinsic architectural interest was recognized only later.

ing the organized preservation movement in America, worked from 1853 to 1879 to ensure the rescue and preservation of Mount Vernon, not only because it was the home of George Washington, the nation's preeminent historical figure, but also because it stood as an emblem of American ideals at a time when these were coming into question under the pressures of industrialization, immigration, and civil war. (Fig. 5.8)

The first American preservationists were virtually all amateurs and laypeople passionately interested in history and culture. At the time, there were few American scholars of historical architecture and, with their focus on civic and moral instruction, early restorers were as likely to be guided by imagination as by evidence. The troubled restoration history at Independence Hall in Philadelphia offers a case in point. (Hosmer, 1965, pp. 87–88.) Cunningham, an exception to this pattern, was committed to making Mount Vernon as accurate a presentation of George Washington's home as research and documentation permitted, and she worked tirelessly to keep it that way. (Fitch, 2006, p. 185, and Hosmer, 1965, pp. 41–57.)

A more specialized approach to preservation emerged after the turn of the twentieth century, exemplified by William Sumner Appleton and the Society for the Preservation of New England Antiquities (SPNEA), which he founded in 1910. Appleton viewed the old houses SPNEA acquired as historic documents rather than aesthetic exemplars, but he applied a more scientific method to their investigation and treatment. His conservative approach emphasized buildings as a visible record of change over time, and he aimed to conserve not only their materials but their "documentary value" by making his intentions evident and therefore reversible. (Page and Mason, 2004, p. 99.) The limitation of Appleton's view was a tendency to classify historic buildings individually as "antiques" rather than see them as groupings or as embedded in urban fabric. Many of the SPNEA properties were house museums insulated from the pressures of growth and change faced by structures still in active use. Nonetheless, Appleton's influence slowly led to a growing appreciation in New England for the architectural significance of historic structures apart from their educational or patriotic value.

The American architectural profession was slow to enter the preservation field in a significant way, partly because the strongly European focus of most architectural practice and education through the nineteenth century blinded architects to their own country's heritage, and partly because the needs of new construction in the rapidly expanding nation overshadowed the care of old buildings. As interest in older American architecture grew, so did architects' involvement in preserving its best exemplars. In 1893, architects led the fight to preserve Charles Bulfinch's State House in Boston and the 1910 restoration of New York's City Hall by Grosvenor Atterbury marked the rise of "scientific" restoration as an aspect of American architectural practice. As architects gained experience with restoration projects and as the Colonial Revival became more popular, old buildings took on new value as a canon for emulation by designers. (Page and Mason, 2004, pp. 156, 91.)

By the 1920s, leaders of the profession like Fiske Kimball, John Mead Howells, and William Lawrence Bottomley became involved in campaigns to preserve and restore old buildings and neighborhoods, not solely for their historical or associational interest, but as models of traditional architecture and urbanism. For these designers and many of their peers, preservation and contemporary design formed a fruitful synergy within their practices. Experience in the physical restoration of historic buildings increased the designers' appreciation for the styles they sought to emulate, and the design of new buildings in those same styles yielded insights into the design methods of the original builders. A further benefit of the close relation between restoration and new design at this time was an expanding catalog of publications of measured drawings and documentary photographs, such as the *White Pine Series of Architectural Monographs*, the journal *Pencil Points*, the two-volume *Great Georgian Houses*, and many others. These books were supplemented by the documentation compiled by the Historic American Buildings Survey, established within the National Park Service in 1934, and together made the best models of American architecture—as well as newly appreciated vernacular examples—widely available for study and emulation for the first time. The American Colonial Revival swept the country in large part thanks to these published resources, becoming a truly national vernacular style. For the authors of these publications or the architects who benefited from them, preservation was not an exercise in nos-

5.9. The Capitol, Williamsburg, Virginia, as reconstructed by Perry, Shaw & Hepburn, 1926–35.

The most important restoration project in America was initially inspired by Viollet-le-Duc's approach and has been criticized accordingly. Despite its imperfect verisimilitude, the restored town is an excellent model for new traditional design and New Urbanist TNDs.

talgia, patriotic symbolism, or moral edification, nor was it an antiquarian or technical exercise; rather, it was an essential part of the discipline. The relation between history and contemporary practice was close and fruitful in both directions.

This closeness brought with it special problems, as it had for the followers of Viollet-le-Duc in France. While Cunningham and Appleton—despite having little or no training or specialized knowledge—pursued the best standards of historical accuracy then available to them, the involvement of professional architects introduced new questions about the potential conflict between the architects' fidelity to the historical record and their commitment to the ongoing development of the building tradition in which they worked. While there is no reason why the goals of preservation and new design in the tradition should necessarily diverge, in practice they often clashed because architects, following the French theory, saw historic structures as part of an ongoing tradition and the preservationists, following the English pattern, tended to see them as sacred artifacts to be shielded from further development.

American preservation in the 1920s and 1930s was dominated by the restoration of the former colonial capital of Williamsburg, Virginia, an enterprise profoundly influenced by the writings and example of Viollet-le-Duc. (Fig. 5.9) At the outset, the sponsors, advisers, and architects declared that the purpose of the restoration, along with celebrating the historical significance of an important venue in the founding of the nation, was to demonstrate models of American classical style in order to elevate popular taste. Later directors of Colonial Williamsburg would tip the balance more strongly toward an archeological and anthropological viewpoint, but in the first decades of the restoration project, representing the historical realities of mid-eighteenth-century daily life with exacting verisimilitude was not a high priority. The architects Perry, Shaw & Hepburn were criticized in later years as professional standards and expectations for restoration projects changed, but their achievement should not be underestimated. No other effort in the American preservation movement has had a deeper or more lasting impact on the historical consciousness of Americans, and many of the principles and methods now routinely used in the field were first developed at Williamsburg. (See Chapter 9.)

Elsewhere, the Williamsburg model's focus on urban ensembles rather than individual buildings inspired the pioneering legislation that established historic districts, starting in 1931 with Charleston and followed in quick succession by New Orleans, Boston, Brooklyn Heights, and many others. Rather than focusing on house museums and isolated historic sites, the new zoning ordinances and preservation laws brought broader regulation and protection to many of America's most admired and most threatened neighborhoods, some of which were considered at the time by authorities and planners as slums deserving only demolition. The Charleston ordinance, for example, created an Old and Historic District (subsequently expanded well beyond its original boundaries) and established a Board of Architectural Review with authority over architectural changes to buildings in the district visible from public rights-of-way. The ordinance crucially required new construction to conform to the character of the historic district and prohibited "incongruous" developments. The Charleston ordinance became a model widely imitated prior to the mid–1970s, when preservation policies shifted their emphasis toward differentiation and away from literal or stylistic compatibility.

What began as isolated preservation efforts in America's historic cities grew by the mid-twentieth century into a more coordinated national movement. The founding of the National Trust for Historic Preservation in 1949 institutionalized preservation in the United States and the National Historic Preservation Act of 1966 made it an instrument of federal government policy with broad impacts on the rehabilitation of both historical monuments and older neighborhoods. The 1966 Act also established the National Register of Historic Places as a national inventory of significant cultural properties, modeled after the French efforts of over a century before, and established procedures for review and mitigation of preservation issues whenever federal funds or programs were involved. While the nascent movement was unable to prevent the execrable destruction of Charles McKim's great Pennsylvania Station in New York in 1964, the loss of that landmark—and the galvanizing effect of the protest movement that rallied around it—was an invaluable spur to the legislation that followed, on both the local and national levels. (Fig. 5.10) A decade later the 1976 Tax Reform Act gave economic impetus to preservation by creating incentives for private sponsors to undertake rehabilitation of National Register sites, prompting a groundswell of bricks-and-mortar preservation from house museums to entire Main Streets in small towns, to the sweeping "Back to the City" movement that transformed many of the largest American cities from the mid–1970s onward. The 1978 Supreme Court decision upholding the City of New York's preservation law in the Grand Central Terminal case not only preserved that beloved landmark, but placed the regulation of historic properties on a sound legal footing nationwide. Gradually, preservation became part of the American cultural mind-set and challenged the long-standing and deep-seated predisposition in favor of novelty and change.

The Athens Charter, 1931

This important document, issued by the First International Congress of Architects and Technicians of Historic Monuments meeting in Athens, was the first attempt to achieve international consensus among professionals in the restoration field concerning treatments for historic sites. (ICOMOS, 1931.) Echoing the criticisms of Ruskin and following the lead of Boito, the charter sought to limit additions in the Viollet-le-Duc mode by noting the predominant tendency among the participating countries "to abandon restorations *in toto* and to avoid the attendant dangers" posed by such projects as the nineteenth-century completions of medieval church façades or the removal of historic fabric for purposes of maintaining a stylistic unity. Instead, the charter called for "a system of regular and permanent maintenance" to preserve the buildings without radical restoration. When restoration is necessary, the entire history and artistic significance of the monument should be respected, "without excluding the style of any given period." Reflecting the influence of Giovannoni, the document called for not only the monuments themselves but also their surroundings to be respected, including "certain groupings and certain particularly picturesque perspective treatment." The charter recommended the occupation of buildings "which ensures the continuity of their life" but

only for purposes that respect their artistic or historic character. The charter approved of the reassembly of original fragments at ruined sites (anastylosis) and called for any new materials added to be "recognizable," although without specifying the degree of difference desired—a matter that would be subject to broad interpretation in the field.

The charter reflects a bias toward ancient monuments built of stone, like the Greek sites the participants visited during their conference and which are explicitly identified as models of good conservation practice, and disregards the different problems raised by a heritage constructed of less durable materials. (Fig. 5.11) The charter does not recognize the importance of craft and stylistic traditions that may have survived into the present and instead relies on expert opinion and technical solutions. Regrettably, the charter endorses the use of "modern materials . . . and more especially reinforced concrete" for use in the consolidation of monuments—a practice that proved disastrous in some cases, including the Greek monuments where concrete was introduced, has subsequently failed, and is now being removed at

great expense. (See fig. 1.10.) The document does, however, recognize the importance of preserving the artistic integrity of the monument and diplomatically states that the removal of sculpture from monuments or "from the surroundings for which they were designed is, in principle, to be discouraged." The charter does not specifically address the question of new additions and urban infill but does make a general plea for the preservation of the character of a site when new buildings are planned, including respect for the "external aspect of the cities in which they are to be erected," and preservation of characteristic landscape elements in the neighborhood of the monuments.

Overshadowed in architectural circles by the other Athens Charter of the same year that announced the social and urbanistic agenda of Le Corbusier and CIAM, the Athens Charter for restoration does not mention changing ideals in contemporary architecture but, poignantly, notes that "the best guarantee in the matter of the preservation of monuments and works of art derives from the respect and attachment of the peoples themselves," and that this attachment can be promoted by public authorities.

5.10. Pennsylvania Station, New York, by McKim, Mead & White, 1904–10.

The demolition of this masterwork—only fifty-three years after its completion—prompted legislation to protect other landmarks. These very laws now threaten to immortalize the structures that rose on the rubble of Penn Station itself.

Perhaps the conference participants already recognized that the architects, intellectuals, and experts that had formerly led preservation activities were now increasingly distracted by the allure of a utopian future and that the affections of nonspecialists—that is, of the public—would become a more significant factor in the care of the cultural heritage. Indeed, the rise of heritage tourism, first in Europe and then increasingly in the United States, and the vast numbers of visitors to historic sites and cities proves the authors of the charter prescient, even if massive visitation also brought with it new problems that may be even more difficult to remedy than the technical issues of consolidation and atmospheric pollution that the charter explicitly addressed.

Finally, it should be noted that the charter qualifies its recommendations with the recognition that each case must be treated individually and that preservation measures should be "in keeping with local circumstances." The language of the charter throughout is advisory rather than authoritarian, calling on the participating countries to cooperate with one another in accordance with the spirit of the League of Nations. While the charter still calls upon experts—mostly archeologists and architects—to collaborate closely in the treatment of historic monuments, it saw action by national governments and local authorities as critical to achieving preservation goals, especially in view of the potential conflicts between the interests of preservation and those of private property. The national states were explicitly identified as "wardens of civilization," a chilling thought indeed, considering the horrors that those same states would descend into in the coming decades, with all their devastating consequences for historic cities and human communities alike. Nonetheless, it would be state action, often supported by private financing, that would spur the unprecedented preservation activity that ensued internationally after the Second World War, even in the United Kingdom and the United States, where private action remained decisive in the implementation of conservation programs.

5.11. Ise Shrine, Japan.

Current preservation philosophy disregards the necessity of maintaining a building culture for the conservation of monuments built in wood. The Ise Shrine has preserved its historic form for centuries by being meticulously reconstructed every twenty years.

The Venice Charter, 1964

Based on the Athens Charter but going much further in articulating the modernist view of historical monuments, the founding document of modern international preservation was drafted following a conference in Venice in 1964 and reflects the ascendancy of a more "scientific" and curatorial approach to the field as well as a reaction against postwar reconstruction of cities and monuments. (ICOMOS, 1964.) The language of the Venice Charter abandons the exhortatory and advisory tone of the Athens document in favor of a series of statutory imperatives with little latitude for individual cases. In many respects the charter was a victory for the Ruskin-Morris view and a definitive renunciation of the Viollet-le-Duc approach, turning its attention to the "safeguarding of the architectural heritage," the material "authenticity" of which it sought to protect from devaluation by imitation or insensitive encroachment. With all its strengths and weaknesses, the Venice Charter has been the basis for nearly all professional preservation programs around the world since its adoption and remains in force through the programs and agreements of UNESCO, although its assumptions and implications have increasingly come under critical scrutiny.

In continuity with the Athens statement, the Venice Charter acknowledged the contribution of "modest works" as well as "monuments" and called for preservation of "not only the single architectural work but also the urban or rural setting." It called for these works to be maintained permanently in their original locations and, if possible, to be used for "some socially useful purpose." This emphasis on context is one of the charter's strengths, along with its call for "the valid contributions of all periods to the building" to be respected and the removal of later additions to be undertaken only when "the material which is brought to light is of great historical, archaeological, or aesthetic value."

The charter has proved less helpful in its insistence that restoration "must stop at the point where conjecture begins" and that additions to historic settings "must be distinct from the architectural composition and must bear a contemporary stamp." Parts added to monuments are to "integrate harmoniously with the whole, but at the same time must be distinguishable from the original so that

restoration does not falsify the artistic or historic evidence." Going much further than the Athens Charter, the Venice statement declared "All reconstruction work should . . . be ruled out 'a priori,'" and "only *anastylosis*, that is to say, the reassembling of existing but dismembered parts, can be permitted." While anastylosis has been a useful practice at many ancient sites, it clearly falls short of the objectives of maintaining a historic monument in good repair and in beneficial economic use. This provision would prohibit such painstaking and didactically valuable reconstructions as the Athenian Stoa of Attalos (1952–56). (See fig. C.16.) It further fails to recognize the need for periodic replacement of materials in kind or the wholesale replacement of entire buildings, especially those made of wood, as

5.12. Markets of Trajan, Rome, second century, with glass infill, 2007.

Reflecting the stark differentiation required by the Venice Charter, the new glazing in the openings of the ancient market creates a bizarre appearance. The insertions call attention to their alleged technical sophistication rather than promoting a harmonious setting.

5.13. Old Town Market Place,
Warsaw, as reconstructed
after World War II.

Despite official
condemnation of the
practice elsewhere, the
rebuilding of the historic
center of Warsaw was a
necessary act of cultural
healing. Sadly, the
reconstruction was limited to
the oldest quarters, and the
rest of the city was rebuilt
on Corbusian principles.

in the case of Scandinavian vernacular build-ings or the famous Ise Shrine in Japan, rebuilt every twenty years. The effect of these charter provisions has been to cut off historic build-ings from the building cultures that produced them, even when these traditions remain oper-ative in the present, resulting in a growing collection of isolated and decontextualized fragments throughout the world. (See Chapter 12.) (Fig. 5.11.)

The charter was itself a document of its time, embodying the reaction of younger Ital-ian conservators and theorists against the post-war reconstructions of bombed structures such as the Abbey of Montecassino and the bridges of Florence. (Ceschi, 1970, p. 203.) (See fig. C.18.) While nonprofessionals saw such recon-structions as commonsense responses to tragic wartime damage, the new theorists, drawing on Cesare Brandi's influential book, *Teoria del Restauro*, of 1963, viewed them as "false his-tory." (Brandi, 2000.) The principal authors of the Venice Charter, Roberto Pane and Pietro Gazzola, had themselves just completed the restoration of monuments damaged by the war.

But viewing these postwar reconstructions as exceptional and otherwise impermissible con-cessions to popular demand, they drew a sharp distinction between a strictly curatorial care for the artifact and any treatment that would "falsify" the historical record by filling in miss-ing elements or adding new parts in the same style, as Giovannoni and others had done suc-cessfully in the decades before the war. (Ceschi, 1971, p. 208.) (I consider Brandi's theory in more detail in Chapter 6.)

From the viewpoint of the charter's authors, the reconstruction of a bombed structure was tantamount to forgery, even if much of the original material was salvaged and reused in the reconstruction and despite the fact that many of the monuments of Italy (as in Europe generally) had been restored and reconstructed already numerous times in the past. Their insistence that the authenticity of the monu-ment lay in its material and date rather than in its form was consistent with the authors' positivistic, materialistic view of art. It also reflected the prevalent revolutionary tenor of the time, in which modernist architecture was viewed as a bulwark against any recurrence of traditional design, which was viewed—counterfactually—as tainted by Fascism. The charter also paradoxically ignored the experience of eastern Europe, where Communist governments lavished extraordinary care on postwar reconstructions. The rebuilding of the historic center of Warsaw, for example, has consistently been viewed as an exceptional case because of its deliberate destruction by the Nazis, despite its clear violation of the sweeping ban on reconstruction imposed by the charter. (Fig. 5.13)

The Venice Charter was also drafted at a time when it appeared certain that historic architecture would never again inform contemporary practice. With historic and contemporary architecture seen as radically discontinuous in time, it made sense that they be discontinuous in space as well—the physical sequestering of different periods being a logical consequence of the charter's emphasis on differentiation. But the most important development of the decades since the charter was written has been the emergence of new traditional architecture that seeks to heal that separation between historical and contemporary design. Today we can no longer assume that "contemporary" automatically means "modernist." If historic and contemporary architecture can be seen as continuous in time, it makes sense that they be seen as continuous in space also. Reflecting changing views of contemporary architecture, in 2006 the International Network for Traditional Building, Architecture, and Urbanism (INTBAU) convened an international conference in Venice to draft a supplement to the charter, The *INTBAU Venice Declaration on the Conservation of Monuments and Sites in the 21st Century*, which calls for an updating of the charter to recognize a pluralism of building cultures and craft traditions, as well as to recognize the legitimacy of the contemporary practice of traditional architecture in historic settings. (INTBAU, 2008, pp. 657–65.)

The Secretary of the Interior's Standards for Rehabilitation, 1977

The Venice Charter was an important source for *The Secretary of the Interior's Standards for Rehabilitation*, drafted in 1977 by W. Brown Morton III, Gary Hume, Kay Weeks, and Charles Fisher of the National Park Service (NPS) to define the eligibility and compliance of preservation projects under the Tax Reform Act of 1976. (National Park Service, 1995.) The act established tax incentives for the rehabilitation of National Register properties in private ownership and gave an essential economic boost to the vigorous "back to the city" movement that renovated vast tracts of America's historic centers from the late 1970s to the present. According to the National Park Service, by 2005 over $36 billion had been invested in over 33,000 projects nationwide. Historian and preservationist Calder Loth has pointed out that the historic preservation tax-credit program is "the only successful urban renewal program because *it is the only one that has actually renewed urban areas.*" (Loth, 2006, emphasis added.) To qualify for tax benefits, projects must comply with the *Standards*, which govern the eligibility and appropriateness of rehabilitation work, emphasizing repair and renovation rather than restoration or reconstruction. While not in fact subject to them in many cases, local preservation officials have tended to use the *Standards* to guide their own programs, lending the *Standards* a far broader authority than originally intended. Indeed, they have become the de facto national standards for preservation activity in the United States. (For local adoption of the *Standards*, see City of Charleston, 2008. Since their inception, the *Standards* have been revised several times, most recently in 1995, and that is the version quoted here. See National Park Service, 1995.)

The *Standards*, while informed by the spirit of the Venice Charter, were in their original version more moderate, having been designed to encourage rehabilitation rather than strict restoration. The NPS provisions define a balanced approach between doing justice to the historical and artistic significance of a site and promoting its continuance in beneficial economic use, which was after all the main intent of the Tax Reform Act. For the most part, the *Standards* are unexceptionable. For example, they call for retaining and preserving the historic character of a site, "recognized as a physical record of its time, place, and use." The *Standards* recognize that "properties change over time; those changes that have acquired historic significance in their own right shall be retained and preserved." Finally, the *Standards* endorse the concept of reversibility, so that contemporary additions or alterations might be removed in the future without permanent damage to the

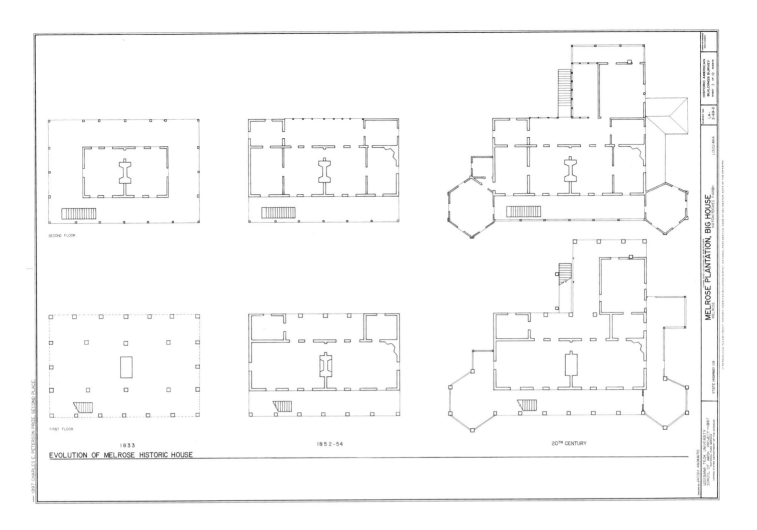

SECOND FLOOR

FIRST FLOOR

1833   1852-54   20TH CENTURY

EVOLUTION OF MELROSE HISTORIC HOUSE

5.14. Melrose Plantation,
Natchitoches, Louisiana,
nineteenth and early
twentieth centuries, floor
plans showing expansion.

Despite prohibitions
against additions using
elements taken from other
buildings or sites, numerous
landmarks are valued
precisely because they
expanded in this way.
Melrose Plantation's main
house expanded with wings
salvaged from nearby
houses.

historic fabric. These provisions parallel the moderate views of Boito and Giovannoni.

Other provisions have proved more troublesome, such as the passage in Standard Three: "Changes that create *a false sense of historical development,* such as adding conjectural features or architectural elements from other buildings, shall not be undertaken." The philosophical subtext of the italicized phrase will be explored in depth in Chapter 6, but the main intent of the provision was to prevent the practice, common in the previous decades, of cobbling together buildings or entire districts by relocating elements or structures from other sites to create "period rooms" or "historical parks." This practice raised the specter of fakery and potentially supported a market in architectural salvage that encouraged demolition or relocation of old buildings. But the reconstructions of medieval Spanish chapels and courtyards at the Cloisters (part of the Metropolitan Museum of Art in New York) or the remarkable Melrose Plantation in Louisiana (with its congeries of wings and pavilions taken from

houses demolished nearby) can be considered historic precisely because of their ingenious integration of salvaged parts. The additions are as important as—or perhaps more important than—the "original" structures to which they were appended. (Fig. 5.14) While the advisability of prohibiting such practices is at least arguable, the language of Standard Three has been interpreted in ways that press well beyond the original intent in order to discourage the addition of new features in the same style as the landmark building or the completion of a building according to its original design. (See Chapters 8 and 9.)

Standard Nine has proved the most problematic provision due to its ambiguity: "The new work shall be differentiated from the old and shall be compatible with the massing, size, scale, and architectural features to protect the historic integrity of the property and its environment." While the *Standards* do not call for new additions to be contrasting or require them to be in a modernist style (in contrast to the implication of the Venice Charter's "contemporary stamp"), they do require new construction to be "differentiated" without defining how or to what degree, and to be "compatible" without offering criteria for achieving this objective. Crucially, the *Standards* do not suggest where the balance between "differentiation" and "compatibility" should be placed. While such guidance does not necessarily go beyond the moderate position of Boito and Giovannoni, the unresolved contradiction between the two terms and the equal weight given to them in the text has produced confusion and widely divergent interpretations in practice.

In NPS reviews of projects applying for tax credits or grants, the "compatibility" requirement was typically met by relying on abstract relationships like size, massing, color, materials, and horizontal façade alignments—such as continuous cornices and string courses linking the new and old buildings—to tie new and old together. Differentiation was usually provided by using a readily identifiable modernist style for the new work, albeit "toned down" to remain "compatible." (This interpretation was personally explained to me by the then-Chief Architect of the Technical Preservation Services Branch of the National Park Service, the official responsible for interpreting the *Standards* and applying them to proposed preservation projects for Federal grants and tax credits, at a National Trust conference in Milwaukee, October 20, 2006. NPS policy in these matters may have changed under new leadership since that time.)

As an aid to designers and officials, the NPS periodically published *Guidelines* highlighting preservation treatments as either "recommended" or "not recommended." In these examples, a clear preference for modernist additions was long apparent; indeed, no traditional additions were illustrated. (See Chapter 11.) The ambiguous language of the *Standards* and the exclusively modernist examples illustrated in the *Guidelines* have allowed officials to err on the side of "differentiation," and some preservation commissions and local officials have interpreted the *Standards* as actually mandating modernist design for new construction in historic settings.

The confusion created by varying interpretation of the *Standards* goes well beyond projects submitted for federal grants or tax credits, but has infused the preservation movement nationally and percolated to the local level. A proposal in 2007 to rewrite the pioneering 1931 Zoning Ordinance in Charleston, removing the existing requirements for conformance with the historical character of the district and instead referencing the *Standards*, can be seen as an attempt by the Board of Architectural Review in that city to operate under the more elastic language of the National Park Service. Wisely, the city chose to adapt the language of the *Standards* to its own needs, producing a text less likely to be interpreted in favor of harsh contrast in new construction. (City of Charleston, 2008.) On the other hand, growing opposition to the imposition of modernist interventions in historic districts has led to calls for further revisions to the *Standards* to clarify their intent in a way that is not prejudicial to new traditional design. (Semes, 2007.) (I revisit the issue of "differentiation" and "compatibility" in Chapter 7.)

Preservation and Modernism

Over the course of the last century, preservation efforts in the United States succeeded beyond the wildest dreams of Pamela Cunningham or William Sumner Appleton. Beginning in the 1930s, thousands of individual structures were granted landmark status and historic districts were designated in dozens of cities. European regulatory oversight was even more extensive. But the movement's postwar successes in the United States occurred against the backdrop of widespread demolitions for the sake of federal urban renewal programs and highway construction schemes. Hardly any sizable city avoided the demolition of a significant portion of its central business district or inner residential neighborhoods in the interest of misguided and often unrealized redevelopment schemes. The scale of the planned destruction of American urban centers approached that of the devastation of World War II in Europe, and the frequent failure of replacement construction to win public acceptance fueled the rapid expansion of the preservation audience.

The rise of populist protest movements in the 1960s and 1970s brought a new focus to the movement. In the protests against the destruction of New York's Pennsylvania Station in 1964 or the struggle of Jane Jacobs and her Greenwich Village neighbors against the highway schemes of Robert Moses, for example, nonprofessional preservationists were motivated not by patriotic idealism or antiquarianism, but by fierce resistance to what the participants saw as misguided progress and the arrogance of unchecked government bureaucrats and real estate developers. They fought for the physical survival of their homes and neighborhoods against the imposition of the utopian visions of modernist urbanism. For preservation activists like Henry Hope Reed, modernist architecture itself was the enemy and preservation an effective weapon against it.

Much of the lay public was sympathetic to this view: They loved old buildings and neighborhoods, but, even more, they hated the modernist buildings that replaced the old ones. Paul Goldberger has correctly noted that the preservation movement was often motivated by "not so much love of what is being preserved as fear of what will replace it. No wonder people feared the new forty years ago; architects were giving them every reason to." (Goldberger, 2005.) In what may have at times been overzealous preservation, many old structures were given landmark protection with little regard for architectural quality. An uncritical valuation of anything old and aversion to anything new was an entirely reasonable response to the madness of the city-destroying architectural and planning doctrines of the time, but it established precedents that are now being exploited by a new generation of preservationists seeking protection for the very buildings that replaced the landmarks whose destruction inspired the preservation movement in the first place.

With the ascendancy of modernism after the Second World War, architects in the process of reinventing their discipline had no further need of historical exemplars and instead viewed the historical city as a vast redevelopment site. A sentimental attachment to old buildings was still strong, but their modernist convictions led architects to see historical buildings as having little or nothing to teach them about contemporary design. As the old cities were destined to be torn down and rebuilt anyway, there was no need to make new buildings fit in with older ones. Rarely did a new modernist structure positively engage its neighbors and rarely did an architect's rendering even show any neighbors. At the same time, architects continued to support preservation in principle—for example, through the work of the Historic Resources Committee of the American Institute of Architects—so long as such support did not come at the expense of opportunities for new building

projects or undermine the commitment of the general culture to the artistic and social aims of modernism.

Ultimately, and with a few notable exceptions, the architectural profession all but abandoned the conservation of historic sites to the care of historians, archeologists, museum curators, art conservators, and other specialists. This group brought a new preservation culture to the forefront, committed to a more exacting and scientific analysis of evidence to reveal historical conditions as accurately as possible. Sites of all periods were now viewed as cultural artifacts subject to a rigorously "value-free" anthropological approach. The new preservation culture had little interest in the continuance of architectural traditions, but only in the stabilization and preservation of the artifacts produced by those traditions, which had now been superseded by modernism. Architects who chose to pursue preservation as a professional specialty were, with a few exceptions, committed modernists who strictly separated conservation of historic fabric and design of new elements, as if working simultaneously in two distinct and formally unrelated worlds. This continues to be the dominant pattern today among contemporary practitioners: restoration work is typically undertaken with considerable knowledge and skill and yet juxtaposed with new elements bespeaking an antithetical aesthetic sensibility. (See Chapter 11.)

To be sure, the technical advances brought by scientific preservation have vastly increased our knowledge of historic building methods and materials, computer technology has enabled the management of vast amounts of research data, and high-tech equipment and procedures have made possible types of noninvasive and reversible preservation undreamed of in the time of Cunningham and Appleton. The Association for Preservation Technology (APT) has played a major role in refining methods for building analysis, diagnostics, and conservation techniques by means of conferences, research, and publications. But these gains do not compensate for the widespread loss of aesthetic understanding of the building cultures that produced the monuments under preservation. While a number of gifted and conscientious architects devoted their careers to thoughtful and historically informed restoration work and developed national practices in this area—John Milner in Pennsylvania and John Waite in New York being among the leading exemplars—the general abdication of responsibility for the care and interpretation of its own heritage by the architectural profession effectively removed architectural judgment from the professional practice of preservation.

An unspoken truce of sorts seems to have been brokered between the professional preservationists and the modernist architectural establishment from the 1970s onward, as each agreed not to interfere with the core interests and activities of the other. This did not go unnoticed by the grass-roots activists. James Marston Fitch, in a late essay recalling the history of American preservation, noted the gradually emerging conflict between the lay and professional classes, but he underestimated how well founded this lay skepticism was. As the professional experts began to demonstrate not only a tolerance for but an active encouragement of modernist insertions in historic settings in the 1980s and 1990s, the skepticism of the grass-roots preservation constituency only deepened. (Fitch, 2006, p. 193.)

The divergence between the two camps was strikingly revealed as early as 1977 at a conference sponsored by the National Trust for Historic Preservation, the Society of Architectural Historians, and the Washington Chapter of the AIA, the proceedings of which were published in 1980 as *Old and New Architecture: Design Relationship.* (National Trust, 1980.) In their commentaries, the architects praised inappropriate and oppositional new buildings as "contextual," while nonarchitects tended to express skepticism about the motivations of the architects. Jean Paul Carlhian, for example, praised the "slim elegance" of the immense John Hancock Tower in Boston (I. M. Pei & Partners, 1976) "rising majestically" above Trinity Church—designed by the founder of Carlhian's firm, Henry Hobson Richardson—which was reflected in the glass tower's curtain wall. Carlhian complained that the church's silhouette is "destroyed" by the "bulk" of the older eclectic John Hancock Building by Cram & Ferguson (1948) just beyond. He had it backward, of course—it is the new Hancock that destroys the character of Richardson's church, not the vastly more sympathetic older one. (National Trust, 1980, pp. 49–68.) (See fig. C.15.)

In contrast, nonarchitect Pringle Hart Symonds of Historic Annapolis spoke candidly about her skeptical view of architects' preoccupations. She and her fellow lay preservationists looked at proposed projects in the context of the city as a whole, while the architects tended to focus only on formal experimentation within the confines of their particular sites. On the other hand, classical architect Samuel Wilson, Jr., from New Orleans presented a number of sympathetic additions and infill buildings in the Vieux Carré designed by his firm and continuing the styles of the neighboring buildings. Wilson's approach demonstrated the kind of architecture that might develop out of a fundamental respect for the historic resource, but his minority report was offered almost apologetically, being clearly outside the mainstream. From our vantage point today it looks prescient and deserves closer study. (National Trust, 1980, pp. 203–16, 151–61.) (Fig. 5.15) In my view the 1977 conference underscores the most important lesson of the last four decades for architects and preservationists—that "compatibility" must be grounded in formal grammar and syntax, not mute abstract qualities or inarticulate shapes of similar size. Lay activists like Symonds and traditional architects like Wilson understood this, but their viewpoint was always a minority position within the upper levels of the preservation community and is only now beginning to grow in influence.

We gain some insight into the conflicting motives of many preservation architects in the writings of Fitch, who exhorted his audience "to save historic buildings from the savage spread of modern urbanism" while heaping scorn on the "historicist eclecticism" that had produced the very historic buildings and districts he worked tirelessly to preserve. Fitch, an admirer and defender of the Bauhaus—he authored a 1960 monograph on Walter Gropius—as well as an outspoken partisan of the political Left, saw no contradiction in preserving the products of period revival design while denouncing the architectural culture that had produced them. He vehemently denied any logical connection between the act of preserving old buildings and the desire to design new ones with similar qualities. Fitch seemed unaware of an apparent double contradiction in his position: celebrating modernist architecture in general while damning its urbanism, and damning historical "eclecticism" while fighting to preserve its built products. (Fitch, 2006, pp. 183, 194.)

In my experience Fitch's attitudes are widely shared by the professional and academic elite of preservation, and this raises an important question: Why would one devote one's career

5.15. Royal Sonesta Hotel,
New Orleans, Louisiana, by
Samuel Wilson, Jr., of Koch
& Wilson Architects, 1968.

Wilson was among the few
architects of the 1960s and
1970s who gained wide
recognition as a designer in
historic styles. The new hotel
maintains historic character
by respecting the size,
scale, materials, typologies,
and styles of the Vieux
Carré Historic District.

to the preservation of architecture that one no longer believes in? And, if one values historic urbanism and traditional buildings, why would one actively discourage attempts to build more of what one values in favor of experimental models that frequently result in failure? This apparent split between an intellectual commitment to modernism (based on an ideology to be examined in Chapter 6) and a sentimental attachment to historic architecture (which underestimates both the rational basis of traditional design and the Romanticism of modernism) has become a prominent feature of contemporary preservation discourse. (Fitch, 2006, pp. 26–40, and Bland, 2004.)

American Preservation Today

Despite some infamous losses early on, the preservation movement in the United States

since the mid–1970s has met with astonishing success, largely due to continuing popular resistance to perceived or real threats to beloved landmarks and neighborhoods, the federal program of tax credits for rehabilitation established in 1977, and the Supreme Court's 1978 decision upholding New York's preservation ordinance. The movement metamorphosed from a small collection of antiquarians, patriots, and community activists into a multi-billion-dollar industry with an extensive political, institutional, professional, and academic infrastructure. At the same time, the scope of preservation activity expanded geographically, typologically, and chronologically to include increasing segments of the common built heritage. (Choay, 2001, pp. 140–41.)

Preservation now looked beyond individual buildings to include whole neighborhoods, towns, and landscapes; new building types, not previously deemed "historic," were scrutinized, including industrial and engineering structures; and the chronological window of eligible sites expanded to include buildings fifty years old or less, including modernist buildings that had arisen on the rubble of the historic buildings preservationists had fought unsuccessfully to save. Preservationists began to value vernacular, folkloric, and transient landscapes and sites, as well as environments identified with ethnic and immigrant communities. By the late 1990s, what had begun as a movement to protect a collection of important historic sites and a few exceptional urban ensembles now seemed to embrace the totality of the premodern, preindustrial world and was quickly moving into the "recent past." (Lambin, 2007.) The criteria for historical or artistic significance seemed to be up for grabs as the concept of "heritage" expanded to include almost any human artifact or cultural practice that was deemed significant to some community with sufficient political clout to make itself heard. Preservation, rather than being an instrument of cultural resource conservation based on informed judgment of what constituted "historic" aspects of the built environment, seemed on the verge of becoming merely a ratification of the status quo, as if its highest aim were to retain indiscriminately the evidence of whatever happened to have happened. (Leigh, 2001, p. 41, and Adam, 2003.)

At the same time, the split between professional preservationists and grass-roots volunteers over the place of modernism in preservation widened. The resistance of the nonprofessional preservationists to contrasting styles for interventions in historic settings was contained as long as there appeared to be no alternative to mainstream modernism in contemporary architecture. As preservation commissions in New York and elsewhere increasingly approved contrasting modernist designs for new buildings in some of the nation's most prized historic districts, critics of these approvals were dismissed as "knee-jerk preservationists" or told that they "didn't understand the process." (Barstow, 2000.)

The advent of new traditional architecture and New Urbanism, however, opened a schism within the ranks of the architects themselves. As the leading modernist architects in the 1990s became more aggressive in their rejection of history and context, growing awareness of new traditional design and New Urbanism emboldened neighborhood activists to oppose with greater force and confidence what they considered to be inappropriate new construction in historic settings. In Charleston, the Committee to Save the City headed a citizen revolt against the modernist preservation elite through its publication *The Guardian*. In Rome, resistance to the Richard Meier design for the Ara Pacis Museum, while unsuccessful in stopping the project, initiated a broad and ongoing debate about proposed skyscrapers and other modernist interventions in several Italian cities. (Younes, 2004 and Maltese, 2007.) (See fig. 1.3.)

At this point my historical narrative arrives at the present moment and the debate that is now joined among architects and preservationists regarding new architecture in historic settings. I take up these questions again in later chapters, but must first undertake a critique of the ideology that has united the modernist architectural establishment and the professional class of preservation in opposition to the recovery of traditional languages in the design of buildings and cities, a deeply entrenched and often uncritically assumed philosophy called historicism.

**6.1. Bibliothèque Ste.-
Geneviève,** Paris, by Henri
Labrouste, 1845–51.

The library is often
celebrated as a
"progressive" forerunner
of modernism. Some of
Labrouste's sources were
indeed foreign to the
academic orthodoxy of the
time, but he nonetheless
displays a profound
continuity with the classical
tradition.

CHAPTER 6

Historicism and the Search for an Architecture of Our Time

Architecture is not the product of materials and purposes—nor by the way, of social conditions—but of the changing spirits of changing ages. It is the spirit of an age that pervades its social life, its religion, its scholarship, and its arts. The Gothic style was not created because somebody invented rib-vaulting; the Modern Movement did not come into being because steel frame and reinforced concrete construction had been worked out—they were worked out because a new spirit required them.

—SIR NIKOLAUS PEVSNER, *An Outline of European Architecture* (1943)

One of the most persistent ideas that architects and preservationists have inherited from the nineteenth century is the idea that art and architecture express, or ought to express, the spirit of the age. Whenever we hear contemporary design described as "the architecture of our time"—meaning not that it is the product of people living today but that it consciously embodies themes or concerns specific to this historical moment—we are under the influence of a complex of ideas philosophers call historicism. Essentially, this is the doctrine that each era or period in history has a unique and exclusive "spirit" or set of ideas and concerns exclusive to it within a greater temporal sequence that aims at the realization of some ideal of progress.

In the historicist philosophy of Georg Wilhelm Friedrich Hegel, the spirit of the age (*Zeitgeist*) is revealed by developments in art, as much as by political, social, and technological change, and an individual artwork is little more than a symptom of its social and cultural context. The main task of the artist, critic, or historian is, therefore, to discern the spirit of the time and give it adequate expression. Hegel's descendant, Karl Marx, viewed works of art and culture as either "progressive"—for facilitating class struggle and the ultimate fall of capitalism—or "reactionary"—for inhibiting or obscuring that process. In both philosophies, art is judged according to whether it advances or retards the "imperatives" of a given age, however they may be defined.

By the turn of the twentieth century, historians indebted to Hegel and Marx (as well as to the evolutionary ideas of Darwin and Spencer) had classified world history into temporal periods, which they saw as subject to distinct phases of rise, development, and decadence. This historiographic program was perhaps best summed up by Oswald Spengler, whose *Decline of the West* (first published in 1918) posits a multiplicity of distinct and unique cultures rising and falling in temporal waves: "Each culture has its own new possibilities of self-expression which arise, ripen, decay, and never return. There is not one sculpture, one painting, one mathematics, one physics, but many, each in its deepest essence different from the others, each limited in duration and self-contained, just as each species of plant has its peculiar blossom or fruit, its special type of growth and decline. . . ." (Spengler, 1932, pp. 21–22.) In this view each historical period has its own exclusive concerns, methods, and

145

goals expressive of the spirit of the age, and it is the job of the historian to sort these out. Each period must only be judged by the criteria proper to it as a time-bound, never-to-return phenomenon. Conformance with the historicist program superseded any claim to universal values or criteria applying beyond the boundaries of a given period. Those artists or thinkers whose work seemed to epitomize their time were identified as the major figures; those who did not conform to expectations of their period could probably be safely ignored.

"Architecture is the will of an epoch translated into space." "The new architecture is the inevitable logical product . . . of our age." "The architect's task consists in coming into agreement with the orientation of his epoch." These statements, respectively from Mies van der Rohe, Walter Gropius, and Le Corbusier, "are among the cruder outcroppings of a theory of historical determinism, a sort of *Reader's Digest* version of Hegel which was abundantly taken in by the architectural and planning professions in the earlier years of [the twentieth] century." (Rowe and Koetter, 1978, pp. 28, 95–99.) These sentiments, with their underlying progressive social and political commitments, placed modernist architecture "on the side of the future." History was a series of significant ruptures or revolutions in which new forces and new ideas from time to time broke through the straitjacket of tradition. Moreover, the ruptures were the inevitable outcome of the historical process itself; the ultimate triumph of progress was assured. Modernism was the most recent—and perhaps final—instance of such cultural breakthroughs, one capable of realizing at last "the age-old promise to drag us out of the Dark Ages." (Ouroussoff, 2007.) But what is the end toward which progress in architecture aims? Until two decades ago it might have been the consummation of Marxist revolution; today it seems to be the perfection of technology. Architects have staked their profession and their individual reputations on experimentation with new construction methods and materials, as well as new ways of conceiving and representing architectural designs, so that technology itself—or at least the appearance of it—is no longer a means of environmental improvement but has become an end in itself.

Architectural education supported the progressive program, especially in the teaching of architectural history. Generations of students have absorbed the historicist narrative from Sir Bannister Fletcher's *History of Architecture on the Comparative Method*, first published in 1896 and still a standard textbook in the field. (Fletcher, 1928.) The influential writings of Sigfried Giedion and Nikolaus Pevsner presented the genesis of modernist architecture as the inevitable product of the spirit of the age and then retroactively identified as "pioneers" those historical designers whose work seemed to point toward modernism. Those architects or artists whose work either did not contribute to the founding of the Modern Movement or who continued to work in historical styles after 1925 were summarily excluded from the history of architecture. (Giedion, 1954, and Pevsner, 1960 and 1977.) Pevsner, for example, recounting the leading architects of the modern era, simply declares that for the first forty years of the twentieth century, "no English name need here be mentioned," thereby consigning the splendid work of John Belcher, Edwin Lutyens, Giles Gilbert Scott, Reginald Blomfield, Beresford Pite, Charles Holden, Charles Townsend, and many others to an oblivion that has only recently been remedied. (Pevsner, 1977, p. 394, and Watkin, 1977, pp. 114–15.)

Since the early 1990s, global confidence in a predetermined—or at least clearly identifiable—pattern of progress in history has largely disappeared from the world of politics, economics, and international affairs. Since the fall of Communism—the political expression of Marx's historical determinism—it seems that nothing is inevitable after all. But while the philosophical and political implications of historicism were abandoned nearly everywhere else, the historicist faith remains strong among contemporary architects and critics, many of whom cling to the idea that every age must distinguish itself from all previous ages by making new buildings look different from any previously built. This assumption not only drives much of the culture of novelty visible in contemporary design, but also provides the philosophical framework for mainstream preservation policies: the projection of "difference" between new construction and historic fabric arises from the historicist view that every period must present itself in terms uniquely expressive of its particular moment. Without making this difference conspicuous, it is thought, the clarity of the historicist narrative might become obscured and its authority undermined. (For a thorough review of the history and influence of historicism in architectural theory, see Watkin, 1977.)

Historicism and Historical Architecture

The historicist viewpoint in architecture rests on the axiom that buildings and cities are to be seen primarily as *documents of their times*. This is not an unreasonable assumption for a historian, for whom architectural artifacts can be an endlessly rich source of information about the designers, builders, and inhabitants of a historic place. Buildings and cities seem to be even more revealing than written documents or other evidence our predecessors might have left behind, disclosing substantial information about the larger culture of the time and place, including social organization, economic structure, political apparatus, technologies, and religious observances. For the architect or historian approaching historical fabric in this way, buildings and sites can indeed be splendid documents of their times. Difficulties arise when historic buildings and sites are seen as documenting a time for which a general framework has been established in advance by the historicist narrative. The human tendency, shared even by professional historians, is to find what we are looking for. By defining what they supposed a given period to have been about and focusing on those buildings that corroborated this characterization and deemphasizing those that did not, historians of the historicist school constructed an elaborate, but incomplete, picture of Western architecture based on an evolutionary model. Chronological criteria replaced aesthetic criteria for making judgments of quality, and conformance to period-stylistic templates supplanted the investigation of actual historical development for writing history. (Collins, 1967, p. 157.)

In order to keep the various periods distinct, historians emphasized the differences between them; ultimately it was these differences that defined history in disregard of the predominant continuity that binds one period to its predecessors and successors. For example, the differences between the thought and culture of the medieval and Renaissance periods in Europe, and concomitant differences between Gothic and Renaissance architecture, tended to be exaggerated. On closer scrutiny, the two traditions are more difficult to separate than their conventional presentation in standard histories would suggest, but a clean division between them better suits the historicist parcelization by period. Works that seem to combine or straddle two periods or styles are especially disadvantaged because they frustrate a historicist evaluation; they are typically seen, at best, as examples of "transition." The Church of St.-Eustache in Paris, for example, is dismissed by Pevsner as "not amongst the historically leading works" because he values more highly those buildings that seem to "lead" to subsequent, even more esteemed, works. (Pevsner, 1977, p. 310.) (See fig. 3.1.) Valuing buildings primarily in terms of how well they conform to the presumed profile of their period or how clearly they seem to prefigure some later development imposes on the past a sort of temporal typecasting that deprives us of an accurate or complete picture of any historical epoch.

Every historian approaches the subject matter at hand with a point of view, historicist or otherwise; but an entirely different picture of history can be painted depending on whether one sees continuities or discontinuities as normative. If ruptures, revolutions, and daring innovations are what define the spirit of the time—as Spengler thought—then the historian will emphasize those and ignore the vast preponderance of buildings that continue along stylistic lines established earlier. This partially explains the standard critical approach to two other landmarks of Paris, Henri Labrouste's Bibliothèque Ste.-Geneviève (1845–51) and Charles Garnier's Opéra (1861–74). Labrouste's library, both technically challenging and stylistically innovative, is seen by many historians as progressive and a precursor to later modernist developments. Garnier's Opéra, on the other hand, falls outside the historicist narrative despite its vast inventiveness and technological sophistication, because its more retrospective neo-Baroque style had no influence on the development of modernism, except as an example of what the Modern Movement deplored. But what is most striking about these two works is what they have in common—a strong commitment to the ongoing development of the classical tradition, a specific interest in ornament, the further exploration of their respective building types, and an incorporation of the most advanced technology their rapidly developing building culture afforded them. (Fig. 6.1) (See fig. 2.2.) Giedion, who claimed that "there are whole decades in the second half of the nineteenth century *in which no architectural work of any significance is encountered*," devoted an entire chapter to Labrouste but ignored Garnier. (Giedion, 1954,

p. 292, emphasis added.) Nineteenth-century architecture is treated with more respect by more recent historians, but the conventional view still holds much of the architectural community in its grasp. (For more balanced views of Labrouste and Garnier, see Bergdoll, 2000, and Watkin and Middleton, 2003.)

The historicist narrative fails to recognize the extent to which the art and architecture of any moment in history is driven by multiple impulses, even contradictory ones, that compete and combine in a continually jostling marketplace of works and ideas. Developments and new styles tend to come from the initiatives of individuals and groups, not from blind forces, abstract ideas, or steady evolution. (Collins, 1967, p. 28.) Architectural traditions, operating as described in Chapter 3, are motivated by the ongoing conversation about the models rather than by a desire to subsume the built evidence under some abstract idea or presumed *Zeitgeist*. Sometimes a building culture evolves slowly, almost imperceptibly; at other times a single building or event can seem to revolutionize a culture's entire conception of architecture and urbanism. In any case, there is no "spirit of the time" independent of the acts and works that are thought retrospectively to have embodied it, and these are typically too numerous and diverse to fit neatly in any temporal pigeonhole. (Scott, 1924, p. 27.) Despite Pevsner's claims to the contrary, it was because someone invented rib-vaulting that the Gothic style emerged, not because the spirit of the time required it. (Pevsner, 1977, p. 17.)

Like most clichés, the historicist view of architectural progress does contain a kernel of truth. There are many cases when a particular and well-defined line of development, once initiated, is pursued by a number of architects working on a specific problem over the course of a few generations or more. The development of the Greek Doric temple from Agrigento in Sicily to the Parthenon; the succession of Gothic cathedrals from Chartres to Beauvais; the recovery and extension of the classical language from Brunelleschi to Michelangelo; and the refinement of the American skyscraper from Louis Sullivan to Raymond Hood and William F. Lamb are all instances of progress along a clear line of refinement. Two caveats must be noted, however: First, these sequences do not necessarily fit into a grander scheme of development embracing them all, and second,

it would be wrong to see the earlier stages in any of these examples as being necessarily inferior to the later ones. Chronological placement in the sequence of development does not determine the aesthetic merit of individual works.

A corollary to historicism's emphasis on evolutionary progress is its emphasis on "ideas" and "meanings" at the expense of formal design. When architecture is seen as an expression of the spirit of the age, the indirect meaning associated with the political or social values held by the architects or believed to be represented by the building can outweigh consideration of the physical properties of the design as it actually appears. Examples of this are the commonplace nineteenth-century identification of the Greek temple form with democracy, the association of axial plans like Versailles with political absolutism, or the postwar tendency to view even the most abstract references to classical composition as representing Fascism. While one cannot deny the many connections between a given building and the ideas that may have been significant for its designer or that became attached to it during its subsequent history, neither can one assume that these ideas or associations determined the forms, are given univocal expression by them, were used exclusively by the persons or groups we associate with them, or will retain the meanings we impute to them in the future. The value of any building considered from the viewpoint of its status as a work of art ultimately rests on its relationship to perennial values that transcend, while still respecting, the concerns of any historical moment. (Olsen, 1986, pp. 281–85.)

In truth, only within a style can a specific form become reliably associated with a specific content or idea. Outside of a style, the correspondence between forms and the ideas they are thought to express is either accidental or perhaps projected onto the forms by a critic with a vested interest in proving a particular theory. Despite their frequent reluctance to do so, historians and critics of architecture must pay attention to the forms buildings and urban ensembles present to us—to what buildings look like rather than only the ideas they are thought to express—in order to understand how style allows forms to communicate ideas. Style, not "meaning," is the key to understanding the aesthetic achievements of historical architecture.

But this inquiry is hampered by the historicist identification of "style" with the temporal category of "period." Each style is identified with the historical moment when it first appeared and developed its characteristic features; knowing this allows the historian to use style in dating works, since buildings may be assumed to belong to the period in which their style was prevalent. For the historicist, the notion that style might be independent of historical sequence—that one might legitimately build in a particular style decades or even centuries after it first arose—violates the legibility of the historical process and confuses the building's provenance. The deliberate imitation of a style no longer in fashion is therefore considered "false history"—it purports to tell a story contrary to the "true" history of stylistic succession as defined by the historicist narrative. This is the source of the common modernist distaste for stylistic revivals. Subsequent appearances of a style—Colonial Revival works from the early twentieth century, for example—are therefore considered inauthentic and labeled as "pastiche."

This prejudice can distort our evaluation of historic sites under consideration for designation as protected landmarks, tempting us to overlook important sites or overestimate unimportant ones on the basis of ephemeral associations. For example, the Richardson Dilworth House, a Georgian Revival–style building that contributes to the beauty and coherence of the Society Hill Historic District in Philadelphia, was nearly demolished in 2005 with the approval of the city's preservation commission when a new condominium tower designed by Venturi, Scott Brown and Associates and was approved for its site. Because the house was built in 1957 by former mayor Dilworth to encourage the restoration and redevelopment of the then deteriorated neighborhood, it was viewed as potentially "historic"; on the other hand, it was seen as having little or no architectural value because its late Colonial Revival style ran counter to the authorized narrative of Philadelphia's architectural history. The house remains standing, but its future is still in doubt. (See fig. 3.2B.)

The narrow application of the historicist notion of "period" to historical buildings distorts the legitimate idea of authenticity. For example, in Paris, monuments such as the Louvre, the Conciergerie, or the Cathedral of Notre-Dame cannot be securely dated by visual inspection alone because their complicated histories of restoration and repair obscure the chronology of their construction. (See Chapter 5.) In Rome almost nothing we see today is a pure survival from ancient times; everything has been rebuilt, restored, or transformed through the centuries. The Curia in the Roman Forum was last rebuilt in 1928, making it effectively a twentieth-century building rather than the second-century survivor it appears to be. (Fig. 6.2) To the historicist such stylistic anachronism is seen as a form of fakery. Consequently, current preservation policies discourage restorations or reconstructions that might create "a false sense of historical development," as expressed in *The Secretary of the Interior's Standards for Rehabilitation*. But how can we present a true sense of historical development if the facts must be interpreted to save the presupposed narrative rather than allowing the narrative to be constructed in light of the facts? While we might also limit our designs for new interventions into the historic setting to the style of our time, what if the style of our time is in dispute? And how do we maintain the formal integrity and historic character of monuments if we are obliged to add to a preexisting setting only what is alien to it or in apparent contrast to it?

In truth, the historicist equation of style and period is a simple tautology: A building looks a certain way because that was the style of the time; we can identify the style of the time because buildings built then looked that way. But that is not what a style properly is. A style is like a literary genre that may be employed at various times and for various reasons, persisting and changing in the development of a literature. As I noted in Chapters 2 and 3, a style is *the conscious and public cultivation of the appropriate as discerned by a community*. Such a community may range widely in both space and time, so that styles often remain applicable in physical and temporal contexts different from those in which they first appeared. To build in a historical style is not to pretend to be living in another time; nor is it an attempt to deceive. It is an exploration of a formal language that may have application in and relevance to any number of times and places, even far removed from its original appearance. The rehabilitation of the concept of style independent of historical sequence is essential if we are to arrive at a "true sense of historical development" because only by means of the development of styles can there be "historical development" in architecture at all.

6.2. The Roman Forum, with Arch of Septimus Severus, Church of San Martino e Luca, and Curia Senatus, Rome.

The Roman Forum is a veritable palimpsest of building and rebuilding. Next to a seventeenth-century church stands the ancient Curia (right), seat of the Roman Senate. Last restored in 1928, it retains significant elements and materials from its antique past.

6.3. Old Court House, Williamsburg, Virginia, eighteenth century, restored twentieth century.

The portico was to have Ionic columns, but these were not installed during the 1770s, and Doric columns added later were removed in the 1930s restoration. While historically accurate, the restoration misrepresents the builders' design intentions.

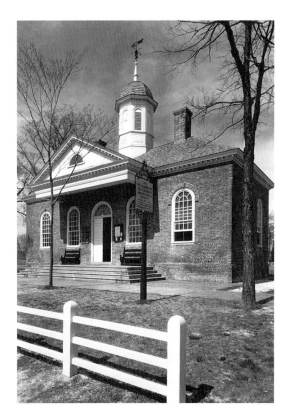

Another consequence of seeing buildings primarily as historical documents is that material authenticity tends to be exaggerated at the expense of formal design. Old buildings stand before us "imbued with a message from the past," as the opening words of the Venice Charter put it, and seem to reveal in their material presence what a particular past time was "really like." The primary goal of preservation or restoration then becomes "verisimilitude" rather than, say, integrity as a work of art. (Fitch, 1982, pp. 225, 241.) For example, the columns of the portico at the old Court House in Williamsburg are missing—the originally intended columns were never installed during the Colonial period and those installed later in the nineteenth century were removed by the restorers—in order to show the building as it would have appeared in 1770. Although there is no doubt that a row of Ionic columns was part of the original design, the historicist viewpoint would forbid installing them now. To do so would be "false history." (Fig. 6.3) Despite

the seeming objectivity of this apparently "scientific" approach, it nevertheless betrays a Romantic fascination with the isolated fragment or the ruin as a metaphorical expression of the irrecoverable past. An excessive emphasis on material authenticity reinforces the historicist alienation of the past from the present as the remains of a bygone time become sacred relics, precious but untouchable, and powerful reminders that we no longer live in their world, nor they in ours. (Lowenthal, 1985, pp. 280, 384, 412.)

This cult of the ruin is illustrated vividly by the nonreconstruction of Benjamin Franklin's house and shop in Philadelphia by Venturi, Scott Brown and Associates, where the surviving brick foundations of Franklin's long-vanished home and the stabilized ruin of the commercial buildings along the street are presented to the public as if they were religious relics or the precious and inscrutable remains of a vanished prehistoric culture. The former structures might have been reconstructed based on

findings from the archeological investigation, documentary evidence provided by letters and descriptions from the period, and knowledge of the local building culture as revealed by contemporary buildings nearby. Even if we could not be sure we had precisely replicated the building Franklin lived in, an informed reconstruction would have been more illuminating than the three-dimensional cartoon that was constructed. The known outlines of Franklin's lost structures were limned in steel tubing, like ghostly intimations of a vanished history. The treatment of the site immortalized the physical evidence connected with a particular moment in time while disregarding the role of the monument in the formation of an enduring sense of place. (Fig. 6.4) While the restoration of the site stopped "at the point where conjecture begins," as the Venice Charter says, we are left with little basis on which to fill in the blanks in our own minds. This presentation of the bare archeological artifacts serves the historicist mission of isolating the past from the present

6.4. Franklin Court, Philadelphia, by Venturi, Scott Brown and Associates, 1976.

Reaction against Williamsburg-style restoration prompted rendering the supposed outlines of Benjamin Franklin's home and workshop in "wireframe." An inaccurate rebuilding was avoided, but at the cost of preventing a view of the site as an element in an urban setting.

A

6.5. Greenwich Village façade renovation (project), New York, by Fairfax & Sammons Architects, 2003.

A. Existing street façade.

B. Proposed renovation.

Preservation authorities ruled against remodeling this insensitively modernized façade in the style of the building, but suggested restoring the offending curtain wall instead. Insisting on "differentiated" new construction immortalizes discordant features of the setting.

ignation or, in cases where "non-contributing" buildings or features may be removed, insert new construction in a contrasting idiom representing "our time." What is not permitted is to add new elements in the style of the historic fabric based on the architect's knowledge of that style; to do so would be "false history" and might confuse observers unable to distinguish the new and the old elements. Loss of continuity and integrity in historical character, therefore, becomes *the inevitable consequence of the preservation activity itself*, which is clearly a counterproductive outcome. (Fig. 6.5)

But why should allowing a place to evolve as it always had in the past be considered "false"? What if the historicist scheme of historical periods with their unique and exclusive styles is a fiction? What if there is no progress in architecture apart from the technical progress that comes from advances in engineering or the response to new programmatic needs? What if style is a genealogical rather than a chronological phenomenon? If there is a *Zeitgeist*, why should it necessarily lead to an iconoclastic rejection of traditions instead of a renewal of them? These questions compel us to examine more critically the historicist assumptions underlying current preservation policies and prompt us to reconsider the way we look at historic resources. Preservation must assure a future for—as well as safeguard the past of—the places we value enough to try to keep alive.

Liberation from the historicist narrative would allow preservation policies to base their judgments on appropriateness—the fitting and the exemplary—rather than on a temporal succession of chronologically defined styles. The differentiation between new construction and historic fabric would be the natural consequence of the different designers, interests, and varieties of craftsmanship involved in the development of a site over time, rather than a self-conscious dramatization of the differences between contradictory conceptions of architecture. Viewed from this perspective, the treatment of historic buildings and districts prioritizes the preservation of historic character over the introduction of new or contrasting character, and the historic district is seen as a zone in which the character-defining elements that give the district its identity are protected and new contributions to the built fabric are not permitted to remove, obscure, or diminish that character.

and keeping the evidence of each period safely contained in its officially determined chronological slot without fear of "false history."

The cumulative effect of the historicist influence on preservation practices is the *decontextualization* of historic buildings— they become museum artifacts instead of remaining part of our living world. The very act of designating a building or district as a landmark subject to preservation regulation seems to place a moratorium on the continued life and change of that fabric and that place. According to present doctrine, preservation commissions can offer architects working in historic settings only three options: strictly restore historic fabric based on physical or other documentation, scrupulously maintain the conditions that existed at the time of des-

Historicism and Contemporary Architecture

Historicist attitudes also strongly color our views of the architecture we produce today. For example, historicism defines "contemporary" architecture largely in terms of opposition to historical practice: Just as each period has its unique concerns and formal language, so contemporary architects seek a characteristic style that expresses our time and vividly projects the "difference" between their work and whatever has been produced in the past. The "difference," naturally, is explored in terms of the conscious rejection of precedent. But the commitment to pursuing innovative and purportedly unprecedented formal gestures seems only to blind contemporary architects to the precedents that nonetheless appear in their work. That virtually no building ever designed can truly be said to be unprecedented is a reality shared by both traditional and modernist architecture, although this reality is only admitted by the former.

While a general critique of contemporary movements in architecture is beyond the scope of this book, the relation between those movements and our attitudes toward historic buildings and cities is indeed relevant. Our view of historic settings is inevitably informed by our aspirations for the architecture of our own day and, therefore, contemporary fashions are of more than passing interest. This is especially the case when current architectural culture is dominated by a commitment to the dramatization of the difference between new and old construction and the fear that compromise in this projection of difference would undermine the philosophical premises upon which modernist architecture rests. The fear of "false history" in restoration work and a restless drive for novelty and originality in new work are opposite sides of the same coin. (See figs. C.2 and C.3.)

The self-conscious search for an architecture uniquely expressive of our time is handicapped by the absence of any single set of ideas or interests that clearly and uniquely defines our time in contradistinction to previous times. On those issues that count the most in human experience, little has changed in the last two and a half millennia, and many of our present discontents have roots stretching back into ancient times. (Sennet, 1993.) What *has* changed is our technology and the ways that its

B

advancement shapes the way we live and think; but architecture, as an exponent and beneficiary of technology, can more easily illustrate than comment on these changes. High technology can carve a Corinthian capital or deform a metal and glass curtain wall, but it no longer determines a priori how buildings ought to look, if indeed it ever did.

The ubiquity of the familiar image of the contemporary world as an arena of iconoclasm and self-invention tends to obscure an equally pervasive fascination with the past in popular culture. While often derided by contemporary architects and critics, traditional art, architecture, and decoration continue to exert a powerful attraction, especially in residential environments. If the "architecture of our time" were to be measured by the kinds of environments that people actually choose to live in when they have the choice, rather than by what establishment architects and critics say it is, it would be a mixture of traditional styles. In truth, many modernist designers themselves choose to live in traditional buildings and historic districts—another instance of the split consciousness in which a sentimental regard for historic buildings competes with an intellectual commitment to their negation. Indeed, the most expensive places to live and work in most European and American cities are now the historic centers, demonstrating intense demand for architecture and urbanism minimally impacted by modernist transformation and placing these environments beyond the means of all but the most affluent.

These reflections lead us to question the definition of the "architecture of our time"—to ask by whom it is to be defined, and how it is to be expressed in material terms. The political dimension of any group's claim to control the definition of progress must be taken into account. We might unmask the agenda underlying the "architecture of our time" by asking, simply: Who is the "we" implied by that "our"? (Brolin, 1981, pp. 12–13.) The imperiousness with which such assumptions are made can be breathtaking: Renzo Piano recently responded to popular resistance to his proposed glass skyscraper in Turin by characterizing his critics as being "afraid of the future," as if it were beyond dispute that "the future" and his designs were synonymous. (Maltese, 2007.) Undoubtedly, it is not the future per se that frightens Piano's critics, but the prospect of a future decided and enforced by architects and their powerful corporate clients without consulting the people whose lives are affected or showing respect for the historic center whose beauty will be diminished by the new tower. In a culture that pays lip service to nonconformity and the questioning of authority, the power of architectural elites has yet to be subject to the kind of public questioning now typically directed at political and economic ones; but perhaps doubts are now beginning to be expressed, and not only among those unsympathetic to modernist aims. (Kunstler, 1994, p. 226. See also Glazer, 2007, and Silber, 2007.)

Indeed, it is not the idea of progress—in the sense of reasonable improvements in technology or civic and social life—that critics of modernist architecture question, but the presumption that progress can be embodied only in certain architectural forms believed by the avant-garde to represent our current stage in the historicist narrative. On the contrary, we are justified in evaluating contemporary design according to the same principles that underlie all architecture regardless of style, based on the familiar Vitruvian trinity of sound construction, accommodation of human need, and beauty. The role of the critic is, therefore, to judge the relative success with which a building or ensemble satisfies those principles and is likely to do so over the long term. From this viewpoint, the style of a new building may well be one drawn from the past but, in any case, should be decided on the basis of appropriateness rather than in subservience to the presumed "imperatives of our age," with all the abuses implied by that notion. (Tiller, 2007.) It is up to us to determine, in the course of the decisions we make on a daily basis, what the "architecture of our time" ultimately will be.

Historicism and "False History"

Ultimately there is no such thing as "false history" in architecture. Truth or falsehood are qualities that we may attribute to historical accounts or interpretations but not to buildings, which may only be judged good or bad, appropriate or inappropriate. Our understanding of the history of architecture at any given time is necessarily provisional, precluding the presumption that any one interpretation is uniquely "true" and therefore determinative of the quality or significance of architectural works simply based on their conformance with that interpretation. One may believe that designs based on historical models are distasteful or antiquated, but they cannot be rejected as "false." Despite this, the fear of "false history" continues to govern much of the discourse in preservation today.

As mentioned in the previous chapter, the argument against "false history" was articulated by Cesare Brandi in his *Teoria del Restauro* (1963). In Brandi's theory an object produced by an artist or craftsman (including a building) that resembles similar objects made in the past can be considered a *copy*, an *imitation*, or a *falsification*. A copy is any new object that reproduces the appearance, the manner, or the style of a historical period not one's own for purposes of documentation; an imitation is the same but for purposes of deriving private pleasure from the reproduced object; a falsification is the same, but with the intention to deceive others as to the date, authenticity, or authorship of the object in order to benefit from a presumably higher market value. A copy or imitation made in the course of training or some scholarly pursuit is benign but, crucially, Brandi labels as falsification any copy or imitation created for public consumption *even without the intention to deceive*—the mere fact of its nonconformance with the historicist narrative makes it false and potentially confusing. Hence, any new work based on the continuity of a tradition, a formal language, or a building culture is deemed a falsification and therefore judged impermissible. (Brandi, 1963, pp. 65–69.)

In keeping with the historicist viewpoint, only a modernist design for a new building or object can avoid falsification because only modernist design is seen as giving truthful expression to the imperatives of our time. For this reason Brandi condemned the rebuilding of the Campanile in the Piazza San Marco in Venice after its collapse in 1901 and the reconstruction of the Santa Trinità Bridge in Florence blown up by the retreating Nazis in 1944 as "an offense against history and an outrage against Aesthetics, as if time were reversible and art works reproducible at will." His preferred option for the Campanile would have been a "vertical element"—presumably an abstracted structure in metal and glass to represent "our time"—to preserve the tower's urbanistic role; the bridge should have been replaced by a new design or left as a ruin but in any case not replaced by a copy. (Brandi, 2000, p. 46.) (See figs. C.18 and 5.4.) But the reconstructions of the Campanile and the bridge were not intended to provide copies of the monuments themselves; rather, they intend to retain the historic urban landscape of which they were essential parts. In its exclusive focus on the artifact, the doctrine of falsification tends to ignore this concern for the larger urban setting, its continuity and coherence, not to mention the deep attachment of the citizens to their historic environment—too often dismissed by the historicist as evidence of sentimentality and nostalgia. (Ceschi, 1970, pp. 105–6, 203.)

It is essential to understand both how radical Brandi's theory was and how contrary to the practice of most artists and architects over the course of the last two thousand years. A consistent adoption of his criteria would con-demn as "false" virtually all the greatest works of art in Western civilization prior to the rise of modernism, most of which are inconceivable without reliance on imitation—either of nature or of other artworks—beginning with virtually the entire output of ancient Roman sculptors, to a great extent copies or adaptations of earlier Greek models. Modernist design, while being no less imitative than its predecessors, fiercely denies that it is so and, in any case, carefully limits its models to its own recent productions, thereby presumably avoiding any "offence to History." But the more we study architecture and building cultures the clearer it becomes that a strict distinction between "copies" and "originals" is impossible. In fact, there is no original, no pure concept, no primordial work compared to which all others are derivatives or copies. Every architectural work is in a sense a copy of some earlier work, which it regards as a precedent; but each new work is also an original in its adaptation to new conditions, presenting itself as a new beginning. (Bruner, 1994, p. 407.)

Brandi's obsession with the threat posed by the circulation of "copies" in the world of fine and decorative art is, in part, motivated by the fear of forgery. In an art world that assigns values (and prices) to art works based on who created them and when, a misattribution or deliberate deception poses a risk to buyers and curators who depend on correct attribution to ensure the market value of their collections. Brandi then introduced this fear into the field of architecture and the city, so that a new building or addition in a historical style is seen as complicating our perception of the building's provenance. But buildings and cities are not artworks whose value depends on authentication. We do not value a good building less because we learn that a lesser-known architect designed it; nor should we value it differently because it was built at a time when its style was unfashionable. The imposition of an inappropriate art-market model of authenticity on the world of architecture and urbanism has only served to promote the alienation of surviving historic fabric from contemporary production. (Marconi, 2003, pp. 28–29, 35.)

Brandi's position also reflected a political commitment that viewed modernist architecture as a form of resistance to Fascism, which was irredeemably but counterfactually linked in his mind with traditional architecture. Like Fitch, Brandi saw architectural style as a battleground in the struggle to overthrow capitalism, an aspect of the progressive program of the historicist worldview that attracted many among the architectural community in the decades after the Second World War. But as a review of the products of various political regimes over the course of the last two centuries proves, no architectural style has a monopoly on expressions of tyranny and exploitation or, for that matter, of freedom and human rights. Nevertheless, the identification of classical columns with Fascist political programs remains an unquestioned article of faith among many modernist architects, despite the absence of historical justification for this view.

The collapse of assent to historicist philosophy does not necessarily imply the end of modernist architecture. Even without historicism we would probably have something like a modernist style, but its adherents would not justify their work on the basis of the presumed historical inevitability of their formal choices, nor argue for its preservation on the basis of its place in a historical sequence of progressive experiments. Outside of the historicist framework, modernist architecture may be seen as a style like any other—albeit one whose premises are the negation of those underlying the traditional styles—and one that architects are free to use or reject, depending on whether or not they deem it suitable for realizing their aesthetic intentions in whatever time or place they work.

A Nonhistoricist Alternative

The emerging conservation ethic offers an alternative to historicism, based on an alternative view of history. Because there is no "spirit of the age" independent of the activities that are perceived to manifest it, the future depends entirely on our own choices, and these are not determined by any historical necessity. (Scott, 1914, p. 27, and Popper, 1963, p. 3.) The architecture of the traditional city, its urban structure and character, and the judgments necessary to maintain and extend that character in space and time, unfold within a history that is neither predetermined nor in need of being "expressed." We are free to judge works of art and architecture on the basis of their *quality*—and their fertility for generating new works—rather than their position on a purported evolutionary timeline. We can reexamine the achievements of artists undervalued or

ignored by historians because their works were not found to have prefigured modernism. We can write a comprehensive history of twentieth-century architecture for the first time.

To deny a preordained program to history is not, however, to deny meaning or the reality of social, political, or cultural goals as motivating forces in our work and judgments. On the contrary, a sense of ultimate direction or moral purpose, a guiding narrative, a commitment to shared goals and publicly supported values—what Aristotle called a *telos*—is essential to any civilized social and cultural life. (Bess, 2006, pp. 11–15, and MacIntyre, 1984, pp. 52, 148.) Whether philosophic, aesthetic, or religious in its foundation, a *telos* is assumed and implied by every cultural act, including the design of buildings and cities. For us, as for Vitruvius, Alberti, or Jefferson, "a building is a form given to a moral proposition. When architecture is not a moral proposition, it is mere fashion." (Westfall, 2006, p. 20.) This "moral proposition" consists of a vision of the nobler ends toward which humans direct their affairs, which is ultimately a vision of the ideal city or a place "in which citizens can pursue justice, elegance, and grace." (Westfall, 2004, p. 20.) Since the *telos* rests not in some purported movement of history but, rather, in our nature, it transcends the contingencies of temporal succession. If, as the concept of *telos* suggests, the world is meaningful already and we need only discover that meaning, we still have no guarantee that we will definitively possess it. Our attempts to understand and describe meaning do, indeed, change over time—hence, we have a history that must be periodically rewritten. Our current knowledge is simply "the best we know so far," and our convictions must be tempered by our recognition that they are inevitably provisional. (MacIntyre, 1990, pp. 64, 88–89, 124–25.)

Here we discover the great advantage of the traditional architectural languages—they are themselves sensible, and they help us to communicate to others whatever sense we find in the world. Our capacity for expressing our ideas and meanings is in direct proportion to our command of the language available to us and its capacity, once we have mastered it, to give adequate expression to our intentions. Of course, even the best language cannot guarantee the truth of what is said in it. Although the *telos* never changes, our inevitably incomplete or contradictory conceptualizations and attempted realizations of it do change. But while art may advance in the short term, it is not progressive. Just when we think we have advanced in one direction, we find ourselves drawn in another or find that we have ended up where we began. We also tend to go off on tangents, which is why artists periodically take a step back, try to untangle the threads, and begin to weave the fabric anew in one of the periodic renascences that have punctuated history. (Settis, 2004.) The resiliency and capacity for change of our formal languages facilitates this process; without them we would be at a loss to know where to begin or how to proceed.

Accordingly, a nonhistoricist architecture seeks to weave the threads of historic and contemporary building into a new wholeness, whether by completing work left unfinished in the past or by the addition of new construction designed to sustain rather than challenge the character-defining elements of a historic place. The architect has the obligation to *recontextualize* historic structures in the life-world in which they are now set. Historic and new architecture can be collaborators rather than antagonists, each enriching and informing the other, but only if the character of place is allowed to overrule the supposed imperatives of time.

An immediate benefit of our liberation from historicism is that art and architectural history become vastly more complex and interesting. Frank Lloyd Wright and Stanford White, Le Corbusier and Auguste Perret, Edwin Lutyens and Gunnar Asplund: we can evaluate these pairs of contemporaries by judging how each opens or closes possibilities for further exploration, how each expands or contracts the formal language of the discipline, and how each probes or disregards perennial concerns that motivate artists in all periods. Our judgments will be based on our cultivation of a sense of the appropriate, or what the eighteenth century called "taste" and which Geoffrey Scott

defined as "the disinterested enthusiasm for architectural form." (Scott, 1914, p. 19.) Of course, by taste I am not referring to subjective individual preference, but to judgments that can be defended and shared with others. At any given time there is a plurality of tastes and styles, all competing for the attention and approbation of the general public and the patrons whose munificence finances the city and its architecture.

The breakdown of historicism offers us hope. What is best in human art and culture is not necessarily or exclusively time-bound; achievements of the past are not necessarily lost to us. As Henry Hope Reed once remarked, "What people have done once, they can do again." It is not the time but the *telos* that needs expressing, and this is hopeful indeed, because while time passes and the past is irretrievable, human nature—with all its potentialities and limitations—remains. The instinctive desire for the ennoblement of human thought and action transcends all times because human nature is the one thing that we take with us throughout our journey in time. It is this nature that traditional architecture, in its nearly inconceivable variety and complexity, seeks to concretize in buildings and cities that aim for beauty, sustainability, and justice.

Architecture without historicism offers a new respect for the character of valued places as works of art persisting in time. More broadly, it offers a rebirth of optimism and a greater appreciation for the contributions of both individual genius and artistic traditions. We are free to make choices about the ways buildings and cities are built, and the architecture of our time, in all its multiplicity of appearance, may be judged by the same standards and criteria used to judge the architecture of any time. As Léon Krier has written, "Authentic architecture is not the incarnation of the spirit of the age but of the spirit, full stop." (Krier, 1998, p. 71.)

7.1. Temple of Hadrian,
Rome, second century,
incorporated into the Stock
Exchange building, 1874.

The colonnade and cella
wall of the ancient temple
were "adaptively reused"
to form the Stock Exchange
for modern Rome. Escaping
the demolitions intended to
isolate Roman monuments,
the site illustrates inclusion
of a monument in the
ongoing life of the city.

CHAPTER 7

Preservation After Historicism

> The task involved in bringing together the petrified remnants of yester-
> day and the life of today provides a vivid illustration of what tradition
> always means: not just the careful preservation of monuments, but the
> constant interaction between our aims in the present and the past to
> which we still belong.
>
> —Hans-Georg Gadamer, "The Relevance
> of the Beautiful" (1977)

For many people, the value of old buildings and neighborhoods lies in what they "say" about life in the past. Historical buildings and sites are preserved, according to this view, primarily for their documentary value and because so many of us have an abiding interest in the life of earlier times. There are, of course, many historic places whose preservation is prompted primarily by their importance as such windows on the past, but this historical value alone would not seem to justify the enormous investment in preservation that our society has made over the last several decades; nor does it account for the fervor with which partisans of the preservation movement have promoted the rehabilitation and restoration of older buildings and neighborhoods.

The more important motive for preservation is that people value old buildings and neighborhoods for what they mean to us in the present. We preserve them because many historic settings are places in which we want to live and work today. This does not mean we want to live in the past but, rather, reflects a belief that the built environment surviving from the past offers qualities and benefits that newer construction often does not. Preserved buildings and districts serve as models from which we might recon-stitute the building cultures, the styles, and the craftsmanship without which we cannot build buildings, neighborhoods, and cities suitable for the conduct of civilized human life. In other words, *we preserve in order to learn how to build.* Recovering the building cultures that gave us the historic settings we now admire allows us to see what is of greatest value in the surviving historic fabric and what aspects of the inherited world are likely to be most fruitful for building new, equally beautiful buildings and cities. Therefore, *we also build in order to understand what and how to preserve.*

The urgent task for traditional designers and sympathetic preservationists, then, is to return historic buildings and districts to the ongoing flow of life, reweave them into a continuous urban fabric, and see them as models for advancing contemporary design in continuity with, rather than in opposition to, valued aspects of the existing built world. The relationship between architects and preservationists will then move from the present mutual skepticism toward a common ground, and architects will reassume their traditional role as both practitioners of historically informed new architecture and conservators of surviving historic fabric. (Fig. 7.1)

Defining the Resource

All preservationists should agree that respect for the historic resource is the fundamental commitment on which all their activity rests, but how do we define the resource and what are our obligations to it? Attempts to define the object of preservation on a purely materialistic basis have led to confusion. A growing international recognition of the need for a more nuanced and inclusive approach to cultural resource conservation has paralleled the growing awareness of historic sites as an aspect of community memory and identity in contrast to the homogenizing pressures of the global economy and corporate culture. (Adam, 2003, and Hardy, 2008.) A more inclusive concept of cultural heritage examines both "tangible" and "intangible" elements. The first category includes objects, buildings, urban environments, and landscapes, while the second embraces perishable cultural products as well as practices, techniques, skills, traditions, and know-how from surviving traditional cultures. Both aspects of culture must be recognized as constituents of the cultural landscapes of our historic places. Living traditional building cultures rightly seek recognition of their ongoing ancient building practices without being constrained by the stark historical distance assumed and enforced by the Venice Charter and the *Secretary's Standards*.

(ICOMOS, 1964, and National Park Service, 1995.) Reflecting the changing perspectives of a more inclusive approach, English Heritage recently published new draft guidelines based on the weighing of "heritage values" rather than merely the treatment of material artifacts, allowing more sensitive responses to often-complex preservation decisions. (English Heritage, 2007.)

The essential insight of these developments in preservation philosophy is that, just as the best way to repair historic structures is with materials and methods closely matching or approximating those used by the original builders, so the best way to ensure a future for valued remnants of the past is to sustain building traditions capable of maintaining them. In many places around the world, traditional building cultures continue to flourish; in many others, such as in Europe and North America, they are recoverable. The focus of preservation activity, then, is properly placed on the process by which the heritage culture defines itself, cares for its old products, and generates new works. New traditional designers, New Urbanists, and historic preservation specialists must have as their common cause a commitment to the sustainability of the traditional building process itself, what Françoise Choay calls "*our competence to build.*" (Choay, 2000, pp. 172–73.) That competence, expressed in the continuously developing historic city, is the true resource that needs our protection. (Fig. 7.2)

Buildings in Context

As all architectural designs involve the insertion of new construction into a preexisting setting, however varied such settings may be, the first task of the architect is to define the boundaries and identify the character of the preexisting context, which may be defined as the scale of the city most relevant to the setting of the proposed building. For example, will a new building be joining an ensemble along a street frontage, or enclosing a square, or terminating a vista? Is the character of that whole suitable or noisome? Does the context exhibit a consistent and valuable character (based on style, scale, materials, and other formal attributes)? Or is it compromised by poor construction, alterations, demolitions, or other negative factors? The preexisting context must be studied to determine its actual and potential formal

7.2. Students at American College of Building Arts, Charleston, studying decorative plaster, 2007.

The recovery of craftsmanship has been led by the restoration industry but is also increasingly supported by new construction in traditional styles. The Charleston school trains artisans in masonry, timber framing, finish carpentry, metalwork, and plasterwork.

properties, assuming remedial action is feasible. Often enough, the preexisting context has been in some way diminished and the architect is challenged to heal it.

Once the character of the context is defined, the architect determines the appropriate response to that context:

• A generally good context is to be improved by reinforcing its strengths and diminishing its weaknesses.

• A consistent and valuable context is to be respected and reinforced.

• An unsuitable context is to be made suitable by the proposed intervention.

• A response that would diminish a positive context is unacceptable.

The architect then evaluates the character of the proposed intervention, asking to what degree the proposed building alters the preexisting context. To the degree that the existing context has a positive, consistent, and valued character, and to the degree that the proposed design would substantially alter that character or introduce nonconforming elements, to that extent the proposed design must bear the *burden of proof* for demonstrating that the benefits to the context—and to the city as a whole—will "outweigh the residual, unavoidable harm that would be done to the significance of the place." (English Heritage, 2007, p. 50.) This location of the burden of proof upon the architect's proposed change is a necessary counterbalance to the temptation of the architect to pursue solutions that might be appropriate in another environment but fail to meet the specific requirements of the historic setting. It specifically proscribes the tendency of the contemporary avant-garde to "subvert the context" as a general strategy when working in historic places.

The conservation ethic for cultural resources is modeled after the defense of natural resources and environmental quality. James Marston Fitch made the analogy between these two fields over two decades ago: "We are beginning to see that the protection of the artistic and historic heritage against the ravages of uncontrolled technology is a fundamental aspect of the curatorial management of the environment as a whole. *The two environments, natural and artificial, are actually complementary halves of the human biosphere.*" (Fitch, 1982, p. 80, emphasis added.) Just as an environmental impact statement assesses the costs and benefits of proposed

TOP

7.3. Washington Square North, New York, circa 1830.

Despite the preponderance of speculative construction, New York boasts numerous ensembles of exemplary civic character. At Washington Square North, the continuity of the row as a composite form is more important than the individual structures.

BOTTOM

7.4. Astor Tower Hotel, Chicago, by Bertrand Goldberg Associates, 1962.

Unlike nearby Art Deco–style apartment buildings, this tower consciously violates every principle of traditional architecture and urbanism. Raising its high-rise volume on Le Corbusier–style concrete *pilotis*, the building virtually destroys the character of the street.

7.5. Baker Street buildings,
London, by Quinlan &
Francis Terry Architects,
2001–2.

Showing a close rapport
between architecture
and urbanism, these new
buildings graciously join
their Georgian neighbors
and reinforce the scale and
character of the district,
reprising some aspects of
the setting while introducing
stylistic innovations. (See
also fig. C.19.)

interventions in terms of their likely ecological consequences, evaluations of proposed new construction in protected historic contexts must justify interruptions or alterations in the preexisting character in terms of their consequences for the historic city. While the introduction of new uses, forms, styles, and scales of building into preexisting urban contexts is both inevitable and welcome, such changes must be managed to prevent the diminishment of valuable contexts—and thereby the city as a whole—by short-sighted decision-making impelled by immediate interests, current architectural fashions, or perceived short-term economic gain. A historic district is properly seen as analogous to a protected wetland or the habitat of an endangered species: certain kinds of development that might be appropriate elsewhere are properly prohibited within its boundaries in order to preserve the character and life of the district. While change over time is inevitable, not all change is good, and it

is up to the curatorial guardians of the environment to manage change. (Figs. 7.3 and 7.4)

It is the task of preservationists and historians to identify those sites deserving of special protection and stipulate their character-defining elements; it is the obligation of architects and urbanists to participate in this process of identification and protection, and to direct their design work toward sustaining these aesthetic achievements that support the character of the city, securing them for the future. Finally, it is the responsibility of preservation commissions and architectural review boards to be the curators and guardians of the architectural and urbanistic heritage of the city, protecting it from outright demolition, but also from more insidious loss from gradual erosion as a result of inappropriate alterations and interventions. The Charleston Charter, a statement by a gathering of lead architects and urbanists in Charleston in March 2005, included the following call for revisions to current policies.

"New construction in historic settings, including alterations and additions to existing buildings, should not arbitrarily impose contrasting materials, scales, or design vocabularies, but clarify and extend the character of the place, *seeking always continuity and wholeness in the built environment*." (Charleston Charter, emphasis added.) (Fig. 7.5)

Significance and Treatments

If the character and significance of a historic setting is what we seek to preserve, a range of options is open to us, from placing a historical marker or plaque on the site of a demolished building to detailed restoration or reconstruction of a structure and its interiors as they are documented to have appeared at some time in the past, with many intermediate possibilities between these two poles. The choice of an option along that spectrum can only be made with confidence once we have clearly defined and agreed on a site's *significance*, which is to say, what we value in that site and want to take with us into the future. Significance can be evaluated with respect to four types:

• Evidential: the building or site is valued primarily for the information it reveals about conditions in the past—for example, at archeological sites or especially well-preserved museum environments.

• Historical: the building or site is valued primarily as the location of historical events or as the residence or workplace of a historic personage.

• Aesthetic: the building or site is valued primarily as a work of art and design, or as good urban fabric, and is therefore considered exemplary.

• Communal: the building or site is valued primarily for its association with symbolic, religious, national, or other social values and ideas. (English Heritage, 2007.)

There is no single formula for preservation treatments that will fit all these types of significance. Rather, we need to choose in each individual case the set of criteria most appropriate to apply, based on the nature of the setting, recognizing why the site has been designated, keeping in mind that many sites may present more than one type. The sources of significance for most historic sites is not a mystery: In the United States, they are defined for properties on the National Register of Historic Places by the nomination forms and their supporting docu-

mentation; other authorities similarly record the character-defining elements that make a given site worthy of preservation in the first place.

Having ascertained the significance of a site, we can then evaluate the preservation treatments available to us in light of that significance. The terms and definitions below are essentially those of James Marston Fitch, although I have edited them slightly to maintain a more style-neutral approach.

• Preservation is "the maintenance of the artifact in the same physical condition as when it was received by the curatorial agency. Nothing is added or subtracted from the aesthetic corpus of the artifact."

• Conservation and consolidation are the "physical intervention in the actual fabric of the building to ensure its continued structural integrity."

• Restoration includes "returning the artifact to the physical condition in which it would have been at some previous stage of its morphological development."

• Reconstitution involves "piece-by-piece reassembly, either in situ or on a new site."

• Adaptive use concerns "adapting old buildings to the requirements of new tenants."

• Reconstruction is "the re-creation of vanished buildings on their original sites."

• Replication entails "the construction of an exact copy of a still-standing building on a site removed from the prototype . . . (such that) the replica coexists with the original." (Fitch, 1982, pp. 46–47.)

All of these treatment types are legitimate instruments in the tool kit of the preservationist; at the same time, they differ in the kinds of knowledge and skill required, the probable costs associated with them, their physical impact on the site, their longevity, and their likelihood of generating debate or controversy. No a priori assumptions or rules can be given for the selection and execution of the appropriate treatment. While each of the approaches listed above will be appropriate in some instances and not in others, we are wise to avoid proscribing any of them solely on theoretical grounds. For instance, the categorical prohibition of reconstruction written into the Venice Charter would deprive us of an essential tool for the sustainability of cultural heritage. We must also recognize that there is no such thing as a "no-effect" option; all treatments impact the resource, including the decision to do nothing at all. (Fig. 7.6)

We must clearly define what it is we value

7.6. Basilica of San Lorenzo fuori le Mura, Rome, thirteenth century, reconstructed after 1945 by Alberto Terenzio.

The meticulous postwar reconstruction of San Lorenzo fuori le Mura, or that of San Giorgio in Velabro after a bombing in 1991, illustrate the compelling need to sustain the form of some monuments, even if much new material is inroduced and despite the prohibitions of charters and standards.

in the site and want the public to understand about it after the work we propose to undertake has been completed. While no one would likely approve of an addition or undocumented alteration to Mount Vernon or Monticello today, these and similar sites are themselves the resultants of repeated additions and alterations by their owner-designers, and changes made by subsequent owners have quite properly been removed. Thousands of more modest structures are significant simply because they have grown, changed, and developed over time, and this must be recognized in deciding their proper treatment, although there is no reason to assume that they should not continue to change and grow in accordance with the typological and stylistic patterns that have informed their development so far. (See fig. 5.14.)

On the whole, I believe preservationists are well advised whenever possible to respect the familiar principle enunciated in 1839 by the French archeologist A. N. Didron: "*It is better to preserve than to repair, better to repair than to restore, better to restore than to reconstruct.*" (Quoted in Brand, 1994, p. 94, and Jokilehto, 1999, p. 138.) The maintenance of original or historic fabric when possible is the *sine qua non* for any conscientious program of restoration

and, naturally, should be maximized in rehabilitations and adaptive use projects as well. While the retention of aged fabric is not the only value to be considered, in the absence of compelling reasons to do otherwise it is best to observe the Didron principle out of respect for the resource in the fullness of its significance. At the same time, we should not interpret Didron's precept as *precluding* restoration or reconstruction, especially when the significance of the resource is closely tied to a particular stage of its morphological development.

Such careful navigation among important but possibly irreconcilable values involves a synthesis of the philosophical positions of both Viollet-le-Duc and Ruskin, in which the artistic impulse toward wholeness and completion is tempered by respect for the historic fabric that we have inherited. At the same time, our regard for authentic materials should not prevent our weaving of the surviving old into the promising new work. Nuanced judgment of this kind requires a degree of tact and respect that no standard, charter, or guideline alone can supply. The process for resolving these decisions will, naturally, vary depending on the social and political apparatus in place in particular settings.

It is in this context that we should judge the achievement of many past restoration efforts that have struck the kind of balance among sometimes irreconcilable values urged here. In particular, the Italian School of restoration, including Gustavo Giovannoni, his colleagues and students, deserves special mention for its commitment to balance among values and its embrace of an urbanistic rather than an exclusively artifact-based approach to preservation problems. The restorations and reconstructions of bombed monuments after the Second World War in Italy, like the rebuilding of the historic centers of Warsaw and Dresden, are models of scholarship and good judgment, as well as acts of courage in the defense of culture. (See figs. 5.13 and 7.9.) Not to be forgotten are the civic authorities and untold thousands of anonymous property owners in historic centers worldwide who have transformed abandoned or decayed buildings and neighborhoods into flourishing communities, rehabilitating old structures and managing their growth and change with tact and loving care. These acts demonstrate genuine citizenship and an investment in permanence in defiance of a contemporary building culture dedicated to novelty, ephemerality, and waste. (Fig. 7.7)

Reversibility

If every intervention in a preexisting context is like entering a conversation already in progress, we must recognize that even the most attentive listener may still misunderstand what others have to say. The principle of reversibility is a safety net for historic sites in the event our view of them and the future we create for them turns out to be mistaken or incomplete. Buildings may indeed outlast our knowledge or feelings about them, and advances in research may bring to light new understandings not accessible to us at present. Will the preservation decisions we make today still make sense a generation or more from now? Reversibility means that whatever we do, conservators in the future with a different interpretation, with different documentation, or with different materials and techniques might be able to recover the fabric that we inherited and treat it differently. We can hope that they will show the same consideration to our work that we have tried to show to that of our predecessors. Above all, the concept of reversibility is a reminder that

modesty, not audacity, is the great virtue of the preservation architect.

Naturally, reversibility has practical limits. "It is unreasonable," the English Heritage guidelines state, to take reversibility "to the point that new work in significant places diminishes their aesthetic values by appearing contrived, awkward, or ugly." Nor should places "be rendered incapable of a sustainable use because of a reluctance to make modest but irreversible changes." (English Heritage, 2007, p. 40.) Reversibility is not simply a matter of making our interventions temporary; it is more properly a way of thinking about our work, understanding that we will probably not have the last word on any building in our care. We are always only stewards of our cultural heritage; we should not, therefore, preempt the con-

7.7. Urban rehabilitation, Astor Square, New York.

Since the mid–1970s vast swaths of American cities have been the beneficiaries of rehabilitation tax credits, their abandoned industrial or commercial buildings converted to new uses, their formerly deteriorated streets now pulsating with economic life.

7.8. Glass elevator at the Vittorio Emanuele II monument, Rome, 2007.

The "temporary"—hence, theoretically reversible—glass elevator at the rear of the monument appears as a piece of equipment that can be removed at a moment's notice, but this only partly compensates for its unsightly intrusion into the setting.

tributions that our descendants might make in the future by making alternative outcomes impossible. (Fig. 7.8)

Authenticity and Appropriateness

In the wake of historicism the concept of authenticity has value only as a judgment regarding the probity of the intentions that have brought some cultural product into being, irrespective of style or date. A work of architecture may be considered authentic as long as it arises out of a building culture appropriate to its place. Contrary to Brandi, if a building was made to imitate an older building or style—either because the earlier model was thought beautiful or out of a desire to sustain the tradition that produced the earlier work—

it cannot be considered inauthentic as long as there has been no intent to deceive. Curiously, we seem to understand this perfectly well with respect to modernist sites now considered historic, such as Eero Saarinen's Dulles Airport, Skidmore, Owings & Merrill's Lever House, or the United Nations Headquarters. In these cases the building culture that produced the monuments more or less continues in effect, so even the total replacement of the curtain wall of the Lever House in a recent restoration was not seen as a loss of authenticity. (See figs. C.17 and 8.6.) (Fixler, 2006.) Why would we not make similar judgments about other building cultures that remain alive or are recoverable, such as a Georgian Revival building from the 1920s or a new classical building completed this year?

Calling into question the modern idea of authenticity is not to deny the importance of a commitment to accuracy. A restoration or reconstruction is properly esteemed for its fidelity to the available evidence of a no-longer-visible historical condition, but this is not the same as requiring that surviving evidence of the past be presented only as fragmentary and decontextualized. On the contrary, an act of restoration and reconstruction might be partly conjectural and still be legitimate and valuable, so long as it is not inconsistent with what we know of the history of the site or what the site itself reveals to us, the reasoning and procedures of the restorers are properly documented, and as long as the preexisting historic material remains recognizable and recoverable. It is in this more limited sense that we may describe an architectural work as authentic—that is to say, it is true to the facts of its own making and sustains the integrity of the character of its place. Something like this is implied by the guidelines of English Heritage, which describe authenticity as the resultant of attitudes "which most truthfully reflect and embody the heritage values attached" to a place. (English Heritage, 2007, p. 18.)

Perhaps we should worry less about authenticity and instead concern ourselves with appropriateness—with the fitting and the exemplary. In a historic district, for example, the fitting is whatever reinforces the character-defining elements that inspired the designation of the district in the first place; the inappropriate would be whatever diminishes, obscures, or disfigures those character-defining elements. This is not a subjective or personal decision, but one that ordinary people can usually be relied upon to make correctly, without theoretical investigations or lengthy deliberation. Nor is it a judgment of the ultimate aesthetic worth of a particular proposal: an architect might design the most beautiful building in the world but may propose to build it in the wrong place. Even so, the fitting does not preclude interventions intended to alter the character of a setting, as I discuss in Chapter 11, but such oppositional responses must be defended on the basis of their long-term effects on the city rather than on an appeal to current fashion or some other short-term gain.

The exemplary intervention is one that offers itself as a precedent. Every design act should set a good example for imitation by others: *We should only build what we would like to see more of.* Appropriate individual buildings can, indeed, have a powerful effect on an entire building culture, making successful buildings easier to build and more likely to be built. (Davis, 2006, p. 299.) The reverse, of course, is also true, in that bad examples can poison a building culture. Accordingly, the "curatorial management of the built environment" called for by James Marston Fitch involves, at a minimum, promoting the good examples and preventing the bad. The pursuit of this goal requires a further virtue, identified by Vitruvius as that of *authority*—not the authority of power or command, but the authority of knowledge and mastery of a discipline, the trustworthiness that comes from the conspicuous exercise of good judgment informed by a tradition. Preservation commissions and architectural review boards are charged with exercising precisely this kind of authority in the defense of historic character in the built environment. (Vitruvius, 1999, p. 24, and Bess, 2006, p. 8.)

Reconstruction

Of all the various treatments available to the preservation architect, thorough restoration and reconstruction have been the most controversial. Reconstruction and replication have been discouraged by modern preservation authorities because "all attempts to reconstruct the past, no matter what academic and scientific resources are available to the preservationist, necessarily involve subjective hypothesis." (Fitch, 1982, p. 47.) But if our intention is not to reconstruct the past but to construct the present and future, we have no reason to fear "subjective hypothesis." What, after all, is *design* if not "subjective hypothesis"? The extrapolation of a building tradition or a formal language beyond the limits of available documentation is a legitimate exercise in many instances, as long as the "conjecture" is acknowledged and as long as valued historic fabric is not destroyed in the process. In truth, the best way to learn how historic buildings were designed and constructed is to try to build new fabric the same way. For example, we can better understand the construction of the Parthenon if we attempt to cut stone and fit it together as the ancient masons did. (Hardy, 2008, pp. 714–718.)

Reconstructions, whether thoroughly supported by documentation or "conjectural," are an essential mode of sustaining the knowledge base and craft skills required to maintain a building culture. We simply must be candid about the extent to which our work represents some known previous condition in the life history of the building. The principle of reversibility requires that the reconstruction be done in such a way that the remaining historic fabric, if there is any, is identifiable and recoverable. The rebuilt Stoa of Attalos in the Agora in Athens, sponsored by the American School of Archeology in the 1950s and incorporating original fragments, is an excellent example of the didactic use of reconstruction. (See fig. C.16.) Similarly, the reconstruction of the Old and New Towns of Warsaw, of the historic center of Dresden, or, if undertaken, the proposed rebuilding of the Tuilleries Palace or the Berliner Schloss, are acts of curatorship intended to conserve the city as a living entity persisting in time. Such reconstructions—whether of a vanished monument or a modest street—are essentially acts of regeneration rather than of nostalgia, assertions that "the way the building came down to us in history"—that is, its destruction by war or violence—is not what is most important about it. (Fig. 7.9) Acts of reconstruction like these are among the most hopeful things that we can do to recover beauty and significance in the public realm.

As a practical matter, partial reconstruction offers the best way to preserve a ruined building by rendering it whole and giving it the constructive means to defend itself against the ravages of weather, material deterioration, and use. Just as conservation specialists now understand that the best way to consolidate

7.9. The Neumarkt and the Frauenkirche, Dresden, as reconstructed after World War II.

Like the center of Warsaw, historic Dresden is being rebuilt, and the remarkable Frauenkirche once again dominates the Neumarkt.

OPPOSITE

7.10. Two ways of connecting new and old.

A. Murphy Memorial Building, Chicago, by Marshall & Fox, 1923–26.

B. Old Masonic Temple, Washington, D.C., by Adolph Cluss and Joseph von Kammerhueber, 1867–69, with adjacent Gallup Building, Martinez & Johnson Architects, 1999–2002.

Excessive differentiation leads to awkward conjunctions between new and old buildings, such as the use of "glass gaskets." In the past, new buildings abutted their neighbors with respect, preserving the continuity of the street and maintaining the character of the place.

fragments of old building fabric is to insert the same materials and use the same methods as were used in the original construction, so completing missing fabric and providing a proper roof are essential to the long-term conservation of a ruined structure exposed to the elements. The restoration of missing or deteriorated masonry in the monuments of the Athenian Acropolis, for example, is commendable as far as it goes, but only the reconstruction of the roofs will ensure the structure's integrity. (See figs. 1.10 and 12.2.) (Economakis, 1994 and 2006.)

Differentiation and Compatibility

When we turn from the treatment of existing or reconstructed structures to the broader problem of adding new construction in historic settings—either additions to individual buildings or infill construction within historic districts or ensembles of buildings—consensus on basic principles is notably lacking among professional preservationists, architects, and officials. Attitudes toward the design of additions and infill buildings inevitably reflect one's preferences in the architecture of the present

day, and battles over style and language in contemporary design have made debate on this issue increasingly heated. At the center of the debate is the question of the proper balance to be struck between continuity and difference when adding new work to old. Should new elements be obviously distinct from the pre-existing construction or attempt to harmonize with them and so conceal their newness? What harmful consequences, if any, might come from either an excessive distinction or an excessive imitation?

The language of the *Secretary's Standards* calls for a balance between the opposing values of differentiation and compatibility intended to maintain clarity about the construction history of a site without necessarily altering its character. (National Park Service, 1995.) In practice, the "transgressive" attitude toward traditional architecture taken by many contemporary designers inevitably threatens that balance. The recovery of traditional architecture in contemporary practice further complicates matters by presenting the possibility of legitimate new architecture that is in stylistic harmony with the historic setting from the outset, suggesting to some a danger of insufficient differentiation. Ultimately, judgments about appropriate new construction in historic contexts hinge on what priority is given to sustaining the preexisting character of the site (assuming that is valued) as opposed to promoting the interests of contemporary design (however that might be defined at the time). There will be no magic formula for determining the appropriate outcome; rather, a range of approaches will be necessary to address the issues on a case-by-case basis.

In truth, the doctrine of differentiation has often been used as a mask for stylistic bias. The *Secretary's Standards* and the Venice Charter on which they were based assumed that the modernist aesthetic would be normative for contemporary building culture forever and sought to discourage any suggestion that preservation was an antimodernist enterprise. But use of an antithetical style as an instrument of differentiation is insupportable as a general principle. Preservation regulations, including the *Standards*, should not be construed to require that any specific proposal should be accepted or rejected *solely on the basis of style*. Additions or new construction may be in the same style as the historic buildings, provided that the new style emulates the typologies, composition, scale, proportion, ornament, materials, and craftsmanship typical of the setting. Violation of these same attributes for the sake of a questionable theoretical principle is a recipe for the loss of historic character.

A concrete example of overzealous differentiation is the frequent refusal of new modernist buildings to engage physically with their historic neighbors, as if it were somehow improper for new and old buildings to touch at all. At an architectural scale, new and old buildings are frequently joined by "glass gaskets," or transparent glazed connections—an example is featured as "Recommended" in the National Park Service guidelines—to underscore the uncrossable divide between tradition and modernism. A more straightforward joint would perhaps suggest that the new and old are entitled to establish a relationship based on equality and mutual respect. (Fig. 7.10) At an urban scale the isolation of the new and the old produces cities and landscapes divided into two entirely separate and antithetical worlds—historic settings constituting "the past" and the modernist structures besieging them in the name of "the future." The result is the continued erosion of the character of historic places and an increasingly schizophrenic quality in the total built environment.

A

B

7.11. Nantucket Atheneum,
Nantucket, Massachusetts,
circa 1846, with addition
by Ann Beha Associates,
1995.

Greek Revival buildings
were typically expanded
by adding lateral wings.
Here, the new wing (right)
is subtly differentiated
by its simplified detail.
Astonishingly, current policy
would prefer a modernist
addition at the rear of the
building.

The overemphasis on differentiation between new and old construction runs counter to our intuitions about our own bodies. Just as a surgical team performing an organ transplant seeks a donor whose tissue will not be rejected by the body of the patient, so, too, the restorer properly introduces carefully chosen new materials so that the new "tissue" will render the restored work whole. Rather than making evidence of the surgical procedure itself as visible as possible, our attention, like that of the physician, should be directed toward ensuring a healthy and productive life for the resource over the long term. A differentiation of new from old that would preclude or obscure the continuing role of the resource in the ongoing life of its setting should, therefore, be resisted.

In general, when additions or new construction are proposed for settings of great value,

they should be designed in such a way that the new construction is distinguishable from the historic fabric by *informed observers or trained professionals* but is otherwise continuous in character with the historic setting. No differentiation should be made that would result in an incongruous or ugly contrast. Where the new construction would not be readily distinguishable by the public at large, interpretive materials should clarify the construction history of the site rather than expecting it to be self-evident from appearance alone. As the guidelines published by English Heritage suggest,

> Adding that which may be valued in the future is vital to sustaining cultural values in the historic environment. Owners and managers of significant places should not be discouraged from adding further layers of potential interest and value,

provided that established heritage values are not compromised in the process. . . . There are no simple rules for achieving quality of design in new work, although a clear and coherent relationship of all the parts of the new work to the whole, as well as to the setting into which it is introduced is essential. (English Heritage, 2007, p. 48.)

Deemphasizing differentiation and privileging compatibility means that historic buildings and districts can grow and change in accordance with their historic patterns, styles, and typologies, thereby assuring a continuity of character through time. For example, Greek Revival temple-form buildings historically grew by the addition of lateral wings separated from the main block by hyphens; this is the appropriate way for such buildings to grow today. (Fig. 7.11) The English Heritage guidelines express this as follows:

> New work should aspire to a quality of design and execution related to its setting, which may be valued both now and in the future. This neither implies nor precludes working in traditional or new ways, but demands respect for the significance of a place in its setting. (English Heritage, 2007, p. 18.)

Compatibility is not solely a question of architectural style. As we can see in the great historic urban ensembles examined in Chapter 2, the best way to make buildings from different eras and styles compatible is for them to share the same generative principles so that they sustain a decorous conversation about space, structure, elements, composition, proportion, ornament, and character. If these principles are shared by the buildings along a street or around a square, they will be compatible, regardless of size or style. If the principles of some of the build-

ings are antithetical, no alignment of cornices or adjustments of massing will be sufficient to maintain a relationship of civility between them. What we want is balance between differentiation and compatibility: enough of the former to allow the historic fabric to be identified by interested observers but enough of the latter to prevent the historic portion of the building from suffering the decontextualization that inevitably follows when it is treated as an objet trouvé in an otherwise alien setting.

Applying such broad guidelines as these in specific cases, however, raises many challenging questions. The just balance between differentiation and compatibility will, in fact, vary from case to case, and so the architect-preservationist must approach each project with a range of options rather than a single rule. Putting aside questions of particular style or language, we can define a set of four possible attitudes toward the relationship of new and old, ranging from maximum compatibility to maximum differentiation, with two intermediate positions that favor one or the other:

1. Literal Replication
2. Invention Within a Style
3. Abstract Reference
4. Intentional Opposition

These four options define a range of treatments, and each lends itself to some kinds of significance and some existing conditions better than others. None of the four can be considered normative, nor can any be considered a falsification: Together, they are instruments in the toolbox of the preservation officials and architects charged with the proper care of the historic built environment, and they must be used wisely, like any set of tools. The four strategies are examined in more detail in the following chapters.

8.1. Piazza Ss. Annunziata,
Florence. Ospedale degli
Innocenti, by Filippo
Brunelleschi, 1419–24.

The replication of one
architect's work by another
is often the key to creating
an urban ensemble
with unified character.
Brunelleschi's façade
became the model for
matching facades added
to two other sides of the
piazza by later architects.

CHAPTER 8

Literal Replication

Each of the four strategies strikes a different balance between the values of differentiation and compatibility. The strategy of Literal Replication prioritizes the latter and minimizes the former. This is the strategy of the "seamless addition" that seeks to expand a preexisting structure or ensemble by directly reproducing or closely imitating the original form, material, and detail. If the designer has mastered the language of the architecture to be replicated, and adequate means to replicate the materials and craftsmanship of the original fabric are available, this strategy has often been successful in sustaining the character of existing settings, as long as the scale of the replication is modest relative to the overall composition of the building or ensemble. There is a limit to how much more of the same thing one can add to an existing context without creating monotonous or—at an extreme—preposterous results.

Despite the frequently expressed disapproval of this strategy by contemporary preservation theorists and officials, it has the sanction of history. Architects have often chosen to add to existing buildings by reproducing some previous architect's work, sometimes even centuries afterward, usually for the sake of a compositional goal, such as completing an intended

but unrealized symmetry or maintaining a pattern already strongly established. This strategy has often been used to complete the building façades that form the walls of a public space, whether as part of an original conception for the whole ensemble or as a result of unforeseen sympathetic additions by later builders. For example, Filippo Brunelleschi's Ospedale degli Innocenti—considered the first realized design of the Italian Renaissance—was constructed on the southeast side of the Piazza Santissima Annunziata between 1419 and 1424. The façade, with its elegant arcade and Della Robbia medallions, was a marked departure from its medieval neighbors, although Brunelleschi's design draws from significant local precedents. (Fig. 8.1) Only the middle nine arches of the arcade are original, however. Over the following two centuries, the disparate buildings around the square were successively unified by the addition of similar arcades. Antonio da Sangallo the Elder cleared and enlarged the square and built the Loggia of the Confraternità dei Servi di Maria between 1516 and 1525, placing a matching arcade directly opposite that of Brunelleschi. (Fig. 8.2A) Between 1601 and 1607, a similar arcade was extended across the front of the preexisting church of Santissima Annunziata. (Fig. 8.2B) As a result, the piazza

A

8.2. Piazza Ss. Annunziata,
Florence.

A. Loggia of the
Confraternità dei Servi
di Maria, by Antonio
da Sangallo the Elder,
1516–25.

B. Church of Santissima
Annunziata, fifteenth century,
with loggia added 1601–7.

C. Plan drawing, from A.
Grandjean de Montigny
and A. Famin, *Architecture
Tuscane*, 1815.

Over the course of two
centuries, three sides of
the piazza received a
uniform treatment based on
Brunelleschi's Ospedale (right
in plan). The subsequent
designers believed the
character of the ensemble
more important than the
individual building or
architect.

(or at least three sides of it) appears to be an integrated design by a single hand. (Fig. 8.2C)

The length of time usually required to complete major buildings, coupled with the shorter life expectancies of previous centuries, meant that important monuments were often not completed by the architect who first designed them. These conditions led to what we might call "delayed completions." Several of the works of Michelangelo were completed by others, sometimes centuries later. (See fig. 11.3.) Of his design for the Piazza del Campidoglio in Rome—proposed in 1537—the Palazzo dei Conservatori was completed by Giacomo della Porta in 1564, the Palazzo Senatorio in 1592, and the Palazzo del Museo Capitolino around 1650. The remarkable paving pattern around the statue of Marcus Aurelius was installed for the first time in 1940. That the square we see today is still considered the work of Michelangelo testifies to the fidelity of his successors

to the master's original vision across the centuries.

These examples demonstrate what Edmond Bacon called the "The Principle of the Second Man": Coherent urban ensembles often depend on subsequent architects subordinating their own design agendas to fulfill the potential suggested by an earlier architect's efforts, extending the original pattern through replication and sometimes in ways unforeseen by the earlier designer. (Bacon, 1967, pp. 108–9.) Bacon was simply updating Alberti's call for architects to complete faithfully what another had begun well. (Alberti, 1988, pp. 318–19.) We owe to the operation of this process much of the beauty we find in the great urban sequences of European and American cities, both monumental and modest, amply justifying our continued use of the practice today despite the resistance of some preservation officials who see such imitation as "false history."

The Louvre, Paris

The monumental complex of the Louvre, constituting both a building and a series of urban spaces, illustrates three of the four strategies for adding new architecture to old in a single built example. In 1515, François I returned to Paris from Italy determined to plant the Italian Renaissance in France. In 1546, Pierre Lescot designed for him the southern half of the present west façade on the Cour Carré. After François's death Henri II completed Lescot's façade with its richly carved ornament and statuary by Jean Goujon. The nine bays are punctuated by three projecting pavilions with segmental pediments, and the two main stories are regulated by tiers of Corinthian columns and pilasters, the whole topped by an attic story—the first completely formal and regular classical façade in French architecture. (See fig. C.22.)

In the following century, Louis XIII commissioned Jacques Lemercier to complete the west side of the Cour begun by François I. At the center, immediately north of Lescot's façade, Lemercier added a new projecting pavilion, the Pavillon de l'Horloge. The elevation of this towerlike pavilion continues the horizontal bay articulation and classical orders of Lescot's design but amplifies them, culminating in tall arched windows framed by pairs of monumental caryatids and topped with a *dôme française*, the precursor of the familiar mansard roof.

B

North of the center pavilion Lemercier faithfully replicated Lescot's façade to complete the symmetrical composition on the Cour. The earlier façade is repeated in all its details and embellished with new sculptures closely imitating those on the original wing. Note also that the tripartite divisions of Lescot's façade are reprised at a larger scale by Lemercier, who rendered the entire elevation on the Cour as an overarching three-part façade composed of the new central pavilion flanked by the earlier and later "twins." This nesting of scale levels elevates what might have been a monotonous range of similar bays into a rhythmic composition. Content to imitate the design of his predecessor a century before, Lemercier made a grander design out of the fragmentary condition he inherited and set the tone for still grander works to follow.

There may yet be further forays into the field of Literal Replication at the Louvre—to

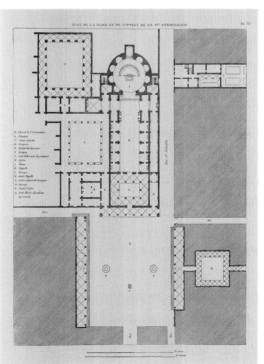

C

8.3. Carson Pirie Scott Store, Chicago, by Louis Sulllivan, 1899–1903, with additions by Daniel Burnham & Company, 1906, and Holabird & Root, 1960.

A. Detail of ornament.

B. Expanded elevation on State Street.

Despite being regarded as proto-modernist, Sullivan's traditional compositions are rooted in classical, Celtic, and Islamic sources. His masterwork was expanded once by Sullivan himself and twice by other architects, each time precisely replicating the original details.

A

address its future expansion needs and the vast increase in visitation since the opening of the Grand Louvre in 1989, the museum is studying proposals to reconstruct the Tuilleries Palace destroyed in 1871. (See Chapter 11.) If the plan proceeds, it will mark a resumption of the interrupted tradition of continuity in Parisian architecture and urbanism.

Carson Pirie Scott Store, Chicago

The Literal Replication strategy may also be employed for the simple purpose of extending an existing building by adding more of whatever repeatable units the original design presents. As architectural design became increasingly rationalized in response to the industrialization of building materials and methods in the final decades of the nineteenth century, the nested composite forms of classical composition were gradually supplanted by the iteration of repeated units, especially for commercial building types like the department store and the tall office building.

Louis Sullivan's pioneering essays in these types represent the encounter between a highly developed ornamental sense rooted in traditional composition and motifs and the regularity imposed by engineering efficiency and the standardized floor space needed by the new commercial buildings. Sullivan's combination of mystical ornamentalism and constructive rationalism produced splendid buildings but was widely misunderstood by historians eager to identify him as a precursor of the Modern Movement. With closer study we can see that Sullivan's ornament was consistently based on traditional motifs—albeit drawn from a wide variety of sources, including Arabic, Persian, and Celtic—and the nuanced regularity with which he expressed the structural frame in the middle floors of his buildings is still far from the industrial imagery of the Modern Movement figures with whom Sullivan is often associated in the standard histories. Sullivan's rationalism and ornamentalism are entirely consistent with his École des Beaux-Arts training, which, despite his fervently antiacademic rhetoric, continued to inform his work throughout his career. Like many of his contemporaries, Sullivan was an artist for whom memory and invention were equal and essential partners; like all traditional architects, his individual buildings reveal the same dialogue between new and old

B

architecture that also distinguishes urban settings built up over long periods of time. (Sullivan, 1924.) (Fig. 8.3A)

This same quality is given a curiously literal form in Sullivan's masterpiece, the Carson Pirie Scott store. This building in fact comprises several separate structures, and despite usually being credited to Sullivan alone, the primary street elevation is the work of three different firms over the course of six decades. Sullivan's initial building, three bays wide and nine stories high, was built along Madison Street in 1899 for the Schlesinger & Mayer Company. In 1903 he added the main portion of twelve stories, including the round corner tower—apparently modeled after similar corner entrance towers at the Parisian department store Le Bon Marché, completed shortly before—and the eight bays extending south along State Street. The store was sold to Carson Pirie Scott & Company, which added the next five bays to the south in 1906. For this, the store engaged Daniel Burnham & Company, which made a literal replication of Sullivan's exterior treatment. Finally, the southernmost three bays were added as late as 1961 by Holabird & Root, similarly replicating the previous designs although only

eight floors high. The later replications are so faithfully done that the joints between the four sections are almost imperceptible, and the fact that half the building we see today was not personally designed by Sullivan is rarely mentioned in the literature. (Fig. 8.3B)

The question of authenticity in Literal Replication is, naturally, of great importance to preservation theory, but the issue becomes more complicated when we cross the boundary from handicraft to industrially produced works. The carving of new stones to resemble old ones in Florence or Paris involves the subordination of the artist to the model being repeated, the chisel following lines determined by a previous artisan or designer. Sullivan's building, with its uniform grid of piers and spandrels, its cast ornament, and its standardized "Chicago windows," is a product of industrial systems and components. By its nature, industrial production lends itself to the use of interchangeable parts and their extrapolation through mechanical repetition. The architects who followed Sullivan had only to extend the bays of the structural frame and cast new units of its ornamental drapery from the original molds or from casts made at the building site.

Where, then, does authenticity lie in the case of industrialized building systems, where there is no "hand of the craftsman" and replication may be extended at will? Strictly speaking, every piece of cast ornament on the building is a copy. How, then, does the date on which any particular casting was struck bear on the quality of the form or our perception of it? If it does not, does the phased expansion of Sullivan's building constitute a "true" or a "false" historical development? Could the Carson Pirie Scott store's expansion have continued indefinitely? Fortunately, it stopped short of the Mentor Building of 1906 by Howard Van Doren Shaw on the corner of Monroe Street, another example of expressive rationalism clad in industrially produced glazed terra-cotta. In 2007, Carson Pirie Scott & Company vacated the premises, and the building has been comprehensively restored—requiring additional new casts of missing ornamental elements—to house a variety of retailers on the ground floor and office space on upper floors. The question of the meaning of authenticity with respect to industrial building products is still with us.

The Lambs Club, New York

Judging by the examples reviewed so far, it might seem that the Literal Replication strategy guarantees success if one simply reproduces an architectural condition already identified as masterful. The doubling in 1915 of McKim, Mead & White's 1905 Georgian Revival–style Lambs Club on West 44th Street in New York demonstrates that this is by no means assured. The fine brickwork and stone trim of the addition perfectly replicate the original façade, but the second architect should have known better than to ignore the canon of number: Mirroring the façade of the original building inflated a well-proportioned three-bay Georgian townhouse into an unresolved six-bay minipalazzo with a noticeably weak center. The resulting duality has pragmatic difficulties, too, leaving us with two identical front entrances to the building. (Fig. 8.4)

The differences between the Lambs Club and the Carson Pirie Scott store are worth noting: What was replicated on Sullivan's façade was a modular unit consisting of a single bay, part of an additive system of identical units without an overarching compositional framework. The construction of additional units enlarged the

aggregation without fundamentally changing it. At the Lambs Club, the addition repeated the whole of a classical composition that was already complete in itself. If the former was like adding cars to a train, the latter was like cloning; the first instance is a simple expansion, the second produced a monster.

The Jewish Museum, New York

The previous examples suggest that the Literal Replication strategy works best when what is replicated is a repeatable fragment in an additive arrangement, not an entire composition. Where an entire composition is replicated, it must be separated from the original model by a third distinctive element, like Lemercier's Pavillon de l'Horloge. Perhaps even better are extrapolations rather than simple repetitions of an existing structure. This was the basis for Roche-Dinkeloo's addition to the French Gothic–Revival Felix Warburg mansion at Fifth Avenue and 92nd Street, designed by C. P. H. Gilbert in 1908 and home to The Jewish Museum since 1945. The architects' initial schemes called for a "sliver building" as a distinct—and oppositional—addition to the original mansion, but because both the architects and the museum directors saw the mansion as part of the museum's identity, they agreed to expand it—literally—rather than add a contrasting new element. (Fig. 8.5)

Kevin Roche's addition occupies a former sculpture court, expanding the façade of the mansion northward by two bays. The southernmost of the new bays is recessed slightly to preserve the symmetry of the original elevation on the avenue, but the pleasing overall asymmetry of the new elevation reinforces the primacy of the entrance façade on East 92nd Street. Matching Indiana limestone was used for the new exterior finish, and the original carved ornament was exactly duplicated by use of computer-assisted drafting and manufacturing (CAD/CAM) technology. Some original elements from the north (rear) elevation of the mansion were removed and incorporated into the new façade. The new stonework was tooled and distressed to match the weathered material in the older building, producing a seamless addition and requiring close inspection to identify the joint between the two structures. (Barreneche, 1993.) What is less immediately apparent is that the addition, while reproducing the materials and details of the original building, nonetheless had to be designed and composed—it is not a simple mirroring or pure repetition of the original structure. As a result, the completed building looks as if it were designed from the beginning to be the whole composition we now see rather than being the recipient of a mechanical implant.

Curiously, the precise replication of the Warburg mansion's details was endorsed by the New York City Landmarks Preservation Commission even though doing so flouts the principles of the Venice Charter and the *Secretary's Standards* and contradicts the commission's own decisions in other cases. Indeed, the Roche-Dinkeloo addition suggests a "false sense of historical development" by giving the impression that the Warburg mansion has always looked the way it does now. But despite this departure from established preservation policies, the extension of the building in kind was clearly the right move to preserve the museum's identity and maintain the character of the historic setting. The enlarged building also makes sense urbanistically because it transforms the former private residence into a more substantial presence on Fifth Avenue in

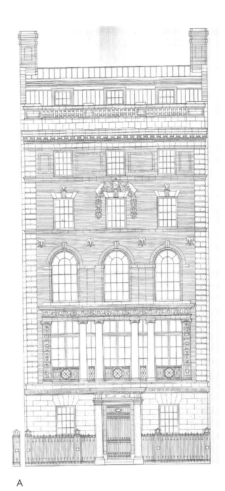

A

8.4. Lambs Club, New York, by McKim, Mead & White, 1906, with addition by George Freeman, 1912.

A. Elevation of original Lambs Club from *A Monograph of the Works of McKim, Mead & White.*

B. Façade as extended.

The doubling of the Lambs Club ignored the canon of number, resulting in an awkward center-occupied façade and two identical entrances. The interiors of the building have now been replaced by a high-rise building on the site in an act of "facadism."

B

A

8.5. Jewish Museum, former Felix Warburg residence, New York, by C. P. H. Gilbert, 1908, with addition by Roche-Dinkeloo Architects, 1993.

A. General view from Fifth Avenue.

B. Detail of joint between new and old.

Both the original Warburg mansion (right) and the adjacent lot were too small for a conspicuously different addition. Wisely, the architect expanded the building horizontally, replicating the mansion's style, materials, and details in the new recessed center bay and northern bay (center and left in B).

B

keeping with the decorum of its present public use as a museum. It is also a point in the addition's favor that it is relatively small and does not make a large impact on either the original building or on the urban setting, as a distinctive or contrasting addition would have. For relatively small incremental additions, this strategy may be the best option.

Nonetheless, some professional preservationists criticized the project for the way it obscures the expanded building's construction chronology, lamenting "the confusion it engendered as to what was truly old architecture and what was imitation." Some critics viewed the project as the product of a society that "doesn't want to know the difference between the imitation and the real." (Byard, 1998, p. 162.) But how was the original Warburg mansion, itself a "copy" of a European model, not also "imitation architecture"? What architecture is not imitative? The achievement of the expanded

8.6. Dulles International Airport Terminal, Chantilly, Virginia, by Eero Saarinen, completed 1962, extended by Skidmore, Owings & Merrill, 1997.

Saarinen's original terminal was doubled in length by adding identical new units at either end (as he had intended), but probably no further expansion is possible without irretrievably compromising the design.

home for The Jewish Museum is not that it fools the public into thinking that the building visible today was built in 1908, but that it proves that a building which reinforces the character of a valued 1908 building can, in fact, be built today, all theories and criticisms to the contrary notwithstanding.

Dulles Airport Terminal, Chantilly, Virginia

Le Corbusier's declaration in *Vers une Architecture* that a house is "a machine for living in," reflects the modernist vision of industrialized buildings assembled from interchangeable parts

intended to be replaced as fatigue or wear take their inevitable toll. (Le Corbusier, 1924, p. 89.) We do not typically see such replacement harming the integrity of the machine. Moreover, the modernist emphasis on the conceptual basis of the work rather than its concrete realization, on its "meaning" rather than "what the building looks like," suggests that the modernist building is less dependent on the pieces of which it is made than a fifteenth-century masonry building might be. For this reason the total replacement of an aluminum-and-glass curtain wall was not thought to diminish the integrity of a modernist landmark like the Lever House in New York. (Fixler, 2006.) (See fig. C.17.) But how, then, is an addition to be made "distinct from the architectural composition" (as the Venice Charter requires) if the composition is itself an additive series and the architect's original intention was that it grow by adding more modules? Are there limits to such expansion or, rather, does even a modular composition have an implied limitation that allows it to be perceived as a whole? To what extent is the original structure or concept "diluted" when a Literal Replication strategy adds more of the units from which the building is made?

Controversy around these very questions was prompted by a proposed addition to the Kimbell Art Museum in Fort Worth by Louis Kahn (1972), a building also composed of repeated structural-spatial units. Romaldo Giurgola's 1989 proposal would have expanded the museum by adding slightly modified versions of Kahn's vaulted concrete modules at either side of the original building. The proposal was withdrawn because it seemed impossible to resolve the inherent ambiguity in Kahn's original design between the modularity of the structural units and the sense of wholeness and completion created by Kahn's balanced composition of them. "Dilution" of the original building concept seemed inevitable as a consequence of the addition. A similar controversy arose in 1991 around a proposed expansion of Kahn's Salk Institute in La Jolla, California (completed in 1967), although in this case the addition was constructed despite protests from the architectural community. (See Byard, 1998, pp. 99–101, and Crosbie, 1993.)

The expansion of the main terminal building at Dulles International Airport near Washington, D.C., raises all of these issues and, as a result, provoked controversy between preservation professionals and transportation officials. The original terminal, designed by Eero Saarinen and completed in 1962, was a 600-foot-long linear structure of identical structural bays defined by a distinctive combination of massive concrete piers and a cable-suspension roof system that together formed perhaps the most impressive large-scale example of architectural expressionism realized in the twentieth century. (Fig. 8.6) It was apparently always Saarinen's intention that the terminal expand in response to increased demand, and so he located his sculptural air-traffic-control tower at the center of the terminal and proposed that the terminal itself grow by adding bays equally to both ends to maintain the symmetry of the overall composition. Over the years, various improvised alterations were made that compromised both visual integrity and efficient use, so that three decades after its construction the airport's increasing traffic made a comprehensive overhaul necessary. In 1997, under the supervision of Skidmore, Owings & Merrill, the terminal building was restored and doubled in length from 600 to 1200 feet, maintaining the symmetry about the air traffic control tower by adding equally to the two ends, in accordance with Saarinen's intentions. (Merkel, 2005, pp. 217–26.)

Like Sullivan's Carson Pirie Scott building, Saarinen's terminal at Dulles could be added to because it was designed to allow addition; his earlier TWA Terminal at John F. Kennedy Airport in New York, another exercise in architectural expressionism, was conceived as a closed form that did not readily accommodate change or addition. That building, no longer gracefully accommodating the needs of contemporary airport functions, has had a different history, including the threat of demolition. The price of Dulles's accommodation to expansion, of course, is the risk of disorientation or monotony in the repetition of similar units. At nearly a quarter-mile long, have the aesthetic or pragmatic limits to further expansion of such a linear system been reached? If further terminal space were required, presumably a new structure would make sense, but even a separate building would still raise the question of how to add to such a historic setting, with or without a continuity of language.

As in the case of the Lambs Club, there remains the risk with the Literal Reproduction strategy that merely repeating a composition will alter our perception of the original piece. On the other hand, the Jewish Museum shows how replication, not of a whole composition but of materiality and detail—and, most importantly, formal language—can allow a valued landmark to expand without dilution or distortion. Whether the building in question is traditional or modernist, the matter is the same. The limit imposed on the Literal Replication strategy is not the risk of deception but, rather, the risk that the scale and character of the original work as conceived by the architect will be diminished or lost.

Kennedy-Warren Apartments, Washington, D.C.

There is no concern about dilution of the original intent in the "delayed completion" subset of the Literal Replication strategy, which proposes to realize an earlier architect's conception long after the fact. Construction of the Kennedy-Warren Apartments in northwest Washington began in 1929 to the designs of Joseph Younger, at a site on fashionable Connecticut Avenue overlooking Rock Creek Park and the National Zoo. Younger's design is in a fully articulated Art Deco style, featuring stylized mechanical and vaguely Aztec motifs. The buff brick exterior is trimmed in Indiana limestone and features decorative spandrel panels in cast aluminum. Younger's concept placed three tall wings around a central courtyard and fountain, providing an elegant entry court at the center of the building. After two of the three wings were completed, the Depression brought a halt to construction and the building remained in truncated form for three-quarters of a century. The incomplete Kennedy-Warren was designated a historic landmark by the District of Columbia in 1989 and added to the National Register in 1994. (Fig. 8.7A)

Completion of Younger's building became a possibility upon the discovery in the late 1980s of a number of the architect's original drawings for the project, including perspective renderings and some construction drawings. Hartman-Cox Architects were engaged to piece together the originally intended design for the parts of the new wing visible from the entry court and Connecticut Avenue. They also created new elevations overlooking the park to conform to the contemporary apartment layouts to be used inside the new wing. The replicated parts of the new wing, completed in 2004, are a reasonably close match to the architect's drawings and the existing wings, with a few minor changes to account for differences in construction methods and standards in the intervening decades. For example, the original brick was no longer available and so the brick used is slightly different in color, and the change from a load-bearing to a curtain-wall construction system required the introduction of control joints in the brick surfaces. Within the constraints of contemporary construction practices, the level of finish and quality of workmanship of the completed project produces a respectful, if belated, completion of Younger's concept, while the differences allow a knowledgeable and close observer of the new wing to detect its more recent completion date. (Fig. 8.7B)

The architects, owner, and local review boards had all agreed that the addition should follow as closely as possible the style, materials, and design of the historic structure, but when the owners applied to the National Park Service for rehabilitation tax credits, the NPS determined that the addition violated the *Secretary's Standards* proscription against creating "a false sense of historical development." The NPS saw the preexisting truncated state of the Kennedy-Warren as a part of its significance—showing "how the building came down to us in history." An appropriate addition, from the NPS viewpoint, would have been one sited so as to be invisible from the public street, or one that, if it must be in plain view, would have departed sufficiently from the original architectural style and materials to differentiate it unambiguously from the historic fabric and avoid any confusion regarding its date of construction—solutions that would have precluded the recovered integrity of Younger's design. (This interpretation was personally explained to me in October 2006 by the chief architect of the NPS at the time of the decision.)

Such an interpretation of the *Standards*, in my view, distorts the original intent of Standard Three's prohibition against a "false sense of historical development." What, after all, would a "true" sense of historical development be, if not the realization of the building according to the original architect's design? Is it not the architect's intent that counts in assessing the site's significance for us, rather than the mere happenstance that the structure was left incomplete? The standard of preserving "how the building came down to us in history" is no standard at all; it is simply an attempt to place a moratorium on change and avoid the necessity of judging which aspects of that history are significant and which are not.

In recent years such "delayed completions" have become more common. In addition to the Kennedy-Warren, the spire of the Roman Catholic cathedral of Dallas, the dome of the state capitol in Oklahoma City, and the cupola of Memorial Hall at Harvard University are highly visible examples. All of these projects completed buildings left unfinished at the time of their construction by following the architect's original designs, and all of them have won awards for preservation. And yet all of them presumably violate the same interpretation of the *Standards* that disqualified the Kennedy-Warren's application for rehabilitation tax credits.

The application of the NPS interpretation historically would have deprived us of the successive completions of the Louvre, the Piazza

A

8.7. Kennedy-Warren Apartments, Washington, D.C., by Joseph Younger, 1929, with added south wing by Hartman-Cox Architects, 2004.

A. Original structure, showing entrance.

B. Addition by Hartman-Cox.

The unbuilt south wing of the building (right in B) was added seventy years after construction was halted by the Depression. The new and old portions are almost indistinguishable. In a bizarre decision, the NPS disapproved because the addition altered perception of "how the building came down to us in history."

Santissima Annunziata, the Piazza del Campidoglio, and countless other valued monuments. It was not the fact of its incompletion that made the Kennedy-Warren building worthy of preservation; rather, it was the importance of its design, its representation of the Art Deco style, its workmanship and decorative arts, and its appositeness as a typological model of urban housing. None of these values is in the least diminished by the completion of the missing wing; on the contrary, we now see as never before the full import of an architectural conception whose quality had already been recognized by virtue of the site's designation as a landmark in the first place.

Many professionals and officials in historic preservation continue to oppose Literal Replication because they believe that new construc-

B

tion must, as the Venice Charter expressed it, "bear a contemporary stamp." A broader view of the resource to be preserved, a more pluralistic view of contemporary design, and more attention to our obligation toward wholeness in architectural and urbanistic compositions would not only permit but encourage Literal Replication when the context and the scale of the proposed construction make it appropri-

ate. From that viewpoint, the "contemporary stamp" might be simply the date of construction carved into one of the stones or noted on a bronze plaque commemorating the work. The standard of "what has come down to us in history" must give way to a larger and more demanding standard—what will contribute to the building of beautiful, sustainable, and just cities.

9.1. Office buildings for the French Senate, Rue Vaugirard, Paris, by Christian Langlois, 1965–74.

A new design in a style already characteristic of the context promotes continuity in a historic setting without replication. Langlois's adaptation of Percier & Fontaine's façades on the Rue de Rivoli appropriately addresses the Palais de Luxembourg opposite.

CHAPTER 9

Invention Within a Style

The second of the four strategies yields a new addition or infill building which, while not replicating the original design elements, nonetheless adds new elements in either the same style or in a closely related one, sustaining a sense of general continuity in architectural language. The intention of the strategy is to achieve a balance between differentiation and compatibility, but weighted in favor of the latter. This, too, is a strategy with a long history. In fact, it is what most architects have always done—discontinuity and deliberate contrast having been more the exception than the rule except during those atypical moments when architectural culture pursued the deliberate cultivation of "difference."

Historically, the second strategy was often followed unselfconsciously as a consequence of working within a tradition or a recognized style. Even for buildings or urban districts whose construction extended over long periods, the development and succession of styles did not always occur so rapidly that builders could not maintain stylistic continuity with their predecessors. The styles themselves provided sufficient latitude to allow varied responses to individual building tasks without sacrificing harmonious relationships with neighboring buildings. When styles did develop or succeed one another during the course of a building's or district's construction, the underlying consonance in formal principles allowed different styles to be harmonized in varied ensembles, as discussed in Chapter 2. While there are examples of stark contrasts between an older building and a new addition—especially during the Renaissance, as I show in Chapter 11—the traditional building cultures of Europe and the Americas have more often promoted a gradual process of change by accretion with few instances of stark and radical contrast. Especially from the early nineteenth century on, when a conscious choice of style could be made in response to a given program or context, architects more often than not selected their styles, materials, and formal languages to maintain a harmonious continuity rather than to introduce a conspicuous contrast. (Fig. 9.1)

The attitudes of nineteenth-century revivalist architects toward their historical sources were varied and complex. In the 1830s, Karl Friedrich Schinkel proposed perhaps the greatest Greek Revival project of all—a vast royal palace in classical style to be built atop the Athenian Acropolis that would have incorporated and restored the ancient ruins of the Propylaea, the Erechtheum, and the Parthenon. The project displays an extraordinary sense of

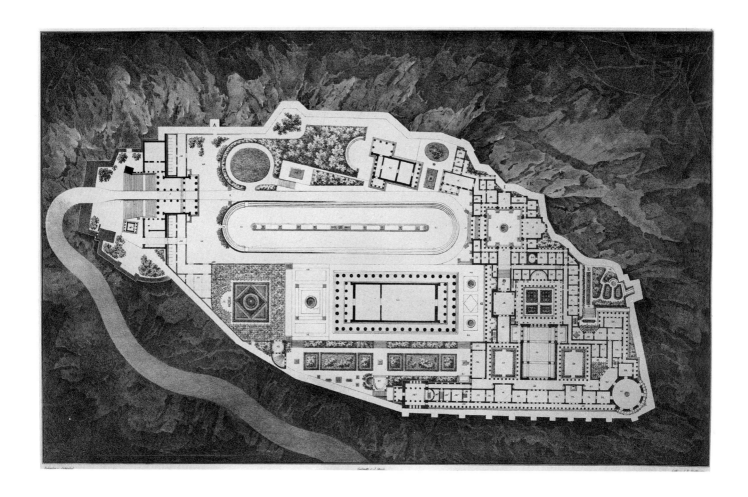

9.2. Site plan, proposed palace on the Acropolis, Athens, Karl Friedrich Schinkel, 1834.

Good judgment sets strict limits to the scale of intervention in places of transcendent importance. Schinkel's project for the Acropolis demonstrates extensive knowledge of Greek architecture but would have overwhelmed the ancient monuments. (See fig. 1.1.)

continuity with antiquity—as well as breath-taking audacity—although many admirers of classical architecture are undoubtedly grateful the project remained unbuilt. (Fig. 9.2) Other essays in continuity, albeit less audacious in their scope, were commonplace throughout the nineteenth century and right up to the time of the Venice Charter.

Santa Maria Novella, Florence, and San Petronio, Bologna

Renaissance architect and author Leon Battista Alberti makes a poignant argument for continuity of style when adding to a preexisting building:

> The brevity of human life and the scale of the work ensure that scarcely any large building is ever completed by the same man as begins it. While we, the innovative architects who follow, strive by all means to make some alteration, and take pride in it, as a result, something begun well by another is perverted and finished incorrectly.

I feel that the original intentions of the author, the product of mature reflection, must be upheld. Those who began the work might have had some motive that escapes you, even though you examine it long and thoroughly, and consider it fairly. (Alberti, 1988, pp. 318–19.)

Alberti followed his own principle in designing the unfinished façade of Santa Maria Novella in Florence, where the medieval stone façade had risen only to the first tier of arcades, leaving most of the elevation in rough masonry. Around 1458, Alberti provided designs for the completion of the façade in a manner calculated to uphold the "original intentions of the author," while at the same time allowing Alberti to make his own unique contribution. (Fig. 9.3)

Under the influence of historicism we tend to exaggerate the difference between medieval and Renaissance architecture; Alberti's work at Santa Maria Novella demonstrates that the border between them was broad and pervious. In the twelfth century the Tuscan proto-Renaissance, represented by the beautiful

Church of San Miniato al Monte overlooking Florence from the south, presents nearly all the materials and motifs that Alberti would use in completing his church three centuries later, not least of which is a geometrical stylization of classical composition rendered in charming patterns of dark green and white marble. Other local antecedents for his design appear in the eleventh-century Baptistery of Florence as well as the fourteenth-century campanile designed by Giotto adjacent to the Duomo. But Alberti does not simply assemble the materials he inherited; he weaves them together with new materials gleaned from his knowledge of Roman antiquity and his reading of Vitruvius. As the new façade rises, the architectural language is subtly and gradually transformed. With precise control of proportional relationships, just regulation of moldings and details, and graceful patterns in green and white marble, the façade moves upward from the Gothic arches of the ground floor through an abstracted classicism in the midsection to arrive at its crowning tetrastyle temple

front and the marvelous volutes that connect the central feature with the flanking volumes of the aisles. Continuity and invention collaborate in this respectful determination to bring to fruition what another has begun well.

A century later, the Renaissance masters Giacomo Barozzi da Vignola, Baldassare Peruzzi, and Giulio Romano, among others, submitted Gothic designs for the unfinished façade of the Basilica of San Petronio in Bologna. The façade of the large medieval church, occupying a commanding location on the city's principal square, had been carried out only to the top of a "ground floor" tier of pink and white marble cladding, including the tympanum of the arch enclosing the center portal housing Jacopo della Quercia's sculptural relief of the Madonna and two saints. The Gothic designs submitted by these classicists of the Renaissance demonstrate the open-mindedness of the architects, despite their convictions about the superiority of the *stile antico*. It is noteworthy that Palladio alone broke the pattern by proposing a fully classical scheme that would have

9.3. Church of Santa Maria Novella, Florence, thirteenth century, with façade completed by Leon Battista Alberti, 1458–78.

Alberti followed his own advice when completing the medieval façade by adding sympathetically to what another builder-architect had begun. The new façade incorporated materials and motifs of the existing lower tier, subtly transforming the style as it rose.

A

9.4. Basilica of San Petronio, Bologna.

A. Existing state.

B. Proposed completion of façade by Giacomo Barozzi da Vignola, 1545.

Vignola, a central figure of the Italian Renaissance, proposed completing the basilica façade in the Gothic style in which it had started, demonstrating that the medieval and Renaissance building cultures were less antagonistic than is usually thought.

B

replaced the existing medieval work entirely. (Faietti and Medica, 2001.) (Fig. 9.4)

Among the lessons we can draw from the cases of Santa Maria Novella and San Petronio are the simultaneous coexistence of different stylistic traditions, the permeability of the boundaries separating different traditions, and the value of remaining open to the promptings that the monument itself can provide, rather than imposing on it a fixed notion of style or meaning. We must acknowledge the legitimacy of working in a tradition, even a tradition not one's own, if we, following Alberti's call, are to be sympathetic and wise curators of our historic urban environments.

The Louvre, Paris

The key to the remarkable continuity of the vast building complex of the Louvre we see today is the commitment of the architects and royal patrons to make it so; once the vision of the classical palace had been introduced by Lescot, all that followed was a set of elaborate and increasingly opulent variations on the themes he introduced. (See fig. C.23.) In the 1560s, Henri II's widow, Catherine de Médicis, ordered construction of a second palace for her own use—the Tuilleries—nearly 1,500 feet (450 meters) west of the Louvre, in what was then the country outside of Paris. Designed by Philibert Delorme, Jean Bullant, and Jacques Androuet du Cerceau, the new palace adapted the architectural language pioneered at the Cour Carré by Lescot. Because of the distance between the two structures, Henri III commissioned a "Grand Design" to link the two palaces with pavilions and galleries, a project that continued under construction for the remainder of the sixteenth century and into the seventeenth. The connection began with

9.5. Grande Galerie du Bord de l'eau, the Louvre, Paris, by Louis Métezeau, 1574–89.

The long façades overlooking the Seine use elements and motifs drawn from Lescot's design for the Cour Carré. The same style was followed when the western half of the wing was rebuilt in the nineteenth century.

9.6. East front, the Louvre,
Paris, by Louis Le Vau,
Claude Perrault, and
Charles Le Brun, 1667–72.

Perrault's great façade
introduces a grander scale
and more monumental
character—essentially a
Baroque sensibility—to
French architecture. At the
same time, it maintains
continuity with the materials,
formal language, and
ornament of the earlier
wings.

Delorme's Petite Galerie and was joined by the Grande Galerie du Bord de l'Eau, a narrow covered passage extending along the Seine to the Tuilleries. To break the monotony of this long façade, the work was split between Louis Métezeau (who was responsible for the eastern half) and Delorme (who designed the western half). The two architects designed different, but coordinated, façades, but only Métezeau's gallery remains today. Its two principal stories, heavily rusticated and lavishly ornamented, are punctuated by paired Doric and Corinthian pilasters, their rhythm reinforced by alternating triangular and segmental pediments. (Fig. 9.5) (See Color fig. C.23.)

Upon moving into the Louvre, Louis XIV ordered his architect, Louis Le Vau, to complete the remaining three sides of the Cour Carré to conform to the Lescot/Lemercier side. The new façades did not reproduce the earlier scheme,

but freely invented within the same style, introducing a variety of different elements and altering the character of the earlier work. Le Vau's north façade continued Lescot's and Lemercier's horizontal lines, but broke them up with a series of projecting pavilions and a central entry bay recalling a Roman triumphal arch. Instead of the tall roofs of the sixteenth century, Le Vau finished the building with a parapet and balustrade. For the south wing facing the Seine, François d'Orbay designed a majestic new façade that introduced to France Michelangelo's colossal order from the Campidoglio and balanced the long horizontal expanse of the façade with a welcome vertical emphasis.

The east wing facing the city caused the most trouble. In 1665, Gian Lorenzo Bernini was invited from Rome and provided two schemes: The first—with a massively undulating façade—was rejected as "too Italian"; the second scheme was accepted and foundations begun, but Bernini left Paris in 1667 and Le Vau was recalled, assisted by Claude Perrault, Charles Le Brun, and d'Orbay. The majestic colonnade of paired Corinthian columns on the façade as built, traditionally attributed to Perrault, sums up all the themes of French classicism. While appropriately deferential to the work that preceded it, Perrault's façade nonetheless introduced a series of new elements that have had an incalculable influence on subsequent architecture, both in France and beyond. (Fig. 9.6)

The Louvre we know today is in large part the creation of the Second Empire, during which Napoléon III completed a vast building program from 1852 to 1870. Louis Visconti's scheme included a full integration of the Louvre and the Tuilleries, uniting them for the first time into a single coordinated complex by means of new wings on the north and south of the Cour Napoléon and the Place du Carrousel. The new façades were consciously modeled after those of the previous centuries but on a grander scale and with even more exuberant ornament. The western portions of the Grande Galerie were rebuilt with broad new entrances for traffic through the Place du Carrousel, but the side facing the Seine consciously imitates the work of Métezeau and Delorme of three centuries earlier.

Hector Lefuel, carrying on after Visconti's death, intensified the ornament and decoration even further in the new wings around the Cour Napoléon, where he adapted Lemercier's design of the Pavillon de L'Horloge—including the tall roofs and *dôme Français*—for his new Pavillons, not forgetting the caryatids. To be sure, the nineteenth-century Louvre lacks the relative intimacy of the old Cour Carré and the majestic repose of the east front, but its grandeur is clearly derived from those earlier models. The Louvre of the Second Empire was a kind of fulfillment of the older Louvre, three hundred years after Lescot. (Fig. 9. 7)

The emperor and his architects had planned to follow their work at the Louvre with a nearly complete reconstruction of the Tuilleries, but this was cut short by the Franco-Prussian War and the Paris Commune. The Tuilleries wing was burned by the communards in 1871, and the blackened ruins of the palace stood for a dozen years while the authorities debated their future. Lefuel's reconstruction schemes were set aside by the Assembly in 1883, the ruins were pulled down, and a public garden was

installed on the site of the former palace. The development of the Louvre finally seemed to be at an end.

Façades of the Cathedrals of Milan, Florence, and Cologne

Countless numbers of tourists visit historic cathedrals throughout Europe and gaze admiringly at the façades which, naturally, they take to be representative of medieval design and artistry, unaware that many of them are only a century or two old. The fronts of the cathedrals at Milan, Florence, and Cologne were left unfinished until the nineteenth century, when they were completed in their original styles according to newly made designs based on close study of the completed portions of the original buildings.

9.7. Façades on the Cour Napoléon, the Louvre, Paris, by Louis Visconti and Hector Lefuel, 1852–70.

The nineteenth-century buildings around the Cour Napoléon are based on Lemercier's work of two centuries before. The composition is richer, the ornament more robust, and the character more exuberant, but essential continuities unify the sprawling complex.

9.8. The United States Capitol,
Washington, D.C., by
William Thornton, 1793,
Benjamin Henry Latrobe,
1804–17, and Charles
Bulfinch, 1818–29, and
expanded by Thomas U.
Walter, 1851–63.

A. The first Capitol, by
William Thornton.

B. Expanded Capitol, by
Thomas U. Walter.

The original Capitol was
radically expanded by
Walter, though its classical
style was no longer
considered "of its time."
Classical additions to the
Capitol continued into the
1960s. Current preservation
policies would not have
permitted this stylistically
consistent expansion of our
greatest national monument.

A

At Milan Cathedral the intricately detailed late Gothic church, so richly articulated in every part with tracery modeled after the cathedrals of France, had only a plain, bare masonry façade. In 1571, Pellegrino Tebaldi proposed an elaborate classical composition in the spirit of Michelangelo's design for St. Peter's, although only the five portals and the windows above them—all surrounded by elaborate Baroque aedicular frames—were carried out to his design. In the mid-seventeenth century, Carlo Buzzi (recalling Peruzzi's and Vignola's schemes for San Petronio) proposed a return to the Gothic, retaining however the Baroque elements already in place. Additional schemes over the next century oscillated between these styles until the façade was finally realized after 1806 according to the late-eighteenth-century designs of Leopoldo Pollack and his successors Giuseppe Zanoia and Carlo Amati. The executed scheme also retained the Baroque elements and wove around them a texture of Gothic tracery continuing the material and detail of the original side elevations and bringing them to an appropriate culmination. An important example of a large-scale completion in the original style and following the sprit of Alberti's work at Santa Maria Novella, the Duomo of Milan also demonstrates once again the affinities of the two great styles which are here felicitously combined. (See fig. 3.3.)

Similarly, nineteenth-century façades were added to the Duomo of Florence and the Cathedral of Cologne—the latter project by Schinkel, who excelled at both classical and Gothic design. (See fig. C.24.) These completed façades are so convincing as culminations of their respective churches that only those trained in architectural history (or reading the fine print in their travel guides) are aware that they are not viewing medieval work. The success with which the architects achieved their goals would have been inconceivable without—in addition to native talent as designers—a profound sympathy for the styles they employed. While the eclectic revivals that occupied the architects of the nineteenth century still suffer from critical disrepute, it was precisely their conscious study and revival of Greek, Gothic, Romanesque, and Renaissance styles that allowed them to exercise the informed judgment and skillful design that produced the cathedral façades— and much else besides. At the same time, it must be acknowledged that a conscious identification of the contemporary architect with the tradition of the historic monument in his care poses problems of its own, as we saw in the clumsy restorations of English cathedrals that so aroused Ruskin. In truth, restoration and completion *in stile* present complicated problems requiring the highest degree of knowledge, judgment, and tact. On the other hand, the opposite stance—a distanced and "scientific" preservation approach—presents other, equally difficult problems, not least of which

B

is the inability or unwillingness of the architect to complete fragmentary or unrealized designs in accordance with their original intentions.

The United States Capitol

Like the complex of the Louvre, the construction of the most imposing national monument in the United States was prolonged and its present form unforeseen by its original designers; yet the Capitol today is visibly the natural outgrowth of its initial form. In addition to the quality of the architecture, its painted and sculpted decoration, and its employment of advanced building technology, the Capitol is a superb illustration of how buildings can absorb massive growth over extended periods of time while maintaining the styles and character that sustain their identity.

The Capitol achieved its essential character from the start. The country's founders—especially George Washington—were immediately drawn to the 1796 competition-winning scheme of William Thornton, which imaginatively adapted models from Roman antiquity for the various parts of the building. The growth of the building over the following centuries has maintained this formal, visual, and typological linkage between ancient and modern sources. (Westfall and Van Pelt, 1991, pp. 155–60.) The precise contributions of the successive architects who guided the building's

early development are not easily identifiable; successive additions were closely coordinated and subordinated to an overall architectural conception. Henry Hope Reed sorts it out as follows:

> To William Thornton belong the entrance portico (without steps), the two wings set off by pilasters, and the plan of the Great Rotunda. Latrobe has the credit for the two legislative chambers, the Supreme Court Chamber with its vestibule, the small rotundas, the enlarged portico with its steps and cheek-blocks, and the initial design for the Great Rotunda—changes that made for a more imposing building. Bulfinch did the final design of the Great Rotunda, which is there today, and the Crypt as well as the West Front and the first dome. Altogether the result was a handsome, if modest, structure worthy of a young nation. (Reed, 2005, p. 12.)

Thomas Ustick Walter was chosen as architect for the Capitol's greatest expansion in 1851. The first plan was to expand the building with new wings to the north and south to accommodate enlarged House and Senate chambers, without changing Bulfinch's low dome. Walter convinced his clients that such major additions required a proportionally larger new centerpiece to hold the composition together. First proposed in 1851, the new dome was finally "topped off" in 1863. (Fig. 9.8)

The expanded Capitol defies the historicist chronology of neatly defined periods and styles,

9.9. Reichstag, Berlin, by Paul Wallot, 1882–94, with new dome by Foster & Partners, 1992–99.

Foster's glass dome has been praised as differentiating the new German parliament from its prewar predecessor, while offering a degree of continuity. The partial restoration of the building reflects continuing ambivalence about the site and its painful history.

expressing the universality of the classical tradition at a time when most American architects were committed to the Gothic Revival and eclectic styles. Upon its completion in 1863, a contemporary critic might have thought the Capitol failed to express "the architecture of our time." Not only was the great dome stylistically anachronistic, but this resounding symbol of Union and Freedom rose just as the nation descended into the Civil War. From our viewpoint today this "out of time" quality is one of the greatest strengths of the Capitol's design, providing us with a telling illustration of the persistence of classical forms across time, independent of the fluctuations of politics and culture. From Thornton's original design to the completion of the Rayburn Room in the 1960s—a span of 170 years—the expanding building remained remarkably unified and its essential style unchanged.

The Capitol is the paramount American example of how to make additions that reinforce rather than diminish a great architectural work by maintaining stylistic continuity over time. The contributions of the architects who followed Thornton were differentiated by the

varying sensibilities of the designers but made compatible by their fidelity to a common architectural language. Walter's additions more than doubled the size of the building, and his dome transformed the Capitol into a monument capable of dominating the city around it, as it still does. This audacity and scale would undoubtedly render his project unacceptable under most current preservation policies. Imagine for a moment that Walter's Capitol dome had to be replaced today under the rubrics of the *Secretary's Standards* and the watchful eye of preservation authorities: Perhaps the result would resemble Norman Foster's scheme for the Berlin Reichstag—a contrasting steel-and-glass shape protruding from the preexisting form. However appropriate this approach might have been for the seat of the newly reunited German government (and the point is arguable), such radical noncontinuity would be utterly inappropriate for the seat and symbol of American government for a host of symbolic as well as architectural reasons. (Fig. 9.9) While working in the same style as the preexisting historic setting does not guarantee appropriate design, Walter could not have succeeded as well as he did without maintaining a continuity of formal language. Our preservation architects and policy-makers today would be well advised to study this example and model their evaluative criteria upon this, our nation's preeminent historical monument.

St. Bartholomew's Church, New York

Bertram Grosvenor Goodhue's design for St. Bartholomew's Church on Park Avenue in New York epitomizes the search for continuity between distinct though closely related styles. The original building of 1872, designed by James Renwick in a Pisan-Lombardic Romanesque style, was located on Madison Avenue and 44th Street. In 1903, Stanford White added new entrance portals for the church in a scholarly adaptation of the twelfth-century abbey church of St.-Gilles in southern France, a change in style that did not obscure the character of Renwick's church. When the congregation decided to relocate farther uptown a decade after White's death, they asked Goodhue to design a new building incorporating White's entrance. Goodhue's 1918 church—with its reminiscences of Romanesque, Venetian, and Byzantine styles—is both an imaginative evocation of its historical and stylistic sources and a rationally assembled composition of carefully articulated elements. (See fig. C.25.)

Goodhue incorporated White's former entrance into an independent limestone block housing the narthex, standing free of the taller mass of the new church behind it. He then used a subtle polychromy of salmon-colored brick and buff limestone to tie together the two architects' works while at the same time distinguishing them. The limestone of White's portal is woven into the texture of the brick walls in apparently random patterns, but on closer inspection we see that the pattern results in a literal "weaving" of disparate threads into a tapestry uniting and harmonizing the constituent parts without in any way diminishing them.

Following Goodhue's death, his successor firm, Mayers, Murray & Phillip, added the Community House south of the church in 1927. In 1931, Cross & Cross completed the fifty-one-story RCA Victor (now General Electric) office tower, which rises in graceful stages directly behind the dome of Goodhue's church like a magnified campanile. What might have

been a shocking juxtaposition in scale instead seems a natural completion of the block. The tower uses the same salmon brick as the church and has an ornamental richness that Goodhue himself might have displayed had he lived into the era of Art Deco. The brick and terra-cotta tracery in its crown suggests not only flamboyant French Gothic, but electricity and radio waves—an appropriate nod to the building's original sponsor. In contrast to the designs of Marcel Breuer and Norman Foster mentioned earlier, the RCA tower shows that a skyscraper need not be a destructive addition to a low-rise historic setting, but can be an instrument of urban continuity. (See figs. 1.4 and C.4.) A mid-rise 1970s office building behind the Community House, though not distinguished, continued the pattern of deference and used the same brick.

The parish did not follow this pattern when it proposed in 1984 to construct a massive office building on the site of the Community House. Peter Capone of Edward Durrell Stone Associates proposed a fifty-nine-story glass tower partially cantilevered above the church. The design was, if anything, even more of an "aesthetic joke" than Marcel Breuer's scheme for Grand Central Terminal. The proposal was rejected by the Landmarks Preservation Commission, as was a second scheme a year later. The parish then sued, claiming the landmarks law imposed intolerable burdens on religious institutions and violated religious freedom, but the courts decided in favor of the city, further strengthening the legal foundation of preservation laws.

ICP Social Housing Developments and the Work of Armando Brasini, Rome

As one might expect, robust traditional architecture and urbanism flourished in Rome in the years prior to the rise of the Fascist dictatorship in 1922, most notably in the exemplary social housing projects of the Instituto per Case Popolari (Institute for Social Housing, or ICP) sponsored by the pre-Fascist liberal government. While all of the ICP projects were constructed outside the center of Rome, where land prices allowed for affordable development, they nonetheless represent the strategy of Invention Within a Style with respect to the wider context of the city as a whole and offer essential lessons in how this strategy can

9.10. Housing project for the Istituto per Case Popolari at San Saba, Rome, by Quadrio Pirani, 1921–23, corner detail.

The housing projects of the 1920s in Rome are models of invention within the styles characteristic of the historic city. The complexes incorporated progressive social amenities and were so well built that eighty years later they have not needed restoration.

OPPOSITE

9.11. INA Building, Rome, by Armando Brasini, 1928–34.

Brasini brought to the classical language a fantasy and invention that nonetheless respected the underlying grammar. This project for a complex urban site displays skillful manipulation of mass and scale in response to views from varying distances.

be used at an urban scale for social housing in and near historic centers. Projects at San Saba, Testaccio, Città Giardino Aniene, and Garbatella, to name only a few, were designed by such masters of the Roman "barochetto" (an early-twentieth-century urban vernacular of the "minor baroque") as Quadrio Pirani, Innocenzo Sabbatini, and Gustavo Giovannoni. The principles of traditional architecture are consistently employed, beginning with the enclosure and animation of urban space and proceeding to the character-defining details of doorway or window surrounds and judicious ornament. Each of the developments is remarkable for its sophisticated architectural invention, impressive craftsmanship, and generous social amenities, including landscaped internal courtyards, street-level retail spaces, and playgrounds. (Fig. 9.10)

The traditional styles of these projects were not embraced by the Mussolini regime, which was more interested in projecting the imagery of modernity and progress proposed by the Italian Rationalists, and in the 1930s literal use of traditional and classical languages was all but

banned by government decree. Despite this, the ICP projects came to be associated with the regime in the minds of architects and critics and are still today commonly referred to as representing "Fascist" architecture; as a result, the projects were badly neglected by postwar administrations and allowed to deteriorate. Today these developments are being privatized, restored, and sold as condominiums at high prices in response to intense demand. The ICP projects deserve greater critical and scholarly attention and should be closely studied by New Urbanists, architects, housing advocates, and preservationists as examples of sensitive architectural design in historic settings and as evidence of a lively and socially progressive traditional practice of public housing prior to the ascendancy of the Modern Movement. (See Mazzola, 2004.)

The outstanding classical designer in this period in Italy was without question Armando Brasini. An artist of prodigious talent from a modest background, Brasini was entirely self-trained and began designing spectacular architectural projects as a teenager. Attracting the attention of important patrons, he was soon producing sculptural decoration for the completion of the monument to Vittorio Emanuele II and designing new churches commissioned directly by the pope. His transformation of the Palazzo Chigi from a private residence to the seat of the Italian Council of Ministers and his addition of the Museum of the Risorgimento on the eastern flank of the Capitoline Hill are extremely sensitive interventions made possible by his seemingly innate understanding of classical and Baroque architecture.

The more constrained the site, the more complex the program, and the more daunting the artistic challenge of the project, the more Brasini seemed to excel in his design solutions. The INA Building of 1928–34 is his outstanding contribution to the urban fabric of the historical center and represents a vital continuity with the classical building culture of the city. A work of extraordinary architectural and urbanistic imagination, the building is replete with recollections of Mannerism and the Baroque, but is memorable above all for its homage to Michelangelo. It is also superbly pragmatic in the way it skillfully fits a substantial new structure into a hopelessly constrained hillside site surrounded by historical buildings and gardens. The architect's mastery of scale is demonstrated by the division of the building

façade into two registers: the lower, in travertine, providing a suitable entrance scaled to the near view; the upper, in brick with stone trim, offering a clever termination of the distant vista from the Via del Plebiscito and appearing to be a far larger structure than it in fact is. Brasini's urban scenography is matched by his command of classical detail: The massive Doric order of the base is perfectly complemented by the elegant Corinthian at the upper part of the façade flanking the arches. The composition's apparent solecisms—the two-bay composition of the upper façade and the misalignment of the centerlines of the upper and lower registers—are consciously designed to address visual relationships even at the cost of defying the academic canon. (Fig. 9. 11)

Brasini undoubtedly merits inclusion in the tradition of idiosyncratic classicists from Michelangelo and Giulio Romano to John Soane and C. R. Cockerell, to Jože Plečnik and Edwin Lutyens. Brasini's full-bodied classicism was not supported by the regime, however, and he received no important state commissions after 1931. After the war, Brasini was all but forgotten and was only "rediscovered" by Robert Venturi in the mid-1960s, despite an oeuvre rich in lessons for a renewed practice of traditional architecture and urbanism. (Venturi, 1977, pp. 65–66, 77, 92–93.)

Merchants Square, Williamsburg, Virginia

No historic site in the United States better demonstrates the divide between popular American culture and elite taste-makers than Williamsburg, Virginia. The restored Colonial town is second only to Disneyland—with which it is frequently unflatteringly compared—as an object of derision by mainstream critics, architects, and preservationists uneasy with what they see as a veritable pageant of "false history." Ada Louise Huxtable, for example, condemned Williamsburg as "the replacement of reality with selective fantasy." The restored town, according to Huxtable, has led Americans "to prefer—and believe in—a sanitized and selective version of the past" rather than "the real thing." (Huxtable, 1992.) Echoing the theories of Cesare Brandi, Huxtable is concerned with the distinction between "original" and "copy"—and the purportedly damaging consequences of confusion between them—

although closer scrutiny of eighteenth-century architecture immediately reveals this distinction to be spurious. After all, the "original" Williamsburg was itself a "copy" of models brought over from England, which were in turn based on Palladian models imported from Italy by Inigo Jones. Palladio thought he was designing in the manner of the ancient Romans, who modeled their temples after those of the Greeks. The search for an authentic original leads inevitably to an infinite regress, revealing that all architecture is made up of previous architecture. (See fig. 5.9.)

The display of an authentic "original" artifact was in any case not the intention of the founders of Colonial Williamsburg, the Reverend William A. R. Goodwin and John D. Rockefeller, Jr., who planned the restoration in order to acquaint Americans with their architectural heritage and elevate popular taste. Following the ascendancy of modernism, such models were seen by leading professionals and academics as having little to offer, except perhaps a didactic window onto the past. The restored town was transformed into a "living history" museum promising as authentic an interpretation of eighteenth-century life in Virginia as public health and safety regulations would permit. But from the viewpoint of "verisimilitude," Huxtable and other critics of Williamsburg were undoubtedly correct: The streets are not full of mud, no pigs and chickens run loose, the buildings are all immaculately maintained, and African slaves are rarely visible. In response to accusations that they presented "sanitized" versions of history, the displays and reenactments produced for visitors have recently introduced a greater diversity of historical characters and even explored such unpleasant historical realities as slave auctions. But from the point of view of architecture and urbanism, the demand for historical verisimilitude is beside the point: Refusal to see the place as an essential model for humane building and place-making apart from its specific—and not always edifying—history deprives us of a resource of great value. The architecture, landscapes, and decorative arts of Williamsburg no longer belong to the eighteenth century—they are available as a source of lessons for contemporary design and deserving of the attention of architects, urbanists, and preservationists today.

Colonial Williamsburg's streets, buildings, and gardens were restored or reconstructed between 1926 and 1935 under the direction of

architects Perry, Shaw & Hepburn, largely as an application of the principles of Viollet-le-Duc to an American site. The restoration program undertaken there dominates the history of American preservation and, while the results were not always consistent with the standards adopted by the profession subsequently, there can be no doubt that those who criticize Williamsburg today base their critique in large part on the methods and knowledge that the restoration itself developed and made possible. To be sure, subsequent research revealed that some aspects of the restoration departed from available documentation, especially in the apparent misreading of the archeological evidence for the reconstructed Capitol. (Lounsbury, 1990.) Despite these faults, the restored town has had a greater and more enduring influence on American taste in architecture, landscape, and decorative arts than any other single source, just as its original sponsors hoped it would. The Colonial Revival, a style that both derived from and contributed to the Williamsburg restoration, remains an active force in contemporary design today. (Wilson, 2004.)

While the restored Colonial fabric remains a topic of critical discussion, less attention has been directed to the modern buildings in Colonial Revival style that the restoration architects designed to serve as a new town center, housing functions relocated from the buildings removed or restored elsewhere in the town. Perry, Shaw & Hepburn's designs for Merchants Square at the west end of Duke of Gloucester Street demonstrate the adaptation of the historic language and materials of the Colonial town to its modern expansion. (Fig. 9.12) The new structures—offices, shops, a theater, and a post office—display a continuity of language, scale, and materials with their historic and restored neighbors, but also show significant innovations—larger shop windows, more varied building types, and new uses. The new buildings introduced post-Revolutionary architectural features that illustrate the development of the classical tradition after the Colonial period right up to the time of the restoration itself. For these newly invented structures, the architects also permitted themselves a broader eclecticism, drawing from English, Atlantic Seaboard, and Anglo-Caribbean sources. Most important, the architects applied to the new buildings what they had learned about Virginia's Colonial

A

9.13. New Merchants Square buildings, Williamsburg, Virginia, by Quinlan & Francis Terry, completed 2004.

A. General view.

B. Detail of façade.

The new buildings suggest how the local style might have developed if Williamsburg had remained the state capital after 1777. This "false history" allows expansion of the setting without the loss of character that would result from intervention in a contrasting style.

B

building culture, proving the value of the restorations for making new architecture. (Chappell, 2003, p. 87.)

More recently, when a corner site became available on the main street, Colonial Williamsburg sought to build an extension of Merchants Square that would continue the pattern set by the earlier buildings. The new commercial structures, designed by Quinlan & Francis Terry, Architects, and completed in 2004, fulfilled this goal with great skill and distinction. Terry's buildings, like Perry, Shaw & Hepburn's, are deeply contextual, not just in the superficial sense of replicating details and elements found nearby, but in the more profoundly historical sense of suggesting what Williamsburg might look like had it remained an English colonial capital and had new buildings added by architects who had developed their language in the decades after 1770. Elements new to the town are introduced, such as the dark rusticated sandstone base on the corner building, tall brick pilasters on another, or the Federal character recalling Latrobe in a third. (Fig. 9.13)

The town center of Williamsburg is an urban neighborhood continuing to develop within an ongoing stylistic tradition and building culture. One misses only the presence of multiple uses, of apartments above the stores, and services other than those strictly directed to the needs of tourists. It is conceivable that these features would appear if Williamsburg successfully transformed itself from a large-scale historical entertainment into what it surely was meant to be—a well-designed small American city with superb architecture and urbanism, gracefully accommodating modern life, and serving as a model for other towns. Were it to reassume this more didactic and exemplary role, the restoration and the present-day center of Williamsburg might yet fulfill its founders' original objectives and embody the town's official motto: "That the future may learn from the past."

A

B

The Frick Collection, New York

Among the best and clearest examples of continuity of style over the course of successive additions is the transformation of the Henry Clay Frick residence in New York into one of the city's premier art museums. Two successive building campaigns did not simply add to the existing fabric, but subtly transformed it, each time underscoring the character of its predecessor while introducing relevant new features and refinements. Facing Central Park across Fifth Avenue in the Upper East Side Historic District of Manhattan, the Frick Collection illustrates at a smaller scale the kind of stylistically continuous expansion and growth displayed by the United States Capitol and the Louvre. Designed by Carrère & Hastings in 1912, the original structure comprised a substantial urban residence based on the Parisian townhouse type. Designer Thomas Hastings punctuated his elegant façades with a relatively chaste form of the Ionic order and strategically placed sculpted ornament. (Fig. 9.14A)

In 1931, John Russell Pope converted the house into a public museum. He refashioned the ground-floor rooms as art galleries and added an auditorium and supporting service areas. Most important, he transformed the former carriageway into one of the great interior spaces of New York—the Garden Court—with its graceful paired Ionic columns supporting a translucent, glazed vault. Along 71st Street, Pope stitched together his new structure with the long, windowless wall of the original gallery wing, matching Hastings's original bays. He then added a new structure for the Frick Art Reference Library, a building both deferential to the original landmark and a masterful work in its own right. (Stern, Gilmartin, and Mellins, 1987, p. 137.)

Pope's attitude betrays neither willfulness in imposing his own stamp on the project nor timidity in making his own contribution on an equal footing. In truth, it is difficult to tell where Carrère & Hastings leave off and Pope begins. On closer view the stylistic "fingerprints" of the two generations of designers can be discerned: Hastings brought a strong French classical sensibility to his work, as well as an ornamental richness and delicacy, reflecting his training at the École des Beaux-Arts. By comparison, Pope's taste is more austere and neoclassical. His genius lay in abstract massing and unornamented surfaces, as demonstrated in his masterpiece, the National Gallery of Art in Washington. For the Frick Collection, Pope tempered his own instincts, achieving continuity by means of a shared language and a great sensitivity to scale; differentiation came as the natural and inevitable result of the different sensibilities of the two architects.

In the 1970s the Frick commissioned a modest new wing from architects Harry Van Dyke and G. Frederick Poehler, who were joined by the classical designer and cofounder of Classical America, John Barrington Bayley. Their addition, completed in 1977, followed Pope's example by maintaining the existing style. The new pavilion repeats the rusticated limestone, Ionic order, and horizontal lines of the original house, but the detailing is consistently more robust than that of either Hastings or Pope. The Ionic capitals on the new garden elevation are the more sculptural Scamozzi type, with a convex face and drops below the volutes.

The bold entablature with modillion cornice breaks forward above the pilasters, casting strong shadows. The curvilinear character of the order is nicely reinforced by the curved, reentrant corners of the new addition on 70th Street. None of these features are present in Hastings's or Pope's designs for the building, which are chaste and reticent by comparison. The bolder details on the new addition reveal the hand of Bayley, whose classical taste was far more robust—virtually unaffected by neoclassicism—than that of either of his two predecessors. As in Pope's additions, compatibility comes from the use of the same materials, scale, and formal language as the previous work; differentiation arises from a subtle modulation in character. Today visitors to the Frick Collection experience a unified architectural whole composed by three teams of designers over the course of three generations, each adapting the genetic material bequeathed by their predecessors and producing beauty undisturbed by theories of rupture.

The Carhart Mansion, New York

The Carhart Mansion at 3 East 95th Street, designed between 1913 and 1916 by Horace Trumbauer, leads an elegant parade of townhouses that, despite their variety of styles, massing, and materials, compose a congruent urban streetscape. To the east is another city landmark, the intriguing Fabbri Mansion, designed by Egisto Fabbri and Grosvenor Atterbury between 1914 and 1916, with its neo–Italian Renaissance detailing and unusual entry courtyard. The elegant ensemble was almost ruined by an unattractive 1950s building rising on the lot between the two landmarks but, happily, its replacement has raised the tone of the whole street. (See fig. C.27)

The owners of the building, which had been occupied for many years by a private school, asked architect Brian Connolly to prepare feasibility studies for converting the building into luxury apartments and constructing an addition on the site next door, sympathetic in style, scale, and materials. (Fig. 9.15A) In 2001, a new owner of the property engaged Beyer Blinder Belle Architects and Planners to continue the project. They proposed a frankly modernist—albeit "sympathetic"—façade for the addition with a gridded veneer stone cladding and a large central bay of aluminum-and-

OPPOSITE

9.15. 3–5 East 95th Street, New York.

A. First phase: Addition proposed by Brian Connolly, 2000.

B. Second phase: Addition proposed by Beyer Blinder Belle Architects and Planners, 2001.

C. Third phase: Addition proposed by Zivkovic Connolly Associates with John Simpson & Partners, 2002.

The design of the new townhouse (right) passed from one closely related to Trumbauer's to modernist abstraction to a sympathetic style without direct imitation. Both the second and third schemes were approved by the Landmarks Commission, and the third was built. (See also fig. C.27.)

glass curtain wall. (Fig. 9.15B) The Landmarks Preservation Commission approved the Beyer Blinder Belle scheme with only minor modifications, but the developer-owner and the real estate broker had difficulties preselling the units in the addition and decided to reconsider the design along classical lines.

In 2002, Zivkovic Associates Architects—of which Connolly was now a principal—were asked to prepare plans and elevations for the new building based on their earlier studies. They invited the London firm of John Simpson & Partners to join their team and give particular attention to the exterior of the new wing. Their new façade was a strongly classical composition along the lines of Connolly's earlier proposal, but it gave the new building greater independence from its historic neighbor while maintaining a closely related style. (Fig. 9.15C) When the team returned to the Landmarks Commission with the revised design in 2003, the commission approved the design but expressed concerns about the "authenticity" of the new construction—they were concerned that it be executed with the highest level of craftsmanship. (Curiously, this had not been an issue with the modernist design.) In this case the architects used thick, load-bearing masonry walls on the two façades visible from the street, eliminating telltale expansion joints, and articulated the wall surfaces with carefully studied moldings, rustication, keystones, cornices, and carved ornament. The concerns of the commission were amply satisfied.

Perhaps the strongest aspect of the completed building is the way it works three-dimensionally in its urban setting. The elevation facing the courtyard of the Fabbri Mansion next door establishes a vertical emphasis, anchoring the street façade like a little tower. While the new building maintains key horizontal alignments with the older building, the new street façade subtly detaches itself from its historic neighbor by changing the scale of the rustication on the ground floor and separating the piano nobile and third floors, in contrast to Trumbauer's linkage of these two floors by pilaster strips and recessed spandrels. These contrasts are subtle but effective and give the new building a sense of mass and dignity that allow it to hold its own as a partner, rather than an adjunct, to Trumbauer's robust house next door. The new structure is a model for new traditional architecture, urbanism, and historic preservation working together to bring civility and continuity to the city.

A

B

C

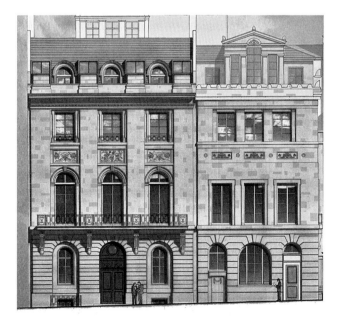

9.16. Proposed hotel, Marion Square, Charleston, by Fairfax & Sammons Architects, 2005–7.

A proposed hotel at the northwest corner (center) reintroduces familiar Charleston models while being scaled to the surrounding buildings and the space of the square itself. Preservationists opposed the building's height, despite the much taller 1920s hotel on the southwest corner of the square.

Marion Square, Charleston

A battleground for the competing interests struggling over the character of new building in the Historic District of Charleston has formed around the proposed redevelopment of Marion Square, where a series of imaginative new traditional designs have been proposed to rejuvenate this nineteenth-century public park on the north side of the city's historic center. The proposals, by a group of designers including Fairfax & Sammons, Ralph Muldrow, Randolph Martz, Goff D'Antonio, and Evans & Schmidt, include New Urbanist prescriptions for regulating traffic, increasing density, promoting mixed use, defining the public space of the square, and maintaining a pedestrian scale, but they go beyond these familiar recommendations to address the issue of style. New buildings on vacant lots and replacement buildings for modernist structures—including a public library and a federal office building, both abandoned for several years—reestablish a stylistic identity around the square, reinforcing the architectural patterns native to Charleston.

A proposed hotel on the site of the former federal building on the east boundary of the square features a colossal colonnade recalling the Charleston Hotel designed by Robert Mills in the 1830s and demolished in the 1960s. New structures on the south side of the square define a "gateway" to the historic district, while a new "liner" building provides a new retail façade for an existing parking garage on the west side. Finally, a new hotel on the site of the former library adjacent to the Gothic Revival Citadel Building is proposed to complete the north side of the square. These proposals have elicited strong support from citizens but have encountered skepticism from design professionals and preservation officials.

Designed by Fairfax & Sammons Architects with the local firm Goff D'Antonio, the hotel on the north side of the square has a cast-stone rusticated base with arched entries and retail storefronts. The pale stucco walls above are punctuated by awnings, shutters, cornices, and a hip roof. (Fig. 9.16) The height of the proposed hotel prompted some local resistance, although the new building is consistent with the historic Mills House Hotel, which was of a similar height, and is overshadowed by the Francis Marion Hotel on the southwest corner of the square, built in the 1920s and considered a city landmark. The setting of the square calls for buildings of sufficient scale to maintain the enclosure of the expansive space, but determined opponents of new buildings are understandably defensive after decades of fighting inappropriate proposals.

Charleston is the special place it is today because of the foresight of preservation leaders like Albert Simons and Susan Pringle Frost, who over eighty years ago understood that what is to be preserved is not isolated structures but *ensembles*—entire streets and neighborhoods. Achieving this goal does not preclude growth and new construction, but new buildings must generally adopt materials, methods, and styles similar to those that created the historic character of the place. This is not a proposal for uniformity or for making all new buildings look the same; rather, it is a call for stewardship of the building culture of the place. The designs for Marion Square show that this can be done while maintaining a high level of design quality and without replication. As the public becomes increasingly aware that this alternative to current orthodoxy exists, they will increasingly press for a more historically informed and inclusive attitude toward the architecture of their time and place.

Whitman College, Princeton University

New exercises in the Invention Within a Style strategy are not limited to the classical tradition; Gothic invention is also flourishing again. Dimitri Porphyrios's Magdalen College, Oxford (1994–98), showed the possibilities for the expansion of a complex of medieval academic buildings and demonstrated the feasibility of the Gothic tradition for contemporary architecture. Whitman College, the new residential complex designed by Porphyrios for Princeton University, has both a physical and a cultural context of importance: Physically, the Princeton campus, with its Federal, Victorian, Collegiate Gothic, and modernist buildings, is among the most architecturally distinguished in the United States. Part of the cultural context for the new college is the overwhelming preference of students for the Collegiate Gothic dormitories erected in the early twentieth-century and designed by such notable architects as Ralph Adams Cram. In an age when the "branding" of institutions is a key element in their financial health and the maintenance of their mission, the university's return to the Gothic tradition was both a sound aesthetic judgment and a prudent investment. (Fig. 9. 17)

Like its Princeton and Oxford precedents, Whitman College encloses a series of courtyards, surrounding them with façades enlivened by the syncopated, asymmetrical composition typical of the style. The buildings are punctuated by towers and open archways that link the enclosed spaces to the surrounding campus. In comparison to the early twentieth-century residence halls that inspired them, Porphyrios's buildings are simpler, more regular, less rich in incident and decorative detail. However, they are not bereft of these: String courses, window surrounds, oriels and bays, buttresses, and dor-

mers perform their familiar roles with realism and tact. The architect has thoughtfully provided places for the statuary, memorials, and other decorative features that so animate the familiar landmarks of Collegiate Gothic or medieval construction. With time, Whitman College will undoubtedly display its fair share of such ornamental detail.

Standing in the center of Chester Court, one has the sense that a continuous and ongoing sense of place is no romantic fantasy but a present reality. We do not think we have stumbled into a time warp and stepped into the year 1908. Rather, we have entered a present relieved of the compulsion to overthrow those cultural continuities that still speak to contemporary students, teachers, parents, and alumni. The buildings are not mere stage sets, but have been detailed and constructed with unusual care. That Whitman College was initiated and partially funded by the founder of one of the most successful Internet businesses underscores the appeal of traditional architecture even to the most technologically sophisticated audience. Perhaps it is because they are technologically sophisticated that the place is so attractive to today's students. What Whitman College's architectural style represents to its contemporary residents is not medievalism or antiquarianism, but comfort, scholarship, and—most important—Princeton. It would be difficult to find a stronger illustration of the power of architectural character to create an enduring sense of place even in the midst of change.

9.17. Whitman College, Princeton University, Princeton, New Jersey, by Porphyrios Associates, 2004.

The new college is organized around a series of courtyards that knit the new buildings gracefully into the scenic, predominantly Gothic campus. The popular new dormitories are neither abstract nor nostalgic, but lovingly crafted new Gothic Revival work.

**10.1. Goldman & Salatsch
Building (Looshaus),** Vienna,
by Adolf Loos, 1910.

Loos's attempted
compromise intends an
abstract relationship to
its historic setting while
asserting itself as "of its
time." But times changed
and recent interventions in
Vienna, as elsewhere, have
become more adversarial.

CHAPTER 10

Abstract Reference

The third strategy is a modern innovation that seeks to defer to the historic setting while consciously avoiding literal resemblance or working in a historical style. The approach seeks to balance differentiation and compatibility, but with the balance tipped toward the former. It is the attempt of the modernist designer to maintain visual continuity with traditional architecture without actually practicing or reproducing it. The objective of the strategy is to maintain a superficial visual continuity within an urban context—to pass the "first-glance test"—by means of compositions and elements that appear consonant with the traditional adjacent buildings but which, upon closer scrutiny, bear only an analogical relationship to traditional architectural language. The product of this approach is generally the simulacrum of a traditional building rendered with modernist materials and details. Because it attempts synthesis between what are, ultimately, irreconcilable values, this is undoubtedly the most internally problematic strategy; nevertheless, it has been consistently promoted by preservation authorities over the last several decades.

A modernist addition to a traditional setting using this strategy will typically conform in its overall silhouette to the massing of neighbor-ing historic structures, important horizontal divisions of their elevations will be registered with simplified moldings or material changes, and new openings may be aligned horizontally and vertically with the older ones, but the details undergo a process of simplification, editing out the small-scale incident provided by ornament. Familiar traditional elements are transformed by reducing their composite form to abstract shapes, eliminating intermediate subdivisions or scale levels until only indivisible units remain. These, in turn, become components in a collage arranged to resemble a traditional composition when viewed as a whole, but without the nested relationships linking parts and wholes typical of traditional work. For example, the traditional canon of punctuation might be acknowledged by maintaining a species of moldings in those locations where moldings are expected, but the molding profile might be reduced to a simple semicircle or a flat fascia.

We might say that the Abstract Reference strategy seeks to retain the decorous rhetoric of traditional architecture without the formal grammar or material rendering; alternatively, it seeks to retain the formal grammar and material rendering of modernist architecture without the oppositional rhetoric. The difficulty in either case is the tendency to emphasize abstract relationships and disregard character or, perhaps more accurately, to assume that a sympathetic character can be rendered by means of abstract relationships alone. Often left out of the reference are the character-defining materiality, depth, and texture that we associate with traditional construction but which are foreign to the sleek, diaphanous, and evanescent character typical of modernist construction. Of course, there is no reason why modern materials should necessarily be incapable of producing a character analogous to traditional design, or at least to those examples of traditional architecture that themselves made use of such materials. Too often, in my view, exercises in the Abstract Reference strategy present a schematic version of traditional architecture that ultimately evokes a sense of loss more keenly felt because the work declines to deliver the character it promises at first glance.

The Looshaus, Vienna

Adolf Loos's 1910 Goldman & Salatsch Building (now referred to as the Looshaus) on the Michaelerplatz in Vienna is perhaps the first realized example of the strategy and has served as a much-imitated model. Loos's building makes reference to its setting through massing, materials, scale, and very restricted articulation, allowing it to be both "modern" (in the sense of using a minimum of historical detail) and "contextual" (in the sense of fitting in physically with the scale, materials, and urban typology of the preexisting setting). Apart from the appearance of a simplified Doric order in its lower stories and the suggestion of a rusticated base, the detailing of the building avoids explicit use of the classical grammar, relying instead on simplified shapes and profiles to make visual connections with traditional neighbors. The grid of unarticulated window openings in the middle stories has been identified as revealing Loos's modernist sensibility by virtue of its abstraction of the more inflected window patterns of the largely Baroque surrounding buildings. (Fig. 10.1)

Loos's work epitomizes the widespread early-twentieth-century movement to apply an increasing level of abstraction to traditional architectural language. Similar goals were pursued by his fellow Viennese Otto Wagner, the Parisian Auguste Perret, the French-American Paul Cret, and the Italian Marcello Piacentini, to name only a few. In the work of these designers before the Second World War, the Abstract Reference strategy was an attempt to hold on to essential principles of traditional design in the face of the Modern Movement's general repudiation of any but the most generalized application of them.

Modestly scaled buildings like the Looshaus were reasonably successful in insinuating aspects of the new aesthetic into the historic environment with minimal disruption, but as the scale of such buildings increased, the omission of multiple scale levels and elimination of fine-grained articulation and ornament made compatibility between new and historic buildings more difficult to achieve. All the while, buildings using the strategy faced the risk that they would look either incomplete or as if their former ornamental richness had been stripped away in an insensitive remodeling. Rarely would the balance between traditionalism and modernity be as skillfully maintained as at the Looshaus, perhaps because its architect was content to retain the classical order as a generator of proportion and ornament—at least for the lower stories. Without this vestige of the classical language, Loos's building would be deprived of an essential means of relating to the context at the middle scale. This is an important lesson for designers today: Meaningful compatibility requires that new and old buildings observe similar protocols of scale—throughout a full complement of scale levels, not just the scale of the whole.

Urban Infill, EUR, and the Via della Conciliazione, Rome

Perhaps the most extensive application of the Abstract Reference strategy for new architecture in a historic city was carried out during the 1920s and 1930s in Rome. When it came to new construction in the historic center, the Fascist government never gave unequivocal support to any of the competing styles of the time, from the Rationalism of the early Modern Movement to the classicism of Brasini or Giovannoni. The closest thing to an official style was the "stripped classicism" of Marcello Piacentini and his colleagues, along with a subspecies characterized by a minimalist evocation of Renaissance building types rendered with modern detail. Some of the new infill buildings erected in the historic center in this latter style play their roles in the urban ensemble with considerable tact, while others hover more uncomfortably between classical reminiscence and modernist abstraction. The difference between the stronger and weaker examples of this approach depends on the space-making quality of the buildings in conformance with the historical streetscape, the maintenance of a full complement of scale levels, and the closeness with which the articulation of detail approximates elements and relations of the classical language. The buildings designed in the 1920s along the newly built Corso del Rinascimento, overlooking Largo Giuseppe Toniolo, and around Piazza Nicosia, for example, are reasonably effective on these counts, exhibiting the principles of traditional design in most respects, except for their tendency to omit the smaller scale levels and to eliminate ornament. (Fig. 10.2)

The most complete demonstrations of the government's official style were the large state-sponsored projects for the Città Universitaria (1932–35), the Esposizione Universale di Roma (known by its acronym EUR, 1937–42), and the Via della Conciliazione (1936–50), all three of which were planned and executed under the supervision of Piacentini. The first and second of these were planned for sites outside the historical center—a new American-style campus for the University of Rome and a world's fair whose 1942 opening was preempted by the war—and demonstrate a grandiose but ultimately unsatisfying attempt at a synthesis, or compromise, between the classical and modernist sensibilities. But, in truth, it was not much of a compromise: The classical contribution to these projects is limited to a generalized bilateral symmetry in the site plan and in most (though not all) of the individual building plans and elevations; the buildings' exterior articulation generally reflects the reductivist language of Modern Movement functionalism or—especially in those designed by Piacentini himself—an extremely abstracted and minimalist version of classical composition from which all the smaller scale levels and ornament have been eliminated. (Rossi, 2005, pp. 94–101.)

At EUR the modernist sensibility dominates in the vast open spaces scaled to the automobile, widely dispersed object-buildings, and a Cartesian grid of boulevards descended from Le Corbusier's Plan Voisin for Paris of the pre-

vious decade. (The site plan of EUR also bears a close resemblance to Le Corbusier's Cité Mondiale at Geneva of 1929, which had similar programmatic and symbolic aims. See Etlin, 1991, pp. 513, 563–68.) From a distance we can see what appear to be columns and arches on the earliest buildings, but on closer view these are revealed to be without articulation, punctuation, inflection, or ornament. The monotonous regularity of the original designs for EUR is often seen by critics as a reminiscence of classical monumentality, but where in the classical tradition does one find such mechanical reiteration of identical components bearing no

10.2. Buildings on Largo Giuseppe Toniolo, Rome, by Mario De Renzi, circa 1928.

Much urban construction in Fascist Rome sought a compromise between modernist and classical design by means of simplification in detail. Despite some relative successes, this approach is limited by its omission of character-giving smaller scale levels and ornament.

organic relationship to one another or to the whole? EUR's iconic buildings—such as the Palazzo della Civiltà Romana, also known as the "square Colosseum"—are closer in spirit to the Rationalism of Terragni's Casa del Fascio in Como than to anything produced by the classical tradition in Rome. (Rossi, 2005, pp. 133–49; Frampton, 1980, pp. 203–9, 214–15.) (Fig. 10.3)

The Via della Conciliazione, a new boulevard linking the Ponte Sant'Angelo to the Piazza San Pietro built to commemorate the concordat between Mussolini and the Vatican, cut a merciless swath through the ancient *borgo*, entailed the demolition of dozens of medieval and Renaissance buildings, and pro-foundly altered the scale of the city and the approach to Bernini's piazza at the west end of the new thoroughfare. Another of the broad, ramrod-straight avenues which to Mussolini represented modernity, efficiency, and power, the Via della Conciliazione is not so much a classical conception rendered in traditional architecture as it is a modernist conception rendered in a camouflage of abstracted classical design. Piacentini's plan could not be further from the spirit of Giovannoni's *diradamento*, and indeed Giovannoni himself protested against Piacentini's plan, but to no avail. (See Chapter 5.) (Ceschi, 1971, p. 114.) It is as if Piacentini imposed the standards of the Via dell'Impero—as the main boulevard at EUR

10.3. **Palazzo della Civiltà Romana**, EUR, Rome, by Ernesto La Padula, Giovanni Guerrini, and Mario Romano, 1939–42.

The "square Colosseum" mechanically piles up over two hundred identical arches, but these mere simulacra of classical arches violate the principle of fictive structure, disregard the canons of punctuation and inflection, and are devoid of ornament.

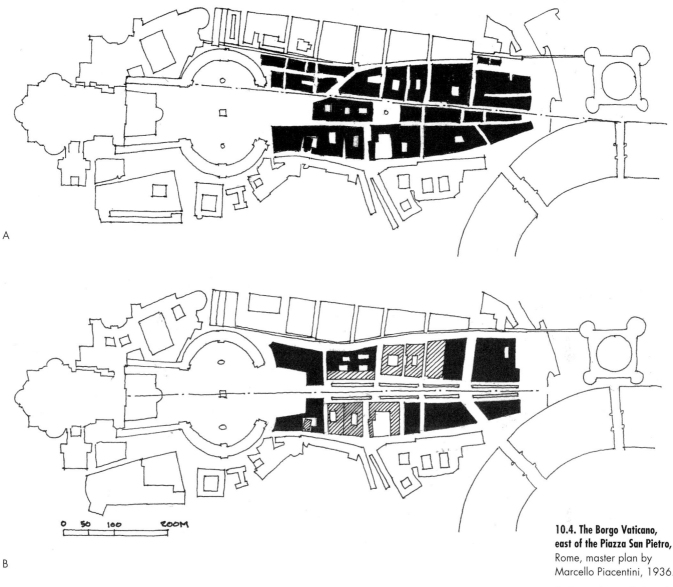

A

B

10.4. The Borgo Vaticano, east of the Piazza San Pietro, Rome, master plan by Marcello Piacentini, 1936.

A. Figure/ground plan of preexisting neighborhood, after Marconi, 2003.

B. Figure/ground plan of neighborhood after construction of the Via della Conciliazione.

The Piazza San Pietro (left in plans) was originally approached through narrow streets—the Borgo Vecchio and the Borgo Nuovo, separated by the *spina* and punctuated by the piazze Rusticucci and Scossacavalli. Some of the surviving—albeit modified—historic structures are indicated by hatching in the lower diagram.

was originally named—on the intricate grain and intimate scale of the old borgo, gutting the neighborhood and remaking it according to an alien model for the city. (Fig. 10.4)

The removal of an entire historic neighborhood was dictated by the Duce's determination to liberate Rome from the "mediocre construction," the "picturesque and so-called local color," that he believed disfigured the grandeur of the city. (Benito Mussolini, quoted in Kostoff, 1973, pp. 9–10.) The new street tries to rationalize the irregular alignments of the surviving medieval and Renaissance façades, substituting a regimented streetscape for the more fine-grained character of the

old *borgo*. As a consequence, the surviving Renaissance palazzo façades are viewed across spaces too large for them. But if the axial vista to St. Peter's Basilica, obelisklike streetlamps, and classicizing new façades of the avenue were intended to recall the glory of papal Rome, comparison of the Via della Conciliazione with the scale, proportions, and architectural richness of Julius II's Via Giulia or Sixtus V's "trident" of streets fanning out from the Piazza del Popolo should disabuse us of any such notion. (See figs. 3.4 and 3.10.) On the contrary, the trapezoidal expanse of Piacentini's transitional Piazza Pio XII spoils the intended drama of entering Bernini's col-

10.5. Views of the Via della Conciliazione, Rome, by Marcello Piacentini and others, 1936–50.

A. East end of the Via della Conciliazione.

B. West end of the Via Conciliazione.

Piacentini's replacement for the old *borgo* begins with an edited classicism at the east end (A) but lapses into abstract reference where it meets Bernini's colonnades (B). New and historic classicizing façades line a boulevard conceived according to modernist urbanism and scaled to the automobile. (See also fig. 3.5.)

A

onnades by placing at this crucial point a vast undifferentiated expanse full of traffic and parked cars.

If Piacentini's urban plan is disastrous, the architecture of his infill façades, despite obvious weaknesses, is not so easily dismissed. Framing the entrance to the avenue at the Tiber are a pair of matching classical buildings finished in travertine, raising a plain Tuscan order above a ground-floor podium—a faint echo of Bernini's colonnades at the opposite end of the street. Around the corner, the façades are simpler, with brick wall planes bordered by travertine trim and plain piers replacing the order. (Fig. 10.5A) At the west end of the axis the new elevations facing the Piazza Pio XII are further edited: Brick predominates and the travertine trim is reduced to squarish, flat profiles. (Fig. 10.5B) Piacentini's stiff references to Borromini's most abstract brick façades sacrifice the Baroque master's vitality for a regimented orthogonality that is altogether too prim and deferential. Had these façades been intended as infill along the Corso del Rinascimento or elsewhere in the dense and intimately scaled Campo Marzio, one might find them entirely fitting. But here, at the entrance to the great piazza of St. Peter's, the

anticlimactic lapse in decorum is astonishing, since it is here that one would expect a grand gesture of connection to Bernini's colonnades. The site demands Michelangelesque flourishes like those of Armando Brasini's INA Building or, at the very least, a repeat of the travertine classical pavilions facing the Tiber at the other end of the street. Perhaps Piacentini thought it best "not to compete" with Bernini's monument across the street; but, faced with the challenge of adding new buildings to a setting like the entrance to the Vatican, an exaggerated deference is no solution. (See Marconi, 2003, pp. 94–100.)

Lafayette Square, Washington, D.C.

In the United States after the Second World War, the Abstract Reference strategy underwent a reversal of intention, becoming a means of holding on to the design legacy of the Modern Movement in the face of rising popular and critical resistance to modernist urbanism and large-scale planning schemes. A movement within modernism began exploring allusions to historical building and formal types, experi-

B

menting with decoration, and reintroducing materials and methods that retained some connection to handicraft. John Carl Warnecke was among those architects in the 1960s who tried to bring a measure of warmth to functional modernist buildings through the use of traditional materials, decorative finishes, and allusions to recognizable building elements. His office buildings flanking Lafayette Square in Washington are an illuminating example of this approach, applied within a highly charged historic environment at a moment when the interests of historic preservation and modernist architecture were still in open conflict. The compromise reached at Lafayette Square, however tentative and ambiguous, became the basis for numerous interventions in the following decades.

Pierre-Charles L'Enfant's 1791 plan for Washington imagined a square in front of the President's House on the model of the Place de la Concorde, surrounded by coordinated classical buildings. The MacMillan Plan of 1902 ratified this idea and proposed a new formally designed Executive Group of office buildings around the square. Cass Gilbert's Treasury Department Annex, constructed in 1917, was the inaugural building in this intended series

of façades. With its continuous upper-level colonnades, Gilbert's design recalls Ange-Jacques Gabriel's buildings on the Parisian place that had served to inspire L'Enfant. The annex was never joined by the intended office buildings, and by the late 1920s, planners had selected the Federal Triangle as the preferred location for expanding executive departments. Nonetheless, proposals to redevelop the square continued to be discussed into the 1960s. (Gutheim and Lee, 2006, pp. 154, 175.)

Preservationists moved to protect Latrobe's Decatur House, St. John's Church, and several other historical and architectural landmarks on the square. While there was an urgent need for more office space near the executive mansion, the likely outcome of a modernist rebuilding of the square in the architectural climate of the 1960s was precisely what its most important residents wished to avoid. In response to the direct intervention of President and Mrs. Kennedy, Warnecke was asked to develop a plan for new executive branch office buildings that preserved the existing low-rise historic buildings on the square. Warnecke's plan fitted two tall office buildings to the rear of the existing houses and added sympathetic low-rise buildings to fill gaps between the surviving historic

10.6. New Executive Office Building, Lafayette Square, Washington, D.C., by John Carl Warnecke, 1964–69.

A. Executive Office Building.

B. Infill façade, west side of the Square.

For sites opposite the White House, the architect sought a compromise between traditional and modernist styles. Warnecke's buildings are skillfully sited to "mitigate their impact," but at the cost of eliminating elements that lend character through detail. Infill façades (center, B) are more successful.

A

B

structures facing the square. After a lengthy review and construction process, the complex was completed in 1969. (Fig. 10.6)

Warnecke's towers, clearly inspired by the Looshaus with their "punched" window openings and metal "mansard" roofs, previewed the differentiated-but-compatible manner of syn-

thesizing traditional references and modernist building types that would be enshrined in the *Secretary's Standards* in the following decade. The buildings' modernity was indicated by their height, inarticulate surfaces, and absence of traditional detail, while their sensitivity to the context was evoked by the use of brick and a selection of abstracted architectural features analogous to traditional elements, like the tall bay windows rising through the upper stories and the pitched roofs. At the largest scale, Warnecke's towers show a schematic tripartite composition, but the next-smaller scale level is missing: The window openings of the typical office floors form a tartan grid applied without inflection across the thirteen identical bays of the façades facing the park. These windows are set flush with the brick veneer to reinforce the thinness and planarity of the exterior envelope, which is not further articulated except by small-scale brick details at the top and bottom of the towers. The absence of a full range of scale levels reinforces the reading of the towers as object-buildings rather than space-defining participants in a composed ensemble; at the same time, their inarticulateness contributes to the neutral and unassuming character that was sought by the architect and preservationists alike.

Since neither a fully articulated traditional building nor a confident modernist one would be accepted at that time and place, the best the architect could do, so the thinking went, was to "mitigate the impact" of new buildings by minimizing the attention they attract to themselves at first glance. This was the birth of the "background building," an implicit recognition by architects and preservationists that conventional modernist buildings were incompatible with traditional settings unless they conceded their customary oppositional stance and adopted formal neutrality. Like Piacentini's buildings across from the Piazza San Pietro, Warnecke's buildings were designed to avoid competition with their historic neighbors. The towers were, in fact, seen by many as a victory for preservation, demonstrating that new and old buildings could coexist—even if only on ambiguous and ambivalent terms—while others considered the project a bland and characterless compromise. This critical dilemma is inescapable in the Abstract Reference strategy, caught as it is between a prohibition against adopting "literal" traditional language and an acknowledged need to dilute and pacify the modernist language in the interest of visual consonance.

Seamen's Church Institute, New York

In the following decades Colin Rowe and his followers of the "Cornell School" sought a more intellectually rigorous way to reconcile the spatial and urbanistic models of the historical city with the elevational and constructional typologies of Le Corbusier. As the consequences of modernist large-scale planning schemes became more apparent and prompted increasing popular and critical resistance, theorists like Rowe and his colleagues sought a way to retain the modernist visual culture descended from Cubism while jettisoning the disastrous effects of modernist urbanism on the traditional city. Rowe meticulously analyzed the compositional patterns of traditional and classical architecture, particularly of the Italian Renaissance, and translated the architectonic grids and sculptural layering of façades by Baldassare Peruzzi, Giulio Romano, and Andrea Palladio into diagrams revealing their underlying formal order in terms of figure/ground, layering, transpar-

ency, solid/void, and hierarchy. The resulting diagrams, presenting the rationalized order of the original composition without ornamental articulation, were then available for translation into modern materials. A case for the theoretical metamorphosis from Palladio to Le Corbusier was most clearly presented in Rowe's essay, "The Mathematics of the Ideal Villa," and it spawned an entire generation of similar translations of classical plan and elevation diagrams into modernist buildings clad in curtain walls and punctuated by pipe railings. (Rowe, 1976.)

An example of this analytical approach applied to an infill structure in a historic setting is the Seaman's Church Institute at New York's South Street Seaport Historic District, designed by James Stewart Polshek & Partners and completed in 1992. The façade references its early-

10.7. Seamen's Church Institute, New York, by James Stewart Polshek & Partners, 1992.

In a contextualism based on diagrammatic analogies to historic forms, the brick-clad screen wall abstracts adjacent nineteenth-century commercial buildings, and the metal-clad superstructure behind and above it refers to early modern maritime design.

nineteenth-century neighbors by aligning its principal façade with the adjacent buildings and repeating their pattern of window openings. In fact, the historic façade to the north is all that remains of the building formerly behind it: The new building entirely occupies the space behind the preserved street wall. The façade of the new addition is distinguished from the adjacent historic one by being entirely rendered in industrial materials—the principal plane is clad in brick veneer, the thinness of which is underscored by the absence of sills or lintels at the openings. Openings are formed of steel frames set into the brick plane; within these metal frames are windows with rounded corners resembling ships' bulkhead doors. A major opening above the entrance reveals the metal-clad secondary plane, which rises to a rooftop penthouse and recalls the superstructure of a modern ship. The diagrammatic conformance of the building to the adjacent historical buildings passes the first-glance test, while, upon closer inspection, the abstracted shapes and shallow planarity of the façade maintain a modernist aesthetic at the level of detail. (Fig. 10.7)

The Polshek building is more successful than most of the other examples of this strategy because of its modesty and consistency. In keeping with the best intentions of the Abstract Reference strategy, the Seamen's Church Institute avoids radical departures from its surroundings while yet introducing industrial materials and detailing that are identifiable as belonging to the modernist tradition in general and, in this case, expressing a specific utilitarian and maritime character. Perhaps the new building fits in as well as it does because the historic buildings next door are themselves utilitarian vernacular structures of a workaday character—elegant and modest, but sparse in ornament and simple in composition. The characters of the new and old buildings are similar enough (if we overlook differences in tectonic expression or materiality) to avoid a major rupture. In summary, the anonymity that the strategy typically imposes on the modernist work in this instance assists the architect to harmonize with an already anonymous (or nearly so) vernacular context. The same correspondence in character would not be possible in a more formalized, high-style, or monumental setting, where the absence of a common formal language would be more pronounced.

The Scholastic Building, New York

The ten-story building designed for the Scholastic Corporation by Aldo Rossi (with Gensler & Associates) and completed in 1997 represents the Abstract Reference strategy from a postmodern viewpoint while also revealing its limitations. Filling a gap between the Rouss Building (Alfred Zucker, 1888–90) and the Little Singer Building (Ernest Flagg, 1903) in the SoHo–Cast Iron Historic District, the new building uses abstract evocations of nearby nineteenth-century cast-iron architecture and utilitarian industrial buildings to maintain a visual relationship with its setting. The Broadway façade features several floors marked by heavy entablaturelike steel beams (aligned with the floors of the adjacent Rouss building) supported by thick two-story-high tubular white columns that stand in front of a curtain wall detailed to resemble industrial sash. (Figs. 10.8 and C.26)

Despite his status as a celebrity designer, author of the seminal book *The Architecture of the City*, and 1990 winner of the Pritzker Prize, Rossi proved to be remarkably expeditious. "It took him only five minutes to come up with the solution," reported Richard Robinson, head of Scholastic Inc., whose headquarters would occupy the new building. Perhaps Rossi's design process was facilitated by his characteristic recycling of a small group of visual motifs, in this case a design for the Hotel Il Palazzo in Fukuoka, Japan, from 1989. The New York City Landmarks Preservation Commission was similarly rapid in arriving at its decision, deliberating less than an hour before approving the design, unanimously and unaltered. (Dunlap, 2000.)

Critical reception of the completed building was largely worshipful. The chair of the commission stated that the Scholastic Building "offered a 'textbook example' of how to build in a historic district. 'Mr. Rossi was able to design a new façade that respected the character of Broadway but didn't inappropriately try to mimic it.'" (Dunlap, 2000.) Paul Goldberger agreed, finding the Rossi design "subtle, brilliantly inventive . . . the sort of building that . . . will teach generations of architects the proper way to respond to historic contexts." He concluded, "This is one of the most distinguished pieces of new architecture to be proposed for

10.8. Scholastic Building, New York, by Aldo Rossi with Gensler & Associates, completed 1997, detail.

Rossi's building (right) passes the "first glance test" for compatibility with its historic neighbor (left) largely by means of horizontal alignments and a similar bay spacing. A second glance reveals how differentiation is achieved through reduction of composite form to cartoonish shapes: Rossi's elements refer to the adjacent traditional one but lack the punctuation and inflection—and scaling coherence—that reward close observation in the older structure. (See also Color figure C.26.)

any New York City historic district in the last generation." He suggested the lesson to draw from this success is simply "Respect, take cues from what is around you, but do not copy directly." (Goldberger, 1996.)

Not everyone was delighted with the new building, however. As the *New York Times* noted, "Margot Gayle, the moving force behind the creation of the SoHo–Cast Iron district in 1973, said she could not understand the Landmarks Commission's enthusiasm. 'Those large, intrusive columns just don't fit,' she said. 'They're not friendly to the neighboring buildings.'" (Dunlap, 2000.) Gayle, who knew more about cast-iron architecture than anyone and had been instrumental in the designation of the district, had a point that the commis-

sioners and critics missed: While the building as completed does indeed pass the first-glance test, the mute abstraction, stolid proportions, and Rossi's characteristic caricature of architectural elements separate it from its historic neighbors.

The comments of the commission chair and Goldberger are revealing: On one hand, the architect is exhorted to "respect" the historic buildings but not to "mimic" or "copy" them. Logically, the most effective way to "respect" the preexisting context would be to use the same language, just as the architects who originally designed the buildings composing the historic district had done among themselves; the best way to avoid "copying" would be to use that language to say new things, again as the

original architects had. But deprived of a formal language in common with the buildings he was joining, Rossi was forced to walk an aesthetic tightrope: Move too far in one direction and the referenced formal relationships would become so abstract as to be trivial, but too far in the other and a stylistic literalism in the handling of the smaller-scale details would be condemned as "copying." As long as a recovery of the traditional formal languages remained out of the question, the commissioner and the critic had no choice but to insist on the aesthetic compromise that Rossi provided and Gayle questioned.

Jorge M. Perez Architecture Center, University of Miami

We may ask how the Abstract Reference strategy might be applied in the case of an addition to a modernist setting. What would prevent a traditional architect from approaching the dilemma Rossi faced in the Scholastic Building from the other side, as it were? Can one show respect

for qualities of massing, materiality, flowing space, and rational construction without copying the formal or constructive means used to achieve them? What compromises might a traditional architect face in applying the strategy to a modernist work based on antithetical principles? The Jorge M. Perez Architecture Center at the University of Miami, designed by a team led by the architect, urbanist, and theorist Léon Krier and completed in 2005, suggests an answer. (Figs. 10.9, C.28, and C.29)

The University of Miami was founded in 1925 by George Merrick, visionary developer of Coral Gables, the planned suburb of Miami that established the Mediterranean Revival as the most important architectural style in South Florida during the years before the Second World War. Construction of the university campus began in 1926, but the devastating hurricane in September of that year brought the vision to a halt, along with the whole booming economy of South Florida. When construction of the university resumed in 1950, the campus design was recast in the

International Style. The buildings now occupied by the School of Architecture were among the twenty or so designed as student dormitories by Robert Law Weed and Marion Manley (Florida's first woman architect) in the late 1940s as part of their postwar master plan for the university. The simple functionalist buildings are two-story concrete frame structures with metal sash windows, flat roofs, and exterior stairways, and these define the irregular site into which the new Krier building has been inserted.

Krier viewed the existing campus, a collection of object-buildings in an undifferentiated spatial field, as potentially transformable into an urban fabric of streets and squares, and sited his building to introduce the kind of intimate spaces characteristic of early Coral Gables but missing from the contemporary campus. The new building, divided into a large octagonal volume for a lecture hall and a long, low wing for gallery and classroom spaces, is calibrated to the scale of the existing buildings it joins. The end elevation of the gallery wing nicely mirrors the similar dimensions of the neighboring structures, while the octagon, with its two towers and arcaded porch, terminates vistas from different directions. What at first glance appears as an axial composition gradually reveals itself as a subtle and picturesque arrangement. The exterior of the building is finished in white stucco with wide buttresses, deep-set windows, and repeated rows of bold string-course moldings. While the building's exterior features recall traditional architecture, they remain defiantly idiosyncratic. Krier's abstraction works in two directions, creating visual analogies with the white stucco finish and bold shadows visible on the preexisting modernist buildings and broadly connecting the new building with the abstract qualities to be found in the Mediterranean Revival architecture of early Coral Gables.

More precisely, the building is eclectic, incorporating a variety of styles, including neoclassical, Byzantine, Spanish Mission, and Moorish—some have even seen allusions to Miami Beach Art Deco—but forming them into a fabric from which the constituent threads are difficult to unravel. Its eclecticism allows the building to offer itself not as a rebuke to the modernist buildings around it, but as a mediator. If the building sacrifices much on the classical side, it is a sacrifice the designers have been willing to make for the sake of synthesis. Indeed, the building represents a curious reversal of mainstream preservation assumptions: Instead of the new building drawing its visual interest parasitically from the greater inherent interest of the historic buildings around it, here the old buildings take on a new life in their dialogue with their new neighbor. The new building raises the tone of the whole ensemble, and the older buildings benefit from the juxtaposition. Krier seems to be saying that modernism is over, but one can still build in the midst of a modernist setting with tact and, in the process, heal some of the wounds caused by its oppositional stance.

The Abstract Reference strategy may have served its purpose for modernist designers and is perhaps no longer an attractive option for them. On the other hand, the strategy may yet have further application as a means of bringing the increasing numbers of modernist landmarks—the historic sites of the "recent past"—into relationship with the restored townscape posited by the recovery of traditional architecture and New Urbanism. Krier's Perez Center is likely the harbinger of a new generation of Abstract Reference projects in modernist settings still to come.

11.1. Brooklyn Museum, Brooklyn, New York, by McKim, Mead & White, 1895, with new entrance pavilion by James Stewart Polshek & Partners, 2000–2004.

Oppositional approaches exaggerating the difference between new and old can result in the disfigurement of historic landmarks. The new entry pavilion deliberately violates its classical setting with jarringly contrasting shapes, materials, and movement patterns.

CHAPTER 11

Intentional Opposition

The fourth strategy for relating new and old architecture is one of conscious departure from the character of the pre-existing setting and the determination to alter that character through contrast, an approach that privileges differentiation at the expense of compatibility. Modern architects did not invent this idea: Suetonius tells us that the Emperor Augustus found Rome a city of brick and left it a city of marble, but whether this transformation encountered resistance from preservationists is not recorded. (Suetonius, 1979, p. 61.) Sometimes stark contrast is the appropriate response to a context that is found to be in some way unsatisfactory. Architecture is not always obligated to blend into a preexisting condition—sometimes a critique is called for.

Such judgments must be made with care, however. If we are to safeguard the cultural resources represented by our historic built environments, the most suitable use of the Intentional Opposition strategy within them will be to repair damage to the historic setting brought about by previous insensitive or oppositional interventions and to reconnect segments of the historic environment to the context that formerly gave them coherence. Examples of this approach include the rebuilding of a block on the Rue de Laeken in Brussels by a team of architects led by Gabriele Tagliaventi following the demolition of a 1960s glass skyscraper formerly on the site. Similarly, Piotr Choynowski designed new traditional façades for modernist buildings in Oslo to recover the consistent character of a historic streetscape marred by the earlier interventions. (Fig. 11.2) While these interventions were oppositional with respect to the preexisting conditions of their individual sites, they were highly consonant with that part of their contexts that was to remain, reinforcing the character that had been damaged by the buildings they replaced. Alternatively, an intervention using this strategy can be oppositional to the context that is to remain in order to establish a new norm for the surrounding environment, setting a new pattern to be followed by others, as in the examples that follow.

There are innumerable historical examples of additions and infill structures whose projection of difference is plainly intended in the interest of presenting a new or newly fashionable style. (See fig. 1.2.) This opposition of styles, no less than the continuity that we also find in historical practice, tends to be seen today as adding value to historical sites that have survived with their varied layers and additions intact. The common underlying formal principles shared by traditional styles tend to harmo-

nize superficial differences; the extent to which
this traditional layering of styles and additions
through time is disrupted by the introduction
of a new style depends on the degree to which
the contrast between the new and old expressions arises not solely from stylistic differences
but from divergent conceptions of architecture. Because of its potentially greater impact
on historic surroundings, use of this strategy
by modernist designers in traditional contexts
requires extraordinary finesse and tact. Success
is then largely a matter of scale and the degree
to which the contrasting new work impinges
on the observer's perceptions of the original
setting. Paul Spencer Byard is undoubtedly correct in suggesting that, regardless of style, the
meaning of the historic resource must predominate in any "combined work" that incorpo-
rates both historical and modernist elements.
(Byard, 1998, pp. 85.) Judgments as to how
successfully the primacy of the historic character has been maintained will vary, but in cases
where the historic setting is publicly recognized
as one of great cultural value, the imposition of
conspicuous contrast that alters the preexisting
character—irrespective of the purported meanings of the new or old buildings—is very likely
to be inconsistent with the fundamental aims
of preservation. (Fig. 11.1.)

The Capitoline Hill, the Vittorio Emanuele II Monument, and the Piazza del Campidoglio, Rome

The Intentional Opposition strategy almost
makes no sense in Rome. What radical or
adversarial gesture would make any difference in competition with the weight of so
much history? But Michelangelo's dome at St.
Peter's Basilica, rising majestically still over the
city, was clearly intended by its designers and
patrons as a radically new vision, even if rendered in familiar classical forms. What could
be more oppositional than the destruction of
the Constantinian basilica to make way for
that of Bramante, Michelangelo, and Bernini?
And yet, typically for the sixteenth- and seventeenth-century architects involved in that long
and complex project, what appears to us as a
sweeping removal of late-antique or medieval
fabric was seen by them as reestablishing a
deeper continuity with an even older tradition.
What stood between the present and the distant
past (hence, called the Middle Ages) was seen
as a barbaric defacement of the splendor of
antiquity. Intentional Opposition in the hands
of the Renaissance masters was, therefore, not

the imposition of something new, but a deliberate return to something old.

On the Capitoline Hill one finds an example of the Intentional Opposition strategy at its most subtle, in which the preexisting character of a site is transformed in order to reinforce deep connections with the history of the place. In his design for the Piazza del Campidoglio, Michelangelo undoubtedly intended a visible rupture with the former condition of the site, though in truth the contrast was not as great as it might seem. Views of the Campidoglio before Michelangelo's work began reveal that the shift of orientation of the Capitoline buildings from the east (where they had overlooked the Forum) to the west (where they now faced the medieval town along the Tiber) had already occurred, and by the thirteenth century the Palazzo Senatorio, the Palazzo dei Conservatori, and the Church of Santa Maria in Aracoeli had all been given the form in which

Michelangelo inherited them. (Krautheimer, pp. 285–86.) His arrangement determined in part by existing buildings, Michelangelo created a new model of urban space-making that drew together the ancient and modern cities and expanded the expressive capabilities of the classical language in the process. (Fig. 11.3)

Pope Paul III commissioned the artist-architect in 1537 to create a setting for the monumental equestrian statue of Marcus Aurelius (erroneously thought to depict the first Christian emperor, Constantine, hence its preservation) in the civic square atop the Capitoline Hill, which had in ancient times been the symbolic heart of Roman religion and which, in medieval times, had become the political center of the city. In Michelangelo's scheme the existing medieval Palazzo Senatorio atop the ruined Tabularium received a refined new elevation dramatized by a centralized staircase and bell tower and embellished by ancient statues. The

11.3. Piazza del Campidoglio, Rome, by Michelangelo, designed 1537.

A definitive change to an existing context is sometimes appropriate. Here Michelangelo created the first great "urban interior" of the Renaissance and gave us a model widely imitated elsewhere. Completion of his design took four centuries to accomplish.

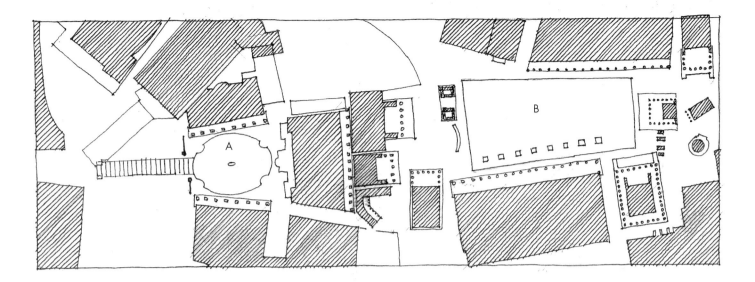

11.4. Plan diagram of the
Roman Forum and the Piazza
del Campidoglio, after David
Mayernik, *Timeless Cities,*
2003.

Michelangelo's plan of the
piazza is a metaphorical
bridge across space and
time. His new civic square
(A) mirrors the ancient
Forum to the east (B),
reversing its trapezoidal
shape and adapting the
ancient classical language
to new purposes and
meanings.

adjacent Palazzo dei Conservatori, which had
already received a colonnaded loggia, was given
a new monumental façade, and this was in turn
mirrored by a new matching building placed
symmetrically about the axis of the Palazzo
Senatorio. While transforming the character of
the medieval buildings, the architect nonetheless chose for his new façades a material palette
rooted in the place, combining the Roman brick
of the medieval town with the mellow travertine of so many ancient structures. The bronze
statue of the emperor was set as a freestanding
element in the center of the new square, whose
distinctive oval paving plan and subtle domical
surface superbly symbolize Rome as the *caput
mundi* while unifying the irregular geometry
of the surrounding buildings. Finally, the *scali-
nata,* a broad flight of ramped steps, led up to
the new piazza from the west, linking the new
civic square with the contemporary city. Further tokens of Roman antiquity were arrayed
along the balustrade that formed the edge of
the terrace, including the colossal figures of
Castor and Pollux. The whole group of buildings was deftly inserted against the flank of
the medieval Church of Santa Maria Aracoeli,
itself occupying the site of an ancient temple.
(See Bayley, 1984, pp. 5–9.)

Michelangelo's architecture, displaying a
contrast with the preexisting buildings that any
contemporary observer would have instantly
recognized, nevertheless remains faithful to the
classical language of architecture, a circum-
stance that makes its designer's innovations
possible and at the same time guarantees the
work's ultimate coherence and relationship to
its ancient site. These buildings are in no sense

"revivalist" but represent a further development of the language and literature of classicism. At the same time, the "rule-breaking"
character of Michelangelo's designs has often
been exaggerated. In truth, the Campidoglio
represents both allegiance to the classical tradition and a determination to contribute to
it, *to take it further*—which is the particular
prerogative of the master. (MacIntyre, 1990,
pp. 64–66.) Michelangelo's buildings and the
space they enclose, like many of the architect's
works, were soon recognized as constituting a
new model that subtly but irrevocably redrew
the centerline of the whole classical tradition.
(Norberg-Schulz, 1980, pp. 151–52.)

The entire composition offers a further connection between the distant past and the present: the trapezoidal space of the piazza mirrors
the similarly trapezoidal (but reversed) space
of the Roman Forum below and to the east.
The Palazzo Senatorio thus became a "hinge"
between the ancient and modern worlds at the
scale of the city as a whole. (Mayernik, 2003,
pp. 55–58.) In sum, Michelangelo's conception of the Campidoglio is nothing less than an
extraordinary weaving of the threads of time
into the fabric of place. It is therefore fitting to
recall that Michelangelo's design for the complex was carried out after his death by a series
of subsequent architects, culminating in the
completion of the intended pavement design
only in the twentieth century. (See Chapter 8.)
(Fig. 11.4)

An entirely different use of the Intentional
Opposition strategy is the monument to Vittorio
Emanuele II (also known as the Vittoriano) at
the north end of the Capitoline Hill, designed

in 1885 by Giuseppe Sacconi and inaugurated in 1911. The designer's choice of dazzling white marble and the style and scale of Imperial Rome signals a deliberate break with the Baroque and its association with papal power symbolized by Michelangelo's dome and Bernini's colonnades at St. Peter's. The Risorgimento was determined to reshape Rome as a suitable capital for the newly united and secular Kingdom of Italy, and this explains the overweening nationalism of the monument. Subtlety in the design of the new structure or sensitivity to the character of the existing context—including the Campidoglio next door—would have diluted the rhetorical force of the nonarchitectural program behind Sacconi's conception, but the audacity of the architect's design has come at the price of the continuity of the millennial fabric of the city. (See fig. 5.6.)

Despite the nearly unanimous detestation of the monument by historians and critics, Sacconi's building is a masterful exercise in classical composition in the tradition of the great Roman sanctuary at Palestrina. Rising in a series of terraces toward a subtly curved monumental Corinthian colonnade crowned with heroic sculpture, the monument is a treasury of inventive classical detail richly embellished with figurative sculpture and ornament. There is no doubt whatever of its seriousness of purpose, its self-conscious majesty as the Altare della Patria—the Altar of the Nation. While it appears out of scale with the city around it today, period photographs reveal the extent to which the Vittoriano has suffered from the removal of its immediate context in the 1930s, when surrounding buildings were demolished to isolate the monument—along with its ancient neighbors. If the Vittoriano were still embedded in the urban fabric that formerly surrounded the Capitoline and, ideally, were the Temple of Jupiter Capitolinus and its ancient companion structures still standing, we would probably not find it out of scale.

At the same time, the uncompromising object-quality of the monument—its refusal to engage the city around it except as a backdrop to its own rhetorical exhortation—precludes the physical links to its place one expects to find in parallel with its use of the classical language. Indeed, it is only this continuity of formal language that saves the Vittoriano from being utterly disastrous for the city. (Imagine if it had been instead designed in some alien and exotic style but retained the same scale and material

contrast!) Unlike the sixteenth-century design of the Campidoglio, the Vittoriano is trapped in the same contradiction that entangles most modern applications of the Intentional Opposition strategy—the desire simultaneously to promote and subvert connections in space and time without which no building can join an ensemble of other buildings to compose a city.

Castelvecchio, Verona

In a 1978 speech, Carlo Scarpa said: "I want to make a confession: I'd like some critic to discover in my works certain intentions I've always had. I mean an immense desire to belong inside tradition, but without having capitals and columns, because you just can't do them anymore. Not even a god could design an Attic base nowadays." (Quoted in Dal Co and Marriol, 1985, pp. 286–87.) Scarpa's words illuminate for us the combination of alienation and nostalgia he felt toward historical architecture, expressed as if one's love of old buildings were a guilty secret to be hidden from one's peers. This illicit longing for tradition is the key to understanding both this architect's work and the contradictory attitudes of many others in the preservation field today.

The Castelvecchio, a medieval fortress that had been substantially remodeled in the early nineteenth century, had previously been converted from military to museum use between 1923 and 1926 by Antonio Avena, director of the museum at the time, and architect Ferdinando Forlati. They restored the crenellations and medieval towers and created new façades for the Napoleonic barracks facing the old central parade ground, which they transformed into an Italian garden of lawns, walks, and decorative planting. Their rebuilt garden façades featured a picturesque arrangement of openings framed by antique medieval and early Renaissance elements salvaged from Veronese buildings that had been demolished. In the center of the north side, opposite the entry from the street, a three-bay loggia served as entrance to the museum, with an array of windows above, punctuated by stone balconies and balustrades. (Fig. 11.6) Forlati, whose distinguished postwar career in restoration included participating in the conference that drafted the Charter of Venice in 1964, was before the war considered a master for his work at the Castelvecchio; but by the late 1950s, Avena and Forlati's work was considered completely out of date. (Ceschi, 1970, p. 141.)

In 1957 museum director Licisco Magagnato invited Scarpa to undertake another remodeling of the museum, intended to bring it into conformance with current architectural and interpretive standards. Scarpa's work, undertaken in two phases, 1957–64 and 1967–73, began with an archeological examination of the site to bring to light its original medieval fabric and proceeded into a campaign of "creative demolition," ultimately removing a substantial amount of nineteenth- and early-twentieth-century material. (Murphy, 1991, pp. 4, 9.) In the process he obliterated virtually every trace of Avena and Forlati's work inside the building. He retained Forlati's "fake" garden façades (as Scarpa described them) but relocated the museum entrance off-center to disturb the "false" symmetry his predecessor had introduced. He located a new system of windows and doors recessed behind the existing Gothic stone frames and arches and designed asymmetrically gridded divisions for these recessed curtain-wall units, inspired, no doubt, by the contrapuntal geometrical compositions of Piet Mondrian. Throughout the complex, the curvature and irregularity of the older walls and openings are juxtaposed with the new, strictly orthogonal pieces inserted by Scarpa, which are rendered so as to be clearly distinguishable from the original fabric on first glance.

As attractive as many of Scarpa's ingenious details are, they consistently reinforce our perception of the Castelvecchio as a fragment—poetic and suggestive, no doubt, but a ruin nonetheless. This decontextualization of the monument is enforced by means of his confrontation of the old buildings with all of the principles of modernist architecture: the restless space in which objects seem to be suspended as in a fluid flow, the dramatization and miniaturization of structural components and materials, the invention of elements from assemblies of abstract shapes, the collagelike juxtaposition of new and old elements, and the use of joints and connections between materials as a form of ornament. But why should we accept a decontextualized fragment as being more truthful or authentic than a recomposed whole? Is Scarpa's preference for the fragment over the whole simply a self-fulfilling prophesy—one destined only to produce more fragments? (Fig. 11.5.)

11.5. Castelvecchio, Verona, fourteenth to nineteenth centuries, remodeled by Carlo Scarpa, 1957–73, view from across the Adige River.

Scarpa's gutting of the old castle is most evident inside, but in this riverside view one of his incisions separating the Napoleonic-era wall from the medieval towers shows the "creative demolition" that he used to present the monument as a series of fragments.

11.6. Castelvecchio, Verona, remodeled by Ferdinando Forlati, 1923–26 and by Carlo Scarpa, 1957–73, view across garden courtyard toward loggia.

Scarpa erased most of what Forlati did, except for a "fake" garden façade where he had incorporated sculptural fragments into the building fabric. Instead, Scarpa treated the entire building as a collection of decontextualized artifacts.

In the context of these questions, Scarpa's declaration (quoted at the beginning of this section) of emotional attachment to a tradition that his intellectual commitments require him to reject takes on deeper meaning. He cannot reconcile the divorce between the head and the heart, and so the traditional and the modernist worlds must remain suspended in irresolvable confrontation. While in logic it is not possible simultaneously to posit a proposition and its antithesis, it may perhaps be possible in art. If any modernist architect had the artistry to synthesize historic and modernist aesthetics, it was Carlo Scarpa; but even he could not do it. Perhaps if he had understood the rational basis for traditional architecture and recognized the

A

Romanesque Revival style, first popularized by Henry Hobson Richardson, the five-part façade features projecting center and end pavilions united by rhythmic tall window bays with semicircular arches. It is clear that the building was intended to fill the entire block, but when construction stopped, only the half facing the square was completed, leaving a rough brick back elevation overlooking a parking lot. The rear corners of the building were left incomplete so that the stone cladding could be keyed in whenever construction resumed. (Fig. 11.7A)

When a ten-story stack and storage addition was built in 1982, the architect, Harry Weese, elected to forgo extending the old building according to its original design or material palette and instead produced a windowless volume clad in red brick with a cylindrical corner tower. (Fig. 11.7B) The addition, matching the height of the original library, is set out of alignment with the street wall of the original building, which it joins by means of deep and broad recesses, further reinforcing the distinction between the new and old structures. These recesses—a commonplace in modernist additions to traditional buildings—suggest that the addition was intended not to compete with the original structure. For visual interest on the blank wall facing Clark Street, the architect designed patterns in the brick surface that suggest an arrangement of interlacing arches, but the relationship of these arches to the arcades enlivening the original building is obscure.

The Newberry Library addition would be of little interest outside its local context had it not been featured for several years as an example of "recommended" practice for additions to historic buildings in the *Guidelines* published by the National Park Service to supplement the *Secretary's Standards*. (National Park Service, 1995.) This official sanction likely inspired numerous similar additions conceived as mute "background buildings" and considered "compatible" by virtue of occupying a volume matching the bulk and height of the adjacent historic structure, though it has virtually nothing else in common with the historic building. By defining the criteria for compatibility in terms of mere dimensional similarity, this interpretation of the *Standards* tries to avoid the contradiction otherwise inherent in the Intentional Opposition strategy. Instead, the example of the Newberry Library demonstrates that a meaningful compatibility cannot

11.7. Newberry Library,
Chicago, by Henry Ives Cobb, 1893, with addition by Harry Weese, 1982.

A. Original façade.

B. View of addition and older building.

The characterless addition to the library, long used by the National Park Service as an example of "recommended" practice, reveals the contradictions in current preservation philosophy. Weese's addition disregards indications that the building was intended to be continued in kind.

Romanticism implicit in modernist design, he might have been able to reach a more fruitful balance. Scarpa's Castelvecchio finally reveals the dilemma of an artist who can neither embrace nor turn his back on the tradition that he guiltily admits he loves, and so instead he disfigures it.

The Newberry Library, Chicago

The Newberry Library, one of the leading research libraries in the United States, occupies a landmark building designed by Henry Ives Cobb (1893) providing a stately backdrop to Washington Square, Chicago's oldest surviving park. An essay in Cobb's preferred

B

be achieved in the absence of a common architectural language.

The Grand Louvre, Paris

Over the course of more than four hundred years, the Louvre gradually expanded from its original medieval footprint into a complex of vast size. Starting in the middle of the sixteenth century, the buildings grew in essentially the same style. Then, in 1989, President François Mitterand opened the Grand Louvre, an enlarged and renovated museum complex commissioned from the Chinese-American architect I. M. Pei. Pei's master plan placed a large central entry hall below the Cour Napoléon, lighted by and entered from the famous glass pyramid. This structure is a technical tour de

force: The supporting steel framework is light and airy and the glass volume viewed from outside is nearly transparent during the day, unlike many other glass envelopes which, represented as transparent in renderings, turn out to be opaque. The pyramid may have been the best possible shape for the new entrance structure if one accepts the premise that anything should be constructed in the Cour Napoléon, and its reflectivity and transparency under different light and weather conditions often create striking images. The pyramidal shape itself—recalling symbolically the ancient Egyptian monuments and Napoleon's campaigns on the Nile—allows views of the historic façades around it and is therefore less intrusive in the space of the Cour than a cube or sphere would have been. These alternatives were evidently

placement of smaller pyramid-skylights in front of the entrances to the Pavillon Denon and Pavillon Richelieu, and the curious blankness of the portion of the Cour behind the cluster of pools and pyramids lend the Pei intervention the character of a banal American corporate office building plaza.

Pei's gesture of Intentional Opposition brought High Modernism into the heart of the complex as confidently as François I had brought classicism to it in the sixteenth century, a gesture equally motivated by a desire to transform the preexisting character. Pei's intervention would seem to be a definitive break with four centuries of continuous development, but the future chapters in the story are uncertain. In 2005, Pei was invited back to update his master plan to handle a level of visitation double that anticipated by his earlier plan. A proposal to reconstruct the Tuilleries is on the table. At this point the question is whether the architects and directors of the museum will return to the historical pattern of imitation and invention or will pursue further assertions of difference in defiance of the overwhelming expression of continuity that makes the Louvre the great monument it is.

Greenwich Village Townhouse, New York

The townhouse at 18 West 11th Street in Greenwich Village, remodeled in 1978 by Hardy Holzman Pfeiffer Associates, signals the appearance of an irreverent new attitude toward historic settings. (Fig. 11.8) In this case the Intentional Opposition to the previously existing form of the landmark building was a response to a historical event. The new façade replaces a unit in a row of six Greek Revival townhouses built by Henry Brevoort in 1844. No. 18 was destroyed by a terrorist bomb in the 1970s—the basement of the building had housed a bomb-making laboratory and the fatal explosion was evidently an accident. Rather than restoring the old façade, the new design breaks out in a Cubistic eruption that recalls the violence done to the older building. The lower two floors of the elevation form an aggressive, angular projection whose shape, large blank openings, and minimalist detailing constitute an unmistakable visual sign of rupture. The semantic ambiguity of the design allows it to evade the question of whether it

11.8. Townhouse at 18 West 11th Street, New York, 1844, remodeled by Hardy Holtzman Pfeiffer Associates, 1978.

Now widely considered a landmark in its own right, Hardy's façade remains a violent intrusion on a civilized street, immortalizing the terrorist bombing that leveled the original house. Restoration of the original façade probably would not be permitted today.

considered and then rejected by the architect and client before settling on the pyramid. Also rejected, for reasons of "historical rigor," were proposals to build new structures in the Cour more in harmony with the architecture of the surrounding buildings. (Soulié, 2003, pp. 37–39.) (See fig. C.1.)

On the other hand, the detailing of the surrounding pools, fountains, pavements, and four smaller pyramids strikes a less happy note in contrast to the embodied geometry and sculptural richness of the historic setting. What was conceived as a mirage-like vision of an "eternal" shape hovering above the fountain pools presents, in actuality, a more banal reality in terms of materiality and detail. The bull-nose profiles of the walls around the pools, the unsightly gutter into which the sloping walls of the main pyramid descend, the unfortunate

is the violence of those who destroyed the old house or the traditional building itself that is the subject of the architect's protest. (National Trust, 1980, pp. 260–61.)

Hugh Hardy's design has been almost uniformly praised by critics and preservation professionals as marking the tragic historical event that reduced the old townhouse to rubble, giving expression to contemporary architectural ideas, and maintaining respect for the historical context (by means of its use of matching brick and containing its explosive shapes within the frame of the former structure). Paul Goldberger voiced a common sentiment when he commented that reconstruction of the destroyed Greek Revival house would have "denied history." (Goldberger, 2005.) By now, this has become a familiar refrain: It is assumed that an appropriate way to commemorate tragic events is to reflect the tragedy literally in architectural form. This temptation, employing architectural design as a form of protest, borrows from movements in modern art the notion of "attacking the awful by increasing the awfulness." (Glazer, 2007, p. 81.) A similar approach, on a much larger scale, was taken in the chosen design for rebuilding the World Trade Center site nearly three decades later. (Stephens, Luna, and Broadhurst, 2004.) But by violating the decorous harmony of the preexisting row of townhouses, Hardy's design doesn't so much memorialize as perpetuate the effects of the bomb blast on the historic block.

I do not believe that repair or reconstruction of historic environments damaged or destroyed by tragic events—whether man-made or natural disasters—is a "denial of history" any more than for a physician to treat a wounded or sick human being is a denial of the reality of suffering. The rebuilt historic centers of Warsaw and Dresden offer contrary examples of the potentially healing effects of recovering valued historic places. (See figs. 5.13 and 7.9.) In my view a more appropriate way to commemorate the violence done to West 11th Street would have been to restore the house and erect a historical marker in front of it or place a memorial in a nearby park. A more puzzling issue is why many preservationists feel that Hardy's intervention should now itself be accorded landmark protection: The New York City Landmarks Preservation Commission would probably not allow this building to be restored to its original Greek Revival design. Such a position institutionalizes rupture and disconti-

nuity at the expense of the values that made the street worthy of historic district protection in the first place.

The Morgan Library and Museum, New York

The precedent set by the Hardy townhouse challenged the superficial contextualism of the 1980s, which was soon abandoned by fashionable architects in favor of a newly aggressive posture toward existing historic contexts. Recent additions to three masterworks of McKim, Mead & White in New York—the Harvard Club, the Brooklyn Museum, and the J. Pierpont Morgan Library—illustrate this more confrontational attitude. These projects were endorsed by the same Landmarks Pres-

11.9. The Harvard Club, New York, by McKim, Mead & White, 1892, with addition by Davis Brody Bond Architects, 2004, detail of new and old façades.

Demonstrating the modernist practice of reducing composite form to abstract shape, the addition (left) continues horizontal lines from the original classical building. But the juxtaposition of the gridded curtain wall and the finely scaled masonry original isolates the landmark and interrupts the otherwise continuous streetscape. (See also figs. C.30 and C.31.)

11.10. J. Pierpont Morgan Library and Museum, New York, by McKim, Mead & White, 1906, with Annex by Benjamin Wistar Morris, 1928, and additions by Renzo Piano Workshop, completed 2006.

A. New entrance from street.

B. Detail of glass "gasket."

C. Original library building by Charles McKim.

Piano's metal and glass additions decontextualize the three historic buildings on the site, reducing them to the status of museum artifacts. Worse, the McKim building and the Annex have lost their historic relationship both to the street and to each other.

A

ervation Commission that thirty years before had argued before the Supreme Court to prevent similarly insensitive proposals. That it was another McKim, Mead & White masterwork—Pennsylvania Station—whose loss in 1964 galvanized the preservation movement nationwide makes the present treatment of these buildings even more disturbing. Indeed, the destruction of Penn Station may not have ended: As of this writing, the needlessly aggressive posturing of SOM's proposed new station within the surviving Farley Post Office opposite the site of the demolished station still threatens to overwhelm the last remaining structure from that grand civic complex. (Ballon, 2002, pp. 153–96.) While the fabric

of these landmark structures has, in fact, been preserved, the historic character of the monuments and their roles in architecturally and historically significant urban ensembles have been seriously compromised. (Figs. 7.1, 11.9, C.30, and C.31) The story of the Morgan Library project is symptomatic of the current contemporary approach—and reveals the continuing legacy of the theory of Brandi and the Venice Charter.

The original library building is one of the masterpieces of the period now known as the American Renaissance. (Fig. 11.10C) Designer Charles McKim, with his customary mastery of massing, proportion, and detail, took what is programmatically a windowless box and

B

C

A

11.11. Soldier Field, Chicago, by Holabird & Roche, 1924–26, with new stadium by Wood & Zapata, 2003.

A. East side.

B. West side.

The original stadium's noble Doric colonnades are now dwarfed by an architectural train wreck. On the west side, an alien form hovers above the peristyles as if about to destroy them. In 2006 the site was removed from the National Register of Historic Places.

rendered it as a pavilion in a garden. (Stern et al., 1983, p. 103.) The entrance façade, with its recessed porch and Serliana based on the garden façade of the Villa Medici in Rome, is austere but welcoming. The marble blocks of the exterior walls are exquisitely laid in the ancient Greek manner, without mortar. Set in its residentially scaled garden behind Morgan's brownstone house, the Library "created a uniquely Arcadian idyll in the midst of the city's street grid." (Stern et al., 1983, p. 103.) Nothing could be more unlike "the world of robber barons and dust-coated scholars" that the critic of the *New York Times* saw in it. (Ouroussoff, 2006.) The library's first addition, Benjamin Wistar Morris's Annex, which also provided an accommodating entrance after the Library opened to the public, is thoughtfully detailed

and proportionally congruent with McKim's pavilion, to which it was originally joined by a handsome link featuring a Palladian window and enclosing a small garden court. The surviving Victorian brownstone home of Jack Morgan on the opposite corner completed the preexisting three-building complex.

Additions to the Library group, designed by the Renzo Piano Workshop and opened in 2006, have permanently altered our perception of the entire site. The new construction is starkly differentiated in both style and character from the three preexisting landmark structures and compatible with them only with respect to size: Piano's new structures are about the same height as the older buildings, with much of the new space concealed below grade. In explanatory notes accompanying the inaugural exhibition of his designs, Piano revealed that he was inspired by utilitarian buildings along the old New York waterfront. While these vestiges of a more heroic industrial age inspire many, one wonders why the architect chose a precedent irrelevant to the building to which he was making the addition. Perhaps, as some critics suggested, the architect's allusions to the city's industrial past were meant to evoke the "gritty" character of "authentic" New York in contrast to the "elitist" world of Morgan and his collection. If true, this is a remarkably patronizing attitude toward the institution and the collection the addition is intended to serve, and yet this characterization rings true for the visitor to the completed project. (Goldberger, 2006, and Ouroussoff, 2006.) (Fig. 11.10A.)

Indeed, the character of Piano's new entrance and atrium could not be more different from the three historic buildings it intends to join together. The basic parti of a central public space in the form of a generously scaled metal-and-glass conservatory is not an inappropriate gesture and would offer some relief from the solidity and opacity of the Library and Annex buildings. (Previously, in 1991, Voorsanger & Mills likewise had placed an oddly curvilinear glazed atrium between the buildings, but this was removed in favor of the Piano scheme.) But Piano's insistent industrial aesthetic, without any concession to McKim's building and its historic neighbors that would draw them into dialogue as equal and respected partners, decontextualizes the historic structures, as if they were themselves artifacts in the Museum's collection. Piano departs from the pattern of classical composition displayed by the landmark structures by giving his two principal street elevations an even number of identical bays, thereby denying the center and underscoring their contrast with McKim's and Morris's façades.

Crucially, the architect's relocation of the public entrance from the Annex on 36th Street to the new atrium on Madison Avenue changes the relationship of the historic buildings to the public realm. Visitors now enter the Library and Museum through Piano's atrium and proceed into the original McKim building from the back—what is obviously the former service entrance—without seeing McKim's façade, thereby robbing the building of much of its meaning. (The previous public entry to the McKim building was likewise from the back, but by means of Morris's link after having passed through the Annex from 36th Street.) The architect's cultivation of difference at every scale, from the overall site plan to the smallest detail, ensures that visitors to the museum will never mistake the new construction for part of the historic ensemble it was supposed to organize and celebrate, but this radical differentiation comes at the cost of diminishing our understanding of the historic resources themselves.

Soldier Field, Chicago

In the case of the 2003 intervention at Soldier Field, the Intentional Opposition of the new construction so attacked the integrity of the historical monument that it produced a backlash. The new structure, erected inside the 1926 classical peristyles of the war memorial stadium designed by Holabird & Roche, caused the site to be removed from the National Register of Historic Places, a rare and drastic step. (Hill, 2006.) The new stadium—the work of architects Wood & Zapata—displays two distinct faces: On the east, a horizontally banded glass and stainless-steel bowl sits primly inside of the Greek Doric colonnades of the historic stadium; on the west, an immense, cantilevered seating structure extends out far above the granite peristyle, which seems about to be crushed beneath the angled planes of the massive, alien shapes hovering above it. (Fig. 11.11) The eastern and western halves of the new structure come together at the centers of the two ends of the stadium in an astonishing collision—it is not a stretch, nor would it probably offend the

B

designers, to call it a train wreck—while on the north the stadium extends a broad pedestrian entry trench, casually off-axis, toward the classical Field Museum opposite.

The intervention at Soldier Field illustrates Andrés Duany's characterization of modernist buildings in historic settings as parasitic: The designers evidently took particular pleasure in violating the formal order of the original stadium and its classical setting to produce a juxtaposition that is conspicuously more advantageous to the new elements than to the original structure. The removal of the site from the National Register was justified because the historic and architectural significance of the classical stadium had been effectively nullified. This admittedly extreme example demonstrates that Intentional Opposition does indeed have its limits, and although the architectural and preservation community has recognized that these limits were exceeded in this case, they have not yet established the place where suitable boundaries might be drawn.

Hearst Tower, New York

Recalling the 1978 United States Supreme Court decision upholding the decision of the New York City Landmarks Preservation Commission in the case of Grand Central Terminal, it is difficult to understand how the same commission in 2001 could approve—with a single abstention—a forty-story glass and stainless-steel tower designed by Norman Foster on top of the 1929 Hearst Building at Broadway and West 57th Street, designed by Joseph Urban. (See fig. C.4 and page 23.) The decision was not in the least controversial and sparked little protest, despite the similarity of the Foster design—in material, bulk, and impact on the landmark building below—to the rejected Breuer design of three decades before. The commission's chairman went so far as to declare it an appropriate addition that "completes" the original landmark building. (Dunlap, 2001.) The new tower, opened in 2006, was described by Paul Goldberger as "gorgeous, gemlike . . . sleek, refined, and filled with new technology," in contrast with what he described as Urban's "six stories of megalomaniacal pomp" down below. (Goldberger, 2006, pp. 98–100.) Clearly, there had been a change in attitude toward the suitability of modernist skyscrapers on top of traditional landmark buildings.

At issue in these cases was not whether an office tower should be built above either building—both had reputedly been intended to accommodate later towers, although no specific plans from the time of their construction existed. Rather, the issue was *what kind* of tower addition would be acceptable now, given that architectural styles had changed radically in the years since the original buildings were built. Given the similarities in bulk, scale, and materials of the two tower proposals, one can only conclude that a style and massing that the commission rejected as an "aesthetic joke" in 1968 had become more palatable by 2001. The *New York Times* reported that the commission's acceptance of the Foster project represented a shift from the "contextualism" that had long dominated the board's thinking

toward an embrace of designs that frankly juxtaposed the landmark with a radically different modernist aesthetic. (Dunlap, 2001.)

Upon second glance, Urban's building reveals much more than "megalomaniacal pomp." (One suspects Goldberger was thinking not of the building but of its sponsor, William Randolph Hearst, who by all accounts was both pompous and a megalomaniac.) The building, if we see it not as the short, squat structure it was in 2001, but as an intended base for a skyscraper, is not to be dismissed so easily. Urban himself was an architect of standing, a Viennese student of Otto Wagner who is remembered today for his designs for the Moderne auditorium of the New School in Greenwich Village and unbuilt schemes for a new Metropolitan Opera House when it was first proposed as a centerpiece for the embryonic Rockefeller Center. The Hearst Building is remarkably restrained in its architectural treatment, betraying more than a little sympathy with the "stripped classicism" popular at the time, though it is clearly governed by canonical classical composition and proportions. The only features that might remotely be considered pompous—but are really only exuberant—are the ornamental fluted column shafts supporting urns and flanked by sculptural figures, placed at the corners and above the entrance.

Foster gutted the entire interior volume of Urban's building, leaving only the exterior façades. Inside this empty shell the architect inserted an interior of Piranesian scale containing vertiginous mezzanines, multistory fountains, and ranks of escalators all rendered in contemporary minimalist style. Indeed, the historic building virtually ceases to exist; it is no more than a freestanding façade, a ghostly vestige of itself. Breuer's scheme for Grand Central Terminal had proposed a similar gutting of the building's interior. To be sure, Urban's Hearst Building did not possess a great public space like Whitney Warren's superb Main Concourse; still, the similarity of the proposals is as marked as the divergence in their reception by the Landmarks Commission and the preservation community.

One can plausibly argue that any skyscraper above Grand Central Terminal would have been unacceptable, but this is not true of the Hearst Building. Grand Central, whatever may have been the architect's intention for a subsequent tower, appears to us as an entire composition complete in itself; it does not inflect toward a missing part of the building for which it is a preparation. The original Hearst Building was, contrary to Goldberger's assessment, not so much pompous as servile; it did indeed inflect to a missing tower above it and the entrance was obviously scaled to be the entry to a much larger building.

Instead of Foster's glass sculpture, Urban's building could have received an office tower sheathed in matching stone and articulated in details consistent with those of the base. Although no design of Urban's for a tower survives, he must have had in mind something like the stripped classical-style towers of the 1920s in Lower Manhattan. Or, demonstrating that such conceptions can still be imagined today, consider the tower proposed in 2005 by Fairfax & Sammons Architects as part of a counterproject for the Hudson Yards site on the west side of Manhattan. Such a scheme truly would have completed the original building in a way sympathetic to the original architect's intention. (Fig. 11.12)

"Façadism" in Historic Districts

The Hearst Building demonstrates the increasing incidence of the demolition of the interiors of protected buildings, leaving only their façades and incorporating them into new, larger, and more economically profitable buildings. This practice has resulted in a series of travesties in which intimately scaled historic buildings have become ornamental frontispieces, masks, or bases to massive new structures completely different in composition, materials, style, and scale. This has been widely considered a victory for preservation but is, from the point of view argued in this book, a betrayal of the fundamental aims of the preservation movement, to say nothing of ideas of quality in architecture. (Gutheim and Lee, 2006, p. 331.) (Fig. 11.13) "Façadism," as this practice is known, is a logical consequence of the modernist decontextualization of historic architecture and the narrow focus of preservationists on material fabric in disregard of a building's formal design, structural integrity, use, interior space, or urban context. The familiar prohibition against "false history" means that historic façades *cannot* be integrated into new buildings in similar style to form greater visual wholes—they can only be submerged in architectural expressions that are conspicuously different, with an inevitable

11.12. Proposed office Tower for Hudson Yards, New York, by Fairfax & Sammons Architects, 2005.

Urban's base might have received a tower like one proposed by Richard Sammons for Hudson Yards. Traditionally composed and proportioned, and sheathed in a matching stone, such a tower would indeed have been a "completion" of the original landmark.

loss of their historic character as the necessary result.

All preservation must arise from respect for the historic resource, proceeding to a thoughtful assessment of its public value and significance. In some cases preservationists must recognize that the meaningful life of a designated building has passed and open up the site for reasonable new development. But by insisting on the routine retention of historic façades in visually lobotomized form, preservationists have served the interests of neither historic buildings nor quality new ones. This is not preservation, but a crude form of architectural taxidermy.

198–202 Piccadilly, London

This final example is a remarkable illustration of the bizarre logic often used by preservation authorities confronting a complex and highly sensitive site. Adjacent to the new structure stands the former Simpson's building, a pioneering modernist design of the 1930s that stood in marked contrast to its older eclectic neighbors. Recognizing that the Intentional Opposition

strategy was an essential component of the protected modernist building's historic character, preservation authorities required that this original relationship be maintained when an adjacent building was cleared for redevelopment. Accordingly, the architects used the Invention Within a Style strategy in relation to the nonmodernist surrounding buildings in order to preserve the rhetorical force of the Intentional Opposition represented by the modernist building in their midst.

The new building, designed by Robert Adam Architects, continues the eclectic but predominantly classical character of the preexisting setting as required by the authorities, but goes well beyond this to assert itself as an important work in its own right. The eight-story structure presents three different street elevations to reflect the different character of the surrounding streets. Piccadilly, an important thoroughfare serving the West End of London, receives the most elaborate classical treatment, including ornamental details modeled by the classical sculptor Alexander Stoddart, while the other two frontages are more restrained. Indeed, the new building meets all our expectations of an urban neighbor, in contrast to the protected

A

11.14. 198–202 Piccadilly, London, by Robert Adam Architects, 2007.

A. General view with adjacent landmarked modernist building.

B. View from opposite corner showing tower element.

Preservation authorities required a traditional style for the new building adjacent to a modernist landmark in order to maintain its original "oppositional" relationship to its context. Why would they not then require a new traditional building in a traditional context to maintain a congruent relationship?

modernist building, whose indifference to its setting has now become the focus of the preservationists' mandate. (Fig. 11.14.)

In this case the importance of protecting the oppositional character of the landmark building outweighed the usual commitment of preservation authorities to promoting the "architecture of our time" for new construction. We can speculate about the application of this London precedent to landmarks in other locations: If the authorities were willing to go to this length to preserve the original *oppositional* relationship between a modernist landmark and its traditional setting, why would they not also require new development to retain a formerly *consonant* relationship between a traditional landmark and surrounding traditional buildings? The case of the Piccadilly project reveals the unacknowledged double standard that has produced one set of rules for interventions in modernist landmark settings and another for traditional settings. A consistent conservation ethic toward the historic built environment requires a single set of values governing the appropriate care of all cultural resources regardless of architectural style. The London authority has gone halfway toward addressing this imbalance.

B

12.1. West Fourth Street, Greenwich Village, New York.

Despite many changes in demographic and economic profile over the last two centuries, Greenwich Village retains its bohemian character and diverse population because of, not in spite of, its designation as the largest historic district in the city.

CHAPTER 12

A Conservation Ethic

When we realize that past and present are not exclusive but inseparable realms, we cast off preservation's self-defeating insistence on a
fixed and stable past. Only by altering and adding to what we save
does our heritage remain real, alive, and comprehensible.

—DAVID LOWENTHAL, *The Past Is a*
Foreign Country (1985)

Previously, I expressed the view that every intervention in a preexisting urban composition, whether a new work or the modification of a building or site already there, is like joining a conversation already in progress. Every new building enters a context already established, unavoidably affecting it and also becoming a precedent, for better or worse, for subsequent interventions. When we introduce a new element or structure into a setting whose character is highly valued, we must proceed with the utmost caution and tact. Creating or conserving an urban district with a strong historical character requires that changes introduced promote conforming and minimize nonconforming features, placing the burden of proof on those interventions that would alter or redefine the preexisting character, however fascinating they may appear to be when considered in isolation.

An objection might be raised that such deference imposes mediocrity on new design, that placing comity and respect ahead of originality and novelty would cripple innovation and produce either characterless replication or Disneyland-like unreality. But these dangers do not arise within a continuing building tradition in which architects do not try to invent a new architecture *ex nihilo* or try to imitate historic models without understanding their formal language and historical significance. The untrained, speculative builders who produced most of the nineteenth-century urban housing stock so prized today in New York, London, Paris, or in smaller towns everywhere, often built structures that can only be considered mediocre if judged one building at a time; it is the way such buildings compose larger urban ensembles that makes them worthy of our study and preservation. The argument advanced here is not necessarily a call for all new architecture and urbanism to embrace the principles of traditional practice. My program is more limited: Deference and continuity of building cultures are particularly indicated in those places where traditional principles of design have been the predominant force in their formation. If, in those instances, restraint in the projection of "the architecture of our time" is called for in order to sustain the integrity and wholeness of valued historic environments, this is a sacrifice that the public has the right to demand and that architects must be willing to make. Daring formal experimentation, programmatic innovation, and technological progress are an inescapable part of the heritage of modernity, but they need not be pursued in ways injurious to historic buildings and cities. (Fig. 12.1)

Listening to History

There are two ways that we should look at historic places: First, we should view them as historians do, as the record of how individuals and communities built their homes, their monuments, their cities, for all sorts of varied reasons and in all kinds of varied circumstances. We want to know why they are the way they are. Second, as architects and citizens, we want to know what we can learn from them and what will happen to them next. We want to integrate them into the new world we are always in the process of making. Those of us who are in a position to make decisions about the future of historic environments need to view them according to a trajectory stretching from the past into the future. The longer the arc along which we envisage the history of a site, the deeper our understanding of it as both a historical and a future reality will be. In this way preservation gives the past a future.

There are two errors to be avoided, each represented by the more extreme positions associated with the names of Viollet-le-Duc and Ruskin, though not necessarily advocated by them. The first is to see the historical fabric as a mere pretext for the formal invention of the artist, ostensibly to "correct" or amplify the stylistic qualities of the original construction. The second is to see the original building as a quasi-sacred relic that may not be touched, but which must simply be respected as it traverses the inevitable life cycle of any organism from birth, to maturity, to decadence and death. While each of these attitudes might be the appropriate approach in some instances, neither can be adopted as a general principle, and the point between these extremes that we choose in any specific case cannot be predetermined. Each of these two extremes makes the mistake of seeing the historic setting as a fixed entity, as material to be used or safeguarded as the case may be, but strictly from the viewpoint of the present. But a living thing entrusted to our care cannot be treated in this way. Each monument or district will have its own life story and will require a different response.

In practice, we must look for balance between the preciousness and vulnerability of highly significant sites on one hand, and their suitability to accommodate *that part of their history still to come* on the other. Monuments of such importance that we view them as unal-

terable and inviolate are few; for most preservation sites, and especially for vernacular contributing buildings in historic districts, we need not attempt to arrest the process of growth and change that made them what they are now. Our task is to allow our historic building traditions to do their work and let time take its course in the same way that it always has, but now with thoughtful management of change to ensure, to the extent feasible, the survival of valued character and significance without unacceptable loss.

Rather than imposing a stylistic or ideological template on the historic resource, the conservation ethic enjoins us to allow the building itself to tell us what it is about, what kind of character it has or is capable of, and what kinds of interventions will help it to become "more itself." A historically informed architect sifts through the physical and documentary evidence, ensuring the closest reading of the tectonic, pragmatic, and aesthetic character of the site, both as architecture and as urbanism. The architect enters into a conversation with the work, interrogating it, probing its character, while at the same time imagining it playing an ongoing role in its context and in contemporary life. Perhaps the building does not corroborate conventional ideas about history or typology, in which case the architect must allow the building itself, rather than a priori theory, to suggest the appropriate treatment. The conversation between architect and historic building or district is a *hermeneutical* one that requires a reciprocal relationship of mutual self-disclosure and mutual interpretation between the historical work and the present day. But when dealing with sites of great importance, we can assume that the monument has more to offer us than we have to offer it. Indeed, "when the architects confront the monument in order to adapt it to new requirements, to substitute some part of it, or to complete it, it is always the monument itself that must enter into the vision of the architect and never vice versa." (Ceschi, 1970, p. 13.)

With deep respect for the hermeneutical conversation that ensues between the architect or restorer and the historic site, we also recognize an obligation toward beauty and wholeness. In cases where we have reasonable certainty about the previously whole state of the site—or the state intended by its designers—it is legitimate to restore or reconstruct the damaged or missing parts. (Fig. 12.2) A preferential option

12.2. Erectheum, Acropolis, Athens, fifth century B.C., restored 1994.

Restorers repaired the surviving masonry by inserting new Pentelikon marble to maintain the physical integrity of the fabric and reveal the form of the walls. Completing the missing masonry and constructing a roof would further protect the structure.

for wholeness means that we see the site as a work of cultural heritage that remains relevant to our present world rather than as simply a vestige of a world now lost to us (unless, of course, that is what it is, as in the case of a ruin from a now vanished society such as the Anasazi or the Etruscans). A predilection for wholeness means we remain open to the possibility that historic cultural insights and expressions may yet teach us something. The task of preservation is, therefore, not merely to ensure the survival of artifacts in isolation, but to *recontextualize* the remnants of the past and ensure their future as living parts of our world.

Wholeness is not uniformity. The buildings in a district or ensemble are not necessarily all alike; indeed, variety within a style or group of related styles is often the basis for deeming a place worthy of preservation. We also recognize that discontinuities and disruptions are real and valuable, in the city as in life, but they are not the norm. Our great cities are not lacking in evidence of disappointment and failure, nor do they deny a multiplicity of values and voices. Aspiring to continuity and wholeness is not a denial of history, but a desire to heal the sometimes unpleasant consequences of history. Our historic cities offer us a panoramic vision

of diverse human possibilities that is nonetheless keyed to the *telos*—that vision of the beautiful, sustainable, and just city, however imperfectly realized and however various the models suggested for realizing it. In preserving the wholeness of the historic building or ensemble, we also contribute to the wholeness of the entire city in which it is set, a city that we are still in the process of building.

The Legacy of Jane Jacobs

A powerful motive to conserve our historic cityscapes arises from our recognition that historic cities at their best offer diversity in the uses and ages of buildings, in economic and social life, and in the classes and livelihoods of their inhabitants. Jane Jacobs, who set the agenda for large-scale urban conservation in the United States over four decades ago, made such diversity the cornerstone of her analysis of success and failure in American cities. An economist rather than an architect or planner, she discussed urban preservation issues in terms of the "economic effects of time." The buildings and the mixture of uses and inhabitants constantly change and yet the life of the city continues. (Jacobs, 1962, p. 189.) In 1962, Jacobs did not foresee the extent to which rehabilitation tax credits or the renovation of abandoned industrial buildings into artists' lofts would transform historic neighborhoods in many American cities, narrowing or reversing the difference in cost and value between new and older buildings. Nevertheless, her argument for diversity proved correct and formed the basis for the New Urbanist alternative that would emerge two decades later.

In my view Jacobs underestimated the extent to which an aesthetic appreciation for old urban neighborhoods and landmark buildings would motivate the "urban renaissance" that has remade so many American cities since her book appeared. Historic districts—many of which were considered unsalvageable blighted areas forty years ago—are today often the most expensive real estate in their respective cities, largely because of their attractiveness to a generation raised in postwar suburbs. Jacobs's old neighborhood of Greenwich Village, or the Upper East and Upper West Sides of Manhattan, the Back Bay of Boston, Society Hill in Philadelphia, Georgetown in Washington, much of Charleston and Savannah, and the Gold Coast of Chicago are cases in point. In almost every case, the designation of a historic district results in a boost in property values and demand for real estate within the district. (City of New York, 2003.) Jacobs would undoubtedly counter that aesthetic interest alone, however important a consideration, would have been insufficient to produce these changes in the absence of economic incentives like rehabilitation tax credits and other public policies that have spurred investment and revitalization. Detroit, for example, had housing stock and public buildings as well designed as those in Milwaukee, and yet the former city continues to experience physical and economic decline while the latter has been singularly successful in revitalizing inner-city neighborhoods. There are many reasons for this difference, and architectural style is not prominent among them. An aesthetic appreciation of the city, a sense of confidence in its future, and the economic means to ensure that future must go hand in hand. The challenge today is to keep our historic centers from being spoiled by their own successes—the process of gentrification that Jacobs called "the self-destruction of diversity"—and to create new urban places that extend the benefits of historic neighborhoods to everyone who desires them. (Jacobs, 1962, p. 251.)

Finding inspiration in the emerging new paradigms of the life sciences, Jacobs identified the city as a problem in *organized complexity* requiring new ways of thinking. (Jacobs, 1962, p. 440.) She identified the misplaced metaphors and inappropriate models that distorted expert understanding of historic cities. Architects, she wrote, made the error of "substituting the order of art for the very different order of life." (Jacobs, 1962, p. 375.) Instead, Jacobs proposed an astonishing and illuminating metaphor that has not yet entered the popular consciousness as some of her other pronouncements have, but it should: A city is like a large field in darkness, in which a few random fires are burning: "Each fire, large or small, extends its radiance into the surrounding murk, and thus it carves out a space. But the space and the shape of that space exist only to the extent that the light from the fire creates it. . . . Where the murk between the lights becomes deep and undefinable and shapeless, the only way to give it form or structure is to kindle new fires in the murk or sufficiently enlarge the nearest existing fires." (Jacobs, 1962, pp. 376–77.) This image of the city as a collection of fires in the darkness in various stages of growing or expiring, puts the focus on the process of keeping cities alive rather than on fixed forms, products, and outcomes; it parallels the idea of cultural heritage as a set of traditions and practices rather than a collection of objects. All the successes of our cities and towns in the last decades can be understood as successful stewardship of the community fires; all the failures as forms of dereliction of civic duty, allowing fires to go out.

We can thank Jane Jacobs for the paradigm shift that finally institutionalized incremental, small-scale change instead of megaprojects that destroy the vitality of neighborhoods. The big issues of regional planning, transportation, utility infrastructure, land use, and balanced development transcend neighborhood boundaries and city limits and must be dealt with at the appropriate scale, but the little issues of street life, civic-minded neighborhoods, and people taking care of their homes, their streets, and their blocks are just as vital to the life of the city and cannot be neglected. Today a resurgent avant-garde expresses its admiration for the audacious redevelopment projects of the pre-Jacobs era and its frustration with the obstacles placed in the way of such plans by the reaction Jacobs and her followers inspired. (Ballon and Jackson, 2007, pp. 65–66, and Haskell, 2006.) But the vitality of our streets and neighborhoods must not be put at risk in the interest of competition with global capitals elsewhere, especially those—like the newly affluent cities of the Middle East and Eastern Asia—that have obliterated their historic centers in favor of architectural menageries designed by the current avant-garde. A great city remains great only as long as it manages to take care of both big and little matters and, at the same time, to balance continuity and change at both the large and small scales.

Preservation and New Urbanism

While sprawl was extending its monotonous placelessness across vast tracts of the American landscape, historic cities and towns were undergoing a similarly destructive transformation: they were being *suburbanized* as development patterns, codes, and redevelopment standards devised for the suburbs were imposed on urbanized areas. Central business districts became clusters of high-rise office buildings surrounded by empty plazas and mammoth parking garages. Zoning laws prohibited residential uses on upper stories above ground floor retail and disallowed conversion of redundant office or commercial space to residential apartments. Live-work units were proscribed in districts exclusively dedicated to commercial or residential uses. High space-per-square-foot or space-per-dwelling-unit parking requirements limited in-town housing and commercial development. Traffic engineers focused solely on "level of service" to drivers passing through downtown areas, turning formerly thriving retail centers into traffic corridors of one-way streets, limited parking, and narrow sidewalks—an unattractive place for pedestrians. (Kunstler, 1994 and Emerson, 2006.)

New Urbanism sought to reverse these ill effects by reintroducing the diversity of uses, income groups, building types, densities, and scales that Jacobs saw as giving life to cities. Desuburbanization of the city center requires replacing single-use monocultural zoning with multiuse neighborhoods showing a balance of housing, office, retail, and institutional occupancies. A landmark in this kind of redevelopment was Alexander Cooper and Stanton

A

B

12.3. Battery Park City, New York, various architects, 1978–2008.

A. View of South End Avenue.

B. View of newer buildings at north end.

The build-out of the Battery Park City master plan started well, with streets and blocks modeled after the best examples in historic Manhattan neighborhoods. Later development abandoned historic models for inarticulate abstraction, impoverishing the resulting urban fabric. (See fig. 1.8.)

Eckstut's 1978 master plan for Battery Park City in New York. (See fig. 1.8.) Their scheme was as radical as it was simple: The city would simply make more of itself. By extending the street grid of Manhattan onto their landfill site, they created additional blocks of New York fabric that could be developed over time by different builders and architects. Their master plan laid out streets and public spaces and established design guidelines for the new con-

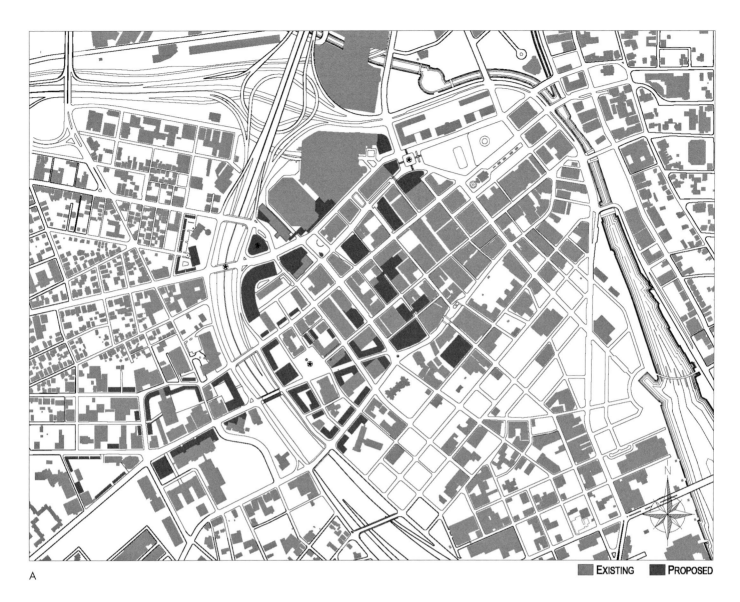

A

EXISTING   PROPOSED

12.4. Revitalization of the Downcity district, Providence, Rhode Island, by Duany Plater-Zyberk & Company, 1991–2004.

A. Master plan.

B. General view of Downcity, Providence, from the Providence River.

The convergence of New Urbanism and historic preservation is evident in the urban plan for Providence, which proposes locations and massing for new construction that reinforces the network of streets and public space in the historic downtown district.

struction. While the original portions of the plan were realized with buildings based on historic New York precedents, more recent construction has, disappointingly, departed from the original concept and regressed into banal abstraction.

This and other examples demonstrate that "good urbanism"—in the form of an urban code specifying mixed uses, a "walkable" configuration of streets and blocks, and building volumes regulated to define and enclose public space—is not enough to produce a beautiful townscape. The architectural scale must be considered or there will be little to attract the eye of the pedestrian, whose presence in those streets and spaces is so essential to achieving New Urbanist objectives. The stylistic implications of the urban design plan must find a reciprocal expression in the individual buildings, and the buildings must rise on an urban plan that disposes them to best advantage. This

is simply to say that New Urbanist practice cannot be style-neutral. The styles of the urban design plan and the buildings raised on it need not be the same, but they cannot be antithetical. (Fig. 12.3)

New Urbanist plans for greenfield sites like Battery Park City—or the hundreds of new traditional neighborhood developments (TNDs) on the suburban fringes—have been widely publicized, but proposals for the reurbanization of historic centers have begun to have significant impact on decision-making and planning processes in already built-up areas. In 1991, Duany Plater-Zyberk & Company prepared a revitalization plan for the Downcity neighborhood of Providence, Rhode Island, integrating new construction and historical resources into a continuous fabric that could be constructed incrementally. (The plan was revisited and augmented with additional detailed proposals in 2004 and is currently being implemented.)

B

(Miller, 2006.) Similar plans prepared by this and other firms in Norfolk, West Palm Beach, Minneapolis, Baltimore, and Philadelphia have led to the redevelopment of former industrial zones, abandoned commercial waterfronts, and decommissioned military installations, and their reintegration into the city as new mixed-use neighborhoods. New master plans and urban codes for Los Angeles and Miami have begun the process of "urban reurbanization" in those sprawling cities. The historic centers of our cities, if they are to remain vital settings for contemporary life while preserving their surviving historic character, must become urban laboratories in which the insights of Camillo Sitte and Gustavo Giovannoni and their followers are brought together and tested. Opportunities for the fruitful collaboration of urbanists and preservationists will undoubtedly expand as environmental distress gradually forces a reversal in the growth of suburban sprawl and the planned contraction of urban areas increasingly becomes the focus of planners and architects throughout the developed world. (Fig. 12.4)

Sustainability

It is becoming increasingly clear that the demand for environmental sustainability will ultimately supersede all other issues in the management of the built environment, with respect to both new construction and preservation. James Marston Fitch, who was remarkably prescient on this subject, called attention to the relationship between preservation and energy conservation decades ago. (Fitch, 2006, pp. 254–55.) No preindustrial society could afford to throw away its old clothes, let alone buildings and entire urban neighborhoods. Recycling and adapting buildings to new uses, often multiple times, has been the rule throughout history. As Quinlan Terry has observed, "Real sustainability is a four-hundred-year-old building still in active use." (Terry, 2005.) Preservationists must take the lead in educating the public, as well as developers and policy-makers, in the economic and environmental benefits of adaptive use, long-term occupancy, and permanent maintenance of older buildings and developed urban areas. Historic preservation is sustainable development because traditional architecture and urbanism are, to a large degree, already "green." So far, the official organs of "sustainable design"—preeminently the LEED certification process of the U.S. Green Building Council—have only begun to recognize the value of reusing historic structures and rehabilitating historic neighborhoods. (Rypkema, 2006.)

A substantial reduction in energy waste would follow from a simple moratorium on demolitions of viable existing buildings except when they present a threat to public health and safety and present no feasible option of beneficial economic use. The embodied energy—that is, the total expenditure of energy involved in the creation and maintenance of a building and its constituent materials—of older building stock represents an enormous investment. When older buildings are destroyed, we not only lose the embodied energy of the demolished building, but we contribute to the estimated quarter of the material in solid-waste facilities derived from construction debris. We typically replace the old building with one built of materials vastly more consumptive of energy, such as plastic, steel, vinyl, and aluminum, but the prudent stewardship of existing built resources and use of traditional, locally produced materials must be key components in any programs designed to mitigate the effects of climate change and energy depletion. (Rypkema, 2006, p. 31.)

There is no question that countering the impending effects of environmental degradation and climate change will require more than the use of recycled materials, planted roofs, wind turbines, and other fashionable high-tech gadgetry currently promoted by the "green design" movement. A "sustainable" single-family house isolated in a rural setting or on a suburban lot that remains dependent on automobiles has not risen to the challenge. (Home Improvement, 2007.) The claims for the energy performance of new "green" skyscrapers, too,

rest on so-far-unsubstantiated data and in any case raise serious questions about their effects on the surrounding environment, transportation systems, and housing. (Addington, 2007.)

In truth, the battle for a sustainable built environment will ultimately be won not by making more efficient individual buildings but by relearning the lessons of traditional urbanism, as it is the city—with its efficiencies of scale, transportation networks, compact development, and pedestrian-based densities—that will allow us to live together in sustainable fashion. We need only look at the historic centers of our cities to see models that can promote the truly radical changes in building patterns that will be necessary for the survival of modern culture, should the prognostications of the more pessimistic commentators prove even partially correct. (Kunstler, 1994, 1996, 2005.) Traditional architecture, New Urbanism, and a reconceived historic preservation can find common cause in guiding the apparently inevitable contraction that our cities and suburban regions will undergo in the coming decades as we approach the end of the era of plentiful and inexpensive fossil fuels. Ultimately, I believe, a sustainable architecture will look more like a renewed and critically improved version of the traditional city than like a utopian and hyper-industrialized vision of the modernist future. What is now criticized as New Urbanism's "nostalgic" evocation of historical models of the city and traditional building materials and methods will very likely look prescient instead when viewed from the perspective of a post-petroleum future. (Fig. 12.5)

Preservation in the early twentieth century was an idealistic campaign of social reform, closely allied with the Progressive Movement of Theodore Roosevelt and other reform-minded leaders. (Page and Mason, 2004, pp. 15, 139.) Today it needs to see its role as something more than perpetuating buildings and sites "as they came down to us in history." History is not always right or just, and preservation should not be used to immortalize damaged or destructive environments. Under current preservation philosophy, there looms the threat that *suburban sprawl itself* might fall under the protection of preservation regulation. The current campaign to preserve the architecture of the "recent past" has already prompted identifying key places in the history of suburban development, such as Radburn and Levittown, as landmarks worthy of protection. But the negative impacts

of sprawl—with respect to both environmental sustainability and social cohesion—must not be immortalized in a misguided attempt to preserve the historical evidence of an environmental crisis. Rather, preservation must rediscover its former prophetic and progressive mission and play its part in shaping a sustainable future beyond sprawl. (Lambin, 2007, and National Trust, 1999.)

Justice

In addition to the implications of preservation for the built environment, we must look at its effects on people. The case for historic preservation as a means of promoting social equity and economic development can be argued far more effectively than it has been. Consider the contribution of preservation programs to affordable housing, for example. As architect and preservationist Donovan Rypkema notes, "older and historic homes will continue to provide affordable housing *if we just quit tearing them down.*" (Rypkema, 2006, p. 36,

emphasis added.) Thousands of single-family houses are thrown away or abandoned in cities and towns across the United States every year, while record numbers of new houses have been built in the far fringes of suburbia, far from the jobs and services lower-income people need. It seems likely that there would be no housing shortage today if the resources spent over the last half-century demolishing vast segments of our housing stock had been directed at neighborhood rehabilitation and revitalization instead. Given the amount of underused, deteriorated, or abandoned housing stock in the United States today, rehabilitation rather than new construction makes the most sense, especially for local programs and neighborhood revitalization efforts.

While preservation regulations have faced legal and constitutional challenges, the courts have so far consistently ruled in favor of preservation ordinances and judgments as long as these have "a clearly articulated and demonstrable public interest, demonstrable links to the stated intent, application early in the design or decision process, and allowing and

12.5. Poundbury, Dorset, United Kingdom, master planned by Léon Krier, 1988–2008.

This aerial view shows the overall layout of the new town, an extension of nearby Dorchester. The urban plan observes the traditional pattern of fabric and monuments and is completed by culturally appropriate and environmentally sustainable construction.

encouraging a variety of acceptable decisions." (George and Campbell, 2000, pp. 164–71.) Fulfilling these criteria will assist project sponsors, design professionals, and public officials alike in making fair and defensible judgments and avoiding the pitfalls of processes that are either excessively rigid and formulaic or vague and discretionary.

This being said, some preservation programs may have unfairly burdened the poor, who may be unable to afford expensive rehabilitation or who face dislocation due to rapid increases in property values and taxes—the process known as "gentrification." This is not, of course, specifically a preservation issue, since new construction has also frequently displaced the poor. (Bluestone, 1994.) The issue is not the age or style of the buildings, but rather the politics and economics of the development project and its impact on preexisting residents. Programs like the "scattered-site housing" developments in Charleston and urban restoration in Bologna have shown that gentrification need not be an inevitable consequence of preservation. (See fig. C.10.) (For Charleston housing, see Tung, 2001, pp. 418–20. For the Bologna urban conservation program, see Appleyard, 1979, pp. 178–202.) Fair and equitable accommodation of the disabled, the elderly, and others with special needs allows them to remain in their homes and enjoy the benefits of rehabilitated neighborhoods. Preservation decisions should not deny decent accommodation to any citizen or property owner and should make use of whatever tools are available to assist those impacted, including revolving funds, life tenancies, deferred preservation, and reversible interventions. (Fisher, 2006.)

The Future of Historic Preservation

If a profession is to be a profession, it must have ideals or standards of excellence, and it must have some criteria for making judgments in fulfilling the obligations to society that any profession naturally is supposed to have. Architecture and preservation, accordingly, are not solely a matter of individual artistic preferences, but of judgments having moral and ethical importance. Vitruvius's three conditions of good building—commodity, firmness, and delight—are not simply desirable outcomes, markers of a particular taste, or indicators of a historical period: They are indeed obligations.

(Collins, 1971, pp. 162–63.) In a similar spirit, Jaquelin Robertson observed that the obligation of the architect involves accountability to three "clients": the patron who commissions the architect and pays for the project, the profession as both a social institution and an artistic-intellectual discipline, and the public in the form of some anonymous observer who a generation or more from now will walk past the architect's work and think, "That building is really not too bad." Architects must be especially attentive to this third, anonymous, and unforeseen client if their buildings are to have the longevity and adaptability that our oldest structures still in continuous use have demonstrated. In sum, the audience for architecture today, as always, is not a chorus of contemporary academics and critics, but a multigenerational and largely unknowable company of observers and users. Our arguments for the appropriateness of our designs and preservation proposals must be directed to them.

The most pressing challenge for preservation programs today is to educate young professionals in the building cultures whose products they will be handling. Young preservationists and architects

must develop the capacity to work in modes of stylistic expression which are not their own; to learn to respect the aesthetic criteria of long-dead designers and craftspersons—criteria which might not be at all congruent with their own taste. They must have a willingness to investigate and then respect the historical development of the artifact in hand; an ability to subordinate their own preferences and prejudices to that record; and a readiness to collaborate with other specialists who will often have a more detailed understanding of . . . the artifact in question. (Fitch, 1982, p. 352.)

This kind of stylistic empathy is rare today because in most university preservation programs students are not required to master any of the traditional languages of architecture—few of them study in detail the classical orders, for example—or gain more than a cursory understanding of traditional construction materials and methods. Some programs now focus primarily on the preservation of modernist works. (O'Connell, 2008.) While such training may be relevant to the growing field of modernist preservation, it is inconceivable that professional preservationists would not be expert in the aesthetic as well as the technical issues they face in treating traditional historic sites. The rising generation of preservationists must be trained not only in historical architecture and traditional construction but in the contemporary practices of new traditional architecture and New Urbanism as well; conversely, architects should be trained in preservation so they will develop the expertise and judgment required to care for historic environments, but also to equip them to design and build for longevity. Both preservation and new design must be taught taking into account the full spectrum of scale levels, from the individual building to the urban district and city. The work of students who study traditional architecture and urbanism in those few places where they are taught gives us hope that the split between the head and the heart that afflicted Carlo Scarpa, James Marston Fitch, and so many others will readily heal itself if we simply stop teaching it. (Figs. 12.6 and C.3)

Changing the culture of designers and public officials is essential but, equally important, preservation must promote "recapturing our competence to build" by recovering the building cultures that produced the monuments we now seek to preserve. We should "no longer aim to preserve a heritage which as such has only a relative and limited interest, but instead to develop our capacity to continue and replace the components of such a heritage," leading to "the reactualization of many artisanal and traditional handicraft activities." (Choay, 2001, pp. 177–78.) This has already begun as the fields of preservation and new traditional building jointly reorganize a broad segment of the construction industry to serve the needs of both conservation and sympathetic new construction. (See fig. 7.2.) Additional training programs and the support of the construction trades could do much to ensure the future supply of competent workers and vendors to meet the rising demand for traditional craftsmanship. The social and economic benefits of such a program would potentially surpass its benefits to the physical environment, once again drawing together the neo-Vitruvian triad of beauty, sustainability, and justice.

We love Rome, G. K. Chesterton remarked, because it is beautiful; but it is beautiful because first it was loved. While all our historic cities were founded to promote some conception of the good life, "our greatest cities are products of love." (Bess, 2006, p. 49.) Here is the heart of the conservation ethic: It

is an outward demonstration of civic responsibility, a proof of Hannah Arendt's exegesis of "culture" as "loving care," and an enactment of Jane Jacobs's metaphor of the fires burning sporadically in a dark field. The conservation ethic allows us to extend to our historic built environments a loving care that assists their growth in accordance with their preexisting and character-defining typologies, materials, and styles. From its fundamental premise that continuity rather than rupture is normative in human culture, the conservation ethic seeks to retain whatever we deem valuable from the past that does not obstruct necessary change. While preservation as practiced over the last few decades has tended to reflect a tragic sensibility that nothing new could ever be as good as the past, the conservation ethic works toward a future that might be better than the past. Conservation, as advocated here, is therefore an optimistic strategy in which the care of the historic environment and the design of new places are undertaken as distinct but mutually coordinated segments of a unified architectural discipline. It is up to us to commit ourselves to this course while the narrow and closing window of opportunity still permits us to do so.

12.6. Redevelopment of waterfront district, Brooklyn, New York, a graduate thesis at the University of Notre Dame, by Nana Andoh, 2007.

Architects and urbanists must confront the problem of reurbanizing existing cities in continuity with their historic character. In this case, an abandoned "brownfield" industrial site (existing condition plan, left) is expanded (proposed plan, right) adjacent to the Brooklyn Heights Historic District. A commitment to continuity at the urban, the building, and the detail scales makes it possible to introduce new construction without destroying the character of the neighborhood.

Bibliography

Adam, Robert. "Authenticity and Tradition." An address to the York Civic Trust, May 29, 2003.

———. *Classical Architecture*. New York: Harry N. Abrams, 1991.

———. "Does Heritage Dogma Destroy Living History?" *Context*, May 2003 (www.ihbc.org.uk/context).

Addington, Michelle. "No Building Is an Island: Looking at the Different Scales of Energy." *Harvard Design Magazine*, Spring–Summer 2007, pp. 38–45.

Alberti, Leon Battista. *On the Art of Building in Ten Books*. Translated by Joseph Rykwert, Neil Leach, and Robert Tavenor. Cambridge: MIT Press, 1988; originally published in Venice, 1478.

Alderson, Caroline. "Responding to Context." *APT Bulletin*, vol. XXXVII (April 2006), pp. 22–23.

Alexander, Christopher. *The Nature of Order*. Berkeley, Calif.: Center for Environmental Studies, 2002.

Alofsin, Anthony. *The Struggle for Modernism: Architecture, Landscape Architecture, and City Planning at Harvard*. New York: Norton, 2002.

Appleyard, Donald, ed. *The Conservation of European Cities*. Cambridge: MIT Press, 1979.

Arendt, Hannah. *Between Past and Future: Eight Exercises in Political Thought*. Harmondsworth: Penguin, 1977.

———. *The Life of the Mind*. New York: Harcourt Brace Jovanovich, 1978.

Bacon, Edmund N. *Design of Cities*. New York: Viking, 1967.

Ballon, Hillary, ed. *New York's Pennsylvania Station*. New York: Norton, 2002.

Banham, Reyner. *Theory and Design in the First Machine Age*. London: Architectural Press, 1960.

Barreneche, Raul A. "Computer-Aided Gothic." *Architecture*, November 1993, pp. 123–27.

Barstow, David. "Fifty-Five Million Dollar Face Lift for Brooklyn Museum." *New York Times*, September 20, 2000.

Bayley, John Barrington. *Letarouilly on Renaissance Rome*. New York: Architectural Book Publishing Co., 1984.

Beeby, Thomas. "The Grammar of Ornament/Ornament as Grammar." *VIA III* (Graduate School of Fine Arts, University of Pennsylvania), 1977, pp. 10–29.

Bello, Eddie. "The Real World." *Charleston City Paper*, February 2, 2005.

Bergdoll, Barry. *European Architecture, 1750–1890*. Oxford: Oxford University Press, 2000.

Bess, Philip. *Till We Have Built Jerusalem: Architecture, Urbanism, and the Sacred*. Wilmington, Del.: ISI Books, 2006.

Bland, Frederick. "Designing for the Urban Context: Exploring How Healthy Differentiation Becomes Eroded Character." A paper presented at the APT (Association for Preservation Technology) International Conference, Galveston, Tex., November 4, 2004.

Bluestone, Daniel. "Preservation and Renewal in Post–World War II Chicago." *Journal of Architectural Education*, May 1994, pp. 210–23.

Boito, Camillo. "I Nostri Vecchi Monumenti." *Nuova Antologia*, vol. 87 (1886).

Brand, Stewart. *How Buildings Learn: What Happens After They're Built*. New York: Viking Penguin, 1994.

Brandi, Cesare. *Teoria del Restauro*. Turin: Giulio Einaudi Edizioni, 2000; originally published in Turin, 1963.

Brolin, Brent C. *Architectural Ornament: Banishment and Return*. New York: Norton, 2000.

———. *Architecture in Context: Fitting New Buildings with Old*. New York: Van Nostrand Reinhold, 1981.

Bruner, Edward M. "Abraham Lincoln as Authentic Reproduction: A Critique of Postmodernism." *American Anthropologist*, June 1994, pp. 397–415.

Byard, Paul Spencer. *The Architecture of Additions: Design and Regulation*. New York: Norton, 1998.

———. "Innovation and Insight in the Contemporary Architecture of Additions." *Harvard Design Magazine*, Fall 2005/Winter 2006.

Carey, Michael, ed. "Building Civil Cities." *Traditional Building*, February 2005, pp. 11–19.

———. "Classicism and the American Architectural Tradition," *Traditional Building*, January–February 2004, pp. 12–17.

———. "Raising Standards." *Traditional Building*, April 2007.

Ceschi, Carlo. *Teoria e Storia del Restauro*. Rome: Mario Bulzoni Editore, 1970.

Chappell, Edward. "Merchants Square Meets Quinlan Terry." *Colonial Williamsburg*, Autumn 2003, pp. 86–89.

Choay, Françoise. *The Invention of the Historic Monument*. Cambridge: Cambridge University Press, 2001.

———. *The Modern City: Planning in the Nineteenth Century*. New York: Braziller, 1969.

City of Charleston. *Charleston Standards for the Treatment of Historic Properties*, 2008. (Available online at: http://www.charlestoncity.info/dept/content.aspx?nid=1247.)

City of New York, Independent Budget Office. "The Impact of Historic Districts on Residential Property Values." *IBO Background Paper*, September 2003.

Claridge, Amanda. *Rome: An Oxford Archaeological Guide*. Oxford: Oxford University Press, 1998.

Collins, George R., and Christiane Crasemann Collins. *Camillo Sitte: The Birth of Modern City Planning* (With a translation of the 1889 Austrian edition of his *City Planning According to Artistic Principles*). New York: Rizzoli, 1986.

Collins, Peter. *Architectural Judgment*. London: Faber & Faber, 1971.

———. *Changing Ideals in Modern Architecture: 1750–1950*. Montreal: McGill University Press, 1967.

Colonial Williamsburg. "The Restoration of Colonial Williamsburg in Virginia." *Architectural Record*. December 1935.

Crosbie, Michael J. "Dissecting the Salk." *Progressive Architecture*, October 1993, pp. 40–50.

Curtis, Nathaniel. *Architectural Composition*. Cleveland: J. H. Jensen, 1935.

Dal Co, Francesco, and Giuseppe Marriol. *Carlo Scarpa: The Complete Works*. New York: Rizzoli, 1985.

Davis, Howard. *The Culture of Building*. Oxford: Oxford University Press, 2006.

Del Bufalo, Alessandro. *Gustavo Giovannoni*. Rome: Kappa, 1982.

Doordan, Dennis. *Building Modern Italy: Italian Architecture, 1914–1936*. New York: Princeton Architectural Press, 1988.

Duany, Andrés, "Modernist Buildings out of Place." *Charleston Post-Courier*, November 8, 2005.

———. "Transect Planning." *Journal of the American Planning Association*, Summer 2002, pp. 245–66.

Duany, Andrés, Elizabeth Plater-Zyberk, and Robert Alminana. *New Civic Art: Elements of Town Planning*. New York: Rizzoli, 2003.

Dunlap, David. "A Building Fits In by Standing Out." *New York Times*, April 23, 2000.

———. "Landmarks Group Approves Bold Plan for Hearst Tower," *New York Times*, November 28, 2001.

———. "Plan for Site of '06 Blast on East Side Is Criticized." *New York Times*, August 18, 2007.

Economakis, Richard, ed. *Acropolis Restoration: The CCAM Interventions*. London: Academy Editions, 1994.

———. "Restoration of Buildings or Conservation of Ruins? Reflections on the Current Acropolis Interventions, and How Best to Restitute the Periklean Monuments." A paper delivered at the conference "Issues in Architectural Reconstruction" at the University of Notre Dame, January 20–21, 2006.

Edwards, Arthur Trystan. *Architectural Style*. London: Faber & Gwyer, 1926.

———. *Good and Bad Manners in Architecture*. London: Philip Allan & Co., 1924.

———. *Style and Composition in Architecture: An Exposition of the Canon of Number, Punctuation, and Inflection*. London: J. Tiranti, 1944.

Egbert, Donald Drew. *The Beaux-Arts Tradition in French Architecture*. Princeton: Princeton University Press, 1980.

Eliot, Thomas Stearns. *Selected Prose of T. S. Eliot*. Edited by Frank Kermode. New York: Farrar, Straus & Giroux, 1975.

Emerson, Chad. "Making Main Street Legal Again: The SmartCode Solution to Sprawl," *Berkeley Electronic Press Express Reprint Series*, 2006, no. 954.

English Heritage. *Guidelines for Conservation*. London, 2007.

Etlin, Richard A. *Modernism in Italian Architecture, 1890–1940*. Cambridge: MIT Press, 1991.

Faietti, Marzia, and Massimo Medica, eds. *La Basilica Incompiuta: Progetti Antichi per la Facciata di San Petronio*. Ferrara: Edisai, 2001.

Fawcett, Jane, ed. *The Future of the Past: Attitudes to Conservation, 1174–1974.* New York: Whitney Library of Design, 1976.

Fisher, Marc. "Putting Home's Appearance Ahead of Helping Frail Couple." *Washington Post,* December 21, 2006.

Fitch, James Marston. *Historic Preservation: Curatorial Management of the Built World.* Charlottesville: University of Virginia Press, 1990; originally published by McGraw-Hill, 1982.

———. *James Marston Fitch: Selected Writings.* Edited by Martica Sawin. New York: Norton, 2006.

Fixler, David N. "Material, Idea, and Authenticity: Lessons from the Modern Movement." A paper presented at the Goucher College National Preservation Forum on Authenticity, March 23, 2006.

Fletcher, Sir Banister. *A History of Architecture on the Comparative Method,* 8th ed., New York: Scribner, 1928.

Ford, Edward. "The Theory and Practice of Impermanence: The Illusion of Durability." *Harvard Design Magazine,* Fall 1997.

Frampton, Kenneth. *Modern Architecture: A Critical History.* New York: Norton, 2007; originally published by Oxford University Press, 1980.

Fried, Robert C. *Planning the Eternal City: Roman Politics and Planning Since World War II.* New Haven: Yale University Press, 1973.

Gabriel, Jean François. *Classical Architecture for the Twenty-first Century.* New York: Norton, 2004.

Gartner, Marieke Cassia. "Classicism for Humanity." *Period Homes,* January 2006, p. 12.

George, R. Varkki, and Marcia Caton Campbell. "Balancing Different Interests in Aesthetic Controls." *Journal of Planning Education and Research,* vol. 20 (2000), pp. 163–75.

Giedion, Sigfried. *Space, Time, and Architecture: The Growth of a New Tradition.* Cambridge: Harvard University Press, 1954; first published in 1941.

Gilmartin, Gregory F. *Shaping the City: New York and the Municipal Art Society.* New York: Clarkson N. Potter, 1995.

Giovannoni, Gustavo. *Vecchie Città ed Edilizia Nuova.* Turin: Unione Tipografico Editrice Torinese, 1931.

Glazer, Nathan. *From a Cause to a Style: Modernist Architecture's Encounter with the American City.* Princeton: Princeton University Press, 2007.

Goldberger, Paul. Address to the Nantucket Preservation Trust. Nantucket, Mass., July 27, 2007.

———. Address to the National Trust for Historic Preservation. New York, May 29, 2003 (available at www.paulgoldberger.com).

———. "Eminent Dominion." *New Yorker,* February 5, 2007, pp. 83–85 (2007b).

———. "New York and New Urbanism." Address to the Congress for the New Urbanism. New York, June 9, 2001 (available at www.paulgoldberger.com).

———. "Primers in Urbanism, Written in Cast Iron." *New York Times,* September 22, 1996.

———. "Triangulation." *New Yorker,* December 19, 2005, pp. 98–100.

———. *Up from Zero: Politics, Architecture, and the Rebuilding of New York.* New York: Random House, 2004.

Grandjean, A., and A. Famin (Van Pelt, John, ed.). *Architecture Toscane.* New York: Pencil Points Press, 1923. Originally published in Paris, 1815.

Greenberg, Allan. *Architecture of Democracy.* New York: Rizzoli, 2006.

Gutheim, Frederick, and Antoinette J. Lee. *Worthy of the Nation: Washington, D.C. from L'Enfant to the National Capital Planning Commission.* Baltimore: Johns Hopkins University Press, 2006.

Hamilton, William L. "How Suburban Design Is Failing Teen-Agers." *New York Times,* May 6, 1999.

Harbeson, John. *The Study of Architectural Design.* New York: Norton, 2008; originally published in 1924.

Hardy, Matthew, ed. *The Venice Charter Revisited: Modernism, Conservation, and Tradition in the 21st Century.* Newcastle upon Tyne: Cambridge Scholars Publishing, 2008.

Haskell, David. "Big Urbanism." *New York Times,* December 10, 2006.

Hegemann, Werner, and Elbert Peets. *Civic Art: The American Vitruvius.* New York: Architectural Book Publishing Co., 1922; reprinted, New York: Princeton Architectural Press, 1988.

Hibbert, Christopher. *Rome: The Biography of a City.* Harmondsworth: Penguin, 1985.

Hill, John. "Chicago's Solider Field Loses Landmark Status." *Architecture,* June 2006.

Hitchcock, Henry-Russell. *Modern Architecture: Romanticism and Reintegration.* New York: Hacker Art Books, 1970; originally published in New York: Payson & Clarke, 1929.

"Home Improvement: An Eco-House for the Future." *New York Times,* May 20, 2007.

Hosmer, Charles B., Jr. *The Presence of the Past: A History of the Preservation Movement in the United States Before Williamsburg.* New York: Putnam, 1965.

HRH The Prince of Wales. *A Vision of Britain: A Personal View of Architecture.* London: Doubleday, 1989.

Huxtable, Ada Louise. *Unreal America: Architecture and Illusion.* New York: Norton, 1997.

International Council on Monuments and Sites (ICOMOS). *Athens Charter for the Restoration of Historic Monuments.* Athens, 1931 (available online at www.icomos.org/athens_charter.html).

———. *Venice Charter: International Charter for the Conservation and Restoration of Monuments and Sites.* Venice, 1964 (available online at www.icomos.org/venice_charter.html).

International Network for Traditional Building, Architecture, and Urbanism (INTBAU). *The INTBAU Venice Declaration on the Conservation of Monuments and Sites in the 21st Century,* 2007 (available online at www.intbau.org/venicedeclaration.htm).

Jacobs, Jane. *The Death and Life of Great American Cities*. New York: Vintage, 1962.

Jackson, Kenneth T., and Hillary Ballon, eds. *Robert Moses and the Modern City: The Transformation of New York*. New York: Norton, 2007.

Jencks, Charles. *The Language of Post-Modern Architecture*. New York: Rizzoli, 1981.

Jokilehto, Jukka. *A History of Architectural Conservation*. Jordan Hill (Oxford): Elsevier, 1999.

Kant, Emanuel (J. H. Bernard, trans.). *Critique of Judgment*. London: Macmillan, 1929.

Kohler, Sue, and Pamela Scott, eds. *Designing the Nation's Capital: The 1901 Plan for Washington, D.C.* Washington, D.C.: U.S. Commission of Fine Arts, 2006.

Koolhaas, Rem. "Junkspace." *October*, Spring 2002, pp. 175–90.

Kostof, Spiro. *The Third Rome, 1870–1950: Traffic and Glory*. Berkeley: University of California, Berkeley Art Museum, 1973.

Krautheimer, Richard. *Rome: Profile of a City, 312–1308*. Princeton: Princeton University Press, 1980.

Krier, Leon. *The Architectural Tuning of Settlements*. London: The Prince's Foundation for the Built Environment, 2008.

———. *Architecture: Choice or Fate?* London: Andreas Papdakis, 1998.

———. *The Architecture of Community*. Washington, D.C.: Island Press, 2009.

Kunstler, James Howard. *The Geography of Nowhere*. New York: Touchstone, 1994.

———. *Home from Nowhere*. New York: Touchstone, 1996.

———. *The Long Emergency: Surviving the Converging Catastrophes of the Twenty-First Century*. New York: Atlantic Monthly Press, 2005.

Lambin, Jeanne. *Preserving Resources from the Recent Past*. Washington, D.C.: Preservation Books, 2007.

Lang, Christopher. *Building with Nantucket in Mind*. Nantucket, Mass.: Nantucket Historic District Commission, 1979.

Langdon, Philip. "Architecture Gone Wild." *Hartford Courant*, July 25, 2004.

———. "New Urbanism in the Crosshairs." *New Urban News*, July–August 2006, p. 1.

Le Corbusier (Charles-Edouard Jeanneret). *Modulor I and II*. (Peter de Francia and Anne Bostock, trans.). Cambridge: Harvard University Press, 1980.

Le Corbusier (Charles-Edouard Jeanneret). *Towards a New Architecture*. New York: Dover Publications, 1986; originally published in English in London, 1927.

Leigh, Catesby. "Goethe and the Mess We're In: A Natural History of the Organic Fallacy in Architecture, Art, and Culture." *The Classicist*, no. 5 (1999), pp. 19–36.

———. "Historic Preservation Goes Awry." *American Enterprise*, July–August 2001, pp. 40–43.

Lombardi, Kristen. "Undulating Facades." *Village Voice*, May 10–16, 2006, pp. 18–22.

Loth, Calder. Address to the conference "Architecture of the Whole," National Civic Art Society and the Institute of Classical Architecture & Classical America. Washington, D.C., October 4–5, 2006.

Lounsbury, Carl. "Beaux-Arts Ideals and Colonial Reality: The Reconstruction of Williamsburg's Capitol, 1928–1934." *Journal of the Society of Architectural Historians*, December 1990, pp. 373–89.

Lowenthal, David. *The Past Is a Foreign Country*. Cambridge: Cambridge University Press, 1985.

Lyon, Elizabeth. *Campus Heritage Preservation: Traditions, Prospects, and Challenges*. Eugene: University of Oregon, 2003.

MacIntyre, Alasdair. *After Virtue: A Study in Moral Theory*. Notre Dame, Ind.: University of Notre Dame Press, 1984.

———. *Three Rival Versions of Moral Enquiry: Encyclopedia, Genealogy, and Tradition*. Notre Dame, Ind.: University of Notre Dame Press, 1990.

Marconi, Paolo. *Il Recupero della Bellezza*. Milan: Skira Editore, 2003.

Maltese, Curzio. "Piano: Il Mio Grattacielo? Ecco Perché Fa Paura." *La Reppublica* (Rome), November 14, 2007.

Mazzola, Ettore Maria. *Contrastoria dell'Architettura Moderna: Roma, 1900–1940 / Counter-History of Modern Architecture: Rome, 1900–1940*. Florence: Alinea Editrice, 2004.

Mayernik, David. *Timeless Cities*. Boulder, Colo.: Westview Press, 2003.

Mehaffy, Michael, ed. "A Conversation with Andrés Duany." *Katarxis No. III*, September 2004 (available at www.katarxis3.com/Duany.htm).

Merkel, Jayne. *Eero Saarinen*. London: Phaidon, 2005.

Milani, G. B. *L'Ossatura Murale* (3 vols.). Turin: C. Crudo & Co., 1920.

Miller, Jason. "Rhode Island Renaissance." *New Towns*, Spring 2006, pp. 6–11.

Morris, A. E. J., *History of Urban Form: Before the Industrial Revolutions*. 3rd ed. Harlow: Pearson Education, 1994.

Morrone, Francis. "The New Morgan Library and Museum." *American Arts Quarterly*, Fall 2006, pp. 11–19.

———. "Of Our Time." *The Classicist*, no. 7 (2007), pp. 6–9.

Mouzon, Steven. *A Living Tradition: Architecture of the Bahamas*. Miami: New Urban Guild Foundation, 2007.

Murphy, Richard. *Carlo Scarpa e Castelvecchio*. Venice: Arsenale Editrice, 1991.

National Park Service. *The Secretary of the Interior's Standards for Rehabilitation*. Washington, D.C.: National Park Service, 1995 (available online at www.nps.gov/history/hps/tps/tax/rhb/stand.htm).

National Trust for Historic Preservation. *Challenging Sprawl: Organizational Responses to a National Problem*. Washington, D.C.: National Trust for Historic Preservation, 1999.

———. *Old and New Architecture: Design Relationship*. Washington, D.C.: Preservation Press, 1980.

Norberg-Schulz, Christian. *Genius Loci: Toward a Phenomenology of Architecture*. New York: Rizzoli, 1980.

———. *Intentions in Architecture*. Cambridge: MIT Press, 1965.

O'Connel, Kim A. "Defining Significance," *Traditional Building*, July–August 2004, pp. 10–12.

———. "Pillars of Preservation." *Traditional Building*, April 2008, pp. 8–11.

Olsen, Donald J. *The City as a Work of Art: London, Paris, Vienna*. New Haven: Yale University Press, 1986.

Ouroussoff, Nicolai. "Architecture Review: Pride and Nostalgia Mix in the Times's New Home." *New York Times*, November 20, 2007.

———. "Architecture Review: Renzo Piano's Expansion of the Morgan Library Transforms a World of Robber Barons and Scholars." *New York Times*, April 10, 2006.

Page, Max, and Randall Mason, eds. *Giving Preservation a History: Histories of Historic Preservation in the United States*. New York: Routledge, 2004.

Palladio, Andrea. *The Four Books of Architecture*. Translated by Robert Tavenor and Richard Schofield. Cambridge: MIT Press, 2002.

Perez de Arce, Rodrigo. "Urban Transformations." *Architectural Design*, vol. 4 (1978).

Peterson, Steven Kent. "Space and Anti-Space." *Harvard Architecture Review*, no. 1 (1980), pp. 88–113.

Pevsner, Nikolaus. *An Outline of European Architecture*. Harmondsworth: Pelican Books, 1977; originally published in London, 1943.

———. *Pioneers of Modern Design: From William Morris to Walter Gropius*. London: Penguin, 1960.

———. *Some Architectural Writers of the Nineteenth Century*. Oxford: Clarendon Press, 1972.

Pinker, Steven. *The Blank Slate: The Modern Denial of Human Nature*. New York: Viking, 2002.

Popper, Karl R. *The Open Society and Its Enemies*. 2 vols. New York: Harper Torchbooks, 1963.

Porphyrios, Demetri, ed. *Classical Architecture: The Living Tradition*. New York: McGraw-Hill, 1992.

———. *Classicism Is Not a Style*. New York: St. Martin's Press, 1982.

Reed, Henry Hope. "The Classical Tradition in Modern Times: A Personal Assessment," *Speaking a New Classicism: American Architecture Now*. Northampton, Mass.: Smith College Museum of Art, 1981.

———. *The Golden City*. New York: Norton, 1971; originally published in New York: Doubleday, 1959.

———. *The United States Capitol: Its Architecture and Decoration*. New York: Norton, 2005.

Reiff, Daniel D. "Viollet le Duc and Historic Restoration: The West Portals of Notre-Dame." *Journal of the Society of Architectural Historians*, March 1971, pp. 17–30.

Reps, John W. *Monumental Washington: The Planning and Development of the Capital Center*. Princeton: Princeton University Press, 1967.

Rhodes, Robin Francis. *Architecture and Meaning on the Athenian Acropolis*. Cambridge: Cambridge University Press, 1998.

Robertson, Jaquelin Taylor. "In Search of an American Urban Order, Part II: The House as the City." *Modulus*, vol. 17 (1984), pp. 138–59.

———. "Only Connect: Recognitions of Old and New." *Harvard Architecture Review*, Spring 1980, pp. 115–21.

Rossi, Piero Ostilio. *Roma: Guida all'Architettura Moderna, 1909–2000*. Rome: Editori Laterza, 2005.

Rowe, Colin. *The Mathematics of the Ideal Villa and Other Essays*. Cambridge: MIT Press, 1976.

Rowe, Colin, and Fred Koetter. *Collage City*. Cambridge: MIT Press, 1978.

Rowland, Ingrid D. "From Vitruvian Scholarship to Vitruvian Practice." *Memoirs of the American Academy in Rome*, vol. 50 (2005), pp. 15–40.

Ruskin, John. *The Seven Lamps of Architecture*. New York: Farrar, Straus & Giroux, 1979; originally published in London, 1849.

———. *The Stones of Venice*. London: Penguin, 1960; originally published in London, 1851–53.

Rypkema, Donovan D. "Economics, Sustainability, and Historic Preservation." *National Trust Forum Journal*, Winter 2006, pp. 27–38.

Saunders, William S., ed. *Judging Architectural Value: A Harvard Design Magazine Reader*. Minneapolis: University of Minnesota Press, 2007.

Salingaros, Nikos. *A Theory of Architecture*. Solingen: Umbau-Verlag, 2006.

Sammons, Richard Franklin. "The Anatomy of a Georgian Room," *Period Homes*, March 2006, pp. 12–15.

Santayana, George. *The Sense of Beauty: Being the Outline of Aesthetic Theory*. New York: Dover, 1955.

Scholfield, P. H. *The Theory of Proportion in Architecture*. Cambridge: Cambridge University Press, 1958.

Scott, Geoffrey. *The Architecture of Humanism: A Study in the History of Taste*. New York: Norton, 2003; originally published in London, 1914.

Scruton, Roger. *The Aesthetics of Architecture*. Princeton: Princeton University Press, 1979.

———. *The Classical Vernacular: Architectural Principles in an Age of Nihilism*. New York: St. Martin's Press, 1995.

Semes, Steven W. *The Architecture of the Classical Interior*. New York: Norton, 2004.

———. "The Art of Conversation." *Period Homes*, Fall 2006, pp. 18–22.

———. "'Differentiated' and 'Compatibile': Four Strategies for Additions to Historic Settings." *National Trust Forum Journal*, Summer 2007, pp. 14–25.

———. "Mercury Downloading: Or, the Classicism of Everyday Life." *The Classicist*, vol. 4 (1995), pp. 4–5.

———. "New Buildings Among Old: Historicism and the Search for an Architecture of Our Time." *American Arts Quarterly*, Spring 2008, pp. 8–19.

———. "Preservation's Identity Crisis." *Traditional Building*, August 2005, pp. 214–15.

———. "Paradigm Shift: The New Classicism and Historic Preservation." *Traditional Building,* January–February 1999, pp. 24–28.

Sennett, Richard. *Flesh and Stone: The Body and the City in Western Civilization.* London: Penguin, 1994.

Settis, Salvatore. *Futuro del "Classico."* Turin: Giulio Einaudi Editore, 2004.

Silber, John. *Architecture of the Absurd: How "Genius" Disfigured a Practical Art.* New York: Norton, 2007.

Smith, Peter F. *Architecture and the Principle of Harmony.* London: RIBA Publications, 1987.

Smith, Thomas Gordon. *Classical Architecture: Rule and Invention.* San Francisco: Gibbs-Smith, 1980.

———. *Vitruvius on Architecture.* New York: Monacelli Press, 2003.

Soulié, Daniel. *Les Bâtisseurs du Louvre.* Paris: Musée du Louvre, 2003.

Spengler, Oswald. *The Decline of the West.* New York: Knopf, 1932; originally published in German, 1918–23.

Stephens, Suzanne, Ian Luna, and Ron Broadhurst. *Imagining Ground Zero: Official and Unofficial Proposals for the World Trade Center Site.* New York: Rizzoli, 2004.

Stern, Robert A. M., Gregory Gilmartin, and John Massengale. *New York 1900: Metropolitan Architecture and Urbanism, 1890–1915.* New York: Rizzoli, 1983.

Stern, Robert A. M., Gregory Gilmartin, and Thomas Mellins. *New York 1930: Architecture and Urbanism Between the Two World Wars.* New York: Rizzoli, 1987.

Stern, Robert A. M., Thomas Mellins, and David Fishman. *New York 1960: Architecture and Urbanism Between the Second World War and the Bicentennial.* New York: Monacelli Press, 1995.

Stern Robert A. M., David Fishman, and Jacob Tilove. *New York 2000: Architecture and Urbanism Between the Bicentennial and the Millennium.* New York: Monacelli Press, 2006.

Suetonius (Gaius Suetonius Tranquillus). *The Twelve Caesars.* Translated by Robert Graves. London: Penguin, 1979.

Sullivan, Louis. *A System of Architectural Ornament According with a Philosophy of Man's Powers.* New York: Press of the American Institute of Architects, 1924.

Summerson, Sir John. *Heavenly Mansions, and Other Essays on Architecture.* London: Cresset, 1949; reprinted by Norton, 1998.

Tagliaventi, Gabriele, ed. *L'Altra Modernità, 1900–2000.* Savona (Italy): Dogma, 2000.

Terry, Quinlan. "Leaving an Environmentally Sound, Attractive Legacy." *Quinlan Terry: The Richard H. Driehaus Prize 2005.* Notre Dame, Ind.: School of Architecture, University of Notre Dame, 2005.

Tiller, de Teel Patterson. "Obey the Imperatives of Our Own Moment: A Call for Quality Contemporary Design in Historic Districts." *National Trust Forum Journal,* Summer 2007, pp. 6–13.

Torsello, B. Paolo, ed. *Che Cos'é il Restauro?* Venice: Marsilio Editori, 2005.

Tung, Anthony. *Preserving the World's Great Cities: The Destruction and Renewal of the Historic Metropolis.* New York: Three Rivers Press, 2001.

Turner, Frederick. "Beauty and Imitative Form." *American Arts Quarterly,* Summer 2006, pp. 9–13.

Tzonis, Alexander, and Lianne Lefaivre. *Classical Architecture: The Poetics of Order.* Cambridge: MIT Press, 1986.

Urban Design Associates. *A Pattern-Book for the Mississippi Coast.* Pittsburgh: Urban Design Associates, 2005 (www.governorbarbour.com/recovery/links/documents/PatternBook.pdf).

Venturi, Robert. *Complexity and Contradiction in Architecture.* New York: Museum of Modern Art, 1966.

Venturi, Robert, Steven Izenour, and Denise Scott-Brown. *Learning from Las Vegas.* 2nd ed. Cambridge: MIT Press, 1977.

Verdon, Timothy. *La Basilica di San Pietro: I Papi e gli Artisti.* Milan: Monadori, 2005.

Viollet-le-Duc, Eugène-Emmanuel. *Dictionnaire Raisonné de l'Architecture Française du XIe au XVIe Siècle.* Paris: Morel, 1866–69; reprinted in English translation as *The Foundations of Architecture: Selections from the Dictionnaire Raisonné.* New York: Braziller, 1990.

Vitruvius, Marcus Pollio. *The Ten Books of Architecture.* Translated and edited by Ingrid D. Rowland and Thomas Noble Howe. Cambridge: Cambridge University Press, 1999.

Watkin, David. *Morality and Architecture.* Oxford: Oxford University Press, 1977.

Watkin, David, and Robin Middleton. *Architecture of the Nineteenth Century.* Milano: Electa (distributed in English by Phaidon Press), 2003.

Westfall, Carroll William. "What Are the Preservationists Preserving?" *Traditional Building,* July–August 2004, pp. 225–26.

———. "Why We Need a Third Architectural Treatise." *American Arts Quarterly,* Summer 2006, pp. 14–21.

Westfall, Carroll William, and Robert Jan Van Pelt. *Architectural Principles in the Age of Historicism.* New Haven: Yale University Press, 1991.

Whitehead, Alfred North. *Modes of Thought.* New York: Free Press, 1968; originally published by Macmillan, 1938.

Wilson, Richard Guy. *The Colonial Revival House.* New York: Harry N. Abrams, 2004.

Wilson Jones, Mark. *Principles of Roman Architecture.* New Haven: Yale University Press, 2000.

Younés, Samir, ed. *Contraproggetti: Ara Pacis.* Florence: Alinea Editrice, 2002.

Younés, Samir, and Ettore Maria Mazzola. *Como: The Modernity of Tradition.* Rome: Gangemi Editore, 2003.

Zucker, Paul. *Town and Square: From Agora to Village Green.* Cambridge: MIT Press, 1970.

Index

architectural style (*continued*)
    language and, 72
    modernism and, 92–93
    New Urbanism and, 248
    proportion in, 63–64
    time period and, 72, 148–49
    urban vernacular design and, 84–85
    see also invention within a style
Arch of Titus, Rome, 7, 124
arcuated construction, 52
Arendt, Hannah, 35, 253
Asplund, Gunnar, 99–100
Association for Preservation Technology, 140
association of ideas, 76–77
Astor Square, New York, *165*6
Astor Tower Hotel, Chicago, *161*
Athens Charter, 132–34
Atlantic Coast Line Building, Washington D.C., *240*
Atterbury, Grosvenor, 204
authenticity
    as basis for evaluation of architecture, 166
    continuity and, 200
    replication and, 177–78
Avena, Antonio, 227–28

B

Bacon, Edmond, 174
Baird, Matthew, *10*
Baker Street, London, *10, 162*
Baroque design, 194
Basilica of Neptune, Rome, *64*
Basilica of San Lorenzo fuori le Mura, Rome, 128–29, *164*
Basilica of San Petronio, Bologna, 189–91
Battery Park, New York, *32, 33,* 247–48
Bayley, John Barrington, 37, *203,* 204
beauty, 88–89
Ann Beha Associates, *170*
Benjamin Wistar Morris, *234, 236*
Bernini, Gian Lorenzo, 74, 192–93
Bertrand Goldberg Associates, *161*
Beyer Blinder Belle Architects, 204–5
Bibliothèque Ste.-Geneviève, Paris, *144,* 147
Big Urbanism, 109
John Blatteau Associates, *3, 31*
Boito, Camillo, 124
Borgo Vaticano, Rome, 212–14
Boston Public Library, 111
Bottomley, William Lawrence, 130
Brandi, Cesare, 136, 154–56
Brasini, Armando, 198–200
Breuer, Marcel, 27, *28*
Brevoort, Henry, 232
British Museum, London, 85
Broadacre City, 107–8
Brolin, Brent, 45, 65
Brooklyn Museum, New York, *222*
Brunelleschi, Filippo, *172*
building culture, 38–40, 43
Bulfinch, Charles, *194,* 195
Bullant, Jean, 191
Bunshaft, Gordon, *9, 35*

Daniel Burnham & Company, *176, 177*
Buzzi, Carlo, 194
Byard, Paul Spencer, 224

C

Calza-Bini, Alberto, 128
Cameron Cameron & Taylor, *15*
canons of composition, 58–60
Capitoline Hill, Rome, 225–26
Capone, Peter, 197
Carhart Mansion, New York, *13,* 204–5
Carlhian, Jean Paul, 141
Carolands, California, *4*
Carré d'Art, Nimes, *90,* 102, *103*
Carrère & Hastings, 203
Carson Pirie Scott Store, Chicago, 176–78
Casa del Fascio, Como, 99, *100*
Castelvecchio, Verona, 227–30
Cathedral of Cologne, 194
Cathedral of Notre-Dame, Paris, *118,* 119–20
Centre Pompidou, Paris, 96
Cervellati, Pier Luigi, *5*
Chalgrin, J. F. T., *60*
character
    architectural meaning, 66
    function and, 66
    historic districts, 86
    meaning and, 74
    modernist architecture and, 104–7
    traditional architecture and, 66
    urban district, 85–86
Charleston, South Carolina
    Marion Square, 206, *207*
    preservation trends and, 139, 143, 162–63
    scattered-site housing, 252
    significance of historic preservation efforts in, 132, 206–7
Chesterton, C. K., 253
Choay, François, 160
Choynowski, Piotr, 223
Church of Orsanmichele, Florence, *53*
Church of Our Lady of the Rosary, *32*
Church of Santa Chiara, Naples, 129
Church of Sant'Andrea, Orvieto, 126
Church of San Zanipolo, Venice, *64*
Church of St.-Eustache, Paris, 147
classical orders, 54–55, *56, 57*
Cluss, Adolph, *168*
Cobb, Henry Ives, 230
Codman, Ogden, Jr., 64
collage, 99
Colonial Revival, 84, 130–31, 201
communal significance, 163
Commune di Bologna, *5*
compatibility
    as basis for design, 141
    principles of, 171
    Secretary of the Interior's standards for rehabilitation, 138–39, 230
    strategies for balancing differentiation with, 171, 173, 187, 209, 223
    treatment options, 171

Illustration Credits

Brian Connolly: 9.15A.

Courtesy of Cooper Robertson & Partners, New York: 1.8.

John Critchley photo, courtesy of Robert Adam Architects: 11.14A; 11.14B.

Tim Crane photo, courtesy of John Blatteau Associates: C.5.

© Denver Public Library, Colorado Historical Society, and Denver Art Museum, 1995–2008: 1.11.

Duany Plater-Zyberk & Company: 12.4A.

© The Duchy of Cornwall, photo by Commission Air: 12.5.

© Tomasz Dziubinski: 5.13.

Frank English photo, courtesy of MTA Metro-North Railroad: C.21.

Krister Engström/The Swedish Museum of Architecture: 4.9B.

Fairfax & Sammons Architects, PC: 6.5A; 6.5B; 9.16; 11.12.

© Scott Frances/Esto: 4.3.

© 2008 Frank Lloyd Wright Foundation, Scottsdale, Arizona / Artists Rights Society (ARS), New York / Art Resrouce, NY: 4.13; 4.15.

© The Frick Collection: 9.14A, 9.14B.

Courtesy of John Andrew Gallery, Preservation Alliance for Greater Philadelphia: 3.2B.

© Dennis Gilbert / View / Esto: 9.9

Aaron Helfand photo: C.15; 4.10C; 4.17.

© Hewitt-Garrison Architectural Photograph, courtesy Ann Beha Architects: 7.11.

Ronny Kreutel, Wikimedia Commons: 7.9.

Courtesy of Koch & Wilson Architects, New Orleans: 5.15.

Sheldon Richard Kostelecky: C.6; 2.9.

Léon Krier: 3.9; 4.18.

Elizabeth Frick LaDuke: C.3.

Library of Congress: 6.3; 9.8A

Library of Congress, Prints & Photographs Division, Historic American Buildings Survey: 1.12; 3.2A; 3.6; 5.8; 5.10; 5.14

Barbara Temple Lombardi photo, courtesy of Quinlan & Francis Terry Architects: 9.13A; 9.13B.

Mike Lydon photo: 12.4B.

Robert McKay, McKay Imaging: C.27.

Musei Civici, Como: 4.5.

Museo di San Petronio, Bologna: 9.4B

Frank Nivison photo, courtesy of The Colonial Williamsburg Foundation: 9.12.

© 2008 Estate of Pablo Picasso / Artists Rights Society (ARS), New York: C.7.

Ezra Stoller, © Esto: 8.6

© Hisao Suzuki: 4.7.

By kind permission of Francis Terry, courtesy of Quinlan & Francis Terry Architects: 3.5.

Bruce B. Tolar: C.9.

© 2006, University of Oregon Nolli Map Project, nolli.oregon.edu/: 2.4.

Tom Crane: C.5.

Neil Wavey photo, courtesy of Quinlan & Francis Terry Architects: C.19; 7.5.

Zivkovic Associates Architects with John Simpson & Partners: 9.15C.